An Anthology for Pre-U Philosophy and Theology

Paper 1:
Introduction to Philosophy and Theology

Eds. FRANCES SLEAP

TRISTAN STONE

Copyright © 2016 Frances Sleap and Tristan Stone

All rights reserved.

ISBN: 1537234803
ISBN-13: 978-1537234809

TO THE STUDENTS OF HARRIS WESTMINSTER SIXTH FORM

CONTENTS

5 Conscience, Free Will and Determinism

5.1 Conscience

ACKNOWLEDGMENTS

With the exception of those notes which are the editors' own, the texts reprinted in this anthology are either in the public domain or copied under educational licenses. Where possible, permission to reproduce texts has been sought. The materials in this anthology are intended for academic study and are transmitted for educational purposes.

This Anthology is by no means intended to be a complete survey of requisite reading but it is hoped that students who read these will be given a decent introduction to a range of classic philosophical, theological and ethical texts.

Although the size of this volume is a natural constraint, every effort has been made to preserve the natural flow of the source material and most of the texts include   more material than might be expected to be read by the casual reader looking to glean particular ideas. Indeed, it is hoped this Anthology will inspire students of Philosophy and Theology to read deeper and further and grapple with the full texts of these and other thinkers. The editors would like to thank Charlotte and Peter Vardy in particular for sharing their work and for permission to use texts in this Anthology.

§1: Foundational Debates in Philosophy
(Ancient Greek Philosophy)

PLATO (C.428 BC – 348 BC)

"It's all in Plato! Bless me, what do they teach them in these schools?"
(Professor Kirke in *The Last Battle* by CS Lewis)

British Philosopher AN Whitehead famously observed, that the whole history of Western philosophy was a series of footnotes to Plato. Indeed it is rather difficult to overestimate Plato's legacy – not only in his ideas but also his method.

Most of Plato's works are written as dialogues between different philosophical characters. Socrates features most prominently, although it is difficult to tell whether the Socrates of Plato's dialogues represents the historical Socrates' ideas, those of Plato himself or some middle way between the two.

Dialogue is the very quintessence of philosophy (literally *love of wisdom*) and theology (literally *God-talk*) and Plato's use of the **dialectic** (i.e. discourse between two or more opposing or differing views to arrive at the truth through reasoned argument) forms the basic structure for those who followed him – whether it be in the Thomist use of "Objections…on the other hand…I answer that…", Humean *Dialogues* or a more modern *Symposium*, grappling with disparate axioms, arguments and conclusions..

Only a few works have been selected for this Anthology (in keeping with the requirements of the Pre-U Specification) and most of these sections are found in Plato's seminal work of political philosophy *The Republic* – which is well worth reading in its entirety. Those students who are interested in deciphering Plato's so-called *Theory of the Forms* should approach his oeuvre in the knowledge that Plato produced no such consistent Theory. Nevertheless, those pieces included in this Anthology are highly important first steps to unravelling his ideas about the nature of Ultimate Reality.

Plato's life can be read about in a great many scholarly and popular biographies. Suffice it to say that he was clearly a man of great genius who benefited from being born into a wealthy, aristocratic family in Ancient Athens. Being taught by Socrates and, in turn, teaching Aristotle, Plato epitomises power of education. Ever 'ahead of his time', Plato founded the first Western University (*The Academy*) and it should be noted that his ideal State included equal treatment and education of women.

from *The Republic*
Book I
Polemarchus and Socrates discuss the conventional view of Justice

Polemarchus takes up the argument and maintains that justice is giving a man his due. Socrates draws a series of unacceptable conclusions in order to demonstrate the inadequacy of this conventional view.

"Well then," said I, "as heir to this argument, tell me, what is this saying of Simonides that you think tells us the truth about doing right?"

"That it is right to give every man his due," he replied; "in that, I think, he puts the matter fairly enough."

"It is indeed difficult to disagree with Simonides," I said; "he had the poet's wisdom and inspiration; but though you may know what he meant by what he said, I'm afraid I don't. For he clearly does not mean what we were talking about just now, that we should return anything entrusted to us even though the person asking for it has gone mad. Yet what one has entrusted to another is surely due to one, isn't it?"

"Yes."

"Yet in no circumstances should one return it to a mad-man."

"True."

"So Simonides must mean something different from this when he says that it is right to give every man his due."

"He certainly must," he replied; "for his thought is that one friend owes it as a due to another to do him good, not harm."

"I see," I said; "then as between two friends one is not giving the other his due when he returns a sum of money the other has entrusted to him if the return is going to cause b harm - is this what Simonides means?"

"Certainly."

"Well then, ought we to give our enemies too whatever is due to them?"

"Certainly," he said, "what is due to them; and that is, I assume, what is appropriate between enemies, an injury of some sort."

"It looks," said I, "as if Simonides was talking about what is right with a poet's ambiguity. For it appears that he meant that it is right to give everyone what is appropriate to him, but he called this his 'due.'"

"Of course."

"Yes, but look here," I said, "suppose someone asked him 'How then does medical skill get its name, Simonides? What does it supply that is due and appropriate and to whom?' How do you suppose he would reply?"

"Obviously that it is the skill that supplies the body with remedies and with food and drink."

"And if he were asked the same question about cookery?"

"That it is the skill that supplies the flavour to our food."

"Then what does the skill we call justice supply and to whom?"

"If we are to be consistent, Socrates, it must be the skill that enables us to help and injure one's friends and enemies."

"So Simonides says that justice is to benefit one's friends and harm one's enemies?"

"I think so."

"Who then is best able to benefit his friends and harm his enemies in matters of health?"

"A doctor."

"And in the risks of a sea voyage?"

"A navigator."

"And what about the just man? In what activity or occupation will he best be able to help his friends and harm his enemies?"

"In war : he will fight against his enemies and for his friends."

"Good. Yet people who are healthy have no use for a physician, have they, Polemarchus?"

"True."

"Nor those that stay on land of a navigator?"

"No."

"Do you then maintain that those who are not at war have no use for a just man?"

"No, I certainly don't."

"So justice is useful in peacetime?"

"It is."

"So too is agriculture?"

"Yes."

"For providing crops?"

"'Yes."

"And shoemaking?"

"Yes."

"Presumably for supplying shoes."

"Yes."

"Well then, what is the use of justice in peacetime, and what do we get out of it?"

"It's useful in business."

"And by that you mean some form of transaction between people?"

"Yes."

"Well, if our transaction is a game of chess, is a just man a good and useful partner, or a chess player?"

"A chess player."

"And if it's a matter of bricks and mortar, is the just man a better and more useful partner than a bricklayer?"

"No."

"Well, for what kind of transaction is the just man a better partner than the bricklayer or the musician? Where does he excel the musician as the musician excels him in music?"

"Where money is involved, I suppose."

"Except perhaps," said I, "when it's a question of buying or selling; if, for example, we are buying or selling a horse, a trainer would be a better partner, would he not?"

"I suppose so."

"Or if it's a ship, a shipbuilder or sailor?"

"Presumably."

"Then in what financial transactions is the just man a better partner than others?"

"When we want to put our money on deposit, Socrates."

"In fact when we don't want to make use of it at all, but lay it by?"

"Yes."

"So when we aren't making any use of our money, we find justice useful?"

"It looks rather like it."

"And so when you want to store a pruning-knife, justice is useful both to the community and to the individual; but if you want to use it then you turn to the vine dresser."

"Apparently."

"And if you want to keep your shield or your lyre safe you need the just man, but if you want to use it the soldier or musician?"

"That must follow."

"And so in all spheres justice is useless when you are using things, and useful when you are not?"

"Maybe."

"Justice, then, can't be a very serious thing," I said, "if it's only useful when things aren't used. But there's a further point. In boxing and other kinds of fighting, skill in attack goes with skill in defence, does it not?"

"Of course."

"So, too, does not the ability to save from disease imply the ability to produce it undetected?"

"I agree"

"While ability to bring an army safely through a campaign goes with ability to rob the enemy of his secrets and steal a match on him in action."

"I certainly think so."

"So a man who's good at keeping a thing will be good at stealing it?"

"I suppose so."

"So if the just man is good at keeping money safe he will be good at stealing it too."

"That at any rate is the conclusion the argument indicates."

"So the just man turns out to be a kind of thief, a view you have perhaps learned from Homer. For he approves of Odysseus' grandfather Autolycus who, he says, surpassed all men in stealing and lying. Justice, in fact, according to you and Homer and Simonides is a kind of stealing, though it must be done to help a friend or harm an enemy. Is that your meaning ?"

"It certainly isn't," he replied, "but I don't really know what I did mean. Yet I still think that justice is to help your friends and harm your enemies."

"But which do you reckon are a man's friends or enemies? Those he thinks good, honest men and the reverse, or those really are even though he may not think so?"

"One would expect a man's likes and dislikes to depend on what he thinks."

"'But don't men often make mistakes, and think a man honest when he is not, and vice versa?"

"Yes, they do."

"In that case their enemies are good and their friends bad."

"Certainly."

"Then it's only right that they should help the bad and harm the good."

"I suppose so."

"Yet good men are just and not likely to do wrong."

"True."

"So that by your reckoning it is right to injure those who do no wrong."

"Oh no, Socrates; it looks as if my reckoning was wrong."

"Well then," I said, "it must be right to harm wrongdoers and help those who do right,"'

"That seems more reasonable."

"So when men are mistaken in their judgements, Polemarchus, it will often be right for them to injure their e friends, who in their eyes are bad, and help their enemies, who are good. Which is the very opposite of what we said Simonides meant."

"That is the conclusion that follows, certainly," he said. "But let us put the matter differently. For our definitions of friend and enemy were perhaps wrong."

"How wrong?"

"When we said a friend was one who *seemed* a good, honest man."

"And how are we to change that?"

"By defining a friend as one who both seems and is an honest man: while the man who seems, but is not, an honest man seems a friend, but really is not. And similarly for an enemy."

"On this reckoning the good man is a friend and the bad man an enemy."

"Yes."

"And you want us to add to our previous definition of justice (that justice was to do good to a friend and harm to an enemy) by saying that it is just to do good to one's friend if he is good, and to harm one's enemy if he is evil."

"Yes," he said, "that puts it very fairly."

"But does a just man do harm to anyone?"

"Oh yes," he replied: "one *ought* to harm bad men who are our enemies."

"If we harm a horse do we make it better or worse?"

"Worse."

"Worse, that is, by the standard of excellence by which we judge horses, not dogs?"

"Yes."

"And a dog if harmed becomes a worse dog by the standard of excellence by which we judge dogs, not horses?"

"Surely."

"But must we not then say of a man that if harmed he becomes worse by the standards of human excellence?"

"Certainly."

"But is not justice human excellence?"

"It surely must be."

"So men if harmed must become more unjust."

"So it would seem."

"Well, musicians will hardly use their skill to make their pupils unmusical, or riding masters to make their pupils bad horsemen."

"Hardly."

"Then will just men use their justice to make others unjust? Or, in short, will good men use their goodness[1] make others bad?"

"That cannot be so."

"For it is not the function of heat to cool things, but of its opposite."

"Yes."

"Nor the function of dryness to wet things, but of its opposite."

"True."

"Well then, it is not the function of the good man to do harm but of his opposite."

"Clearly."

"But is not the just man good?"

"Of course."

"Then, Polemarchus, it is not the function of the just man to harm either his friends or anyone else, but of his opposite, the unjust man."

"What you say seems perfectly true, Socrates."

"So it wasn't a wise man who said that justice is to give every man his due, if what he meant by it was that the just man should harm his enemies and help his friends. This simply is not true: for as we have seen, it is never right to harm anyone at any time."

"I agree."

"So you and I," said I, "will both quarrel with anyone who says that this view was put forward by either Simonides or Bias or Pittacus or any of the canonical sages."

"For myself," he replied, "I am quite ready to join your side of the quarrel."

"Do you know whose I think this saying is that tells us it is right to help one's friends and harm one's enemies? I think it must be due to Periander or Perdiccas or Xerxes or Ismenias of Thebes[2], or someone else of wealth and arrogance."

"Very likely," he replied.

"Well, well," said I; "now we have seen that this is not what justice or right is, will anyone suggest what else it is?"

---

[1] Arete (virtue)

[2] The first three of them were tyrants, the typical bad men of Greek tradition; the last took bribes from Persia, the traditional enemy.

The Ring of Gyges

Glaucon gives the following illustration of liberty:

"The best illustration of the liberty I am talking about would be if we supposed [the just and the unjust man] both to be possessed of the power which Gyges, the ancestor of Gyges the Lydian, had d in the story. He was a shepherd in the service of the then king of Lydia, and one day there was a great storm and an earthquake in the district where he was pasturing his flock and a chasm opened in the earth. He was amazed at the sight, and descended into the chasm and saw many astonishing things there, among them, so the story goes, a bronze horse, which was hollow and fitted with doors, through which he peeped and saw a corpse which seemed to be of more than human size. He took nothing from it save a gold ring it had on its finger, and then made his way out. He was wearing this ring when he attended the usual meeting of shepherds which reported monthly to the king on the state of his flocks; and as he was sitting there with the others he happened to twist the bezel of the ring towards the inside of his hand. Thereupon he became invisible to his companions, and they began to refer to him as if he had left them. He was astonished, and began fingering the ring again, and turned the bezel outwards; whereupon he became visible again. When he saw this he started experimenting with the ring to see if it really had this power, and found that every time he turned the bezel inwards he became invisible, and when he turned it outwards he became visible. Having made his discovery he managed to get himself included in the party that was to report to the king, and when he arrived seduced t the queen, and with her help attacked and murdered the king and seized the throne.

"Imagine now that two such rings existed and the just man put on one, the unjust the other. There is no one, it would commonly be supposed, who would have such iron strength of will as to stick to what is right and keep his hands from taking other people's property. For he would be able to steal from the market whatever he wanted without fear of detection, to go into any man's house and seduce anyone he liked, to murder or to release from prison anyone he felt inclined, and generally behave as if he had supernatural powers. And in all this the just man would differ in no way from the unjust, but both would follow the same course. This, it would be claimed, is strong evidence that no man is just of his own free will, but only under compulsion, and that no man thinks justice pays him personally, since he will always do wrong when he gets the chance. Indeed, the supporter of this view will continue, men are right in thinking that injustice pays the individual better than justice; and if anyone who had the liberty of which we have been speaking neither wronged nor robbed his neighbour, men would think him a most miserable idiot, though of course they would pretend to admire him in public because of their own fear of being wronged."

Book VI
Socrates consents to give Glaucon his opinion on the Form of the Good

"But I don't think it's right, Socrates," Glaucon protested, "for you to be able to tell us other people's opinions but not your own, when you've given so much time to the subject[3]."

"Yes, but do you think it's right for a man to talk as if he knows what he does not?"

"He has no right to talk as if he knew; but he should be prepared to say what it is that he thinks."

"Well," I said, "haven't you noticed that opinion without knowledge is always a poor thing? At the best it is blind - isn't anyone who holds a true opinion without understanding like a blind man on the right road?"

"Yes."

"Then do you want a poor, blind, halting display from me, when you can get splendidly clear accounts from other people?"

"Now, for goodness' sake don't give up when you're just at the finish, Socrates," begged Glaucon. "We shall be quite satisfied if you give an account of the good similar to that you gave of justice and self-control and the rest."

"And so shall I too, my dear chap," I replied, "but I'm afraid it's beyond me, and if I try I shall only make a fool of myself and be laughed at. So please let us give up asking for the present what the good is in itself; I'm afraid that to reach i what I think would be a satisfactory answer is beyond the range of our present inquiry. But I will tell you, if you like, about something which seems to me to be a child of the good, and to resemble it very closely - or would you rather I didn't?"

"Tell us about the child and you can owe us your account of the parent," he said.

"It's a debt I wish I could pay back to you in full, instead of only paying interest[4] on the loan," I replied. "But for the present you must accept my description of the child of the good as interest. But take care I don't inadvertently cheat you by forging my account of the interest due."

"We'll be as careful as we can," he said. "Go on."

---

[3] i.e. what *Good* is.
[4] The Greek for 'interest' (the 'offspring' of a loan) is the same as for 'child.'

The Simile of the Sun

This simile compares the Form of the Good to the Sun, and may be set out in tabular form as follows:

Visible World		Intelligible World	
The Sun:	Source of growth and light,	The Good:	Source of reality and truth,
	which gives visibility to objects of sense and		which gives intelligibility to objects of thought and
	the power of seeing to the eye.		the power of knowing to the mind.
The faculty of sight		The faculty of knowledge	

"I must first get your agreement to, and remind you of something we have said earlier in our discussion, and indeed on many other occasions."

"What is it?" asked Glaucon.

I replied, "We say that there are many particular things that are beautiful, and many that are good, and so on, and distinguish between them in our account."

"Yes, we do."

"And we go on to speak of beauty-in-itself, and goodness- in-itself, and so on for all the sets of particular things which we have regarded as many; and we proceed to posit by contrast a single form, which is unique, in each case, and call it "what really is" each thing[5]."

"That is so."

"And we say that the particulars are objects of sight but not of intelligence, while the forms are the objects of intelligence but not of sight."

"Certainly."

"And with what part of ourselves do we see what we see?"

"With our sight."

"And we hear with our hearing, and so on with the other senses and their objects."

---

[5] This is a difficult sentence of which variant translations are given. The version above follows Adam and adopts his emendation cai ideunv cat ideanv. For the last phrase the modem philosopher might well say 'what x really is.'

"Of course."

"Then have you noticed," I asked, "how extremely lavish the designer of our senses was when he gave us the faculty of sight and made objects visible?"

"I can't say I have."

"Then look. Do hearing and sound need something of another kind in addition to themselves to enable the ear to hear and the sound to be heard - some third element without d which the one cannot hear or the other be heard?"

"No."

"And the same is true of most, I might say all, the other senses. Or can you think of any that needs anything of the kind?"

"No, I can't."

"But haven't you noticed that sight and the visible do need one?"

"How?"

"If the eyes have the power of sight, and its possessor tries to use this power, and if objects have colour, yet you know that he will see nothing and the colours will remain invisible unless a third element is present which is specifically and naturally adapted for the purpose."

"What is that?" he asked.

"What you call light," I answered.

"True."

"Then the sense of sight and the visibility of objects are yoked by a yoke a long way more precious than any other - that is, if light is a precious thing."

"Which it most certainly is."

"Which, then, of the heavenly bodies[6] do you regard as responsible for this? Whose light would you say it is that makes our eyes see and objects be seen most perfectly?"

"I should say the same as you or anyone else; you mean the sun, of course."

"Then is sight related to its divine source as follows?"

"How?"

"The sun is not identical with sight, nor with what we call the eye in which sight resides."

"No."

"Yet of all sense-organs the eye is the most sun-like."

"Much the most."

"So the eye's power of sight is a kind of infusion dispensed to it by the sun."

---

[6] Plato says 'gods' here, as he believed the heavenly bodies to be divine.

"Yes."

"Then, moreover, though the sun is not itself sight, it is the cause of sight and is seen by the sight it causes."

"That is so."

"Well, that is what I called the child of the good," I said. "The good has begotten it in its own likeness, and it bears the same relation to sight and visible objects in the visible realm that the good bears to intelligence and intelligible objects in the intelligible realm."

"Will you explain that a bit further?" he asked.

"You know that when we turn our eyes to objects whose colours are no longer illuminated by daylight, but only by moonlight or starlight, they see dimly and appear to be almost blind, as if they had no clear vision."

"Yes."

"But when we turn them on things on which the sun is shining, then they see clearly, and obviously have vision."

"Certainly."

"Apply the analogy to the mind. When the mind's eye is fixed on objects illuminated by truth and reality, it understands and knows them, and its possession of intelligence is evident; but when it is fixed on the twilight world of change and decay, it can only form opinions, its vision is confused and its opinions shifting, and it seems to lack intelligence."

"That is true."

"Then what gives the objects of knowledge their truth and the knower's mind the power of knowing is the form[7] of the good. It is the cause of knowledge and truth, and you will be right to think of it as being itself known, and yet as being something other than, and even more splendid than, knowledge and truth, splendid as they are. And just as it was right to think of light and sight as being like the sun, but wrong to think of them as being the sun itself, so here again it is right to think of knowledge and truth as being like the good, but wrong to think of either of them as being the good, whose position must be ranked still higher."

"You are making it something of remarkable splendour if it is the source of knowledge and truth, and yet itself more splendid than they are. For I suppose you can't mean it to be pleasure?" he asked.

"A monstrous suggestion!" I replied. "Let us pursue our analogy further."

"Go on."

"The sun, I think you will agree, not only makes the things we see visible, but causes the processes of

---

[7] Idea – the term "form" in English is generally preferred but some translators render it "idea"

generation, growth and nourishment, without itself being such a process."

"True."

"The good therefore may be said to be the source not only of the intelligibility of the objects of knowledge, but also of their being and reality; yet it is not itself that reality, but is beyond it, and superior to it in dignity and power."

"It really must be miraculously transcendent," remarked Glaucon to the general amusement.

"Now, don't blame me," I protested; "it was you who made me say what I thought about it."

"Yes, and please go on. At any rate finish off the analogy with the sun, if you haven't finished it."

"I've not nearly finished it."

"Then go on and don't leave anything out."

"I'm afraid I must leave a lot out," I said. "But I'll do my best to get in everything I can in present circumstances."

"Yes, please do."

The Divided Line

The analogy of the Divided Line is, Plato makes clear, a sequel to the Sun simile, its purpose being to illustrate further the relation between the two orders of reality with which the Sun simile dealt. But it does so from a particular point of view, that of the states of mind in which we apprehend these two orders or realms. The purpose of the Line, therefore, is not, primarily, to give a classification of objects. Both of the two states of mind correlated with the intelligible realm deal with the same kind of object (the forms), though each deals with them in a different way; and though in the physical world there is a difference between physical things and their shadows, that difference is used primarily to illustrate degrees of "truth" or genuineness in what is apprehended - we know very little about a thing if our knowledge is confined to shadows or images of it or, for that matter, to its superficial appearance. The simile may be set out in the form of the table below:

(sections)		Mental States	Objects
Intelligible realm *knowledge*	A	Intelligence (noesis) or Knowledge (episteme)	The Good Forms
	B	Reasoning (dianoia)	Mathematical Objects
Visible Realm *opinion*	C	Belief (pistis)	Visible Things
	D	Illusion (eikasia)	Shadows and Images

Broadly speaking, the mental states comprised by the four subdivisions are: (A) Intelligence. Full understanding, culminating in the vision of ultimate truth. This understanding is reached by philosophy, or as Plato often calls it "dialectic"; a term whose modern associations are quite misleading in interpreting the Republic, but which, with that caution, remains a convenient translation. (B) Reason. The procedure of mathematics, purely deductive and uncritical of its assumptions. (C) Belief. Common- sense beliefs on matters both moral and physical, which are a fair, practical guide to life but have not been fully thought out. (Later in the Timaeus, Plato includes the natural sciences in this sub- section, as they can never reach ultimate truth, being concerned with a changeable world.) (D) Illusion. All the various illusions, "secondhand impressions and opinions", of which the minds of ordinary people are full. In this section "illusion" merely appears as the perception of shadows and reflections. But the wider interpretation is demanded by the Cave simile, which elaborates in a more graphic form the classification set out in the Line. And it is also clearly implied in Book X that all works of poetry and art are to be included in this sub-section.

To look forward for a moment, Plato is not entirely consistent in his use of terms. In Part VII the contrast is frequently between doxa *and* gnosis, *another word for knowledge.* Noesis *is sometimes used of sub-section A of the Line, but, perhaps because the content of the whole region AB is called* noeton, *is also used of intellectual operations more generally. And at one place* episteme *is used of subsection A. The content of CD, commonly referred to in the Line as* to horaton, *the visible, is in this diagram also called the physical world. Though there is an emphasis in the simile on purely visual terms, Plato instances animals, plants and manufactured objects as examples in subsection C, and for example a donkey eating hay in a barn is not a purely visual object. Besides, it is made quite clear in Part VIII that CD is the world perceived by our senses (*aistheton*), the world of material change (*genesis*). The diagram assumes that both* noesis *and* dianoia *deal with forms and that* dianoia *has no separate type of object. It is sometimes claimed that Plato implies that there are special mathematical objects in subsection B; but his language suggests rather that the mathematicians deal with forms, but in a not fully adequate way.*

"You must suppose, then," I went on, "that there are these two powers[8] of which I have spoken, and that one of them is supreme over everything in the intelligible order or region, the other over everything in the visible region - I won't say in the physical universe or you will think I'm playing with words.[9] At any rate you have before your mind these two orders of things, the visible and the intelligible?"

"Yes, I have."

"Well, suppose you have a line divided into two unequal parts, and then divide the two parts again in the same ratio, to represent the visible and intelligible orders. This gives you, in terms of comparative clarity and obscurity, in the visible order one subsection of images (D): by 'images' I mean first shadows, then reflections in water and other close-grained, polished surfaces, and all that sort of thing, if you understand me."

"I understand."

"Let the other sub-section (C) stand for the objects which are the originals of the images - the animals around us, and every kind of plant and manufactured object."

---

[8] The form of the good and the sun.

[9] The Greek words for 'visible' and for 'physical universe' (or more literally *heaven*) bear some resemblance to each other, and it has been suggested that there was some connection between them.

"Very good."

"Would you be prepared to admit that these sections differ in that one is genuine,[10] one not, and that the relation of image to original is the same as that of the realm of opinion to that of knowledge?"

"I most certainly would."

"Then consider next how the intelligible part of the line is to be divided."

"How?"

"In one sub-section (B) the mind uses the originals of the visible order in their turn as images, and has to base its inquiries on assumptions[11] and proceed from them not to a first principle but to a conclusion: in the other (A) it moves from assumption to a first principle which involves no assumption, without the images used in the other sub- section, but pursuing its inquiry solely by and through forms themselves."

"I don't quite understand."

"I will try again, and what I have just said will help you to understand. I think you know that students of geometry and calculation and the like begin by assuming there are odd and even numbers, geometrical figures and the three forms of angle, and other kindred items in their respective subjects; these they regard as known, having put them forward as basic assumptions which it is quite unnecessary to explain to themselves or anyone else on the grounds that they are obvious to everyone. Starting from them, they proceed J through a series of consistent steps to the conclusion which they set out to find."

"Yes, I certainly know that."

"You know too that they make use of and argue about visible figures, though they are not really thinking about them, but about the originals which they resemble; it is *not* about the square or diagonal which they have drawn that they are arguing, but about the square itself or diagonal itself, or whatever the figure may be. The actual figures they draw or model, which themselves cast their shadows and reflections in water - these they treat as images only, the real objects of their investigation being invisible except to the eye of reason."

"That is quite true."

"This type of thing I called intelligible, but said that the mind was forced to use assumptions in investigating it, and did not proceed to a first principle, being unable to depart from and rise above its assumptions; but it used as illustrations the very things (C) which in turn have their images and

---

[10] Literally - true

[11] Greek *hypothesis* of which the English 'hypothesis' is a transliteration. But the English word means "something that may be true but needs testing": the Greek word "something assumed for the purpose of argument."

shadows on the lower level (D), in comparison with which they are themselves respected and valued for their clarity."

"I understand," he said. "You are referring to what happens in geometry and kindred sciences."

"Then when I speak of the other sub-section of the intelligible part of the line you will understand that I mean that which the very process of argument grasps by the power of dialectic; it treats assumptions not as principles, but as assumptions in the true sense, that is, as starting points and steps in the ascent to something which involves no assumption and is the first principle of everything; when it has grasped that principle it can again descend, by keeping to the consequences that follow from it, to a conclusion. The whole procedure involves nothing in the sensible world, but moves solely through forms to forms, and finishes with forms."

"I understand," he said; "though not fully, because what you describe sounds like a long job. But you want to distinguish that part (A) of the real and intelligible (A+B) which is studied by the science of dialectic as having greater clarity than that (B) studied by what are called 'sciences.' These sciences treat their assumptions as first principles and, though compelled to use reason and not sense-perception in surveying their subject matter, because they proceed in their investigations from assumptions and not to a first principle, they do not, you think, exercise intelligence on it, even though with the aid of a first principle it is intelligible[12]. And I think that you call the habit of mind of geometers and the like reason but not intelligence, meaning by reason something midway between opinion (C+D) and intelligence (A)."

"You have understood me very well." I said. "So please take it that there are, corresponding to the four sections of the line, these four states of mind; to the top section intelligence, to the second reason, to the third belief, and to the last illusion. And you may arrange them in a scale, and assume that they have degrees of clarity corresponding to the degree of truth possessed by their subject-matter."

"I understand," he replied, "and agree with your proposed arrangement."

---

[12] Plato uses 'intelligible' to describe the whole section A-B, which is the 'intelligible order' or 'region'. But here he seems to be referring to sub-section A only and to be indicating the deficiency of sub-section B, which is none the less dealing with material which if rightly handled is 'intelligible' in the full (A) sense. The meaning of the phrase is, however, uncertain. It reads literally 'it is intelligible' (noeton) with (with the aid of? in conjunction with?) a (first) principle or 'and has a first principle'. The interpretation here suggested gives a particular meaning to this more general wording. It is worth adding that, at Plato emphasizes degrees of clarity linked with truth and that his four 'states' or 'habits' of mind are said to entail different degrees of clarity and truthfulness of apprehension, which need not correspond to a difference of object. Both shadow and object throwing it are in a sense physical things; it is our fault if we confuse them. If we speak of shadow and reflection as less true or genuine than their original this is really a comment on our own tendency to misapprehend them. Similarly, here, the mathematician has, compared to the philosopher, a defective apprehension of the same realities (the forms).

The Simile of the Cave

"I want you to go on to picture the enlightenment or ignorance of our human condition somewhat as follows: Imagine an underground chamber like a cave, with a long entrance open to the daylight and as wide as the cave. In this chamber are men who have been prisoners there since they were children, their legs and necks being so fastened that they can only look straight ahead of them and cannot turn their b heads. Some way off, behind and higher up, a fire is burning, and between the fire and the prisoners and above them runs a road, in front of which a curtain-wall has been built, like the screen at puppet shows between the operators and their audience, above which they show their puppets."

"Isee."

"Imagine further that there are men carrying all sorts of gear along behind the curtain-wall, projecting above it and including figures of men and animals made of wood and stone and all sorts of other materials, and that some of these men, as you would expect, are talking and some not."

"An odd picture and an odd sort of prisoner."

"They are drawn from life," I replied. "For, tell me, do you think our prisoners could see anything of themselves or their fellows except the shadows thrown by the fire on the wall of the cave opposite them?"

"How could they see anything else if they were prevented from moving their heads all their lives?

"And would they see anything more of the objects carried along the road?"

"Of course not."

"Then if they were able to talk to each other, would they not assume that the shadows they saw were the real things?"

"Inevitably."

"And if the wall of their prison opposite them reflected sound, don't you think that they would suppose, whenever one of the passers-by on the road spoke, that the voice belonged to the shadow passing before them?"

"They would be bound to think so."

"And so in every way they would believe that the shadows of the objects we mentioned were the whole truth.[13]"

"Yes, inevitably."

"Then think what would naturally happen to them if they were released from their bonds and cured of

---

[13] Literally, "regard nothing else as true but the shadows." The Greek word *alethes* (true) carries an implication of genuineness, and some translators render it here as 'real.'

their delusions. Suppose one of them were let loose, and suddenly compelled to stand up and turn his head and look and walk towards the fire; all these actions would be painful and he would be too dazzled to see properly the objects of which he used to see the shadows. What do you think he would say if he was told that what he used to see was so much empty nonsense and that he was now nearer reality and seeing more correctly, because he was turned towards objects that were more real, and if on top of that he were compelled to say what each of the passing objects was when it was pointed out to him? Don't you think he would be at a loss, and think that what he used to see was far truer[14] than the objects now being pointed out to him?"

"Yes, far truer."

"And if he were made to look directly at the light of the fire, it would hurt his eyes and he would turn back and retreat to the things which he could see properly, which he would think really clearer than the things being shown him."

"Yes."

"And if," I went on, "he were forcibly dragged up the steep and rugged ascent and not let go till he had been dragged out into the sunlight, the process would be a painful one, to which he would much object, and when he emerged into the light his eyes would be so dazzled by the glare of it that he wouldn't be able to see a single one of the things he was now told were real.[15]"

"Certainly not at first," he agreed.

"Because, of course, he would need to grow accustomed to the light before he could see things in the upper world outside the cave. First he would find it easiest to look at shadows, next at the reflections of men and other objects in water, and later on at the objects themselves. After that he would find it easier to observe the heavenly bodies and the sky itself at night, and to look at the light of the moon and b stars rather than at the sun and its light by day."

"Of course."

"The thing he would be able to do last would be to look directly at the sun itself, and gaze at it without using reflections in water or any other medium, but as it is in itself."

"That must come last."

"Later on he would come to the conclusion that it is the sun that produces the changing seasons and years and con- trols everything in the visible world, and is in a sense p responsible for everything that he and his fellow-prisoners used to see."

"That is the conclusion which he would obviously reach."

---

[14] Or 'more real.'
[15] Or 'true' / 'genuine'

"And when he thought of his first home and what passed for wisdom there, and of his fellow-prisoners, don't you think he would congratulate himself on his good fortune and be sorry for them?"

"Very much so."

"There was probably a certain amount of honour and glory to be won among the prisoners, and prizes for keen-sightedness for those best able to remember the order of sequence among the passing shadows and so be best able to d divine their future appearances. Will our released prisoner hanker after these prizes or envy this power or honour? Won't he be more likely to feel, as Homer says, that he would far rather be 'a serf in the house of some landless man,'[16] or indeed anything else in the world, than hold the opinions and live the life that they do?"

"Yes," he replied, "he would prefer anything to a life like theirs."

"Then what do you think would happen," I asked, "if he went back to sit in his old seat in the cave? Wouldn't his eyes be blinded by the darkness, because he had come in suddenly out of the sunlight?"

"Certainly."

"And if he had to discriminate between the shadows, in competition with the other prisoners, while he was still blinded and before his eyes got used to the darkness – a process that would take some time - wouldn't he be likely to make a fool of himself? And they would say that his visit to the upper world had ruined his sight, and that the ascent was not worth even attempting. And if anyone tried to release them and lead them up, they would kill him if they could lay hands on him."

"They certainly would."

"Now, my dear Glaucon," I went on, "this simile must be connected throughout with what preceded it. The realm revealed by sight corresponds to the prison, and the light of the fire in the prison to the power of the sun. And you won't go wrong if you connect the ascent into the upper world and the sight of the objects there with the upward progress of the mind into the intelligible region. That at any rate is my interpretation, which is what you are anxious to hear; the truth of the matter is, after all, known only to god. But in my opinion, for what it is worth, the final thing to be perceived in the intelligible region, and perceived only with difficulty, is the form of the good; once seen, it is inferred to be responsible for whatever is right and valuable in anything, producing in the visible region light and the source of light, and being in the intelligible region itself controlling source of truth and intelligence. And anyone who is going to act rationally either in public or private life must have sight of it."

"I agree," he said, "so far as I am able to understand you."

"Then you will perhaps also agree with me that it won't be surprising if those who get so far are unwilling to involve themselves in human affairs, and if their minds long to remain in the realm above.

---

[16] *The Odyssey*, XI, 489

That's what we should expect if d our simile holds good again."

"Yes, that's to be expected."

"Nor will you think it strange that anyone who descends from contemplation of the divine to human life and its ills should blunder and make a fool of himself, if, while still blinded and unaccustomed to the surrounding darkness, he's forcibly put on trial in the law-courts or elsewhere about the shadows of justice or the figures^ of which they are shadows, and made to dispute about the notions of them held by men who have never seen justice itself."

"There's nothing strange in that."

"But anyone with any sense," I said, "will remember that the eyes may be unsighted in two ways, by a transition either from light to darkness or from darkness to light, and will recognize that the same thing applies to the mind. So when he sees a mind confused and unable to see clearly he will not laugh without thinking, but will ask himself whether it has come from a clearer world and is confused by the unaccustomed darkness, or whether it is dazzled by the stronger h light of the clearer world to which it has escaped from its previous ignorance. The first condition of life is a reason for congratulation, the second for sympathy, though if one wants to laugh at it one can do so with less absurdity than at the mind that has descended from the daylight of the upper world."

"You put it very reasonably."

"If this is true," I continued, "we must reject the conception of education professed by those who say that they can € put into the mind knowledge that was not there before – rather as if they could put sight into blind eyes."

"It is a claim that is certainly made," he said.

"But our argument indicates that the capacity for knowledge is innate in each man's mind, and that the organ by which he learns is like an eye which cannot be turned from darkness to light unless the whole body is turned; ir the same way the mind as a whole must be turned away from the world of change until its eye can bear to look straight at reality, and at the brightest of all realities which is what we call the good. Isn't that so?"

"Yes."

'Then this turning around of the mind itself might be made a subject of professional skill, which would affect the conversion as easily and effectively as possible. It would not be concerned to implant sight, but to ensure that someone who had it already was not either turned in the wrong direction or looking the wrong way."

"That may well be so."

"The rest, therefore, of what are commonly called excellences[17] of the mind perhaps resemble those of the body, in that they are not in fact innate, but are implanted by sub- sequent training and practice; but knowledge, it seems, must surely have a diviner quality, something which never loses its power, but whose effects are useful and salutary or again useless and harmful according to the direction in which it is turned. Have you never noticed how shrewd is the glance of the type of men commonly called bad but clever? They have small minds but their sight is sharp and piercing enough in matters that concern them; it's not that their sight is weak, but that they are forced to serve evil, so that the keener their sight the more effective that evil is."

"That's true."

"But suppose," I said, "that such natures were cut loose, when they were still children, from all the dead weights natural to this world of change and fastened on them by sensual indulgences like gluttony, which twist their minds' vision to lower things, and suppose that when so freed they were turned towards the truth, then this same part of these same individuals would have as keen a vision of truth as it has of the objects on which it is at present turned."

"Very likely."

"And is it not also likely, and indeed a necessary consequence of what we have said, that society will never be properly governed either by the uneducated, who have no knowledge of the truth, or by those who are allowed to c spend all their lives in purely intellectual pursuits? The un- educated have no single aim in life to which all their actions, public and private, are to be directed; the intellectuals will take no practical action of their own accord, fancying them- selves to be out of this world in some kind of earthly paradise."

"True."

"Then our job as lawgivers is to compel the best minds to attain what we have called the highest form of knowledge, and to ascend to the vision of the good as we have described, and when they have achieved this and see well enough, d prevent them behaving as they are now allowed to."

"What do you mean by that?"

"Remaining in the upper world, and refusing to return again to the prisoners in the cave below and share their labours and rewards, whether trivial or serious."

"But surely," he protested, "that will not be fair. We shall be compelling them to live a poorer life than they might live."

"The object of our legislation," I reminded him again, "is not the special welfare of any particular class in our society but of the society as a whole; and it uses persuasion or compulsion to unite all citizens

---

[17] Arete (virtue)

and make them share together the benefits which each individually can confer on the community; and its purpose in fostering this attitude is not to leave everyone to please himself, but to make each man a link in the unity of the whole."

from *Meno*

Written c.380 B.C.E

Persons of the Dialogue
MENO
SOCRATES
A SLAVE OF MENO

Men. Yes, Socrates; but what do you mean by saying that we do not learn, and that what we call learning is only a process of recollection? Can you teach me how this is?

Soc. I told you, Meno, just now that you were a rogue, and now you ask whether I can teach you, when I am saying that there is no teaching, but only recollection; and thus you imagine that you will involve me in a contradiction.

Men. Indeed, Socrates, I protest that I had no such intention. I only asked the question from habit; but if you can prove to me that what you say is true, I wish that you would.

Soc. It will be no easy matter, but I will try to please you to the utmost of my power. Suppose that you call one of your numerous attendants, that I may demonstrate on him.

Men. Certainly. Come hither, boy.

Soc. He is Greek, and speaks Greek, does he not?

Men. Yes, indeed; he was born in the house.

Soc. Attend now to the questions which I ask him, and observe whether he learns of me or only remembers.

Men. I will.

Soc. Tell me, boy, do you know that a figure like this is a square?

Boy. I do.

Soc. And you know that a square figure has these four lines equal

Boy. Certainly.

Soc. And these lines which I have drawn through the middle of the square are also equal?

Boy. Yes.

Soc. A square may be of any size?

Boy. Certainly.

Soc. And if one side of the figure be of two feet, and the other side be of two feet, how much will the whole be? Let me explain: if in one direction the space was of two feet, and in other direction of one foot, the whole would be of two feet taken once?

Boy. Yes.

Soc. But since this side is also of two feet, there are twice two feet?

Boy. There are.

Soc. Then the square is of twice two feet?

Boy. Yes.

Soc. And how many are twice two feet? count and tell me.

Boy. Four, Socrates.

Soc. And might there not be another square twice as large as this, and having like this the lines equal?

Boy. Yes.

Soc. And of how many feet will that be?

Boy. Of eight feet.

Soc. And now try and tell me the length of the line which forms the side of that double square: this is two feet-what will that be?

Boy. Clearly, Socrates, it will be double.

Soc. Do you observe, Meno, that I am not teaching the boy anything, but only asking him questions; and now he fancies that he knows how long a line is necessary in order to produce a figure of eight square feet; does he not?

Men. Yes.

Soc. And does he really know?

Men. Certainly not.

Soc. He only guesses that because the square is double, the line is double.

Men. True.

Soc. Observe him while he recalls the steps in regular order. (To the Boy.) Tell me, boy, do you assert that a double space comes from a double line? Remember that I am not speaking of an oblong, but of a figure equal every way, and twice the size of this-that is to say of eight feet; and I want to know whether you still say that a double square comes from double line?

Boy. Yes.

Soc. But does not this line become doubled if we add another such line here?

Boy. Certainly.

Soc. And four such lines will make a space containing eight feet?

Boy. Yes.

Soc. Let us describe such a figure: Would you not say that this is the figure of eight feet?

Boy. Yes.

Soc. And are there not these four divisions in the figure, each of which is equal to the figure of four feet?

Boy. True.

Soc. And is not that four times four?

Boy. Certainly.

Soc. And four times is not double?

Boy. No, indeed.

Soc. But how much?

Boy. Four times as much.

Soc. Therefore the double line, boy, has given a space, not twice, but four times as much.

Boy. True.

Soc. Four times four are sixteen-are they not?

Boy. Yes.

Soc. What line would give you a space of right feet, as this gives one of sixteen feet;-do you see?

Boy. Yes.

Soc. And the space of four feet is made from this half line?

Boy. Yes.

Soc. Good; and is not a space of eight feet twice the size of this, and half the size of the other?

Boy. Certainly.

Soc. Such a space, then, will be made out of a line greater than this one, and less than that one?

Boy. Yes; I think so.

Soc. Very good; I like to hear you say what you think. And now tell me, is not this a line of two feet and that of four?

Boy. Yes.

Soc. Then the line which forms the side of eight feet ought to be more than this line of two feet, and less than the other of four feet?

Boy. It ought.

Soc. Try and see if you can tell me how much it will be.

Boy. Three feet.

Soc. Then if we add a half to this line of two, that will be the line of three. Here are two and there is one; and on the other side, here are two also and there is one: and that makes the figure of which you speak?

Boy. Yes.

Soc. But if there are three feet this way and three feet that way, the whole space will be three times three feet?

Boy. That is evident.

Soc. And how much are three times three feet?

Boy. Nine.

Soc. And how much is the double of four?

Boy. Eight.

Soc. Then the figure of eight is not made out of a of three?

Boy. No.

Soc. But from what line?-tell me exactly; and if you would rather not reckon, try and show me the line.

Boy. Indeed, Socrates, I do not know.

Soc. Do you see, Meno, what advances he has made in his power of recollection? He did not know at first, and he does not know now, what is the side of a figure of eight feet: but then he thought that he knew, and answered confidently as if he knew, and had no difficulty; now he has a difficulty, and neither knows nor fancies that he knows.

Men. True.

Soc. Is he not better off in knowing his ignorance?

Men. I think that he is.

Soc. If we have made him doubt, and given him the "torpedo's shock," have we done him any harm?

Men. I think not.

Soc. We have certainly, as would seem, assisted him in some degree to the discovery of the truth; and now he will wish to remedy his ignorance, but then he would have been ready to tell all the world again and again that the double space should have a double side.

Men. True.

Soc. But do you suppose that he would ever have enquired into or learned what he fancied that he knew, though he was really ignorant of it, until he had fallen into perplexity under the idea that he did not know, and had desired to know?

Men. I think not, Socrates.

Soc. Then he was the better for the torpedo's touch?

Men. I think so.

Soc. Mark now the farther development. I shall only ask him, and not teach him, and he shall share the enquiry with me: and do you watch and see if you find me telling or explaining anything to him, instead of eliciting his opinion. Tell me, boy, is not this a square of four feet which I have drawn?

Boy. Yes.

Soc. And now I add another square equal to the former one?

Boy. Yes.

Soc. And a third, which is equal to either of them?

Boy. Yes.

Soc. Suppose that we fill up the vacant corner?

Boy. Very good.

Soc. Here, then, there are four equal spaces?

Boy. Yes.

Soc. And how many times larger is this space than this other?

Boy. Four times.

Soc. But it ought to have been twice only, as you will remember.

Boy. True.

Soc. And does not this line, reaching from corner to corner, bisect each of these spaces?

Boy. Yes.

Soc. And are there not here four equal lines which contain this space?

Boy. There are.

Soc. Look and see how much this space is.

Boy. I do not understand.

Soc. Has not each interior line cut off half of the four spaces?

Boy. Yes.

Soc. And how many spaces are there in this section?

Boy. Four.

Soc. And how many in this?

Boy. Two.

Soc. And four is how many times two?

Boy. Twice.

Soc. And this space is of how many feet?

Boy. Of eight feet.

Soc. And from what line do you get this figure?

Boy. From this.

Soc. That is, from the line which extends from corner to corner of the figure of four feet?

Boy. Yes.

Soc. And that is the line which the learned call the diagonal. And if this is the proper name, then you,

Meno's slave, are prepared to affirm that the double space is the square of the diagonal?

Boy. Certainly, Socrates.

Soc. What do you say of him, Meno? Were not all these answers given out of his own head?

Men. Yes, they were all his own.

Soc. And yet, as we were just now saying, he did not know?

Men. True.

Soc. But still he had in him those notions of his-had he not?

Men. Yes.

Soc. Then he who does not know may still have true notions of that which he does not know?

Men. He has.

Soc. And at present these notions have just been stirred up in him, as in a dream; but if he were frequently asked the same questions, in different forms, he would know as well as any one at last?

Men. I dare say.

Soc. Without any one teaching him he will recover his knowledge for himself, if he is only asked questions?

Men. Yes.

Soc. And this spontaneous recovery of knowledge in him is recollection?

Men. True.

Soc. And this knowledge which he now has must he not either have acquired or always possessed?

Men. Yes.

Soc. But if he always possessed this knowledge he would always have known; or if he has acquired the knowledge he could not have acquired it in this life, unless he has been taught geometry; for he may be made to do the same with all geometry and every other branch of knowledge. Now, has any one ever taught him all this? You must know about him, if, as you say, he was born and bred in your house.

Men. And I am certain that no one ever did teach him.

Soc. And yet he has the knowledge?

Men. The fact, Socrates, is undeniable.

Soc. But if he did not acquire the knowledge in this life, then he must have had and learned it at some other time?

Men. Clearly he must.

Soc. Which must have been the time when he was not a man?

Men. Yes.

Soc. And if there have been always true thoughts in him, both at the time when he was and was not a man, which only need to be awakened into knowledge by putting questions to him, his soul must have always possessed this knowledge, for he always either was or was not a man?

Men. Obviously.

Soc. And if the truth of all things always existed in the soul, then the soul is immortal. Wherefore be of good cheer, and try to recollect what you do not know, or rather what you do not remember.

Men. I feel, somehow, that I like what you are saying.

Soc. And I, Meno, like what I am saying. Some things I have said of which I am not altogether confident. But that we shall be better and braver and less helpless if we think that we ought to enquire, than we should have been if we indulged in the idle fancy that there was no knowing and no use in seeking to know what we do not know;-that is a theme upon which I am ready to fight, in word and deed, to the utmost of my power.

Men. There again, Socrates, your words seem to me excellent.

Soc. Then, as we are agreed that a man should enquire about that which he does not know, shall you and I make an effort to enquire together into the nature of virtue?

Men. By all means, Socrates. And yet I would much rather return to my original question, Whether in seeking to acquire virtue we should regard it as a thing to be taught, or as a gift of nature, or as coming to men in some other way?

Soc. Had I the command of you as well as of myself, Meno, I would not have enquired whether virtue is given by instruction or not, until we had first ascertained "what it is." But as you think only of controlling me who am your slave, and never of controlling yourself,-such being your notion of freedom, I must yield to you, for you are irresistible. And therefore I have now to enquire into the qualities of a thing of which I do not as yet know the nature. At any rate, will you condescend a little, and allow the question "Whether virtue is given by instruction, or in any other way," to be argued upon hypothesis? As the geometrician, when he is asked whether a certain triangle is capable being inscribed in a certain circle, will reply: "I cannot tell you as yet; but I will offer a hypothesis which may assist us in forming a conclusion: If the figure be such that when you have produced a given side of it, the given area of the triangle falls short by an area corresponding to the part produced, then one consequence follows, and if this is impossible then some other; and therefore I wish to assume a hypothesis before I tell you whether this triangle is capable of being inscribed in the circle":-that is a geometrical hypothesis. And we too, as we know not the nature and -qualities of virtue, must ask, whether virtue is or not taught, under a hypothesis: as thus, if virtue is of such a class of mental goods, will it be taught or not? Let the first hypothesis be-that virtue is or is not knowledge,-in that case will it be taught or not? or, as we were just now saying, remembered"? For there is no use in disputing about the name. But is virtue taught or not? or rather, does not everyone see that knowledge alone is taught?

Men. I agree.

Soc. Then if virtue is knowledge, virtue will be taught?

Men. Certainly.

Soc. Then now we have made a quick end of this question: if virtue is of such a nature, it will be taught; and if not, not?

Men. Certainly.

from *Phaedrus*

written c. 370 BC

Socrates uses the image 'figure' of a **chariot** *and its horses to describe the human and divine soul*

Socrates: Let us view the affections and actions of the soul divine and human, and try to ascertain the truth about them. The beginning of our proof is as follows:-

The soul through all her being is immortal, for that which is ever in motion is immortal; but that which moves another and is moved by another, in ceasing to move ceases also to live. Only the self-moving, never leaving self, never ceases to move, and is the fountain and beginning of motion to all that moves besides. Now, the beginning is unbegotten, for that which is begotten has a beginning; but the beginning is begotten of nothing, for if it were begotten of something, then the begotten would not come from a beginning. But if unbegotten, it must also be indestructible; for if beginning were destroyed, there could be no beginning out of anything, nor anything out of a beginning; and all things must have a beginning. And therefore the self-moving is the beginning of motion; and this can neither be destroyed nor begotten, else the whole heavens and all creation would collapse and stand still, and never again have motion or birth. But if the self-moving is proved to be immortal, he who affirms that self-motion is the very idea and essence of the soul will not be put to confusion. For the body which is moved from without is soulless; but that which is moved from within has a soul, for such is the nature of the soul. But if this be true, must not the soul be the self-moving, and therefore of necessity unbegotten and immortal? Enough of the soul's immortality.

Of the nature of the soul, though her true form be ever a theme of large and more than mortal discourse, let me speak briefly, and in a figure. And let the figure be composite-a pair of **winged horses and a charioteer.** Now the winged horses and the charioteers of the gods are all of them noble and of noble descent, but those of other races are mixed; the human charioteer drives his in a pair; and one of them is noble and of noble breed, and the other is ignoble and of ignoble breed; and the driving of them of necessity gives a great deal of trouble to him. I will endeavour to explain to you in what way the mortal differs from the immortal creature. The soul in her totality has the care of inanimate being everywhere, and traverses the whole heaven in divers forms appearing--when perfect and fully winged she soars upward, and orders the whole world; whereas the imperfect soul, losing her wings and drooping in her flight at last settles on the solid ground-there, finding a home, she receives an earthly frame which appears to be self-moved, but is really moved by her power; and this composition of soul and body is called a living and mortal creature. For immortal no such union can be reasonably believed to be; although fancy, not having seen nor surely known the nature of God, may imagine an immortal creature having both a body and also a soul which are united throughout all time. Let that, however, be as God wills, and be spoken of acceptably to him. And now let us ask the reason why the soul loses her wings!

The wing is the corporeal element which is most akin to the divine, and which by nature tends to soar aloft and carry that which gravitates downwards into the upper region, which is the habitation of the gods. The divine is beauty, wisdom, goodness, and the like; and by these the wing of the soul is nourished, and grows apace; but when fed upon evil and foulness and the opposite of good, wastes and falls away. Zeus, the mighty lord, holding the reins of a winged chariot, leads the way in heaven, ordering all and taking care of all; and there follows him the array of gods and demigods, marshalled in eleven bands; Hestia alone abides at home in the house of heaven; of the rest they who are reckoned among the princely twelve march in their appointed order. They see many blessed sights in the inner heaven, and there are many ways to and fro, along which the blessed gods are passing, every one doing his own work; he may follow who will and can, for jealousy has no place in the celestial choir. But when they go to banquet and festival, then they move up the steep to the top of the vault of heaven. The chariots of the gods in even poise, obeying the rein, glide rapidly; but the others labour, for the vicious steed goes heavily, weighing down the charioteer to the earth when his steed has not been thoroughly trained:-and this is the hour of agony and extremest conflict for the soul. For the immortals, when they are at the end of their course, go forth and stand upon the outside of heaven, and the revolution of the spheres carries them round, and they behold the things beyond. But of the heaven which is above the heavens, what earthly poet ever did or ever will sing worthily? It is such as I will describe; for I must dare to speak the truth, when truth is my theme. There abides the very being with which true knowledge is concerned; the colourless, formless, intangible essence, visible only to mind, the pilot of the soul. The divine intelligence, being nurtured upon mind and pure knowledge, and the intelligence of every soul which is capable of receiving the food proper to it, rejoices at beholding reality, and once more gazing upon truth, is replenished and made glad, until the revolution of the worlds brings her round again to the same place. In the revolution she beholds justice, and temperance, and knowledge absolute, not in the form of generation or of relation, which men call existence, but knowledge absolute in existence absolute; and beholding the other true existences in like manner, and feasting upon them, she passes down into the interior of the heavens and returns home; and there the charioteer putting up his horses at the stall, gives them ambrosia to eat and nectar to drink.

Such is the life of the gods; but of other souls, that which follows God best and is likest to him lifts the head of the charioteer into the outer world, and is carried round in the revolution, troubled indeed by the steeds, and with difficulty beholding true being; while another only rises and falls, and sees, and again fails to see by reason of the unruliness of the steeds. The rest of the souls are also longing after the upper world and they all follow, but not being strong enough they are carried round below the surface, plunging, treading on one another, each striving to be first; and there is confusion and perspiration and the extremity of effort; and many of them are lamed or have their wings broken through the ill-driving of the charioteers; and all of them after a fruitless toil, not having attained to the mysteries of true being, go away, and feed upon opinion. The reason why the souls exhibit this exceeding eagerness to behold the plain of truth is that pasturage is found there, which is suited to the highest part of the soul; and the wing on which the soul soars is nourished with this. And there is a law of Destiny, that the soul which attains any vision of truth in company with a god is preserved from harm until the next period, and if attaining always is always unharmed. But when she is unable to follow, and fails to behold the truth, and through some ill-hap sinks beneath the double load of forgetfulness and vice, and her wings fall from her and she drops to the ground, then the law ordains that this soul shall at her first birth pass, not into any other animal, but only into man; and the soul which has seen most of truth shall come to the birth as a philosopher, or artist, or some musical and loving nature; that which has seen truth in the second degree shall be some righteous king or warrior chief; the soul which is of the third class shall be a politician, or economist, or trader; the fourth shall be lover of gymnastic toils, or a physician; the fifth shall lead the life of a prophet or hierophant

[1]; to the sixth the character of poet or some other imitative artist will be assigned; to the seventh the life of an artisan or husbandman; to the eighth that of a sophist or demagogue; to the ninth that of a tyrant-all these are states of probation, in which he who does righteously improves, and he who does unrighteously, improves, and he who does unrighteously, deteriorates his lot.

Ten thousand years must elapse before the soul of each one can return to the place from whence she came, for she cannot grow her wings in less; only the soul of a philosopher, guileless and true, or the soul of a lover, who is not devoid of philosophy, may acquire wings in the third of the recurring periods of a thousand years; he is distinguished from the ordinary good man who gains wings in three thousand years:-and they who choose this life three times in succession have wings given them, and go away at the end of three thousand years. But the others receive judgment when they have completed their first life, and after the judgment they go, some of them to the houses of correction which are under the earth, and are punished; others to some place in heaven whither they are lightly borne by justice, and there they live in a manner worthy of the life which they led here when in the form of men. And at the end of the first thousand years the good souls and also the evil souls both come to draw lots and choose their second life, and they may take any which they please. The soul of a man may pass into the life of a beast, or from the beast return again into the man. But the soul which has never seen the truth will not pass into the human form. For a man must have intelligence of universals, and be able to proceed from the many particulars of sense to one conception of reason;-this is the recollection of those things which our soul once saw while following God-when regardless of that which we now call being she raised her head up towards the true being. And therefore the mind of the philosopher alone has wings; and this is just, for he is always, according to the measure of his abilities, clinging in recollection to those things in which God abides, and in beholding which He is what He is. And he who employs aright these memories is ever being initiated into perfect mysteries and alone becomes truly perfect. But, as he forgets earthly interests and is rapt in the divine, the vulgar deem him mad, and rebuke him; they do not see that he is inspired.

---

[1] Someone e.g. priest who interprets sacred mysteries

Aristotle (384-322 BC)

It is, perhaps, a great compliment to a teacher to have one's student disagree with his/her teaching so much that the student dedicates their whole life to arguing against that teacher. The dialectic nature of Philosophy has a great tradition in just such a project (as we shall see with the Barth/Harnack correspondence later). It is fitting, therefore, that Aristotle should follow Plato in this Anthology, as so much of Aristotle's work directly (or indirectly) attacked that of his former teacher, Plato.

Many commentators categorise Plato as a 'rationalist' to Aristotle's "empiricism" and there is certainly much to be said about such classification. Aristotle rejected Plato's theory of the forms; he might have felt, (as Johnny Cash would sing some millennia later) Plato was "so heavenly minded" to be "no earthly good."

This essential division in the two Greeks' thinking has led to rather different approaches to Philosophy and Theology ever since. Whereas Augustine was more influenced by Plato, Aquinas' interest in 'science' made him something more of an Aristotelian (or vice-versa). Throughout the mammoth *Summa Theologica*, Aquinas refers to Aristotle by the epithet, "the Philosopher" – some indication of the esteem he held for his pagan counterpart.

Unfortunately, Aristotle is rather more difficult to read than Plato. Those extant writings we have of Aristotle are (more-or-less) notes cobbled together by various students (such is the current scholastic consensus). The syntax is very often knotty and there sometimes lacks an obvious system to his thought. Nevertheless, any serious student of Philosophy will want to attempt reading some Aristotle for him/herself (albeit in translation). The embolded words are editorial for Aristotle and are meant to guide the reader to passages of particular import.

from *Metaphysics*
BOOK IV

Part 1

"There is a science which investigates being as being and the attributes which belong to this in virtue of its own nature. Now this is not the same as any of the so-called special sciences; for none of these others treats universally of being as being. They cut off a part of

being and investigate the attribute of this part; this is what the mathematical sciences for instance do. Now since we are seeking the first principles and the highest causes, clearly there must be some thing to which these belong in virtue of its own nature. If then those

who sought the elements of existing things were seeking these same principles, it is necessary that the elements must be elements of being not by accident but just because it is being. Therefore it is of being as being that we also must grasp the first causes."

Part 2

"There are many senses in which a thing may be said to 'be', but all that 'is' is related to one central point, one definite kind of thing, and is not said to 'be' by a mere ambiguity. Everything which is healthy is related to health, one thing in the sense that it preserves health, another in the sense that it produces it, another in the sense that it is a symptom of health, another because it is capable of it. And that which is medical is relative to the medical art, one thing being called medical because it possesses it, another because it is naturally adapted to it, another because it is a function of the medical art. And we shall find other words used similarly to these. So, too, **there are many senses in which a thing is said to be, but all refer to one starting-point; some things are said to be because they are substances, others because they are affections of substance, others because they are a process towards substance, or destructions or privations or qualities of substance, or productive or generative of substance, or of things which are relative to substance, or negations of one of these thing of substance itself.** It is for this reason that we say even of non-being that it is nonbeing. As, then, there is one science which deals with all healthy things, the same applies in the other cases also. For not only in the case of things which have one common notion does the investigation belong to one science, but also

in the case of things which are related to one common nature; for even these in a sense have one common notion. It is clear then that it is the work of one science also to study the things that are, qua[1] being.-But everywhere science deals chiefly with that which is primary,

---

[1] Latin for 'as'

and on which the other things depend, and in virtue of which they get their names. If, then, this is substance, it will be of substances that the philosopher must grasp the principles and the causes. [...]

"It is evident, then, that it belongs to one science to be able to give an account of these concepts as well as of substance (this was one of the questions in our book of problems), and that it is the function of the philosopher to be able to investigate all things.

For if it is not the function of the philosopher, who is it who will inquire **whether Socrates and Socrates seated are the same thing,** or whether one thing has one contrary, or what contrariety is, or how many meanings it has? And similarly with all other such questions. [...]

Evidently then it belongs to the philosopher, i.e. to him who is studying the nature of all substance, to inquire also into the principles of **syllogism**. But he who knows best about each genus must be able to state the most certain principles of his subject, so that he whose

subject is existing things qua existing must be able to state the most certain principles of all things. This is the philosopher, and the most certain principle of all is that regarding which it is impossible to be mistaken; for such a principle must be both the best known (for

all men may be mistaken about things which they do not know), and non-hypothetical. For a principle which every one must have who understands anything that is, is not a hypothesis; and that which every one must know who knows anything, he must already have when he comes to a special study. Evidently then such a principle is the most certain of all;

which principle this is, let us proceed to say. It is, that the same attribute cannot at the same time belong and not belong to the same subject and in the same respect; we must presuppose, to guard against dialectical objections, any further qualifications which might be added. This, then, is the most certain of all principles, since it answers to the definition given above. For it is impossible for any one to believe the same thing to be and not to be, as some think Heraclitus says. For what a man says, he does not necessarily believe; and if

it is impossible that contrary attributes should belong at the same time to the same subject (the usual qualifications must be presupposed in this premiss too), and if an opinion which contradicts another is contrary to it, obviously it is impossible for the same man at the same time to believe the same thing to be and not to be; for if a man were mistaken on this point he would have contrary opinions at the same time. It is for this reason that all who are carrying out a demonstration reduce it to this as an ultimate belief; for this is naturally the starting-point even for all the other axioms.

Part 4

There are **some** who, as we said, both themselves **assert that it is possible for the same thing to be and not to be**, and say that people can judge this to be the case. And among others many writers about nature use this language. But we have now posited that it is impossible for anything at the same time to be and not to be, and by this means have shown that this is the most indisputable of all principles.- Some indeed demand that even this shall be demonstrated, but this they do through want of education, for not to know of what things one should demand demonstration, and of what one should not, argues want of education.

For it is impossible that there should be demonstration of absolutely everything (there would be an infinite regress, so that there would still be no demonstration); but if there are things of which one should not demand demonstration, these persons could not say what principle they maintain to be more self-evident than the present one.

"First then this at least is obviously true, that the word 'be' or 'not be' has a definite meaning, so that not everything will be 'so and not so'. Again, if 'man' has one meaning, let this be 'two-footed animal'; by having one meaning I understand this:-if 'man' means 'X', then if A is a man 'X' will be what 'being a man' means for him. (It makes no difference even if one were to say a word has several meanings, if only they are limited in number; for to each definition there might be assigned a different word. For instance, we might say that 'man' has not one meaning but several, one of which would have one definition, viz. 'two-footed animal', while there might be also several other definitions if only they were limited in number; for a peculiar name might be assigned to each of the definitions. If, however, they were

not limited but one were to say that the word has an infinite number of meanings, obviously reasoning would be impossible; **for not to have one meaning is to have no meaning, and if words have no meaning our reasoning with one another, and indeed with ourselves, has been annihilated**; for it is impossible to think of anything if we do not think of one thing; but if this is possible, one name might be assigned to this thing.)

"Let it be assumed then, as was said at the beginning, that the name has a meaning and has one meaning; it is impossible, then, that 'being a man' should mean precisely 'not being a man', if 'man' not only signifies something about one subject but also has one significance

(for we do not identify 'having one significance' with 'signifying something about one subject', since on that assumption even 'musical' and 'white' and 'man' would have had one significance, so that all things would have been one; for they would all have had the same significance). "And it will not be possible to be and not to be the same thing, except in virtue of an ambiguity, just as if one whom we call 'man', others were to call 'not-man'; but the point in question is not this, whether the same thing can at the same time be and not be a man in name, but whether it can in fact. Now if 'man' and 'not-man' mean nothing different,

obviously 'not being a man' will mean nothing different from 'being a man'; so that 'being a man' will be 'not being a man'; for they will be one. For being one means this-being related as 'raiment' and 'dress' are, if their definition is one. And if 'being a man' and 'being a not-man' are to be one, they must mean one thing. But it was shown earlier' that they mean different things.-Therefore, if it is true to say of anything that it is a man, it must be a two-footed animal (for this was what 'man' meant); and if this is necessary, it is impossible that the same thing should not at that time be a two-footed animal; for this is what 'being necessary' means-that it is impossible for the thing not to be. It is, then, impossible that it should be at the same time true to say the same thing is a man and is not a man.

"The same account holds good with regard to 'not being a man', for 'being a man' and 'being a not-man' mean different things, since even 'being white' and 'being a man' are different; for the former terms are much more different so that they must a fortiori mean different things. And if any one says that 'white' means one and the same thing as 'man', again we shall say the same as what was said before, that it would follow that all things are one, and not only opposites. But if this is impossible, then what we have maintained will follow, if our opponent will only answer our question. […]

"And in general those who say this do away with substance and essence. For they must say that all attributes are accidents, and that there is no such thing as 'being essentially a man' or 'an animal'. For if there is to be any such thing as 'being essentially a man' this

will not be 'being a not-man' or 'not being a man' (yet these are negations of it); for there was one thing which it meant, and this was the substance of something. And denoting the substance of a thing means that the essence of the thing is nothing else. But if its being

essentially a man is to be the same as either being essentially a not-man or essentially not being a man, then its essence will be something else. Therefore our opponents must say that there cannot be such a definition of anything, but that all attributes are accidental; for

this is the distinction between substance and accident-**'white' is accidental to man, because though he is white, whiteness is not his essence.** But if all statements are accidental, there will be nothing primary about which they are made, if the accidental always implies predication about a subject. The predication, then, must go on ad infinitum. But this is impossible; for not even more than two terms can be combined in accidental predication. For (1) an accident is not an accident of an accident, unless it be because both are accidents

of the same subject. I mean, for instance, that the white is musical and the latter is white, only because both are accidental to man. But (2) Socrates is musical, not in this sense, that both terms are accidental to something else. Since then some predicates are accidental

in this and some in that sense, (a) those which are accidental in the latter sense, in which white is accidental to Socrates, cannot form an infinite series in the upward direction; e.g. Socrates the white has not yet another accident; for no unity can be got out of such a sum. Nor again (b) will 'white' have another term accidental to it, e.g. 'musical'. For this is no more accidental to that than that is to this; and at the same time we have drawn the distinction,

that while some predicates are accidental in this sense, others are so in the sense in which 'musical' is accidental to Socrates; and the accident is an accident of an accident not in cases of the latter kind, but only in cases of the other kind, so that not all terms will be accidental. There must, then, even so be something which denotes substance. And if this is so, it has been shown that contradictories cannot be predicated at the same time.

"Again, if all contradictory statements are true of the same subject at the same time, evidently all things will be one. For the same thing will be a trireme, a wall, and a man, if of everything it is possible either to affirm or to deny anything (and this premise must be accepted by those who share the views of Protagoras). For if any one thinks that the man is not a trireme, evidently he is not a trireme; so that he also is a trireme, if, as they say, contradictory statements are both true. And we thus get the doctrine of Anaxagoras, that all things are mixed together; so that nothing really exists. They seem, then, to be speaking of the indeterminate, and, while fancying themselves to be speaking of being, they are speaking about non-being; for it is that which exists potentially and not in complete reality that is indeterminate. But they must predicate of every subject the affirmation or the negation of every attribute. For it is absurd if of each subject its own negation is to be predicable, while the negation of something else which cannot be predicated of it is not to be predicable of it; for instance, if it is true to say of a man that he is not a man, evidently it is also true to say that he is either a trireme or not a trireme. If, then, the affirmative can be predicated, the negative must be predicable too; and if the affirmative is not predicable,

the negative, at least, will be more predicable than the negative of the subject itself. If, then, even the latter negative is predicable, the negative of 'trireme' will be also predicable; and, if this is predicable, the affirmative will be so too. […]

Indeed, those who say that things at the same time are and are not, should in consequence say that all things are at rest rather than that they are in movement;

for there is nothing into which they can change, since all attributes

belong already to all subjects.

"Regarding the nature of truth, we must maintain that not everything which appears is true; firstly, because even if sensation-at least of the object peculiar to the sense in question-is not false, still appearance is not the same as sensation.-Again, it is fair to express surprise at our opponents' raising the question whether magnitudes are as great, and colours are of such a nature, as they appear to people at a distance, or as they appear to those close at hand, and whether they are such as they appear to the healthy or to the sick, and whether those things are heavy which appear so to the weak or those which appear so to the strong, and those things true which appear to the sleeping or to the waking. For obviously they do not think these to be open questions; no one, at least, if when he is in Libya he has fancied one night that he is in Athens, starts for the concert hall.-And again with regard to the future, as **Plato says, surely the opinion of the physician and that of the ignorant man are not equally weighty, for instance, on the question whether a man will get well or not.**-And again, among sensations themselves the sensation of a foreign object and that of the appropriate object, or that of a kindred object and that of the object of the sense in question, are not equally authoritative, but in the case of colour sight, not taste, has the

authority, and in the case of flavour taste, not sight; each of which senses never says at the same time of the same object that it simultaneously is 'so and not so'.-But not even at different times does one sense disagree about the quality, but only about that to which the quality belongs. I mean, for instance, that the same wine might seem, if either it or one's body changed, at one time sweet and at another time not sweet; but at least the sweet, such as it is when it exists, has never yet changed, but one is always right about it, and that which is to be sweet is of necessity of such and such a nature. Yet all these views destroy this necessity, leaving nothing to be of necessity, as they leave no essence of anything; for the necessary cannot be in this way and also in that, so that if anything is of necessity, it will not be 'both so and not so'.

Part 7

"**But on the other hand there cannot be an intermediate between contradictories,** but of one subject we must either affirm or deny any one predicate.

This is clear, in the first place, if we define what the true and the false are. To say of what is that it is not, or of what is not that it is, is false, while to say of what is that it is, and of what is not that it is not, is true; so that he who says of anything that it is, or that it is not, will say either what is true or what is false; but neither what is nor what is not is said to be or not to be.-Again, the intermediate between the contradictories will be so either in the way in which grey is between black and white, or as that which is neither man nor horse is between man and horse. (a) If it were of the latter kind, it could not change into the extremes(for change is from not-good to good, or from good to not-good), but as a matter of fact when there is an intermediate it is always observed to change into the extremes. For there is no change except to opposites and to their intermediates. (b) But if it is really intermediate, in this way too there would have to be a change to white, which was not from not-white; but as it is, this is never seen.- Again, every object of understanding or reason the understanding either affirms or denies-this is obvious from the definition-whenever it says what is true or false. When it connects in one way by assertion or negation, it says what is true, and when it does so in another way, what is false.-Again, there must be an intermediate between all contradictories, if one is not arguing merely for the sake of argument; so that it will be possible for a man to say what is neither true nor untrue, and there will be a middle between that which is and that which is not, so that there will also be a kind of change intermediate between generation and destruction.-Again, in all classes in which the negation of an attribute involves the assertion of its contrary, even in these there will be an intermediate; for instance, in the sphere of numbers there will be number which is neither odd nor not-odd. But this is impossible, as is obvious from the definition.-Again, the process

will go on ad infinitum, and the number of realities will be not only half as great again, but even greater. For again it will be possible to deny this intermediate with reference both to its assertion and to its negation, and this new term will be some definite thing; for its essence is something different.- Again, when a man, on being asked whether a thing is white, says 'no', he has denied nothing except that it is; and its not being is a negation.

. . .

"Evidently, again, those who say all things are at rest are not right, nor are those who say all things are in movement. For if all things are at rest, the same statements will always be true and the same always false,-but this obviously changes; for he who makes a statement, himself at one time was not and again will not be. And if all things are in motion, nothing will be true; everything therefore will be false. But it has been shown that this is impossible. Again, it must be that which is that changes; for change is from something to something.

But again it is not the case that all things are at rest or in motion sometimes, and nothing for ever; for there is something which always moves the things that are in motion, and the first mover is itself unmoved.

BOOK V

Part 1

"'BEGINNING' means (1) that part of a thing from which one would start first, e.g a line or a road has a beginning in either of the contrary directions. (2) That from which each thing would best be originated, e.g. even in learning we must sometimes begin not from the first point and the beginning of the subject, but from the point from which we should learn most easily. (4) That from which, as an immanent part, a thing first comes to be, e,g, as the keel of a ship and the foundation of a house, while in animals some suppose the heart, others the brain, others some other part, to be of this nature. (4) That from which, not as an immanent part, a thing first comes to be, and from which the movement or the change naturally first begins, as a child comes from its father and its mother, and a fight from abusive language.

(5) **That at whose will that which is moved is moved and that which changes changes,** e.g. the magistracies in cities, and oligarchies and monarchies and tyrannies, are called arhchai, and so are the arts, and of these especially the architectonic arts. (6) That from which a thing can first be known,-this also is called the beginning of the thing, e.g. the hypotheses are the beginnings of demonstrations. (Causes are spoken of in an equal number of senses; for all causes are beginnings.) It is common, then, to all beginnings to be the first point from which

a thing either is or comes to be or is known; but of these some are immanent in the thing and others are outside. Hence the nature of a thing is a beginning, and so is the element of a thing, and thought and will, and essence, and the final cause-for the good and the beautiful are the beginning both of the knowledge and of the movement of many

things.

Part 2 [FOUR CAUSES]

"'**Cause**' means

(1) that from which, as **immanent material**, a thing comes into being, e.g. the bronze is the cause of the statue and the silver of the saucer, and so are the classes which include these. (2) The **form** or pattern, i.e. the definition of the essence, and the

classes which include this (e.g. the ratio 2:1 and number in general are causes of the octave), and the parts included in the definition.

(3) That from which the **change** or the resting from change first begins; e.g. the adviser is a cause of the action, and the father a cause of the child, and in general the maker a cause of the thing made and the change-producing of the changing.

(4) **The end**, i.e. that for the sake of which a thing is; e.g. health is the cause of walking. For 'Why does one walk?' we say; 'that one may be healthy'; and in speaking thus we think we have given the cause. The same is true of all the means that intervene before the end, when something else has put the process in motion, as e.g. thinning or purging or drugs or instruments intervene before health is reached; for all these are for the sake of the end, though they differ from one another in that some are

instruments and others are actions.

"These, then, are practically all the senses in which causes are spoken of, and as they are spoken of in several senses it follows both that there are several causes of the same thing, and in no accidental sense (e.g. both the art of sculpture and the bronze are causes of the statue not in respect of anything else but qua statue; not, however, in the same way, but the one as matter and the other as source of the movement), and that things can be causes of one another (e.g. exercise of good condition, and the latter of exercise; not, however, in the same way, but the one as end and the other as source of movement).- Again, the same thing is the cause of contraries; for that which when present causes a particular thing, we sometimes charge, when absent, with the contrary, e.g. we impute the shipwreck to the absence of the steersman, whose presence was the cause of safety; and both-the presence and the privation-are causes as sources of movement.

"All the causes now mentioned fall under four senses which are the most obvious. For the letters are the cause of syllables, and the material is the cause of manufactured things, and fire and earth and all such things are the causes of bodies, and the parts are causes of the whole, and the hypotheses are causes of the conclusion, in the sense that they are that out of which these respectively are made; but of these some are cause as the substratum (e.g. the parts), others as the essence (the whole, the synthesis, and the form). The semen,

the physician, the adviser, and in general the agent, are all sources of change or of rest. The remainder are causes as the end and the good of the other things; for that for the sake of which other things are tends to be the best and the end of the other things; let us take it as making no difference whether we call it good or apparent good.

"These, then, are the causes, and this is the number of their kinds, but the varieties of causes are many in number, though when summarized these also are comparatively few. Causes are spoken of in many senses, and even of those which are of the same kind some are causes in a prior and others in a posterior sense, e.g. both 'the physician' and 'the professional man' are causes of health, and both 'the ratio 2:1' and 'number' are causes of the octave, and the classes that include any particular cause are always causes of the particular effect. Again, there are accidental causes and the classes which include these; e.g.

while in one sense 'the sculptor' causes the statue, in another sense 'Polyclitus' causes it, because the sculptor happens to be Polyclitus; and the classes that include the accidental cause are also causes, e.g. 'man'-or in general 'animal'-is the cause of the statue, because

Polyclitus is a man, and man is an animal. Of accidental causes also some are more remote or nearer than others, as, for instance, if 'the white' and 'the musical' were called causes of the statue, and not only 'Polyclitus' or 'man'. But besides all these varieties of causes, whether proper or accidental, some are called causes as being able to act, others as acting; e.g. the cause of the house's being built is a builder, or a builder who is building.-The same variety of language will be found with regard to the effects of causes; e.g. a thing may be called the cause of this statue or of a statue or in general of an image, and of this bronze or of bronze or of matter in general; and similarly in the case of accidental effects. Again, both accidental and proper causes may be spoken of in combination; e.g. we may say not 'Polyclitus' nor 'the sculptor' but 'Polyclitus the sculptor'.

Yet all these are but six in number, while each is spoken of in two ways; for (A) they are causes either as the individual, or as the genus, or as the accidental, or as the genus that includes the accidental, and these either as combined, or as taken simply; and (B) all may

be taken as acting or as having a capacity. But they differ inasmuch as the acting causes, i.e. the individuals, exist, or do not exist, simultaneously with the things of which they are causes, e.g. this particular man who is healing, with this particular man who is recovering

health, and this particular builder with this particular thing that is being built; but the potential causes are not always in this case; for the house does not perish at the same time as the builder.

...

Part 5 "

"**We call 'necessary'** (1, a) that without which, as a condition, a thing cannot live; e.g. breathing and food are necessary for an animal; for it is incapable of existing without these; (b) the conditions without which good cannot be or come to be, or without which we cannot

get rid or be freed of evil; e.g. drinking the medicine is necessary in order that we may be cured of disease, and a man's sailing to Aegina is necessary in order that he may get his money.-(2) The compulsory and compulsion, i.e. that which impedes and tends to hinder, contrary to impulse and purpose. For the compulsory is called necessary (whence the necessary is painful, as Evenus says: 'For every necessary thing is ever irksome'), and compulsion is a form of necessity, as Sophocles says: 'But force necessitates me to this act'. And necessity is held to be something that cannot be persuaded-and rightly, for it is contrary to the movement which accords with purpose and with reasoning.-(3) We say that that which cannot be otherwise is necessarily as it is. And from this sense of 'necessary' all the others are somehow derived; for a thing is said to do or suffer what is necessary in the sense of **compulsory**, only when it cannot act according to its impulse because of the compelling forces-which implies that necessity is that because of which a thing cannot be otherwise; and similarly as regards the conditions of life and of good; for when in the one case good, in the other life and being, are not possible without certain conditions,

these are necessary, and this kind of cause is a sort of necessity.

Again, demonstration is a necessary thing because the conclusion cannot be otherwise, if there has been demonstration in the unqualified sense; and the causes of this necessity are the first premisses, i.e. the fact that the propositions from which the syllogism proceeds cannot be otherwise.

"**Now some things owe their necessity to something other than themselves; others do not, but are themselves the source of necessity in other things.** Therefore the necessary in the primary and strict sense is the simple; for this does not admit of more states than one, so that it cannot even be in one state and also in another; for if it did it would already be in more than one. **If, then, there are any things that are eternal and unmovable, nothing compulsory or against their nature attaches to them.**

Part 7 "

"Things are said to 'be' (1) in an accidental sense, (2) by their own nature.

"(1) In an accidental sense, e.g. we say 'the righteous doer is musical', and 'the man is musical', and 'the musician is a man', just as we say 'the musician builds', because the builder **happens to be** musical or the musician to be a builder; **for here 'one thing is another' means 'one is an accident of another'.** So in the cases we have mentioned;

for when we say 'the man is musical' and 'the musician is a man', or 'he who is pale is musical' or 'the musician is pale', the last two mean that **both attributes are accidents of the same thing**; the first that the attribute is an accident of that which is, while 'the musical is a man' means that 'musical' is an accident of a man. (In this sense, too, the not-pale is said to be, because that of which it is an accident is.) Thus when one thing is said in an accidental

sense to be another, this is either because both belong to the same thing, and this is, or because that to which the attribute belongs is, or because the subject which has as an attribute that of which it is itself predicated, itself is.

"(2) The kinds of essential being are precisely those that are indicated by the figures of predication; for the senses of 'being' are just as many as these figures. Since, then, **some predicates indicate what the subject is, others its quality, others quantity, others relation, others activity or passivity, others its 'where', others its 'when', 'being' has a meaning answering to each of these.** For there is no difference between 'the man is recovering' and 'the man recovers', nor between 'the man is walking or cutting' and 'the man walks' or 'cuts'; and similarly in all other cases.

"(3) Again, 'being' and 'is' mean that a statement is true, 'not being' that it is not true but false -and this alike in the case of affirmation and of negation; e.g. 'Socrates is musical' means that this is true, or 'Socrates is not-pale' means that this is true; but 'the diagonal of the square is not commensurate with the side' means that it is false to say it is.

"(4) **Again, 'being' and 'that which is' mean that some of the things we have mentioned 'are'**
potentially, others in complete reality. For we say both of that which sees potentially and of that
which sees actually, that it is 'seeing', and both of that which can actualize

its knowledge and of that which is actualizing it, that it knows, and both of that to which rest is already
present and of that which can rest, that it rests. And similarly in the case of substances; we say the
Hermes is in the stone, and the half of the line is in the line, and we say of that which is not yet ripe that
it is corn. When a thing is potential and when it is not yet potential must be explained elsewhere.

Part 8 "

"We call 'substance' (1) the simple bodies, i.e. earth and fire and water and everything of the sort, and in
general bodies and the things composed of them, both animals and divine beings, and the parts of
these. **All these are called substance because they are not predicated of a subject but everything else**
is predicated of them. (2) That which, being present in such things as are not predicated of a subject, is
the cause of their being, as the soul is of the being of an animal.-(3) The parts which are present in such
things, limiting them and marking them as individuals, and by whose destruction the whole is
destroyed,

as the body is by the destruction of the plane, as some say, and the plane by the destruction of the line;
and in general number is thought by some to be of this nature; for if it is destroyed, they say, nothing
exists, and it limits all things.-(4) The essence, the formula of
which is a definition, is also called the substance of each thing. "It follows, then, that 'substance' has
two senses, (A) ultimate substratum, which is no longer predicated of anything else, and (B) that
which, being a 'this', is also separable and of this nature is the shape or form of each thing.
…

Part 13

"Let us return to the subject of our inquiry, which is substance.
As the substratum and the essence and the compound of these are called substance, so also is the
universal. About two of these we have spoken; both about the essence and about the substratum, of
which we have said that it underlies in two senses, either being a 'this'-which is the way in which an
animal underlies its attributes-or as the matter underlies the complete reality. **The universal also is**
thought by some to be in the fullest sense a cause, and a principle; therefore let us attack the
discussion of this point also. For it seems impossible that any universal term should be the name of

<u>a substance</u>. For firstly **the substance of each thing is that which is peculiar to it, which does not belong to anything else; but the universal is common, since that is called universal which is such as to belong to more than one thing.** Of which individual then will this be the substance? Either of all or of noddddddne; but it cannot be the substance of all. And if it is to be the substance of one, this one will be the others also; for things whose substance is one and whose essence is one are themselves also one. "**Further, substance means that which is not predicable of a subject, but the universal is predicable of some subject always. "But perhaps the universal, while it cannot be substance in the way in which the essence is so, can be present in this; e.g. 'animal'**

can be present in 'man' and 'horse'. Then clearly it is a formula of the essence. And it makes no difference even if it is not a formula of everything that is in the substance; for none the less the universal will be the substance of something, as 'man' is the substance of the individual man in whom it is present, so that the same result will follow once more; for the universal, e.g. 'animal', will be the substance of that in which it is present as something peculiar to it. And further it is impossible and absurd that the 'this', i.e. the substance, if it consists of parts, should not consist of substances nor of what is a 'this', but of quality; for that which is not substance, i.e. the quality, will then be prior to substance and to the 'this'. Which is impossible; for neither in formula nor in time nor in coming to be can the modifications be prior to the substance; for then they will also be separable from it. Further, Socrates will contain a substance present in a substance, so that this will be the substance of two things. And in general it follows, if man and such things are substance, that none of the elements in their formulae is the substance of anything, nor does it exist apart from the species or in anything else; I mean, for instance, that no 'animal' exists apart from the particular kinds of animal, nor does any other of the elements present in formulae exist apart. "If, then, we view the matter from these standpoints, it is plain that no universal attribute is a substance, and this is plain also from the fact that **no common predicate indicates a 'this'**, but rather a 'such'. If not, many difficulties follow and especially the 'third man'.

"The conclusion is evident also from the following consideration. A substance cannot consist of substances present in it in complete reality; for things that are thus in complete reality two are never in complete reality one, though if they are potentially two, they can be one (e.g. the double line consists of two halves-potentially; for the complete realization of the halves divides them from one another); therefore if the substance is one, it will not consist of substances present in it and present in this way, which Democritus describes rightly; he says one thing cannot be made out of two nor two out of one; for he identifies substances with his indivisible magnitudes. It is clear therefore that the same will hold good of number, if number is a synthesis of units, as is said by some; for two is either not one, or there is no unit present in it in complete reality. But our result involves a difficulty. If no substance can consist of universals because a universal indicates a 'such', not a 'this', and if no substance can be composed of substances existing in complete reality, every substance would be incomposite, so that there would not even be a formula of any substance. But it is thought by all and was stated long ago that it is either only, or primarily, substance that can

defined; yet now it seems that not even substance can. There cannot, then, be a definition of anything; or in a sense there can be, and in a sense there cannot. And what we are saying will be plainer from what follows.

Part 14 "

"It is clear also from these very facts what consequence confronts those who say the Ideas are substances capable of separate existence, and at the same time make the Form consist of the genus and the differentiae. For if the Forms exist and 'animal' is present in 'man' and 'horse', it is either one and the same in number, or different. (In formula it is clearly one; for he who states the formula will go through the formula in either case.) If then there is a 'man-in-himself' who is a 'this' and exists apart, the parts also of which he consists, e.g. 'animal' and 'two-footed', must indicate 'thises', and be capable of separate existence, and substances; therefore 'animal', as well as 'man', must be of this sort.

"Now (1) **if the 'animal' in 'the horse' and in 'man' is one and the same, as you are with yourself, (a) how will the one in things that exist apart be one, and how will this 'animal' escape being divided even from itself?**

"Further, (b) if it is to share in 'two-footed' and 'many-footed', an impossible conclusion follows; for contrary attributes will belong at the same time to it although it is one and a 'this'. If it is not to share in them, what is the relation implied when one says the animal

is two-footed or possessed of feet? But perhaps the two things are 'put together' and are 'in contact', or are 'mixed'. Yet all these expressions are absurd.

"But (2) suppose the Form to be different in each species. Then there will be practically an infinite number of things whose substance is animal'; for it is not by accident that 'man' has 'animal' for one of its elements. Further, many things will be 'animal-itself'. For (i) the 'animal' in each species will be the substance of the species; for it is after nothing else that the species is called; if it were, that other would be an element in 'man', i.e. would be the genus of man. And further, (ii) all the elements of which 'man' is composed will be Ideas. None of them, then, will be the Idea of one thing and the substance of another; this is impossible. The 'animal', then, present in each species of animals will be animal-itself. Further, from what is this 'animal' in each species derived, and how will it be derived from animal-itself? Or how can this 'animal', whose essence is simply animality, exist apart from animal-itself?

"Further, (3)in the case of sensible things both these consequences and others still more absurd follow.

If, then, these consequences are impossible, clearly there are not Forms of sensible things in the sense in which some maintain their existence.

Part 15 "

"Since substance is of two kinds, the concrete thing and the formula (I mean that one kind of substance is the formula taken with the matter, while another kind is the formula in its generality), substances in the former sense are capable of destruction (for they are capable

also of generation), but there is no destruction of the formula in the sense that it is ever in course of being destroyed (for there is no generation of it either; the being of house is not generated, but only the being of this house), but without generation and destruction formulae are and are not; for it has been shown that no one begets nor makes these. For this reason, also, there is neither definition of nor demonstration about sensible individual substances, because they have matter whose nature is such that they are capable both of

being and of not being; for which reason all the individual instances of them are destructible. If then demonstration is of necessary truths and definition is a scientific process, and if, just as knowledge cannot be sometimes knowledge and sometimes ignorance, but the state which varies thus is opinion, so too demonstration and definition

cannot vary thus, but it is opinion that deals with that which can be otherwise than as it is, clearly there can neither be definition of nor demonstration about sensible individuals. For perishing things are obscure to those who have the relevant knowledge, when they have

passed from our perception; and though the formulae remain in the soul unchanged, there will no longer be either definition or demonstration. And so when one of the definition-mongers defines any individual, he must recognize that his definition may always be overthrown; for it is not possible to define such things.

"Nor is it possible to define any Idea. For the Idea is, as its supporters say, an individual, and can exist apart; and the formula must consist of words; and he who defines must not invent a word (for it would be unknown), but the established words are common to all the members

of a class; these then must apply to something besides the thing defined; e.g. if one were defining you, he would say 'an animal which is lean' or 'pale', or something else which will apply also to some one other than you. If any one were to say that perhaps all the attributes taken apart may belong to many subjects, but together they belong only to this one, we must reply first that they belong also to both the elements; e.g. 'two-footed animal' belongs to animal and to the two-footed. (And in the case of eternal entities this is even necessary, since the elements are prior to and parts of the compound; nay more, they can also exist apart, if 'man' can exist apart. For either neither or both can. If, then, neither can, the genus will not exist apart from the various species; but if it does, the differentia will also.)

Secondly, we must reply that 'animal' and 'two-footed' are prior in being to 'two-footed animal'; and things which are prior to others are not destroyed when the others are.

"Again, if the Ideas consist of Ideas (as they must, since elements are simpler than the compound), it will be further necessary that the elements also of which the Idea consists, e.g. 'animal' and 'two-footed', should be predicated of many subjects. If not, how will they come to be known? For there will then be an Idea which cannot be predicated of more subjects than one. But this is not thought possible-every

Idea is thought to be capable of being shared. "As has been said, then, the impossibility of defining individuals escapes notice in the case of eternal things, especially those which are unique, like the sun or the moon. For people err not only by adding attributes whose removal the sun would survive, e.g. 'going round the earth' or 'night-hidden' (for from their view it follows that if it stands still or is visible, it will no longer be the sun; but it is strange if this is so; for 'the sun' means a certain substance); but also by the mention of attributes which can belong to another subject; e.g. if another thing with the stated attributes comes into existence, clearly it will be a sun; the formula therefore is general. But the sun was supposed to be an individual, like Cleon or Socrates.

After all, why does not one of the supporters of the Ideas produce a definition of an Idea? It would become clear, if they tried, that what has now been said is true.

Part 16

"Evidently even of the things that are thought to be substances, most are only potencies,-both the parts of animals (for none of them exists separately; and when they are separated, then too they exist, all of them, merely as matter) and earth and fire and air; for none of them is a unity, but as it were a mere heap, till they are worked up and some unity is made out of them. One might most readily suppose the parts of living things and the parts of the soul nearly related to them to turn out to be both, i.e. existent in complete reality as well as in potency, because they have sources of movement in something in their joints; for which reason some animals live when divided.

Yet all the parts must exist only potentially, when they are one and continuous by nature,-not by force or by growing into one, for such a phenomenon is an abnormality.

"Since the term 'unity' is used like the term 'being', and the substance of that which is one is one, and things whose substance is numerically one are numerically one, evidently neither unity nor being can be

the substance of things, just as being an element or a principle cannot be the substance, but we ask what, then, the principle is, that we may reduce the thing to something more knowable. Now of these concepts 'being' and 'unity' are more substantial than 'principle' or 'element' or 'cause', but not even the former are substance, since in general nothing that is common is substance; for substance does not belong to anything but to itself and to that which has it, of which it is the substance. Further, that which is one cannot be in many places at the same time, but that which is common is present in many places at the same time; so that clearly no universal exists apart from its individuals.

"But those who say the Forms exist, in one respect are right, in giving the Forms separate existence, if they are substances; but in another respect they are not right, because they say the one over many is a Form. The reason for their doing this is that they cannot declare what are the substances of this sort, the imperishable substances which exist apart from the individual and sensible substances. They make them, then, the same in kind as the perishable things (for this kind of substance we know)--'man-himself' and 'horse-itself', adding to the sensible things the word 'itself'. Yet even if we had not seen the stars, none the less, I suppose, would they have been eternal substances apart from those which we knew; so that now also if we do not know what non-sensible substances there are, yet it is doubtless necessary that there should he some.-Clearly, then, no universal term is the name of a substance, and no substance is composed of substances.

Part 17 "

"Let us state what, i.e. what kind of thing, substance should be said to be, taking once more another starting-point; for perhaps from this we shall get a clear view also of that substance which exists apart from sensible substances. Since, then, substance is a principle and a cause, let us pursue it from this starting-point. The 'why' is always sought in this form--'why does one thing attach to some other?' For to inquire why the musical man is a musical man, is either to inquire — as we have said why the man is musical, or it is something else. Now 'why a thing is itself' is a meaningless inquiry (for (to give meaning to the question 'why') the fact or the existence of the thing must already be evident-e.g. that the moon is eclipsed-but the fact that a thing is itself is the single reason and the single cause to be given in answer to all such questions as why the man is man, or the musician musical', unless one were to answer 'because each thing is inseparable from itself, and its being one just meant this'; this, however, is common to all things and is a short and easy way with the question). But we can inquire why man is an animal of such and such a nature. This, then, is plain, that we are not inquiring why he who is a man is a man. We are inquiring, then, why something is predicable of something (that it is predicable must be clear; for if not, the inquiry is an inquiry into nothing). E.g. why does it thunder? This is the same as 'why is sound produced in the clouds?' Thus the inquiry is about the predication of one thing of another.

And why are these things, i.e. bricks and stones, a house? Plainly we are seeking the cause. And this is the essence (to speak abstractly), which in some cases is the end, e.g. perhaps in the case of a house or a bed, and in some cases is the first mover; for this also is a cause. But while the efficient cause is sought in the case of genesis and destruction, the final cause is sought in the case of being also. "The object of the inquiry is most easily overlooked where one term is not expressly predicated of another (e.g. when we inquire 'what man is'), because we do not distinguish and do not say definitely that certain elements make up a certain whole. But we must articulate our meaning before we begin to inquire; if not, the inquiry is on the border-line between being a search for something and a search for nothing. Since we must have the existence of the thing as something given, clearly the question is why the matter is some definite thing; e.g. why are these materials a house? Because that which was the essence of a house is present. And why is this individual thing, or this body having this form, a man? Therefore what we seek is the cause, i.e. the form, by reason of which the matter is some definite thing; and this is the substance of the thing. Evidently, then, in the case of simple terms no inquiry nor teaching is possible; our attitude towards such things is other than that of inquiry. "Since that which is compounded out of something so that the whole is one, not like a heap but like a syllable-now the syllable is not its elements, ba is not the same as b and a, nor is flesh fire and earth (for when these are separated the wholes, i.e. the flesh and the syllable, no longer exist, but the elements of the syllable exist, and so do fire and earth); the syllable, then, is something-not only its elements (the vowel and the consonant) but also something else, and the flesh is not only fire and earth or the hot and the cold, but also something else:-if, then, that something must itself be either an element or composed of elements, (1) if it is an element the same argument will again apply; for flesh will consist of this and fire and earth and something still further, so that the process will go on to infinity. But (2) if it is a compound, clearly it will be a compound not of one but of more than one (or else that one will be the thing itself), so that again in this case we can use the same argument as in the case of flesh or of the syllable. But it would seem that this 'other' is something, and not an element, and that it is the cause which makes this thing flesh and that a syllable.

And similarly in all other cases. And this is the substance of each thing (for this is the primary cause of its being); and since, while some things are not substances, as many as are substances are formed in accordance with a nature of their own and by a process of nature, their substance would seem to be this kind of 'nature', which is not an element but a principle. An element, on the other hand, is that into which a thing is divided and which is present in it as matter; e.g. a and b are the elements of the syllable.

...   (part 8)

"(2) In time it is prior in this sense: the actual which is identical in species though not in number with a potentially existing thing is to it. I mean that to this particular man who now exists actually and to the corn and to the seeing subject the matter and the seed and that which is capable of seeing, which are potentially a man and corn and seeing, but not yet actually so, are prior in time; but prior in time to these are other actually existing things, from which they were produced. **For from the potentially existing the actually existing is always produced by an actually existing thing, e.g. man from man, musician by musician; there is always a first mover, and the mover already exists actually.** We have said in our account of substance that everything that is produced is something produced from something and by something, and that the same in species as it.

"This is why it is thought impossible to be a builder if one has built nothing or a harper if one has never played the harp; for he who learns to play the harp learns to play it by playing it, and all other learners do similarly. And thence arose the sophistical quibble, that one who does not possess a science will be doing that which is the object of the science; for he who is learning it does not possess it. But since, of that which is coming to be, some part must have come to be, and, of that which, in general, is changing, some part must have changed (this is shown in the treatise on movement), he who is learning must, it would seem, possess some part of the science. But here too, then, it is clear that actuality is in this sense also, viz. in order of generation and of time, prior to potency.

Book XII

Part 3 "

"Note, next, that neither the matter nor the form comes to be-and I mean the last matter and form. **For everything that changes is something and is changed by something and into something. That by which it is changed is the immediate mover; that which is changed, the matter; that into which it is changed, the form.** The process, then, will go on to infinity, if not only the bronze comes to be round but also the round or the bronze comes to be; therefore there must be a stop.

"Note, next, that each substance comes into being out of something that shares its name. (Natural objects and other things both rank as substances.) For things come into being either by art or by nature or by luck or by spontaneity. Now art is a principle of movement in something other than the thing moved, nature is a principle in the thing itself (for man begets man), and the other causes are privations of these two.

"There are three kinds of substance-the matter, which is a 'this' in appearance (for all things that are characterized by contact and not, by organic unity are matter and substratum, e.g. fire, flesh, head; for these are all matter, and the last matter is the matter of that which is in the full sense substance); the nature, which is a 'this' or positive state towards which movement takes place; and again, thirdly, the particular substance which is composed of these two, e.g. Socrates or Callias. Now in some cases the 'this' does not exist apart from the composite substance, e.g. the form of house does not so exist, unless the art of building exists apart (nor is there generation and destruction of these forms, but it is in another way that the house apart from its matter, and health, and all ideals of art, exist and do not exist); but if the 'this' exists apart from the concrete thing, it is only in the case of natural objects. And so Plato was not far wrong when he said that there are as many Forms as there are kinds of natural object (if there are Forms distinct from the things of this earth). The moving causes exist as things preceding the effects, but causes in the sense of definitions are simultaneous with their effects. For when a man is healthy, then health also exists; and the shape of a bronze sphere exists at the same time as the bronze sphere. (But we must examine whether any form also survives afterwards. For in some cases there is nothing to prevent this; e.g. the soul may be of this sort-not all soul but the reason; for presumably it is impossible that all soul should survive.) Evidently then there is no necessity, on this ground at least, for the existence of the Ideas. For man is begotten by man, a given man by an individual father; and similarly in the arts; for the medical art is the formal cause of health.

…

"That a final cause may exist among unchangeable entities is shown by the distinction of its meanings. For the final cause is (a) some being for whose good an action is done, and (b) something at which the action aims; and of these the latter exists among unchangeable entities though the former does not. The final cause, then, produces motion as being loved, but all other things move by being moved. Now if something is moved it is capable of being otherwise than as it is. Therefore if its actuality is the primary form of spatial motion, then in so far as it is subject to change, in this respect it is capable of being otherwise,-in place, even if not in substance. But since there is something which moves while itself unmoved, existing actually, this can in no way be otherwise than as it is. For motion in space is the first of the kinds of change, and motion in a circle the first kind of spatial motion; and this the first mover produces. The first mover, then, exists of necessity; and in so far as it exists by necessity, its mode of being is good, and it is in this sense a first principle.
For the necessary has all these senses-that which is necessary perforce because it is contrary to the natural impulse, that without which the good is impossible, and that which cannot be otherwise but can
exist only in a single way. "On such a principle, then, depend the heavens and the world of nature. And it is a life such as the best which we enjoy, and enjoy for but a short time (for it is ever in this state, which we cannot be), since its actuality is also pleasure. (And for this reason are waking, perception, and thinking most pleasant, and hopes and memories are so on account of these.) And thinking in itself

deals with that which is best in itself, and that which is thinking in the fullest sense with that which is best in the fullest sense. And thought thinks on itself because it shares the nature of the object of thought; for it becomes an object of thought in coming into contact with and thinking its objects, so that thought and object of thought are the same. For that which is capable of receiving the object of thought, i.e. the essence, is thought.

But it is active when it possesses this object. Therefore the possession rather than the receptivity is the divine element which thought seems to contain, and the act of contemplation is what is most pleasant and best. If, then, God is always in that good state in which we sometimes are, this compels our wonder; and if in a better this compels it yet more. And God is in a better state. And life also belongs to God;

for the actuality of thought is life, and God is that actuality; and God's self-dependent actuality is life most good and eternal. We say therefore that God is a living being, eternal, most good, so that life and duration continuous and eternal belong to God; for this is God.

Part 8 "

"It is clear, then, why these things are as they are. But we must not ignore the question whether we have to suppose one such substance or more than one, and if the latter, how many; we must also mention,

regarding the opinions expressed by others, that they have said nothing about the number of the substances that can even be clearly stated. For the theory of Ideas has no special discussion of the subject; for those who speak of Ideas say the Ideas are numbers, and they speak of numbers now as unlimited, now as limited by the number 10; but as for the reason why there should be just so many numbers, nothing is said with any demonstrative exactness. We however must discuss the subject, starting from the presuppositions and distinctions we have mentioned. The first principle or primary being is not movable either in itself or accidentally, but produces the primary eternal and single movement. But since that which is moved must be moved by something, and the first mover must be in itself unmovable, and eternal movement must be produced by something eternal and a single movement

by a single thing, and since we see that besides the simple spatial movement of the universe, which we say the first and unmovable substance produces, there are other spatial movements-those of the planets-which are eternal (for a body which moves in a circle is eternal and unresting; we have proved these points in the physical treatises), each of these movements also must be caused by a substance both unmovable in itself and eternal. For the nature of the stars is eternal just because it is a certain kind of substance, and the mover is eternal and prior to the moved, and that which is prior to a substance must be a substance.

Evidently, then, there must be substances which are of the same number as the movements of the stars, and in their nature eternal, and in themselves unmovable, and without magnitude, for the reason before

mentioned. That the movers are substances, then, and that one of these is first and another second according to the same order as the movements of the stars, is evident. But in the number of the movements we reach a problem which must be treated from the standpoint of that one of the mathematical sciences which is most akin to philosophy-viz. of astronomy; for this science speculates about substance which is perceptible but eternal, but the other mathematical sciences, i.e. arithmetic and geometry, treat of no substance. That the movements are more numerous than the bodies that are moved is evident to those who have given even moderate attention to the matter; for each of the planets has more than one movement. But as to the actual number of these movements, we now-to give some notion of the subject-quote what some of the mathematicians say, that our thought may have some definite number to grasp; but, for the rest, we must partly investigate for ourselves, Partly learn from other investigators, and if those who study this subject form an opinion contrary to what we have now stated, we must esteem both parties indeed, but follow the more accurate. "Eudoxus supposed that the motion of the sun or of the moon involves, in either case, three spheres, of which the first is the sphere of the fixed stars, and the second moves in the circle which runs along the middle of the zodiac, and the third in the circle which is inclined across the breadth of the zodiac; but the circle in which the moon moves is inclined at a greater angle than that in which the sun moves. And the motion of the planets involves, in each case, four spheres, and of these also the first and second are the same as the first two mentioned above (for the sphere of the fixed stars is that which moves all the other spheres, and that which is placed beneath this and has its movement in the circle which bisects the zodiac is common to all), but the poles of the third sphere of each planet are in the circle which bisects the zodiac, and the motion of the fourth sphere is in the circle which is inclined at an angle to the equator of the third sphere; and the poles of the third sphere are different for each of the other planets, but those of Venus and Mercury are the same. "Callippus made the position of the spheres the same as Eudoxus did, but while he assigned the same number as Eudoxus did to Jupiter and to Saturn, he thought two more spheres should be added to the sun and two to the moon, if one is to explain the observed facts; and one more to each of the other planets.

"But it is necessary, if all the spheres combined are to explain the observed facts, that for each of the planets there should be other spheres (one fewer than those hitherto assigned) which counteract those already mentioned and bring back to the same position the outermost sphere of the star which in each case is situated below the star in question; for only thus can all the forces at work produce the observed motion of the planets. Since, then, the spheres involved in the movement of the planets themselves are--eight for Saturn and Jupiter and twenty-five for the others, and of these only those involved in the movement of the lowest-situated planet need not be counteracted the spheres which counteract those of the outermost two planets will be six in number, and the spheres which counteract those of the next four planets will be sixteen; therefore the number of all the spheres--both those which move the planets and those which counteract these--will be fifty-five.

And if one were not to add to the moon and to the sun the movements we mentioned, **the whole set of spheres will be forty-seven in number.**

"Let this, then, be taken as the number of the spheres, so that the unmovable substances and principles also may probably be taken as just so many; the assertion of necessity must be left to more powerful thinkers. But if there can be no spatial movement which does not conduce to the moving of a star, and if further every being and every substance which is immune from change and in virtue of itself has attained to the best must be considered an end, there can be no other being apart from these we have named, but this must be the number of the substances. For if there are others, they will cause change as being a final cause of movement; but there cannot he other movements besides those mentioned.

And it is reasonable to infer this from a consideration of the bodies that are moved; for if everything that moves is for the sake of that which is moved, and every movement belongs to something that is moved,

no movement can be for the sake of itself or of another movement, but all the movements must be for the sake of the stars. For if there is to be a movement for the sake of a movement, this latter also will have to be for the sake of something else; so that since there cannot be an infinite regress, the end of every movement will be one of the divine bodies which move through the heaven.

"(Evidently there is but one heaven. For if there are many heavens as there are many men, the moving principles, of which each heaven will have one, will be one in form but in number many. But all things that are many in number have matter; for one and the same definition, e.g. that of man, applies to many things, while Socrates is one. But the primary essence has not matter; for it is complete reality. So the unmovable first mover is one both in definition and in number; so too, therefore, is that which is moved always and continuously; therefore there is one heaven alone.) **Our forefathers in the most remote ages have handed down to their posterity a tradition, in the form of a myth, that these bodies are gods**, and that the divine encloses the whole of nature. The rest of the tradition has been added later

in mythical form with a view to the persuasion of the multitude and to its legal and utilitarian expediency; they say these gods are in the form of men or like some of the other animals, and they say other things consequent on and similar to these which we have mentioned. But if one were to separate the first point from these additions and take it alone-that they thought the first substances to be gods, one

must regard this as an inspired utterance, and reflect that, while probably each art and each science has often been developed as far as possible and has again perished, these opinions, with others, have been preserved until the present like relics of the ancient treasure. Only thus far, then, is the opinion of our ancestors and of our earliest predecessors clear to us.

Part 9

"The nature of the **divine thought** involves certain problems; for while thought is held to be the most divine of things observed by us, the question how it must be situated in order to have that character involves difficulties. For if it thinks of nothing, what is there here of dignity?

It is just like one who sleeps. And if it thinks, but this depends on something else, then (since that which is its substance is not the act of thinking, but a potency) it cannot be the best substance; for it is through thinking that its value belongs to it. Further, whether its substance is the faculty of thought or the act of thinking, what does it think of? Either of itself or of something else; and if of something else, either of the same thing always or of something different. Does it matter, then, or not, whether it thinks of the

good or of any chance thing? **Are there not some things about which it is incredible that it should think?** Evidently, then, it thinks of that which is most divine and precious, **and it does not change**; for change would be change for the worse, and this would be already a movement. First, then, if 'thought' is not the act of thinking but a potency, it would be reasonable to suppose that the continuity of

its thinking is wearisome to it. Secondly, there would evidently be something else more precious than thought, viz. that which is thought of. For both thinking and the act of thought will belong even to one who thinks of the worst thing in the world, so that if this ought to be avoided (and it ought, for there are even some things which it is better not to see than to see), the act of thinking cannot be the best of things. Therefore it must be of itself that the divine thought thinks (since it is the most excellent of things), and its thinking is a thinking on thinking.

"But evidently knowledge and perception and opinion and understanding have always something else as their object, and themselves only by the way. Further, if thinking and being thought of are different, in respect of which does goodness belong to thought? For to he an act of thinking and to he an object of thought are not the same thing. We answer that in some cases the knowledge is the object. In the productive sciences it is the substance or essence of the object, matter omitted, and in the theoretical sciences the definition or the act of thinking is the object. Since, then, thought and the object of thought are not different in the case of things that have not matter, the divine thought and its object will be the same, i.e. the thinking will be one with the object of its thought.

"A further question is left-whether the object of the divine thought is composite; for if it were, thought would change in passing from part to part of the whole. We answer that everything which has not matter is indivisible-as human thought, or rather the thought of composite beings, is in a certain period of time (for it does not possess the good at this moment or at that, but its best, being something different

from it, is attained only in a whole period of time), so throughout eternity is the thought which has itself for its object.

Part 10

"We must consider also in which of two ways the **nature of the universe contains the good, and the highest good,** whether as something separate and by itself, or as the order of the parts. Probably in both ways, as an army does; for its good is found both in its order and in its leader, and more in the latter; for he does not depend on the order but it depends on him. And all things are ordered together somehow,

but not all alike,-both fishes and fowls and plants; and the world is not such that one thing has nothing to do with another, but they are connected. For all are ordered together to one end, but it is as in a house, where the freemen are least at liberty to act at random, but all things or most things are already ordained for them, while the slaves and the animals do little for the common good, and for the most part live at random; for this is the sort of principle that constitutes the nature of each. I mean, for instance, that all must at least come to be dissolved into their elements, and there are other functions similarly in which all share for the good of the whole.

"We must not fail to observe how many impossible or paradoxical results confront those who hold different views from our own, and what are the views of the subtler thinkers, and which views are attended by fewest difficulties. All make all things out of contraries. But neither 'all things' nor 'out of contraries' is right; nor do these thinkers tell us how all the things in which the contraries are present can

be made out of the contraries; for contraries are not affected by one another. Now for us this difficulty is solved naturally by the fact that there is a third element. These thinkers however make one of the two contraries matter; this is done for instance by those who make the unequal matter for the equal, or the many matter for the one. But this also is refuted in the same way; for the one matter which underlies any pair of contraries is contrary to nothing. Further, all things, except the one, will, on the view we are criticizing, partake of evil; for the bad itself is one of the two elements. But the other school does not treat the good and the bad even as principles; yet in all things the good is in the highest degree a principle. The school we first mentioned is right in saying that it is a principle, but how the good is a principle they do not say-whether as end or as mover or as form.

"Empedocles also has a paradoxical view; for he identifies the good with love, but this is a principle both as mover (for it brings things together) and as matter (for it is part of the mixture). Now even if it happens that the same thing is a principle both as matter and as mover, still the being, at least, of the two is not the same. In which respect then is love a principle? It is paradoxical also that strife should be imperishable; the nature of his 'evil' is just strife. "Anaxagoras makes the good a motive principle; for his 'reason' moves things. But it moves them for an end, which must be something other than it, except according to our way of stating the case; for, on our view, the medical art is in a sense health. It is paradoxical also not to suppose a contrary to the good, i.e. to reason. But all who speak of the contraries make no use of the contraries, unless we bring their views into shape. And why some things are perishable and others imperishable, no one tells us; for they make all existing things out of the same principles. Further, some make existing things out of the nonexistent; and others to avoid the necessity of this make all things one.

"Further, why should there always be becoming, and what is the cause of becoming?-this no one tells us. And those who suppose two principles must suppose another, a superior principle, and so must those who believe in the Forms; for why did things come to participate, or why do they participate, in the Forms? And all other thinkers are confronted by the necessary consequence that there is something contrary to Wisdom, i.e. to the highest knowledge; but we are not. For there is nothing contrary to that which is primary; for all contraries have matter, and things that have matter exist only potentially; and the ignorance which is contrary to any knowledge leads to an object contrary to the object of the knowledge; but what is primary has no contrary. "Again, if besides sensible things no others exist, there will be no first principle, no order, no becoming, no heavenly bodies, but each principle will have a principle before it, as in the accounts of the theologians and all the natural philosophers. But if the Forms or the numbers are to exist, they will be causes of nothing; or if not that, at least not of movement. Further, how is extension, i.e. a continuum, to be produced out of unextended parts? For number will not, either as mover or as form, produce a continuum. But again there cannot be any contrary that is also essentially a productive or moving principle; for it would be possible for it not to be. Or at least its action would be posterior to its potency. The world, then, would not be eternal. But it is; one of these premises, then, must be denied. And we have said how this must be done. Further, in virtue of what the numbers, or the soul and the body, or in general the form and the thing, are one-of this no one tells us anything; nor can any one tell, unless he says, as we do, that the mover makes them one. And those who say mathematical number is first and go on to generate one kind of substance after another and give different principles for each, make the substance of the universe a mere series of episodes (for one substance has no influence on another by its existence or nonexistence), and they give us many governing principles; but the world refuses to be governed badly. "

"'The rule of many is not good; one ruler let there be.'

§2: Foundational Debates in Epistemology

Epistemology is the study of knowledge. Since Socrates, philosophers have been engaged in the project of questioning and critically evaluating things which we think we know. Epistemology turns the spotlight directly on knowledge itself. Some of the big questions of Epistemology are these:

- What is knowledge? What does it mean to say that you 'know' that it is a sunny day, that Mo Farah has won four gold medals, or that God exists? What makes distinguishes your so-called 'knowledge' from a lucky guess? Philosophers tend to argue that a statement (proposition) that you know must be not only true but also *warranted*. But what 'warrant' consists of is the subject of much debate.

- How is knowledge obtained? This is the question which is our focus in this anthology and course. Does the special kind of belief which we call knowledge come from reason, or from what we see, hear, smell, taste and feel? Or does it come from a combination of those sources? Or from somewhere else?

- What, if anything, is beyond the reach of our knowledge? Are there some subject areas where we are not competent to judge truth and falsity, or even where anything we say is bound to be meaningless? David Hume, an enormously influential figure in philosophy's Early Modern period, put the whole of theology in that latter category as we shall see.

The connection between this branch of philosophy and the fields of ethics and philosophy of religion is clear, as indeed Hume's position demonstrates. Considering what knowledge is, when we can claim to have it and where it comes from may provide a yardstick against which to assess 'knowledge' of right and wrong, or of God. Even if Epistemology fails to provide a solid and reliable yardstick, it will at least give us some insight into the rational status of beliefs and claims in Ethics and Philosophy of Religion.

Our main concern here is with the debate between Empiricists and Rationalists as to the sources of knowledge.

RATIONALISM

The precise claims of rationalists vary, but the position could fairly be summarized as:

the view that all knowledge starts with the mind.

We owe our knowledge primarily or ultimately to our reason, rather than to the experiences of our five senses.

This section of the anthology focuses on the giants of 17th century European philosophy Descartes and Leibniz, but Plato provides another excellent example of the rationalist approach.

The *a priori*

In their epistemological vision, rationalists give pride of place to *a priori* knowledge – knowledge which **does not depend on sense experience**. The Latin words refer to what is before, prior to. 'Prior to what?' you might ask. Prior to sense experience. *A priori* knowledge is the knowledge we can have before referring to what we are seeing, hearing, smelling, touching or tasting (or indeed what we have seen, heard, smelt, touched or tasted). For instance, my knowledge that 2 + 2 = 4 is *a priori* knowledge. It does not depend on the evidence of my senses. It is a matter of logic. Nothing that happens in the material world – the world made of physical stuff – will change the fact that 2 + 2 = 4. I need to look out of the window in the morning to see if it is a sunny day, but I can trust the basic truths of mathematics before even getting out of bed.

Intuition and deduction

Let us unpack the processes of *a priori* reasoning which lead to *a priori* knowledge. Rationalists hold that we can acquire knowledge through intuition and deduction, without the involvement of sense experience. Peter Markie explains how this works here:.

> **Intuition is a form of rational insight.** Intellectually grasping a proposition, **we just "see" it to be true** in such a way as to form a true, warranted belief in it. **Deduction** is a process in which we derive conclusions from intuited premises through **valid arguments**, ones in which **the conclusion must be true if the premises are true.** We intuit, for example, that the number three is prime and that it is greater than two. We then deduce from this knowledge that there is a prime number greater than two. Intuition and deduction thus provide us with knowledge *a priori*, which is to say knowledge gained independently of sense experience.

That concept of a '**valid** argument' deserves another example. (Note that a 'premise' is just one of the statements which form the basis of your argument) This is a valid argument:

Premise 1: I am thinking

Premise 2: Inanimate blobs of jelly cannot think

Conclusion: I am not an inanimate blob of jelly

If the two premises are true, there is no way that the conclusion can be false. That is not hyperbole. It is a matter of logic. It just is not possible for me to be an inanimate blob of jelly if I am thinking and inanimate blobs of jelly can't think. This argument happens to be **sound** as well as valid. A valid argument in which the premises are true is called a sound argument. The conclusion of a sound argument is true.

To recap, rationalists claim that we can gain knowledge without sense experience through **intuition – direct rational insight** - and **deduction – the process of reasoning through valid arguments.**

Another claim that rationalists make is that we are born with ingredients for *a priori* reasoning already present in our minds. We possess innate ideas – **ideas that are not gained through experience but are inherent in our minds.** For rationalists, these innate ideas are not confined to mathematics. René Descartes, with whom you will soon be getting better acquainted, claimed to have a 'clear and distinct idea of God', which he considered could not possibly have come from experience. Plato believed that we are born with concepts of ideals such as Justice, Beauty and Good, as well as mathematical concepts and indeed concepts of all the creatures and objects we encounter in the world.

The superiority of *a priori* knowledge

Plato exemplifies one other rationalist claim. This is the claim that the knowledge we gain purely through *a priori* reasoning (intuition and deduction) is **superior** to knowledge gained using sense experience. For Descartes this is because *a priori* knowledge is **more certain and secure**; our minds can provide reliable 'clear and distinct' ideas whereas sense experience is often misleading or ambiguous (as you will see in his discussion of candle wax). Plato also considers knowledge yielded by reason alone to be more certain. For Plato, though, this knowledge is also superior because of *what* we can know about through it. Through reason alone we can gain knowledge of the realm of the Forms – the true reality of which the empirical world is just a pale imitation.

EMPIRICISM

Empiricism is, in essence, *the view that all knowledge begins with the senses.* I come to know about the world not through detaching from it and trusting only abstract reasoning, but by experiencing the world. The foundations of all knowledge are the sensations provided by sight, hearing, touch, smell and taste.

Empiricism is closely associated with the English philosophers of the Early Modern Period: John Locke, David Hume, and George Berkeley. It should be noted that each has his own complex philosophical system and that these do not fit neatly into broad categories. A thinker may be thoroughly empiricist in some areas but lean towards rationalism in others. Locke, for example, is very much an empiricist in his discussion of how we obtain concepts and knowledge. However, when he argues that matter could not possibly cause consciousness, and that we can legitimately argue from that premise to the existence of God, he is thinking like a rationalist.

The *a posteriori*

A posteriori **knowledge** is knowledge which **depends on sense experience**. It is 'from what comes after' sense experience. *A posteriori* reasoning relies on premises based on the evidence of sight, hearing, touch, taste or smell. My knowledge that there are no clouds in the sky is an instance of *a posteriori* knowledge. If I reason from that premise to the conclusion that I will not be rained upon if I go outside, then I am engaging in *a posteriori* reasoning.

Induction

Induction is the kind of reasoning on which we rely in much of our daily lives. Unlike deductive reasoning, it relies on probabilities. A sound deductive argument makes its conclusion certain, whereas the strongest of inductive arguments only makes its conclusion extremely likely. Here is an example of an inductive argument:

Premise 1: It has rained in London in September every year since records began (in 1910)

Premise 2: It is September

Conclusion: It will rain this month

It is not a matter of logic that the conclusion is true. It depends on what happens in the world. We feel pretty confident in the conclusion, though, because of past experience.

The mind as initially *tabula rasa*

One empiricist claim, which we will be exploring in John Locke's work, is that we are born with neither knowledge nor concepts. The mind of a new born infant is *tabula rasa,* a blank slate. Locke here is the polar opposite of Plato, who thinks that a newborn child has seen - or rather perceived - it all before in the realm of the Forms. Locke sees no evidence of any ideas or understanding preceding the effects of sense experience on babies and children. We acquire every concept which we possess through repeated experience. You can consider for yourself whether there are any counterexamples to this. Is there anything that we *just know* independent of sense experience?

There are two further concepts worth bearing in mind as you go on to explore and analyse epistemology in more depth:

Analytic

An analytic proposition is **a statement that is true by definition.** In other words, if you understand the meaning of the words, you will see that the statement is true. 'All cats are mammals' is an analytic statement. If I understand what 'cat' means and I understand what 'mammal' mean, I cannot deny the statement. Definitions ('a square is a plane figure with four straight sides and four right angles') are analytic statements. So are tautologies – i.e. statements which essentially say the same thing twice ('Your PIN is a number' – it has to be, because PIN stands for Personal Identification Number).

Immanuel Kant, who introduced the term, said that in an analytic proposition, **the predicate is contained within the subject**. That is to say, what you are saying about the thing you are talking about is part of the definition of the thing you are talking about. In 'all cats are mammals', the subject is 'all cats' and the predicate is 'are mammals'. Being a mammal is part of the definition of 'cat'. So 'all cats' *contains* the idea of 'are mammals'.

As we will see, David Hume considered that all *a priori* propositions are analytic. Essentially, reason on its own (without sense experience) can only really allow you to clarify what words or numbers mean – to draw out the implications of language. It cannot tell us about the world. Pure reason can tell me that a bachelor is an unmarried man (true by definition). But it cannot tell me that God exists, or that there is a physical world.

Rationalists think that *a priori* knowledge extends beyond just analytic propositions. For instance, Descartes and Leibniz agree that it includes the knowledge that God exists.

Synthetic

A synthetic proposition is a statement which **you cannot tell to be true just by analyzing the meaning of the words.** You have to look beyond the words themselves. The predicate is not contained within the subject. To pluck one example out of the infinite possibilities, 'My coffee cup is almost empty' is a synthetic statement.

REFERENCES

Simon Blackburn, *Think* (OUP, 1999).

Daniel Cardinal, Jeremy Hayward and Gerald Jones, *Epistemology: The Theory of Knowledge* (John Murray, 2004).

Peter Markie, 'Rationalism and Empiricism' in *The Stanford Encyclopedia of Philosophy*, http://plato.stanford.edu/entries/rationalism-empiricism/.

René Descartes (1596 – 1650)

Meditations on First Philosophy
in which are demonstrated the existence of God and the distinction between the human soul and the body

What can I know?

First Meditation: On what can be called into doubt

Some years ago I was struck by how many false things I had believed, and by how doubtful was the structure of beliefs that I had based on them. I realized that if I wanted to establish anything in the sciences that was stable and likely to last, I needed – just once in my life – to demolish everything completely and start again from the foundations. It looked like an enormous task, and I decided to wait until I was old enough to be sure that there was nothing to be gained from putting it off any longer. I have now delayed it for so long that I have no excuse for going on *planning* to do it rather than getting to work. So today I have set all my worries aside and arranged for myself a clear stretch of free time. I am here quite alone, and at last I will devote myself, sincerely and without holding back, to demolishing my opinions.

What is Descartes aiming to do?

I can do this without showing that all my beliefs are false, which is probably more than I could ever manage. My reason tells me that as well as withholding assent from propositions that are obviously false, I should also withhold it from ones that are not completely certain and indubitable. So all I need, for the purpose of rejecting all my opinions, is to find in each of them at least *some* reason for doubt. I can do this without going through them one by one, which would take forever: once the foundations of a building have been undermined, the rest collapses of its own accord; so I will go straight for the basic principles on which all my former beliefs rested.

Descartes claims that he does not need to prove his beliefs false; he just needs to show that _____

Why will he start with 'basic principles'?

Whatever I have accepted until now as most true has come to me through my senses. But occasionally I have found that they have deceived me, and it is unwise to trust completely those who have deceived us even once.

Are you convinced by his reason for distrusting his senses? Why?/Why not?

Yet although the senses sometimes deceive us about objects that are very small or distant, that doesn't apply to my belief that I am here, sitting by the fire, wearing a winter dressing-gown, holding this piece of paper in my hands, and so on. It seems to be quite impossible to doubt beliefs like these, which come from the senses.

Another example: how can I doubt that these hands or this whole body are mine? To doubt such things I would have to liken myself to brain-damaged madmen who are convinced they are kings when really they are paupers, or say they are dressed in purple when they are naked, or that they are pumpkins, or made of glass. Such people are insane, and I would be thought equally mad if I modelled myself on them.

Why does Descartes consider he cannot take for granted even his physical surroundings and his own body?

What a brilliant piece of reasoning! As if I were not a man who sleeps at night and often has all the same experiences while asleep as madmen do when awake – indeed sometimes even more improbable ones. Often in my dreams I am convinced of just such familiar events – that I am sitting by the fire in my dressing-gown – when in fact I am lying undressed in bed! Yet right now my eyes are certainly wide open when I look at this piece of paper; I shake my head and it isn't asleep; when I rub one hand against the other, I do it deliberately and know what I am doing. This wouldn't all happen with such clarity to someone asleep.

Even though he has a clear impression of actually shaking his head and rubbing his hands while awake, he cannot trust this. Why?

Indeed! As if I didn't remember other occasions when I have been tricked by exactly similar thoughts while asleep! As I think about this more carefully, I realize that there is never any reliable way of distinguishing being awake from being asleep.

This discovery makes me feel dizzy, which itself reinforces the notion that I may be asleep! Suppose then that I am dreaming – it isn't true that I, with my eyes open, am moving my head and stretching out my hands. Suppose, indeed that I don't even *have* hands or any body at all.

Still, it has to be admitted that the visions that come in sleep are like paintings: they must have been made as copies of real things; so at least these general *kinds* of things – eyes, head, hands and the body as a whole – must be real and not imaginary. For even when painters try to depict sirens and satyrs with the most extraordinary bodies, they simply jumble up the limbs of different kinds of real animals, rather than inventing natures that are entirely new. If they do succeed in thinking up something completely fictitious and unreal – not remotely like anything ever seen before – at least the colours used in the picture must be real. Similarly, although these general kinds of things – eyes, head, hands and so on – could be imaginary, there is no

Descartes suggests that perhaps he can trust his belief in universal properties like shape, colour, number, size.

Why?

denying that certain even simpler and more universal kinds of things are real. These are the elements out of which we make all our mental images of things – the true and also the false ones.

These simpler and more universal kinds include *body*, and *extension*; the *shape* of extended things; their *quantity*, *size* and *number*; the *places* things can be in, the *time* through which they can last, and so on.

So it seems reasonable to conclude that physics, astronomy, medicine, and all other sciences dealing with things that have complex structures are doubtful; while arithmetic, geometry and other studies of the simplest and most general things – whether they really exist in nature or not – contain something certain and indubitable. For whether I am awake or asleep, two plus three makes five, and a square has only four sides. It seems impossible to suspect that such obvious truths might be false.

Summarise his point here

Why might an all-powerful God challenge Descartes' belief in shape, size and colour?

However, I have for many years been sure that there is an all-powerful God who made me to be the sort of creature that I am. How do I know that he hasn't brought it about that there is no earth, no sky, nothing that takes up space, no shape, no size, no place, while making sure that all these things appear to me to exist? Anyway, I sometimes think that others go wrong even when they think they have the most perfect knowledge; so how do I know that I myself don't go wrong every time I add two and three or count the sides of a square? Well, you might say ·, God would not let me be deceived like that, because he is said to be supremely good. But, I reply, if God's goodness would stop him from letting me be deceived all the time, you would expect it to stop him from allowing me to be deceived even occasionally; yet clearly I sometimes *am* deceived.

Descartes notes that we might trust God not to let us be deceived because of his goodness. However, he rejects this argument because _____

_____

Some people would deny the existence of such a powerful God rather than believe that everything else is uncertain. Let us grant them – for purposes of argument – that there is no God, and theology is fiction. On their view, then, I am a product of fate or chance or a long chain of causes and effects. But the *less* powerful they make my original cause, the *more* likely it is that I am so imperfect as to be deceived all the time – because deception and error seem to be imperfections. Having no answer to these arguments, I am driven back to the position that doubts can properly be raised about any of my former beliefs. I don't reach this conclusion in a flippant or casual manner, but on the basis of powerful and well thought-out reasons. So in future, if I want to discover any certainty, I must withhold my assent from these former beliefs just as carefully as I withhold it from obvious falsehoods.

It isn't enough merely to have noticed this, though; I must make an effort to remember it. My old familiar opinions keep coming back, and against my will they capture my belief. It is as though they had a *right* to a place in my belief-system as a result of long occupation and the law of custom. It is true that these habitual opinions of mine are highly probable; although they are in a sense doubtful, as I have shown, it is more reasonable to believe than to deny them. But if I go on viewing them in that light I shall never get out of the habit of confidently assenting to them. To conquer that habit, therefore, I had better switch right around and pretend (for a while) that these former opinions of mine are utterly false and imaginary. I shall do this until I have something to counter-balance the weight of old opinion, and the distorting influence of habit no longer prevents me from judging correctly. However far I go in my distrustful attitude, no actual harm will come of it, because my project won't affect how I act, but only how I go about acquiring knowledge.

So I shall suppose that some malicious, powerful, cunning demon has done all he can to deceive me – rather than this being done by God, who is supremely good and the source of truth. I shall think that the sky, the air, the earth, colours, shapes, sounds and all external things are merely dreams that the demon has contrived as traps for my judgment. I shall consider myself as having no hands or eyes, or flesh, or blood or senses, but as having falsely believed that I had all these things. I shall stubbornly persist in this train of thought; and even if I can't learn any truth, I shall at least do what I *can* do, which is to be on my guard against accepting any falsehoods, so that the deceiver – however powerful and cunning he may be – will be unable to affect me in the slightest. This will be hard work, though, and a kind of laziness pulls me back into my old ways.

Like a prisoner who dreams that he is free, starts to suspect that it is merely a dream, and wants to go on dreaming rather than waking up, so I am content to slide back into my old opinions; I fear being shaken out of them because I am afraid that my peaceful sleep may be followed by hard labour when I wake, and that I shall have to struggle not in the light but in the imprisoning darkness of the problems I have raised.

If there is no God, where does that leave us, according to Descartes?

What does Descartes do to try to avoid the temptation of trusting his own senses?

Candle Wax, Experience and Reason...

From the Second Meditation

Let us consider the things that people ordinarily think they understand best of all, namely the bodies that we touch and see. I don't mean bodies in general – for our general thoughts are apt to be confused – but one particular body: this piece of wax, for example. It has just been taken from the honeycomb; it still tastes of honey and has the scent of the flowers from which the honey was gathered; its colour, shape and size are plain to see; it is hard, cold and can be handled easily; if you rap it with your knuckle it makes a sound. In short, it has everything that seems to be needed for a body to be known perfectly clearly. But as I speak these words I hold the wax near to the fire, and look! The taste and smell vanish, the colour changes, the shape is lost, the size increases; the wax becomes liquid and hot; you can hardly touch it, and it no longer makes a sound when you strike it. But is it still the same wax? Of course it is; no-one denies this. So what was it about the wax that I understood so clearly? Evidently it was not any of the features that the senses told me of; for all of them – brought to me through taste, smell, sight, touch or hearing – have now altered, yet it is still the same wax.

Perhaps what I now think about the wax indicates what its nature was all along. If that is right, then the wax was not the sweetness of the honey, the scent of the flowers, the whiteness, the shape, or the sound, but was rather *a body* that recently presented itself to me in those ways but now appears differently. But what exactly is this thing that I am now imagining? Well, if we take away whatever doesn't belong to the wax (that is, everything that the wax *could* be without), what is left is merely *something extended, flexible and changeable*. What do 'flexible' and 'changeable' mean here? I can imaginatively picture this piece of wax changing from round to square, from square to triangular, and so on. But that isn't what changeability is. In knowing that the wax is changeable I understand that it can go through *endlessly many* changes of that kind, far more than I can depict in my imagination; so it isn't my imagination that gives me my grasp of the wax as flexible and changeable. Also, what does 'extended' mean? Is the wax's extension also unknown? It increases if the wax melts, and increases again if it boils; the wax can be extended in many more ways (that is, with many more shapes) than I will ever bring before my imagination. I am forced to conclude that the nature of this piece of wax isn't revealed by my imagination, but is perceived by the mind alone. (I am speaking of this particular piece of wax; the point is even clearer with regard to wax in general.) This wax that is perceived by the mind alone is, of course, the same wax that I see, touch, and picture in my imagination – in short the same wax I thought it to be from the start. But although my perception of it *seemed* to be a case of vision and touch and imagination, it isn't so and it never was. Rather, it is purely a perception by the mind alone – formerly an imperfect and confused one, but now clear and distinct because I am now concentrating carefully on what the wax consists in.

- *How does Descartes consider he reaches a 'clear and distinct' idea of the wax?*
- *What is his attitude towards sense experience?*

- *Are you convinced by his argument here?*

From the Third Meditation

That lists everything that I truly know, or at least everything I have, up to now, discovered that I know. Now I will look more carefully to see whether I have overlooked other facts about myself. *I am certain that I am a thinking thing.* Doesn't that tell me what it takes for me to be certain about anything? In this first item of knowledge there is simply a clear and distinct perception of what I am asserting; this wouldn't be enough to make me certain of its truth if it could ever turn out that something that I perceived so clearly and distinctly was false. So I now seem to be able to lay it down as a general rule that *whatever I perceive very clearly and distinctly is true.*

- *Here Descartes proposes that where he can clearly and distinctly perceive that something is true, it is. How does he come to this conclusion?*

- *Considering Descartes exploration of his knowledge of the wax candle, what kind of reasoning does he see as providing clear and distinct perception?*

God and the restoration of confidence in the external world

From the Third Meditation

..... The idea that gives me my understanding of a supreme God – eternal, infinite, unchangeable, omniscient, omnipotent and the creator of everything that exists except for himself – certainly has in it more representative reality than the ideas that represent merely finite substances.

Now it is obvious by the natural light that the total cause of something must contain at least as much reality as does the effect. For where could the effect get its reality from if not from the cause? And how could the cause give reality to the effect unless it first had that reality itself? Two things follow from this: that something can't arise from nothing, and that what is more perfect – that is, contains in itself more reality – can't arise from what is less perfect.

And this is plainly true not only for 'actual' or 'intrinsic' reality (as philosophers call it) but also for the *representative* reality of ideas – that is, the reality that an idea represents. A stone, for example, can begin to exist only if it is produced by something that contains – either straightforwardly or in some higher form – everything that is to be found in the stone; similarly, heat can't be produced in a previously cold object except by something of at least the same order of perfection as heat, and so on. (I don't say simply 'except by something that is hot', because that is not necessary. The thing could be caused to be hot by something that doesn't itself *straightforwardly* contain heat – i.e. that isn't itself *hot* – but contains heat *in a higher form*, that is, something of a higher order of perfection than heat. Thus, for example, although God is obviously not himself *hot*, he can cause something to be hot because he contains heat not straightforwardly but in a higher form.) But it is also true that *the idea of* heat or of a stone can be caused in me only by something that contains at least as much reality as I conceive to be in the heat or in the stone. For although this cause does not transfer any of its actual or intrinsic reality to my idea, it still can't be less real. An idea need have no intrinsic reality except what it derives from my thought, of which it is a mode. But any idea that has representative reality must surely come from a cause that contains at least as much *intrinsic* reality as there is *representative* reality in the idea. For if we suppose that an idea contains something that was not in its cause, it must have got this from nothing; yet the kind of reality that is involved in something's being represented in the mind by an idea, though it may not be very perfect, certainly *isn't* nothing, and so it can't *come from* nothing.

…The longer and more carefully I examine all these points, the more clearly and distinctly I recognize their truth….

Among my ideas, apart from the one that gives me a representation of myself, which can't present any difficulty in this context, there are ideas that variously represent God, inanimate bodies, angels, animals and finally other men like myself.

As regards my ideas of other men, or animals, or angels, I can easily understand that they could be put together from the ideas I have of myself, of bodies and of God, even if the world contained no men besides me, no animals and no angels.

As to my ideas of bodies, so far as I can see they contain nothing that is so great or excellent that it couldn't have originated in myself. For if I examine them thoroughly, one by one, as I did the idea of the wax yesterday, I realize that the following short list gives everything that I perceive clearly and distinctly in them: size, or extension in length, breadth and depth; shape, which is a function of the boundaries of this extension; position, which is a relation between various items possessing shape; motion, or change in position.

To these may be added substance, duration and number.

But as for all the rest, including light and colours, sounds, smells, tastes, heat and cold and the other qualities that can be known by touch, I think of these in such a confused and obscure way that I don't even know whether they are true or false, that is, whether my ideas of them are ideas of real things or of non-things….

Such ideas obviously don't have to be caused by something other than myself. If they are false – that is, if they represent non-things – then they are in me only because of a deficiency or lack of perfection in my nature, which is to say that they arise from nothing; I know this by the natural light. If on the other hand they are true, there is no reason why they shouldn't arise from myself, since they represent such a slight reality that I can't even distinguish it from a non-thing.

With regard to the clear and distinct elements in my ideas of bodies, it appears that I could have borrowed some of these from my idea of myself, namely *substance, duration, number* and anything else of this kind. For example, I think that a stone is a substance, or is a thing capable of existing independently, and I also think that I am a substance. Admittedly I conceive of myself as a thing that thinks and isn't extended, and of the stone as a thing that is extended and doesn't think, so that the two conceptions differ enormously; but they seem to have the classification 'substance' in common. Again, I perceive that I now exist, and remember that I have existed for some time; moreover, I have various thoughts that I can count; it is in these ways that I acquire the ideas of duration and number that I can then transfer to other things. As for all the other elements that make up the ideas of bodies – extension, shape, position and movement – these are not straightforwardly contained in me, since I am nothing but a thinking thing; but since they are merely modes of a substance, and I am a substance, it seems possible that they are contained in me in some higher form. That is, I am not myself extended, shaped etc., but because I am a *substance* I am (so to speak) metaphysically one up on these mere *modes*, which implies that I can contain within me whatever it takes to cause the ideas of them.

So there remains only the idea of God: is there anything in *that* which couldn't have originated in myself?

By the word 'God' I understand a substance that is infinite, eternal, unchangeable, independent, supremely intelligent, supremely powerful, which created myself and anything else that may exist. The more carefully I concentrate on these attributes, the less possible it seems that *any* of them could have originated from me alone. So this whole discussion implies that God necessarily exists.

From the Fourth Meditation

Now, when I consider the fact that I have doubts – which means that I am incomplete and dependent – that leads to my having a clear and distinct idea of a being who is independent and complete, that is, an idea of God. And from the mere fact that I exist and have such an idea, I infer that God exists and that every moment of my existence depends on him. This follows clearly; I am sure, indeed, that the human intellect can't know anything that is more evident or more certain. And now that I can take into account the true God, in whom all the treasures of wisdom and knowledge lie hidden, I think I can see a way through to knowledge of other things in the universe.

To begin with, I see that it is impossible that God should ever deceive me. Only someone who has something wrong with him will engage in trickery or deception. That someone is able to deceive others may be a sign of his skill or power, but his wanting to deceive them is a sign of his malice or weakness; and those are not to be found in God.

Next, I know from experience that I have a faculty of judgment; and this, like everything else I have, was given to me by God. Since God doesn't want to deceive me, I am sure that he didn't give me a faculty of judgment that would lead me into error while I was using it correctly.

Simon Blackburn

Think (OUP 1999)

Descartes's Trademark Argument and the Cartesian Circle

THE TRADEMARK ARGUMENT

Trusting clarity and distinctness, Descartes indulges a piece of reasoning. Looking into his own 'self, which is all that he has at this point, Descartes discovers that he has an idea of perfection. He then argues that such an idea implies a cause. However, the thing that caused it must have as much 'reality', and that includes perfection, as the idea itself. This implies that only a perfect cause, that is, God, will do. Hence God exists, and has left the idea of perfection as an innate sign of his workmanship in our minds, like a craftsman leaving a trademark stamped in his work.

Once Descartes has discovered God, the seas of doubt subside in a rush. For since God is perfect, he is no deceiver: deceiving is clearly falling short of goodness, let alone perfection. Hence, if we do our stuff properly, we can be sure that we will not be the victims of illusion. The world will be as we understand it to be. Doing our stuff properly mainly means trusting only clear and distinct ideas.

What are we to make of the 'trademark' argument? Here is a re- construction:

> I have the idea of a perfect being. This idea must have a cause. A cause must be at least as perfect as its effect. So something at least as perfect as my idea caused it. Therefore such a thing exists. But that thing must be perfect, that is, God.

Suppose we grant Descartes the idea mentioned in the first premise. (There are theological traditions that would not even do that. They would say that God's perfection defies understanding, so that we have no idea of it, or him.) Still, why is he entitled to the premise that his idea must have a cause? Might not there be events that have simply no cause? Events that, as we might say, 'just happen'? After all, sitting on his rock, Descartes cannot appeal to any normal, scientific, experience. In his bare metaphysical solitude, how can he deny that events might just happen? And if he thinks the contrary, shouldn't he then worry whether the Demon might be working on him, making him think this although it is not true?

However, it gets worse when we arrive at the next step. Consider my idea of someone who is perfectly punctual. Does this need a perfectly punctual cause? Surely a better thing to think would be this. I can simply define what it is for someone to be perfectly punctual. It means that they are never late (or perhaps, never early and never late). To understand what it would be for someone to be like that, I do not have to have come across such a person. I can describe them in advance. I understand what condition they have to satisfy, without any such acquaintance, and indeed even if nobody is ever like that.

Probably Descartes would reject the analogy. Perhaps he thinks of it more like this. Do I have an idea of a perfect mathematician? Well, I can start by thinking of a mathematician as one who never makes mistakes. But that is hardly adequate. A perfect mathematician would be imaginative and inventive as well. Now' with my very limited knowledge of mathematics, I only have a very confused understanding of what that would be like. In general, I cannot clearly comprehend or understand inventions before they come along- otherwise, I would be making the inventions myself! So perhaps it would take a perfect mathematician to give me a good idea (a 'clear and distinct' idea) of what a perfect mathematician would be like.

Well, perhaps; but now it becomes doubtful whether I do have a clear and distinct idea of a perfect mathematician, and analogously, of a perfect being. Generally, what happens if I frame this idea is that I think more as I did when thinking of someone perfectly punctual. I think of an agent who never makes mistakes, never behaves unkindly, never finds things he cannot do, and so on. I might add in imagination something like a kind of glow, but it is clear that this will not help. It surely seems presumptuous, or even blasphemous, to allow myself a complete, clear, comprehension of God's attributes.

In fact, elsewhere in his writings Descartes gives a rather lovely analogy, but one which threatens to undermine the trademark argument:

> We can touch a mountain with our hands but we cannot put our arms around it as we could put them around a tree or something else not too large for them. To grasp something is to embrace it in one's thought; to know something it is sufficient to touch it with one's thought.

Perhaps we can only touch God's supposed qualities by way of definition, but cannot comprehend them. In that case we cannot argue back to an ideal or archetype that enabled us to comprehend them.

So, the trademark argument is one that strikes most of us as far from demon-proof - so far, in fact, that it seems pretty easy to resist even if we are not at all in the grip of extreme doubt. At this point some suppressed premises suggested by the history of ideas may be used to excuse Descartes. He was undoubtedly more optimistic about the trademark argument than we can be because he inherited a number of ideas from previous philosophical traditions. One very important one is that genuine causation is a matter of the cause *passing on* something to an effect. Causation is like passing the baton in a relay race. So, for example, it takes heat to make something hot, or movement to induce motion. This is a principle that surfaces again and again in the history of philosophy, and we shall encounter it more than once. Here it disposed Descartes to think that the 'perfection' in his idea needed to be secreted into it, as it were, by a perfect cause.

But this principle about causation is scarcely demon-proof. In fact, it is not even true. We have become familiar with causes that bear no resemblance to their effects. The movement of a piece of iron in a magnetic field bears no resemblance to an electric current, but that is what it causes. In fact, it seems as though Descartes (once more influenced by ideas from previous philosophical traditions) may have slipped into thinking that an idea of X actually shares X. So an idea of infinity, for instance would be an infinite idea. (Would an idea of something solid be a solid idea?) Similarly an idea of perfection would be a perfect idea, and would require a perfect cause. But again, it might be the Demon that makes you think any such thing, and again there is no good reason to follow him.

THE CARTESIAN CIRCLE

Descartes convinced himself that the argument was good: every step in it was 'clear and distinct'. So now he has God, and God is no deceiver. Still, remember that to do this he had to trust his clear and distinct ideas as sources of truth. Nevertheless, isn't there an awful hole in his procedure? What happened to the Demon? Might not even our clear and distinct ideas lead us astray? To close off this possibility, it seem, Descartes turns round and uses God – the God whose existence he has just proved – as the guarantor that what we perceive clearly and distinctly must be true.

It was one of his contemporaries, Antoine Arnauld (1612 – 94), who cried 'foul' most loudly at this point, accusing Descartes of arguing in a circle, the infamous 'Cartesian circle'. Descartes seems committed to two different priorities. Consider the view that if we clearly and distinctly perceive some proposition p, then it is true that p. Let us abbreviate this to (CDp -> Tp), reading that if p is clear and distinct ('CD'), then it is true ('T'). And suppose we symbolize 'God exists and does not deceive us' by 'G'. Then the circle is that at some points it seems that Descartes holds: I can know that (CDp -> Tp) only if I first know G. But at other points he holds: I can know that G only if I first know (CDp -> Tp). It is like the familiar impasse in the morning, when you need to have some coffee to get out of bed, and you need to get out of bed to fix the coffee.

One or the other has to come first. There is a whole literature trying to understand whether Descartes actually falls into this trap. Some commentators cite passages in which it seems that he does not really hold the first. The major suggestion is that G is necessary only to validate memory of proofs. So while you actually clearly and distinctly perceive something, you do not need to trust anything at all, even G, to be entitled to assert its truth. But later, when you have forgotten the proof, only G underwrites your title to say that you once proved it, so it must be true.

…

The great Scottish thinker David Hume Q7t-76) criticized Descartes like this:

> There is a species of scepticism, antecedent to all study and philosophy, which is much inculcated by Descartes and others, as a sovereign preservative against error and precipitate judgment. It recommends an universal doubt, not only of all our former opinions and principles, but also of our very faculties; of whose veracity, say they, we must assure ourselves, by a chain of reasoning, deduced from some original principle, which cannot possibly be fallacious or deceitful. But neither is there any such original principle, which has a prerogative above others, that are self-evident and convincing: Or if there were, could we

advance a step beyond it, but by the use of those very faculties, of which we are supposed to be already diffident. The Cartesian doubt, therefore, were it ever possible to be attained by any human creature (as it plainly is not) would be entirely incurable; and no reasoning could ever bring us to a state of assurance and conviction upon any subject.

If Descartes's project is to use reason to fend off universal doubt about the truthfulness of reason, then it has to fail.

Daniel Cardinal, Jeremy Hayward, Gerald Jones

Epistemology: the Theory of Knowledge

Other Rationalists

Hume's claim is that the rationalist enterprise must fail. It fails because reason will provide us only with necessary truths, truths that could not be otherwise, whereas knowledge of the world involves knowledge of CONTINGENT truths – truths that could have been otherwise. However, Descartes was not the only rationalist of the modern era. Others followed in his footsteps and took up the challenge of establishing knowledge through reason. Two of these, Leibniz and Spinoia, avoid Hume's criticism to some extent since both of them claimed that all empirical truths are necessary, and so, in principle, can be established by reason alone.

Leibniz

Gottfried Wilhelm von Leibniz (1646-1716), like Descartes, was another great polymath. Most of his life was spent working in the courts of various European royalty and consequently his studies in philosophy, maths and science were all conducted in his spare time. Much of his philosophy was carried out with correspondents through the exchange of letters - he wrote over 16,000 in his lifetime. He was also a great mathematician and discovered calculus at the same time as Isaac Newton. Leibniz established a complex and contained metaphysical view of the world and it is very easy to misrepresent his views by presenting small segments of his philosophy in isolation. Leibniz believed that God existed necessarily and that by definition God is all-good, all-powerful and all-knowing. He subscribed to a version of what is known as the 'ontological argument' for the existence of God. In outline, this argument claims that if we understand the concept of God properly we will recognise that he just has to exist, that is, his existence is necessary. Since this necessary being is all-good and all-powerful, it follows that the world he created would have to be the best possible world there could be. It would be nonsensical for an all-good and all-powerful God to create a less than perfect world. So the world we live in, and every event that takes place in it, takes place necessarily as part of the divine plan to maximise the good. This may seem implausible initially. We can see perfectly well that a lot of what goes on in the world is not good. We can certainly imagine far better worlds than this one - for example, worlds without famine, or the suffering of innocent children. Leibniz defends himself against this objection by arguing that the apparent imperfections in this world appear only because we have a limited view of the whole of God's creation. Each local piece of evil is necessary in order to maximise the overall perfection of the world. So some suffering is required so that more good can be realised, just as we must sometimes endure the discomfort of taking unpleasant medicine in order to recover from an illness. If we had the mind of God and could grasp the bigger picture, we would see that these apparent imperfections are necessary and so could understand the reason for everything in the universe. So, in principle at least, all empirical truths about the world could be worked out a priori, just by thinking about them. So, we wouldn't need to do any empirical research to know whether there will be a white Christmas this year. We could work it out, just by thinking about whether a white Christmas would be part of God's plan to produce the best possible world. Of course, in reality, humans are not up to the task of working out truths like this by reason alone. Our finite minds can't see whether snow or no snow would be best. This is why we have to do empirical research and why such truths appear contingent.

Spinoza

Benedict de Spinoza (1632-77) was born in Amsterdam. He lived an austere life, refusing to accept his inheritance and earning his living as a humble lens-grinder. He died, in February 1677, of consumption, probably triggered by the fine glass dust that he inhaled every day. While grinding he would contemplate philosophical ideas, often discussing his thoughts with friends and intellectuals who would frequent his workshop. Spinoza, like Descartes and Leibniz, adopted the rationalist view that the essential truths about the world should be established through reason and thus could attain the certainty of maths and geometry. His great work, *The Ethics*, starts by stating a series of definitions and axioms that he believes cannot be doubted. Inspired by the geometric method of Euclid who, using a few axioms and definitions, proves various geometrical propositions, Spinoza proceeds to try to deduce in the same manner all sorts of general or metaphysical truths. As *The Ethics* develops, Spinoza arrives at a strange and complex metaphysical picture of the world. Spinoza was a pantheist, believing that God is one and the same as the universe and, like Leibniz, he claimed that all truths are NECESSARY and nothing is contingent. The appearance of contingency is the result of the fact that our minds are not powerful enough to see why everything is the way it is. Forming only a small part of the universe, each human fails to see how every part of the universe, i.e. God, is connected, and it is from this that the feeling of contingency arrives. So while it may seem to me that some events in the universe just happen to be the case, in fact all are necessary.

I had to have the cup of tea I've just finished, as this was a necessary event. I couldn't have had a cup of coffee instead.

The rationalist views adopted by both Leibniz and Spinoza avoid Hume's criticism by claiming that the truths about the world are necessary rather than contingent, and so could, in theory, be discovered by reason. However, these attempts at the rationalist enterprise raise further difficulties. Chiefly, both accounts claim that every event is necessary through their conception of God as a necessary being, who in turn, confers necessity on the world. As such, they rely on the existence of God, and although both attempt to prove the existence of God using reason alone, neither of their versions of the ontological argument is generally considered successful.

John Locke (1632 -1704)

Essay concerning Human Understanding

Book II ("Of Ideas"), Chapter 1 ("Of Ideas in General, and Their Original") —

Edited by Jack Lynch

1. Idea is the object of thinking. Every man being conscious to himself that he thinks; and that which his mind is applied about whilst thinking being the ideas that are there, it is past doubt that men have in their minds several ideas, — such as are those expressed by the words whiteness, hardness, sweetness, thinking, motion, man, elephant, army, drunkenness, and others: it is in the first place then to be inquired, How he comes by them?

I know it is a received doctrine, that men have native ideas, and original characters, stamped upon their minds in their very first being. This opinion I have at large examined already; and, I suppose what I have said in the foregoing Book will be much more easily admitted, when I have shown whence the understanding may get all the ideas it has; and by what ways and degrees they may come into the mind; — for which I shall appeal to every one's own observation and experience.

2. All ideas come from sensation or reflection. Let us then suppose the mind to be, as we say, white paper, void of all characters, without any ideas: — How comes it to be furnished? Whence comes it by that vast store which the busy and boundless fancy of man has painted on it with an almost endless variety? Whence has it all the materials of reason and knowledge? To this I answer, in one word, from EXPERIENCE. In that all our knowledge is founded; and from that it ultimately derives itself. Our observation employed either, about external

> Whence = from where
>
> Come by = get, obtain
> Furnished = provided

sensible objects, or about the internal operations of our minds perceived and reflected on by ourselves, is that which supplies our understandings with all the materials of thinking. These two are the fountains of knowledge, from whence all the ideas we have, or can naturally have, do spring.

3. The objects of sensation one source of ideas. First, our Senses, conversant about particular sensible objects, do convey into the mind several distinct perceptions of things according to those various ways wherein those objects do affect them. And thus we come by those ideas we have of yellow, white, heat, cold, soft, hard, bitter, sweet, and all those which we call sensible qualities; which when I say the senses convey into the mind, I mean, they from external objects convey into the mind what produces there those perceptions. This great source of most of the ideas we have, depending wholly upon our senses, and derived by them to the understanding, I call SENSATION.

4. The operations of our minds, the other source of them. Secondly, the other fountain from which experience furnishes the understanding with ideas is, — the perception of the operations of our own mind within us, as it is employed about the ideas it has got; — which operations, when the soul comes to reflect on and consider, do furnish the understanding with another set of ideas, which could not be had from things without. And such are perception, thinking, doubting, believing, reasoning, knowing, willing, and all the different actings of our

> Viz = in other words

own minds; — which we being conscious of, and observing in ourselves, do from these receive into our understandings as distinct ideas as we do from bodies affecting our senses. This source of ideas every man has wholly in himself; and though it be not sense, as having nothing to do with external objects, yet it is very like it, and might properly enough be called internal sense. But as I call the other SENSATION, so I Call this REFLECTION, the ideas it affords being such only as the mind gets by reflecting on its own operations within itself. By reflection then, in the following part of this discourse, I would be understood to mean, that notice which the mind takes of its own operations, and the manner of them, by reason whereof there come to be ideas of these operations in the understanding. These two, I say, viz. external material things, as the objects of SENSATION, and the operations of our own minds within, as the objects of REFLECTION, are to me the only originals from whence all our ideas take their beginnings.

5. All our ideas are of the one or the other of these. The understanding seems to me not to have the least glimmering of any ideas which it doth not receive from one of these two. External objects furnish the mind with the ideas of sensible qualities, which are all those different perceptions they produce in us; and the mind furnishes the understanding with ideas of its own operations.

These, when we have taken a full survey of them, and their several modes, combinations, and relations, we shall find to contain all our whole stock of ideas; and that we have nothing in our minds which did not come in one of these two ways. Let any one examine his own thoughts, and thoroughly search into his understanding; and then let him tell me, whether all the

> How great a mass of knowledge soever = however great a mass of knowledge

original ideas he has there, are any other than of the objects of his senses, or of the operations of his mind, considered as objects of his reflection. And how great a mass of knowledge soever he imagines to be lodged there, he will, upon taking a strict view, see that he has not any idea in his mind but what one of these two have imprinted; — though perhaps, with infinite variety compounded and enlarged by the understanding, as we shall see hereafter.

6. Observable in children. He that attentively considers the state of a child, at his first coming into the world, will have little reason to think him stored with plenty of ideas, that are to be the matter of his future knowledge. It is by degrees he comes to be furnished with them. And though the ideas of obvious and familiar qualities imprint themselves before the memory begins to keep a register of time or order, yet it is often so late before some unusual qualities come in the way, that there are few men that cannot recollect the beginning of their acquaintance with them. And if it were worth while, no doubt a child might be so ordered as to have but a very few, even of the ordinary ideas, till he were

grown up to a man. But all that are born into the world, being surrounded with bodies that perpetually and diversely affect them, variety of ideas, whether care be taken of it or not, are imprinted on the minds of children. Light and colours are busy at hand everywhere, when the eye is but open; sounds and some tangible qualities fail not to solicit their proper senses, and force an entrance to the mind; — but yet, I think, it will be granted easily, that if a child were kept in a place where he never saw any other but black and white till he were a man, he would have no more ideas of scarlet or green, than he that from his childhood never tasted an oyster, or a pine-apple, has of those particular relishes.

20. No ideas but from sensation and reflection, evident, if we observe children. I see no reason, therefore, to believe that the soul thinks before the senses have furnished it with ideas to think on; and as those are increased and retained, so it comes, by exercise, to improve its faculty of thinking in the several parts of it; as well as, afterwards, by compounding those ideas, and reflecting on its own operations, it increases its stock, as well as facility in remembering, imagining, reasoning, and other modes of thinking.

21. State of a child in the mother's womb. He that will suffer himself to be informed by observation and experience, and not make his own hypothesis the rule of nature, will find few signs of a soul accustomed to much thinking in a new-born child, and much fewer of any reasoning at all. And yet it is hard to imagine that the rational soul should think so much, and not reason at all. And he that will consider that infants newly come into the world spend the greatest part of their time in sleep, and are seldom awake but when either hunger calls for the teat, or some pain (the most importunate of all sensations), or some other violent impression on the body, forces the mind to perceive and attend to it; — he, I say, who considers this, will perhaps find reason to imagine that a foetus in the mother's womb differs not much from the state of a vegetable, but passes the greatest part of its time without perception or thought; doing very little but sleep in a place where it needs not seek for food, and is surrounded with liquor, always equally soft, and near of the same temper; where the eyes have no light, and the ears so shut up are not very susceptible of sounds; and where there is little or no variety, or change of objects, to move the senses.

22. The mind thinks in proportion to the matter it gets from experience to think about. Follow a child from its birth, and observe the alterations that time makes, and you shall find, as the mind by the senses comes more and more to be furnished with ideas, it comes to be more and more awake; thinks more, the more it has matter to think on. After some time it begins to know the objects which, being most familiar with it, have made lasting impressions. Thus it comes by degrees to know the persons it daily converses with, and distinguishes them from strangers; which are instances and effects of its coming to retain and distinguish the ideas the senses convey to it. And so we may observe how the mind, by degrees, improves in these; and advances to the exercise of those other faculties of enlarging, compounding, and abstracting its ideas, and of reasoning about them, and reflecting upon all these; of which I shall have occasion to speak more hereafter.

23. A man begins to have ideas when he first has sensation. What sensation is. If it shall be demanded

then, when a man begins to have any ideas, I think the true answer is, — when he first has any sensation. For, since there appear not to be any ideas in the mind before the senses have conveyed any in, I conceive that ideas in the understanding are coeval with sensation; which is such an impression or motion made in some part of the body, as produces some perception in the understanding. It is about these impressions made on our senses by outward objects that the mind seems first to employ itself, in such operations as we call perception, remembering, consideration, reasoning, &c.

24. The original of all our knowledge. In time the mind comes to reflect on its own operations about the ideas got by sensation, and thereby stores itself with a new set of ideas, which I call ideas of reflection. These are the impressions that are made on our senses by outward objects that are extrinsical to the mind; and its own operations, proceeding from powers intrinsical and proper to itself, which, when reflected on by itself, become also objects of its contemplation — are, as I have said, the original of all knowledge. Thus the first capacity of human intellect is, — that the mind is fitted to receive the impressions made on it; either through the senses by outward objects, or by its own operations when it reflects on them. This is the first step a man makes towards the discovery of anything, and the groundwork whereon to build all those notions which ever he shall have naturally in this world. All those sublime thoughts which tower above the clouds, and reach as high as heaven itself, take their rise and footing here: in all that great extent wherein the mind wanders, in those remote speculations it may seem to be elevated with, it stirs not one jot beyond those ideas which sense or reflection have offered for its contemplation.

25. In the reception of simple ideas, the understanding is for the most part passive. In this part the understanding is merely passive; and whether or no it will have these beginnings, and as it were materials of knowledge, is not in its own power. For the objects of our senses do, many of them, obtrude their particular ideas upon our minds whether we will or not; and the operations of our minds will not let us be without, at least, some obscure notions of them. No man can be wholly ignorant of what he does when he thinks. These simple ideas, when offered to the mind, the understanding can no more refuse to have, nor alter when they are imprinted, nor blot them out and make new ones itself, than a mirror can refuse, alter, or obliterate the images or ideas which the objects set before it do therein produce. As the bodies that surround us do diversely affect our organs, the mind is forced to receive the impressions; and cannot avoid the perception of those ideas that are annexed to them.

Leibniz's Challenge to the Tabula Rasa

Peter Markie, in the Stanford Encyclopedia of Philosophy

Leibniz (1704) tells us the following:

> The senses, although they are necessary for all our actual knowledge, are not sufficient to give us the whole of it, since the senses never give anything but instances, that is to say particular or individual truths. Now all the instances which confirm a general truth, however numerous they may be, are not sufficient to establish the universal necessity of this same truth, for it does not follow that what happened before will happen in the same way again. … From which it appears that necessary truths, such as we find in pure mathematics, and particularly in arithmetic and geometry, must have principles whose proof does not depend on instances, nor consequently on the testimony of the senses, although without the senses it would never have occurred to us to think of them… (1704, Preface, pp. 150–151):

Leibniz goes on to describe our mathematical knowledge as "innate"…. We have substantive knowledge about the external world in mathematics, and what we know in that area, we know to be necessarily true. Experience cannot warrant beliefs about what is necessarily the case. Hence, experience cannot be the source of our knowledge. The best explanation of our knowledge is that we gain it by intuition and deduction. Leibniz mentions logic, metaphysics and morals as other areas in which our knowledge similarly outstrips what experience can provide. Judgments in logic and metaphysics involve forms of necessity beyond what experience can support. Judgments in morals involve a form of obligation or value that lies beyond experience, which only informs us about what is the case rather than about what ought to be.

http://plato.stanford.edu/entries/rationalism-empiricism/

Daniel Cardinal, Jeremy Hayward, Gerald Jones

Epistemology: the Theory of Knowledge

Locke, Sense Data, Induction

The certainty of sensation or 'sense data'

In the previous chapter we saw that an attractive response to someone who is being sceptical about our beliefs is to claim certainty of those things of which we have had direct experience. This is borne out in everyday life. In response to the question, 'How do you know?' we frequently use answers such as 'Because I was there' or 'Because I saw it'.

So it seems we are often inclined to appeal to our own personal experience when attempting to justify our claims to know things, and this is one point that empiricists stress. However, we have also encountered reasons to be sceptical about the reliability of the senses as a source of justification for our beliefs. Descartes argued that the senses may not be a secure basis for knowledge about the world and pointed to their susceptibility to error. Other considerations such as the possibility of sense deception, hallucinations and dreaming further undermined their reliability. In the worst-case scenario he even claimed that an evil demon could be giving me the sensations I'm having. Also the brain in a vat possibility on page 18 can serve to undermine the certainty of our senses. So it seems that, despite what we might ordinarily think, our own experience of the evidence of the senses is not a firm bedrock, and so could not function as the foundation of knowledge.

However, even if we accept that our senses may deceive us about the world, it seems impossible to deny that we are actually having sense experiences. Whether or not the world exists, I remain conscious of having various sensations. I may be hallucinating or be in a virtual reality machine and thus the purple curtains I am staring at may not actually exist, but despite all this it seems impossible to deny that I am having a purple-curtain-like experience. I'll grant the sceptic that the physical world is a figment of my imagination, but the sceptic still cannot take away the fact that I am now having an experience (albeit in imagination alone) of purple.

As Descartes puts it, even if I am dreaming, 'all the same, at least, it is very certain that *it seems to me* that I see light, hear a noise and feel a heat; and this is properly what in me is called perceiving'. Thus to the extent that sensation or 'perceiving' is treated purely as an aspect of conscious experience, and any judgement about the nature of the world beyond it is suspended, then it has a kind of certainty. This means that while I can doubt the existence of the physical universe, I cannot doubt the existence of the sensations which present themselves to me.

This is a crucially important move for the development of modern philosophy. Descartes' genius was to recognise that even if the entire physical world is a dream, or if there is an evil demon deceiving me, none the less sensations can be viewed purely as an aspect of consciousness. This means that the experience of sensation need not commit us to any beliefs concerning the material things which we may normally associate with it, i.e. our bodies' sense organs and the effects made on them by physical objects. So I can know I'm experiencing sensations regardless of whether

or not objects or even my body really exist. Indeed, Descartes would even say can know with absolute certainty that I have a headache, even though I may not know that I have a head!

The incorrigibility of sensation

Now, if my own sensations are certain, regardless of any doubts that may be raised about their origin, then it seems that I cannot be led to change my mind about them. There is no new evidence which could come to light, in other words, which could lead me to correct my claim to know that I am having a sensation of a certain sort - be it seeing a purple patch, experiencing a smell of lavender, or suffering from a headache. I know I am having them whether or not purple things, lavender or even my own head exist. I cannot be brought to doubt that I have a headache no matter what sceptical scenarios one might raise. And the question, 'How do you *know* you have a headache?' seems a silly one.

It is on the basis of our sensations that we infer the existence of objects and events, mostly without being aware of doing so. I open the fridge and have a yellow and round visual experience - from this I infer there is a grapefruit before me. I have a barking aural experience, and infer the existence of a dog outside. In these cases we move from our basic sense experience to a belief about the world. In moving from one to the other there is the possibility of error: it may be a toy grapefruit; it may be a dog impersonator outside my window. I may even be Because there is an

inference involved, there is always room for doubt. But when it comes to experiencing the sensations themselves no inference is necessary. They are presented immediately to my mind and so knowledge of them allows no room for error. That I am experiencing a yellow, round shape cannot be doubted, regardless of what is actually causing it.

It seems that we have indeed found a second bedrock of beliefs. Those about our own sensations are immune from sceptical doubts and for this reason are often termed INCORRIGIBLE; meaning that they are not correctable. I would not under any conceivable circumstances give them up. In other words, they require no further justification; they are, as it is often put, simply GIVEN. Sensations treated simply as aspects of consciousness are often termed sense data, or sometimes the given.

The idea that all knowledge can finally be justified in terms of immediate experience leads into a second kind of foundationalism, namely empiricist foundationalism. The empiricist foundationalist doesn't think all knowledge can be justified in terms of self-evident truths of reason as the rationalist does, but rather thinks that what is given in experience - the certainties of my own sense data - are the true foundation of human knowledge.

Locke and empiricism

What this came to mean for empiricists like the English philosopher John Locke (1632-1704) is that all experience and all human knowledge can be analysed into simple data of SENSATION. These are the elements out of which experience is constructed. The classic expression of this idea is found in Locke's Essay Concerning Human Understanding (1690). The elements of experience which Locke has in mind are simple sensations of, to use his examples, whiteness and hardness. When we are born, Locke claims, our minds are completely empty of any concepts or beliefs, both of which he terms 'ideas', and it is through experience that our minds become furnished. In one image, he tells us that the mind is originally akin to a blank piece of paper void of all characters - it is a tabula rasa or blank slate onto which our experience through life writes.

Knowledge of sense data

Although we have not yet discussed the concept of knowledge in detail or looked at the different sorts of knowledge that there are, it's worth looking ahead a little at this point, for the kind of knowledge we have of sense data is, in an important way, unlike other sorts of knowledge . One sort of knowledge involves believing facts, expressed in sentences) and so is usually called factual knowledge (sometimes it is called propositional knowledge - a proposition being another word for a factual sentence). For example, I might know that snow is made of crystals, or that Elton John's real name is Reginald Dwight. Such knowledge is often gained from books, teachers or TV. As such we infer the knowledge from the relevant sources or from our other beliefs. However, our knowledge of sense data is different in that it is immediate and present, and not inferred from anything else. We may subsequently use the awareness of the sense data to infer the existence of objects and things, but the sense data themselves are given immediately to us - they do not have to be inferred. We are immediately acquainted with them and so I can know I am having a certain sense datum without having to justify it by reference to any other claim. So we have here a distinction between factual knowledge, which is inferred, and knowledge by acquaintance, which is not.

Now, we can use this distinction between inferred and immediate knowledge to clarify what the empiricist foundationalist is saying. Essentially, the idea is that the knowledge one has of one's own sense data is incorrigible because one is directly acquainted with it. It is the bedrock on which all other knowledge must be based since it involves an immediate awareness. For this reason I cannot be mistaken into thinking that I am acquainted with a certain smell when in fact I am not. Notice however that such knowledge does not require that we are able to say anything about the experience in question. Thus, if I have toothache I am intimately acquainted with a pain, but I may not know that I have a wisdom tooth coming through. That is, I may know very little about my condition. Knowledge by acquaintance in itself remains incommunicable since it lacks what is often called PROPOSITIONAL CONTENT. In other words, while factual knowledge can be expressed in a PROPOSITION, knowledge by acquaintance need not be. So I can know I have a toothache simply by being acquainted with it, but not be able to say anything about it. A dentist, on the other hand, may know all kinds of things about my toothache and be able to communicate them to me and others in the form of propositions. In this sense, factual knowledge appears to be the empiricist foundationalist's idea is that factual knowledge about the world can be built on top of the incorrigible knowledge by acquaintance.

David Hume (1711 – 1776)

An Enquiry Concerning Human Understanding (1772)

Hume's fork

Sect. IV, part 1

All the objects of human reason or enquiry may naturally be divided into two kinds, to wit, relations of ideas, and matters of fact. Of the first kind are the sciences of geometry, algebra, and arithmetic, and in short, every affirmation which is either intuitively or demonstratively certain. That the square of the hypotenuse is equal to the square of the two sides, is a proposition which expresses a relation between these figures. That three times five is equal to the half of thirty, expresses a relation between these numbers.

Propositions of this kind are discoverable by the mere operation of thought, without dependence on what is anywhere existent in the universe. Though there never were a circle or triangle in nature, the truths demonstrated by Euclid would for ever retain their certainty and evidence.

Matters of fact, which are the second objects of human reason, are not ascertained in the same manner; nor is our evidence of their truth, however great, of a like nature with the foregoing. The contrary of every matter of fact is still possible, because it can never imply a contradiction, and is conceived by the mind with the same facility and distinctness, as if ever so conformable to reality. That the sun will not rise tomorrow is no less intelligible a proposition, and implies no more contradiction, than the affirmation, that it will rise. We should in vain, therefore, attempt to demonstrate its falsehood. Were it demonstratively false, it would imply a contradiction, and could never be distinctly conceived by the mind.

Section XII, part 3

If we take in our hand any volume; of divinity or school metaphysics, for instance; let us ask, Does it contain any abstract reasoning concerning quantity or number? No. Does it contain any experimental reasoning concerning matter of fact and existence? No. Commit it then to the flames: for it can contain nothing but sophistry and illusion.

Induction

Sect. XII, Part 2

The passages included here follow closely after the passages above in which Hume introduces his categorization of human study into 'relations of ideas' and 'matters of fact'. Here he raises a question about the second category – 'matters of fact':

It may be a subject worthy of curiosity, to enquire what is the nature of that evidence which assures us of any real existence and matter of fact, beyond the present testimony of our senses, or the records of our memory.

An answer of sort soon follows:

All reasonings concerning matter of fact seem to be founded on the relation of cause and effect. By means of that relation alone we can go beyond the evidence of our memory and senses. If you were to ask a man, why he believes any matter of fact, which is absent, (for instance, that his friend is in the country, or in France) he would give you a reason, and this reason would be some other fact, as a letter received from him, or the knowledge of his former resolutions and promises. A man finding a watch or any other machine in a desert island, would conclude that there had once been men on that island. All our reasonings concerning fact are of the same nature. And here it is constantly supposed that there is a connection between the present fact and that which is inferred from it.

But this answer, for Hume, only raises another fundamental question. Where does our knowledge of cause and effect come from?

Three possible explanations are considered and rejected.

  1. We do not know about cause and effect a priori:

I shall venture to affirm, as a general proposition, which admits of no exception, that the knowledge of this relation is not, in any instance, attained by reasonings a priori, but arises entirely from experience, when we find that any particular objects are constantly conjoined with each other. Let an object be presented to a man of ever so strong natural reason and abilities; if that object be entirely new to him, he will not be able, by the most accurate examination of its sensible qualities, to discover any of its causes or effects. Adam, though his rational faculties be supposed, at the very first, entirely perfect, could not have inferred from the fluidity and transparency of water that it would suffocate him, or from the light and warmth of fire that it would consume him. No object ever discovers, by the qualities which appear to the senses, either from the causes which produced it, or the effects which will arise from it; nor can our reason, unassisted by experience, ever draw any inference concerning real existence and matter of fact.

….But to convince us that all the laws of nature, and all the operations of bodies without exception, are known only by experience, the following reflections may, perhaps, suffice. Were any object presented to us, and were we required to pronounce concerning the effect, which will result from it, without consulting past observation, after what manner, I beseech you, must the mind proceed in this operation? It must invent or imagine some event, which it ascribes to the object as its effect, and it is plain that this invention must be entirely arbitrary. The mind can never possibly find the effect in the supposed cause, by the most accurate scrutiny and examination. For the effect is totally different from the cause, and consequently can never be discovered in it. Motion in the second billiard ball is a quite distinct event from the motion in the first nor is there anything in the one to suggest the smallest hint of the other.

2. *We do not know about cause and effect directly from sense experience; we cannot see forces or powers which connect one billiard ball to another. As explained in the passage above, all you see is the two billiard balls.*

3. *Neither can past experience rationally justify our knowledge of cause and effect:*

…As to past experience, it can be allowed to give direct and certain information of those precise objects only, and that precise period of time, which fell under its cognisance; but why this experience should be extended to future times, and to other objects, which for aught we know, may be only in appearance similar-this is the main question on which I would insist. The bread, which I formerly ate, nourished me: that is, a body of such sensible qualities was, at that time, endued with such secret powers; but does it follow, that other bread must also nourish me at another time, and that like sensible qualities must always be attended with like secret powers? The consequence seems nowise necessary. At least, it must be acknowledged that there is here a consequence drawn by the mind, that there is a certain step taken-a process of thought, and an inference, which wants to be explained. These two propositions are far from being the same: I have found that such an object has always been attended with such an effect, and I foresee, that other objects, which are, in appearance, similar, will be attended with similar effects. I shall allow, if you please, that the one proposition may justly be inferred from the other; I know, in fact, that it always is inferred. But if you insist that the inference is made by a chain of reasoning, I desire you to produce that reasoning.

Hume's Problem of Induction

Without a solid basis for 'knowledge' of cause and effect, Hume is left without a solid basis for any inductive reasoning. His difficulty has come to be known as the 'problem of induction'.

His response is not to abandon it. Indeed, if he rejected inductive reasoning, having also rejected rationalism, he would have to resign himself to knowing nothing beyond his immediate sense perceptions and some bare mathematical and logical facts.

The belief in cause and effect on which induction relies is a matter of habit, not of reasoning. The mind becomes accustomed to expecting one thing when it perceives another. We smell something rich and savoury and expect dinner, because we have gradually become accustomed to the smell being followed by dinner. There is a distinct parallel with the process through which a dog learns to rush to receive food when it hears the clinking of its dishes. The habits of mind on which inductive reasoning depend are inevitable and serve us well. They provide adequate grounds for accepting induction, just not rational ones.

We might in principle recognize that we lack rational grounds trusting induction and have a moment of profound skepticism. Frankly, though, we cannot keep it up, and why should we? If we rejected induction we could not function in the world.

As Hume puts it later in the same section of the Enquiry, 'The great subverter of Pyrrhonism or the excessive principles of scepticism is action, and employment, and the occupations of com- mon life. These principles may flourish and triumph in the schools; where it is, indeed, difficult, if not impossible, to refute them. But as soon as they leave the shade, and by the presence of the real objects, which actuate our passions and sentiments, are put in opposition to the more powerful principles of our nature, they vanish like smoke, and leave the most determined sceptic in the same condition as other mortals.'

Simon Blackburn

Think (OUP 1999)

Hume and Induction

PLAUSIBLE REASONINGS

Formal logic is great at enabling us to avoid contradiction. Similarly, it is great for telling us what we can derive from sets of premises. But you have to have the premises. Yet we reason not only to deduce things from given information, but to expand our beliefs, or what we take to be information. So many of our most interesting reasonings, in everyday life, are not supposed to be valid by the standards we have been describing. They are supposed to be plausible or reasonable, rather than watertight. There are ways in which such an argument could have true premises but a false conclusion, but they are not likely to occur.

Nevertheless, we can go a little further in applying some of the ideas we have met, even to plausible reasonings. Why is it silly, for instance, to be confident that my bet at roulette will be a winner? Because my only information is that I have placed my bet on x, and most ways that the wheel might end up do not present x as the winner. What we are dealing with is a space of possibilities, and if we could show that most possibilities left open by our evidence are ones in which the conclusion is also true, then we have something corresponding to plausible reasoning. In the roulette case, most possibilities left open by our evidence are ones in which the conclusion that x is the winner is false.

Roulette and other games of chance are precisely little fields designed so that we know the possibilities and can measure probabilities. There are fifty-two outcomes possible when we turn up a card, and if we do it from a freshly and fairly shuffled pack, each possibility has an equal chance. Probabilistic reasoning can then go forward: we can solve, for instance, for whether most draws of seven cards involve two court cards, or whatever. Such probabilistic reasoning is precisely a matter of measuring the range of possibilities left open by the specification, and seeing in what proportion of them some outcome is found.

What underlies our assignments of probabilities in the real world? Suppose we think of our position like this. As we go through life, we experience the way things fall out. Within our experience, various generalizations seem to hold: grass is green, the sky blue. Water refreshes; chocolate nourishes. So we take this experience as a guide to how things are across wider expanses of space and time. I have no direct experience of chocolate nourishing in the eighteenth century, but I suppose it did so; I have no direct experience of it nourishing people tomorrow, but I suppose it will continue to do so. Our beliefs and our confidence extend beyond the limited circle of events that fall within our immediate field of view.

Hume puts the problem this way:

As to past Experience, it can be allowed to give direct and certain information of those precise objects only, and that precise period of time, which fell under its cognizance: but why this experience should be extended to future times, and to other objects, which for aught we know, may be only in appearance similar; this is the main question on which I would insist... At least, it must be acknowledged, that there is here a consequence drawn by the mind; that there is a certain step taken;a process of thought, and an inference, which wants to be explained. These two propositions are far from being the same, I have found that such an object has always been attended with such an effect, and I foresee, that other objects, which are, in appearance, similar, will be attended with similar effects. I shall allow, if you please, that the one proposition may justly be inferred from the other: I know in fact, that it always is inferred. But if you insist, that the inference is made by a chain of reasoning, I desire you to produce that reasoning.

Experience stretches no further than limited portions of space and time. In particular, all our experience belongs to the past and present. If we make inferences to the future, then these are inferences, and Hume wants to know the 'chain of reasoning' that they employ.

The inference from what is true of one limited region of space and time to a conclusion true of different parts of space and time is called inductive inference. What Hume is bothered about has become known as the problem of induction.

THE LOTTERY FOR THE GOLDEN HARP

Here is a science fiction. You are disembodied spirits, inhabiting a kind of Heaven. I am God. I tell you that I am about to embody you, to give you lives to lead in a physical universe that I have prepared for you: Earth. At the end of your period in this universe, you will return to Heaven. Unlike normal human life, you will all live the same period: nine acts, let us say.

To make things interesting, I am going to offer you a kind of lottery. Each of you will get a ticket. The tickets correspond to the colour of the clear midday sky for each of the nine acts. I covenant with you, as gods do, that I won't change the colour at any time other than the beginning of an act. Just one of you is going to have a ticket that corresponds to the actual colour of the sky in every act. I also tell you that this person, the winner, will get the Golden Harp when you come back to Heaven. This is a very valuable prize. Heaven is good, but Heaven with the Golden Harp is even better.

So a ticket might look like this:

red

orange   X

yellow   X   X

green   X   X   X

blue   X   X

```
violet                            X

Time
```

This ticket corresponds to the sky starting blue, going green, then yellow and orange, before darkening back to blue and even violet. Call the person with this ticket, Wavy.

Some of you (six of you) get straight tickets:

```
red

orange

yellow

green

blue    X  X  X  X  X  X  X  X  X

violet

Time   1  2  3  4  5  6  7  8  9
```

Call this ticket, Straightie.

If there is going to be just one ticket for each of you, there need to be 6^9 of you, which is a very large number indeed, to have a ticket corresponding to each possible distribution of the colours. And correspondingly, your chance of being the winner is only $1/6^9$, which is a very small number.

Hume insists that we cannot know anything right from the beginning in this situation. We cannot have a priori knowledge which ticket will win. Antecedently, while we are still excitedly discussing tickets, there is no reason to prefer one to another. For all we know God may favour waves, or straight lines. Or he may favour Kinkie:

```
red

orange

yellow                  X  X  X  X

green

blue    X  X  X  X  X

violet

Time   1  2  3  4  5  6  7  8  9
```

The clear midday sky starts off blue for the first five acts, and then turns yellow, and stays like that for the rest. So in heaven, before we get any experience of the world God is about to put us into, no ticket has any better chance than any other.

Well, now we go to Earth.

Immediately, 5/6 of us can throw our tickets away. Any ticket not showing blue in the first square is a loser. And similarly, on the first day of each subsequent act, 5/6 of the survivors can throw their tickets away, until at the beginning of the ninth act, only six remain. And a day after that, there is a single winner. Now let us draw the curtain back towards the end of the fifth act.

Each of Straightie and Kinkie has been doing well. They have seen their competitors fall away, on five previous occasions. In fact, the number of survivors in the lottery has dropped from 6^9 down to 6^4 and their chances of being the winner have risen accordingly.

But suppose they get into an argument with each other. Suppose Straightie urges Kinkie that his ticket is far the more likely winner, so that he will swap it with Kinkie but only for a terrific price. We would probably side with Straightie. But suppose that Kinkie resists, urging that there is no reason in what has happened so far to bet on Straightie rather than on him. What can they say to each other?

Each can point to their track record of success. But it is the same track record for each of them. They each have their five hits. And there is nothing else to go on. After all, neither of them can peer into the future. Like us, they are stuck in time, and cannot peek out of it.

What Straightie would like is an argument in favour of the uniformity of nature. In other words, an argument saying that since God has started off with a blue sky, and stuck with it so far, probably he is going to go on sticking with it. But Kinkie can point out that God has started off with an as-per-Kinkie sky, and by equal reasoning urge that he is probably going to stick with that.

Straightie wants the argument that Hume says he cannot find. But, as I said, in our bones we all side with Straightie. What's wrong with arguing that since nature has been uniform so far, it will probably go on being uniform?

> It is impossible, therefore, that any arguments from experience can prove this resemblance of the past to the future; since all these arguments are founded on the supposition of that resemblance.

Of course, Hume knows that we all learn from experience, and that we all rely upon the uniformity of nature. He thinks we share this natural propensity with animals. It is just that this is all it is: an exercise of nature. It is a custom or habit, but it has no special claim in reason. When we reason inductively there is a way in which our premises can be true and our conclusion false. Nature can change. In fact, there are many ways, since nature can change in many ways. There is no contradiction in imagining this. And now, it seems, we cannot even argue that such changes are improbable. We only think that because they have not occurred within our experience. But taking our experience to be representative, in this regard as in any other, presupposes the uniformity of nature. It seems that we engineer a bridge between past and future, but cannot argue that the bridge is reliable.

Daniel Cardinal, Jeremy Hayward, Gerald Jones

Epistemology: the Theory of Knowledge

Problems with Empiricism

Criticism 1: Difficulties for the empiricist account of concept formation

We've seen that traditional empiricism like that of Locke and Condillac, claims that all our concepts are kinds of copies of sensations. My concept of the colour red is derived from my experience of it; and a more complex concept, like that of coffee, is some sort of combination of simple concepts each ultimately derived from the simple elements of sense. This may seem reasonably plausible at first sight, but once we start looking more closely at how this is supposed to work things begin to look more difficult.

To start, let's examine the simple concept of red. If my concept is a kind of copy of a sensation, which particular sensation is it a copy of? If it is a copy of one particular experience of red, then it will necessarily be a particular shade. However, my actual concept of red is not that of any specific shade. The real concept includes all shades of red. So how does the particular shade which the empiricist regards as my concept come to represent all reds? And how do I distinguish the general concept of red from the concept of the specific shade? In response to this, the empiricist might want to say that the concept must be some sort of collection of all the shades of red we have experienced; but does this idea make any sense? If colour concepts are copies of sensations, they must have a specific shade. A particular image of a colour in my mind cannot be many colours. Even if it did involve some sort of spectrum of all the reds I have so far encountered, another problem arises - namely that I wouldn't be able to recognise any new reds as red since they wouldn't be represented in my concept. The concept of coffee presents similar problems. Is it a collection of every single coffee experience I have ever had? Is it some sort of melange of all these experiences? One odd consequence of this possibility would be that I would have to have a different concept of coffee from everyone else because no two people's set of experiences are identical. So I wouldn't be talking about the same thing when discussing coffee.

Other difficulties arise when we consider that we seem able to have a concept of something without ever having experienced it. I can have the concept of coffee even ifI haven't tasted it, and, similarly, I can form the concept of Spain even though I have never been there. Consider also the concept I have of an atom, something that is too small for us ever to have any sense experience of. When it comes to abstract concepts the difficulties get worse. How do I acquire the concept of justice or freedom? It seems very difficult to relate such concepts merely to patterns within experience and ultimately to patterns of sense data. After all, neither justice nor freedom looks or smells like anything; nor do they make any particular noise. In fact, they don't seem to be things that we have sense experience of at all.

An empiricist could argue that the fact that it is very difficult to explain abstract concepts in this way is why such terms are notoriously vague. They could claim that if we could pin them more closely to experience then we would have greater clarity. Here the idea has to be that we are able to form such concepts as that of justice by observing a series of just acts, but precisely how this is supposed to work remains rather unclear.

Further difficulties arise for relational concepts such as being near or far, next to or on top of. If I form the concept of a cat from seeing a cat, then how do I form the concept of the cat being on the mat. I can't actually see the 'on-ness', all that appears in sensation is the cat and the mat.

Here we have raised a host of problems for the traditional empiricist picture of how we form concepts. Since Locke's day, empiricist philosophers have grappled with these difficulties and in the process developed more sophisticated accounts of concept formation. However, we don't have room here to explore this complex area further.

Criticism 2: Are some ideas innate?

Rationalist philosophers often argued that certain concepts couldn't be acquired from experience. We've already looked at some of Plato's arguments for saying that mathematical concepts had to be innate: we may encounter pairs of objects in the world, but never the number two itself. He similarly argued that concepts like 'beauty' or 'justice' are not things we ever perceive in the world. We encounter beautiful things or just acts, but never beauty or justice as such. He concludes that we must acquire these concepts from somehow observing the essential nature of beauty or justice with our minds.

Descartes also argued that the concept of God, i.e. of a being perfect in every wag couldn't be acquired from experience on the grounds that nothing in experience is ever perfect. Similar problems confront the empiricist in trying to account for our concept of infinity. If everything we ever experience in this life is finite, how could experience be the source of this concept? Descartes also claimed that our concept of 'substance' could not have an empirical source. Leibniz argued that we have implicit knowledge of various abstract principles * such as that nothing can be produced from nothing) or that nothing happens for no reason - that could not be discovered through experience.

Beyond philosophy, many people believe that we may have an innate moral sense, that we are somehow born knowing right from wrong. Noam Chomsky (1928-), contemporary American philosopher and political dissident, even argues that we are born with a capacity to learn language.

In another sense, it is undeniable that we are born with certain instincts and urges - to suckle, to cry, to crawl. Some (behaviourists, for example) may claim that this counts as a sort of knowledge. Certainly there is a sense in which a baby knows how to suckle, but few would want to argue that they know what they are doing or why they are inclined to do it.

So it seems that there are many different ways in which we can be seen to have a sort of knowledge that is not derived from experience. How successful any of these considerations is, is a matter for discussion.

Criticism 3: The trap of solipsism

Another difficulty with the empiricist position is that it threatens to lead us into the trap of SOLIPSISM. To understand the difficulty we need to recall that empiricists, like Locke, follow Descartes in claiming that we perceive the physical world only indirectly. But if this is right then how do I get from the immediate knowledge I have of my own sense data to knowledge of anything beyond them, namely the physical world? If all I can be absolutely certain of is that I experience sense data, then it seems I can never be certain that anything else exists. Beliefs founded in one's own personal experience appear to be incurably subjective, and inferred beliefs about physical objects are always vulnerable to sceptical attack. Moreover, if I can't be sure that the physical world beyond my mind exists, then I cannot be sure that minds other than my own exist either. It seems that I may be completely alone! This sceptical position is known as solipsism. It is the idea that all that we can really be certain of is our own existence and experience. It could be that nothing and no one else exists.

Escaping solipsism was the central problematic of eighteenth-century epistemology. The credibility of both Descartes' and Locke's foundationalism hangs on whether or not it can be solved. If they are unable to escape the trap of solipsism - as many argue they are - then their epistemologies will amount to the claim that knowledge of the physical universe is impossible: a sceptical conclusion which we surely have good reason to try to avoid.

Criticism 4: The problem of *a priori* knowledge

Another difficulty for the empiricist is to account for the special status of our knowledge of maths and logical truths. If all knowledge is gained through experience then how can we account for *a priori* truths? If I don't need to make reference to sense data to know that $2 + 3 = 5$ then we have a class of knowledge that empiricism can't explain.

The empiricist may respond by saying that all *a priori* truths are analytic; and as they tell us only about the meanings of the symbols, such truths are condemned as being able to tell us nothing of interest. Alternatively the empiricist may answer that we do indeed gain such knowledge by experience. She may claim that we observe that two apples and three apples make five apples, that two lizards and three snakes make five reptiles, and so on, and it is from such observations that we can generalise that 2 and 3 make 5. The argument is that mathematical laws are discovered in much the same way as are other laws about the world. For example, just as we see the sun rise each morning and thus generalise that it will rise every morning, or observe that delicate objects dropped from certain heights tend to break, so we observe how objects behave when grouped together and make empirical generalisations, which are the laws of addition. The difference between mathematical truths and other empirical truths is only that the evidence for them is more consistent.

However, this conclusion is not very satisfactory as it places mathematical claims on the same level as empirical generalisations and thus maths loses its status as a body of necessary truths. Not every delicate object is certain to break when dropped from a height, and eventually the sun may not rise. And even if delicate objects did always break, and the sun did always continue to rise, it is at least conceivable that this may not be the case. Yet surely 2 plus 3 will always be 5, and we can't imagine waking up one morning and finding that they were now 6. Such an idea appears to make no sense: 2

plus 3 just has to make 5.

How might an empiricist react to such observations? One approach is to modify empiricism slightly and admit these exceptions to the general principle that all knowledge comes from experience. If we accept that reason alone is indeed the basis for mathematics and logic, we may still claim that truths of reason can never tell us anything new or interesting about the world. An empiricist may recognise that there are truths of reason, but regard them as empty of empirical content and so useless as a basis for knowledge about the physical universe. In so doing the empiricist can retain the basic point that it is only experience that can provide interesting or new information about the world. Reason's usefulness lies in unpicking implications and truths that are already present in the knowledge we have. So, for example, if I knew that Shakespeare wrote Hamlet and I later found out that Hamlet was a tragedy, I would be able to deduce, by reason alone, that Shakespeare wrote at least one tragedy. However, in doing so I would not be gaining any new knowledge but merely teasing out facts I knew implicitly already.

Criticism 5: Scepticism about the future and the past

[The authors begin, here, by referring us to two sceptical arguments previously mentioned in their book. One is Hume's sceptical argument about induction. The other is summarized by them earlier in the book as follows:

How can we be sure that any of the evidence we have about the past is reliable? Indeed, it is conceivable that the world came into existence only yesterday complete with apparent memories, history books and fossil records, all as a cosmic prank made up by some unthinkably powerful deity. Since we can't know that this hasn't happened, we can't have knowledge of the past. (Bertrand Russell, Lecture 9: 'Memory', The Analysis of Mind, Routledge 1989)]

Both these sceptical arguments work by pointing out that knowledge of past and future has to be based on an inference. This is because neither can be observed directly - neither is an immediate part of our present sense experience. Hume's sceptical argument about INDUCTION notes that knowledge of the future is based on and inferred from knowledge given us in the past and present. Russell's argument notes that we have to infer knowledge of the past from knowledge given us in the present. Both suggest that the inferences may be unsound. Both Russell and Hume are empiricist philosophers, and the thrust of their sceptical arguments lies in their insistence that genuine knowledge must come from immediate and present experience or from acquaintance with sense data. If one insists on this, then it is a short step for all other kinds of knowledge, knowledge inferred from sense data, to appear less than certain and even, in the final analysis, unknowable. If this is right, then empiricism leads us further into scepticism and so appears inadequate as an account of how human knowledge is justified.

Modern criticisms of empiricist foundationalism

Criticism 6: ls knowledge of sense data really certain?

A Empiricist foundationalism suggests that our sense data, which cannot be doubted, are the building blocks for all our knowledge. However, one objection to this seeks to undermine the supposed certainty of our sense data. The critic claims that sometimes we can be unsure as to how to characterise much of our immediate experience. For example, I may see a flashy car and be unsure of whether the colour is metallic purple or magenta. Moreover I can make mistakes. I may believe that I am eating smoky bacon crisps, when in fact the crisps are paprika flavoured. But surely, the objection runs, if immediate experience is certain I could never be in such a position?

The empiricist foundationalist may feel that she has been cheated here. The obvious defence is that any uncertainty does not concern the appearance to me of the sense data. Rather the error here has to do with how I categorise or describe them. Since these are examples of possibly misdescribing what one perceives, the defence goes, they do not touch the certainty one can have of the immediate sense data themselves prior to any description. I may not be sure of what this colour or taste is called, but I can none the less be certain of what it is like here and now for me.

Another way of making the point is to say that we can avoid error so long as we resist the inclination to 'translate' the immediacy of experience into categories, or to put them into words. While we may go wrong in trying to conceptualise such experience, surely the immediacy of present sensation remains indubitable. The empiricist foundationalist maintains that this original preconceptual given is the ground for any further superstructure of ordered experience.

However, without some sort of interpretation it is difficult to see how such experience could be anything more than what the American philosopher William James (f 842-I9I0) called a 'blooming, buzzing confusion': an undifferentiated stream of sensations. It is only by placing what is given - the stream of sense data - within certain categories that beliefs can be held as to what is the case, and any knowledge claims about it made. One would be acquainted with one's sense data, but not have any factual knowledge about them. Kant expressed the point with the well-known phrase: 'intuitions [i.e. roughly sense data] without concepts are blind'. This means that sense data in themselves cannot even be experienced: the mind would be 'blind' to them because they have not yet been classified.

Whether or not we want to go so far as to say that experience of the raw, uninterpreted given is impossible, it is certainly the case that we cannot talk directly about it or say anything meaningful about what it is like. In other words, without conceptual organisation there can be no knowledge about one's own sense data. It would seem that we cannot even claim certainty for the proposition that a colour looked magenta or that the taste seemed like smoky bacon to me, here and now, since to do so is to go beyond the immediacy of the moment. This is because to describe the way something appears to you involves categorising it along with other similar experiences. Perceptual beliefs depend (if they are to be intelligible) on our being able to connect them with past experiences that are alike in a certain respect. The word 'magenta' functions to connect the present experience with many others that are not present, and to treat it as equivalent to the others in the relevant respect. In other words, the very effort to identify the immediate data of one's private experience necessarily involves going beyond what is immediate. This reference to what lies beyond the experience being described opens up any such statement to the possibility of error or misdescription. It may turn out that the present experience is not of the sort we had supposed it to be.

These considerations are supposed to establish that the possibility of error accompanies any attempt to place things within conceptual categories. Even apparently basic reports about our sense data such as 'I smell thyme' or 'I see magenta' are embedded within larger frameworks. Consequently, factual knowledge must by its very nature be open to doubt and correction and the idea that there could be an indubitable bedrock of beliefs about our own sensory states is to be rejected. Acquaintance with what is given in sense experience does not constitute any kind of factual knowledge, since factual knowledge concerns propositions about sense data, not simply those data themselves. Prior to receiving conceptual ordering or classification, the given cannot have any propositional form and so it cannot be either true or false. This means that since the given is not the kind of thing that admits of doubt, it cannot be the kind of thing that admits of certainty either, because to acquire knowledge we must run the risk of error. Therefore, it becomes meaningless to say that sense data are indubitable since only propositions about them can be doubted or not doubted. Sense data just 'are'.

Criticism 7: Are beliefs about our sense data incorrigible?

Finally, it has been argued that beliefs about our own sense data are not at all incorrigible. That is, they can be corrected in the light of further evidence and so cannot be self-justifying. For example, if I learn that the crisps I am eating come from a pack labelled 'paprika', I may well decide that I am mistaken in believing the taste I am experiencing to be smoky bacon. I may even start to taste the crisps differently. Here it seems I have corrected my characterisation of the original experience. Thus, contrary to the foundationalist assumptions of traditional empiricism, we can alter our beliefs about our sense data in the light of our beliefs about physical objects.

One's previous experience, and expectations, can also influence what one perceives, even though the raw sensory experience would appear to be the same. Two people looking at the same image can see different things. To take a simple example, consider this figure:

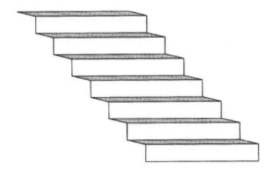

Figure 3.5 What we see depends on what we expect

Most people see this image as a staircase going away from us, up to the left. This is doubtless because we are used to seeing staircases from this angle. But it can just as well be seen as a staircase viewed from beneath. Whichever one it happens to be, the sensory input must surely remain unchanged, so it seems that what we perceive is determined, at least in part, by what we are expecting to perceive. This implies, contrary to foundationalism, that sense data are influenced by our superstructural beliefs about the world.

Here are some other similar examples. Leonardo da Vinci's drawings of the human heart show only three venticles. How could a draughtsman of da Vinci's calibre not see the four ventricles that we now know the heart to contain? One answer is that what one sees is in large part determined by one's background assumptions. Only once people recognise the heart to be a kind of pump are they able to see four ventricles. When scientists first observed human sperm through a microscope, their background assumptions ted them to observe elongated men with beards. Because they believed that sperm would have to contain small versions of the human being they would turn into, this is what they saw.

Examples like these are often taken to show that sense data propositions cannot be the foundation of empirical knowledge. Justification appears to run not exclusively from the sense data up, but in the other direction as well. Our background or superstructural beliefs are often involved in the interpretation of our sense data. If I see pink elephants floating around the room I am liable to suppose that this is a hallucination because of my background beliefs about elephants. Such a perception does not fit into my general pattern of beliefs about the world, and so it is rejected. Indeed it may be that all propositions, whether they concern sense data or not, are open to amendment in the light of other propositions, and consequently that no class of propositions, or beliefs, can be given the privileged status of being the foundations for all others.

§3 Ethics

Absolutism and Relativism

Moral absolutism <u>is the theory that there are certain moral principles that should not be violated under any circumstances.</u> For instance, an absolutist might hold that it is always wrong to kill another human being.

Moral absolutism is subtly different from another position in Ethics:

Moral objectivism: the theory that there are universal moral principles that apply to everyone, in any culture, society or time.

An example might explain the difference. Say that Jack, a moral absolutist, considers that 'Do not kill' is an absolute principle. Jill is a moral objectivist and believes that killing is wrong, but she is not an absolutist as Jack is. Jack and Jill make the mistake of wondering into an Ethics scenario, and find themselves in a town square witnessing the preparations for a mass execution. The captain in charge explains that the twenty people standing against the wall have taken part in an illegal demonstration and are about to be shot. But a strange custom dictates that visitors from abroad be offered the privilege of shooting one of the prisoners themselves and seeing the rest go free. Jack's absolutist pacifist principle tells him that he cannot take up the offer, despite his horror at the situation. But let us assume that the society into which she has stumbled, while brutal, is refreshingly feminist, and the captain gives Jill the same opportunity. She believes that killing is wrong, and the thought of it appalls her. But she also believes in a duty to save life where you can, and the thought of allowing 20 people to die when she had the opportunity of saving 19 appalls her even more. She commits what she considers the lesser evil in the situation, and shoots one of the prisoners, in order to prevent more killing, and fulfill a duty to save life.

If you are an objectivist, you think that there are matters of fact in Ethics. For instance, you might believe that the wrongness of killing is a fact, not a matter of opinion or something that could be legitimately rejected in a different cultural context. Absolutists, who believe in principles that must never be violated, have to be objectivists as well. But not all objectivists are absolutists, as Jill shows us. Absolutism goes a little bit further than objectivism and states that some objective principles are so utterly binding – perhaps sacred – that they cannot be sacrificed whatever other principles or consequences are at stake.

Moral relativism is in opposition to moral objectivism as well as moral absolutism.

<u>Moral relativism:</u> **the theory that:**

1. Actions are right or wrong only relative to some particular standpoint (usually the moral framework of a specific community).

2. No standpoint can be proved objectively superior to any other.

(definition abbreviated from the Internet Encyclopedia of Philosophy)

Let us rewind the situation with Jack, Jill and the mass execution and introduce Jemima, an implausibly committed moral relativist. Like Jack and Jill, she comes from London, but has spent some time living here. She helpfully explains to Jack and Jill that mass execution of peaceful protestors is generally accepted within this society. So there is nothing to be morally outraged about. The execution is right in this society. The same thing might be wrong in Jack and Jill's home society, but that is not relevant here. There is no universal truth about the morality of mass executions, only the individual truths of different societies.

Cultural relativism: the theory that moral principles and values are customs of a particular society, and cannot be understood or judged from outside.

You will notice that what this amounts to is essentially a slightly more specific version of moral relativism.

It is a term particularly associated with anthropologists who have studied different cultures and tried to understand the significance of unfamiliar practices and rituals. Franz Boas (1858-1942) was a highly influential American anthropologist who studied Baffin Island Inuit culture, among others. His studies led him to cultural relativism. He saw difference in values and principles as developing in specific historical and geographical contexts in the interactions between groups. He rejected the idea that societies were all progressing towards the same goal and that Western-European cultures were 'higher' than others.

If you see moral principles as relative not to a society but to an *individual*, you are a **moral subjectivist**.

Moral subjectivism: the view that whether an action is right or wrong depends purely on the beliefs or preferences of the individual. (Note that 'subjectivism' can have several slightly different meanings, of which this is one!)

This position can be seen as falling into the category of moral relativism, but is an area for debate in its own right and is not what philosophers are usually referring to when they discuss moral relativism.

Normative relativism: the theory that because of moral relativism, it is wrong to judge the ethical positions of other cultures.

'Normative' describes a position or theory that prescribes what ought to be done (drawing on some kind of standard or 'norm'). Whereas moral relativism tries to describe how ethical judgements are, normative relativism tells us what we should do about it.

References:

Pojman, Louis P. and James Fieser, *Ethics, Discovering Right and Wrong*, Wadsworth, 2012

Rachels, James, *Elements of Moral Philosophy*, McGraw Hill, 2003

Westacott, Emrys, 'Moral Relativism', in the Internet Encyclopedia of Philosophy
http://www.iep.utm.edu/moral-re/#SH2e

Ethical Theories – Absolutist or Relativist?

Below you will find *the very shortest* of introductions to two normative ethical theories.

A normative ethical theory is a theory about how we ought to live and act. It proposes the basis on which we should make our moral decisions.

Two further definitions are important when we are looking at normative ethical theories:

A theory is consequentialist, or teleological if it holds that it is an action's consequences that make it right or wrong. The Greek word **telos** means 'goal' or 'purpose'. A teleologist holds that if you want to act morally you should have the goal of your action in mind and seek to bring about the best results.

A theory is deontological if it holds that to act rightly we must fulfill our duties and obligations, regardless of the consequences. The Greek word **deon** means 'duty'.

Absolutist or Relativist?

- For each normative theory consider whether it is an example of moral absolutism, or moral relativism, or neither. Consider also whether it fits another category, like objectivism.
- How easy is it to categorise ethical approaches as absolutist or relativist?

Kantian Ethics

Immanuel Kant (1724-1804) is an enormously important figure in modern philosophy. His epistemology disputed the assumptions of empiricists like Locke and Hume. Whereas they saw us as entirely dependent on sense experience for any knowledge, Kant considered that sense experience is ordered by our minds. Gensler explains how Kant sees reason as supreme in ethics as in epistemology:

> Kant looked at old philosophical problems in new ways. For example, we don't derive our notions of space and time from sense experience. Instead, we impose these structures on our sensations. The mind is active.

> Ethics works the same way. Reason imposes its own abstract, formal laws on our actions. **Morality ultimately rests, not on sense experience or feelings, but on reason.**
>
> http://www.harryhiker.com/ms/kant--00.htm

Moral action vs prudent action

Kant sees moral action as contrasting sharply with 'prudent' action. When you act according to prudence, you consider the likely consequences of your action and do whatever you think will have the most advantageous results. If I help a friend because I foresee that I am going to need her help next week and want to make sure I get it, I am acting on prudence.

For Kant, acting morally is not about seeking the right kinds of results. Helping my friend in order to make her happy would not be a moral act either.

Kant's is a deontological theory. Acting morally is about acting for the sake of duty, *not* for the sake of the consequences. What our duty is can be worked out using our reason, which gives human beings their dignity and status as moral beings.

The Categorical Imperative

Whether an action is moral or not is specified by the Categorical Imperative:

'Act only according to that maxim whereby you can, at the same time, will that it should become a universal law.'

A maxim is simply a guide for action. The Categorical Imperative means that you should only do an action if you could will for everyone else to do likewise.

Duty demands that we should not lie, Kant says, because it is impossible to rationally will for everyone to lie. If everyone lied, the very concept of the truth would be lost. And lying depends on the idea of truth, because lying is stating something which is not true. Willing for everyone to lie is inherently contradictory, Kant considers; you are willing for something that would be inherently impossible if attempted by everyone. It is this contradiction that makes lying wrong, not any hurtful consequences it might have.

A 'categorical imperative' is something that must be done, unconditionally, whatever the consequences. When we act according to prudence we are acting on 'hypothetical imperatives'. When I help out my friend my reasoning is 'I must help her *if* I want her to help me.' All actions seeking certain consequences are based on hypothetical imperatives. 'I must go running *if* I want to get fit'; 'I must get him a birthday present *if* I want to make him happy'. But there is no 'if' in the Categorical Imperative.

That is the nature of duty, for Kant. Lying in any circumstance whatever is impermissible, as is killing or stealing. Reason shows us that the action is wrong in itself. There are no exceptions.

Situation Ethics

A summary from Jill Oliphant's *OCR Religious Ethics for AS and A2*

Joseph Fletcher developed Situation Ethics in the 1960s in reaction to Christian legalism and antinomianism (which is the belief that there are no fixed moral principles, but that morality is the result of individual spontaneous acts).

Fletcher argues that each individual situation is different and absolute rules are too demanding and restrictive. The Bible shows what good moral decisions look like in particular situations, but it is not possible to know what God's will is in every situation. Fletcher says: 'I simply do not know and cannot know what God is doing.' As it is not possible to know God's will in every situation, *love* or *agape* is Situation Ethics' only moral 'rule'.

Situation Ethics is midway between legalism and antinomialism, and Fletcher's book, which was published in 1966, reflected the mood of the times – Christians should make the right choices without just following the rules and by thinking for themselves.

Christians should base their decisions on one single rule – the rule of agape. This love is not merely an emotion but involves doing what is best for the other person, unconditionally. This means that other guiding maxims could be ignored in certain situations if they do not serve agape; for example, Fletcher says it would be right for a mother with a 13-year-old daughter who is having sex to break the rules about under-age sex and insist her daughter uses contraception – the right choice is the most loving thing and it will depend on the situation…

According to Fletcher's *Situation Ethics,* this ethical theory depends on four working principles and six fundamental principles.

The four working principles

1. Pragmatism – what you propose must work in practice
2. Relativism – words like 'always', 'never', 'absolute' are rejected. There are no fixed rules but all decisions must be relative to agape. [*Is 'relativism' being used here in the same way as we have defined it?*]
3. Positivism – a value judgement needs to be made, giving the first place to love.
4. Personalism – people are put in the first place, morality is personal and not centred on laws.

J L Mackie

Ethics: Inventing Right and Wrong

Chapter 1, The Subjectivity of Values (abbreviated)

John Leslie Mackie (1917 – 1981) was an Australian philosopher who studied at the University of Sydney before taking up a travelling fellowship to study at Oriel College, Oxford. His most significant work was in ethics, philosophy of religion and metaphysics. He was known for his friendly and courteous approach to philosophical argument. His genial attitude is expressed in the introduction to Inventing Right and Wrong:

> I am nowhere mainly concerned to refute any individual writer. I believe that all those to whom I have referred, even those with whom I disagree most strongly, have contributed significantly to our understanding of ethics: where I have quoted their actual words, it is because they have presented views or arguments more clearly or more forcefully than I could put them myself.

Mackie begins that book by stating and clarifying his central claim:

There are no objective values.

… The claim that values are not objective, are not part of the fabric of the world, is meant to include not only moral goodness, which might be most naturally equated with moral value, but also other things that could be more loosely called moral values or disvalues - rightness and wrongness, duty, obligation, an action's being rotten and contemptible, and so on. It also includes non-moral values, notably aesthetic ones, beauty and various kinds of artistic merit.

After brief discussion of widespread ethical objectivism in philosophical thinkers from Plato and Aristotle to Kant and later thinkers, he notes that ordinary people very commonly assume that there are objective truths about right and wrong

The ordinary user of moral language means to say something about whatever it is that he characterizes morally, for example a possible action, as it is in itself.…

Someone in a state of moral perplexity, wondering whether it would be wrong for him to engage, say, in research related to bacteriological warfare, wants to arrive at some judgment about this concrete case, his doing this work at this time in these actual circumstances; his relevant characteristics will be part of the subject of the judgment, but no relation between him and the proposed action will be part of the predicate. The question is not, for example whether he really wants to do this work, whether it will satisfy or dissatisfy him, whether he will in the long run have a pro-attitude towards it, or even whether this is an action of a sort that he can happily and sincerely recommend in all relevantly similar cases. Nor is he even wondering just whether to recommend such action in all relevantly similar cases. He wants to know whether this course of action would be wrong in itself…

The denial of objective values can carry with it an extreme emotional reaction, a feeling that nothing matters at all, that life has lost its purpose….

Since [Mackie's own theory] goes against assumptions ingrained in our thought and built into some of the ways in which language is used, since it conflicts with what is sometimes called common sense, it needs very solid support. It is not something we can accept lightly or casually and then quietly pass on. If we are to adopt this view, we must argue explicitly for it. Traditionally it has been supported by arguments of two main kinds, which I shall call the argument from relativity and the argument from queerness, but these can, as I shall show, be supplemented…

Mackie first sets out the argument from relativity:

The argument from relativity has as its premiss the well-known variation in moral codes from one society to another and from one period to another, and also the differences in moral beliefs between different groups and classes within a complex community. Such variation is in itself merely a truth of descriptive morality, a fact of anthropology… Yet it may indirectly support… subjectivism: radical differences between… moral judgements make it difficult to treat those judgements as apprehensions of objective truths. But it is not the mere occurrence of disagreements that tells against the objectivity of values. Disagreement on questions in history or biology or cosmology does not show that there are no objective issues in these fields for investigators to disagree about. But such scientific disagreement results from speculative inference; or explanatory hypotheses based on inadequate evidence, and it is hardly plausible to interpret moral disagreement in the same way. Disagreement about moral codes seems to reflect people's adherence to and participation in different ways of life. The causal connection seems to be mainly that way round: it is that people approve of monogamy because they participate in a monogamous way of life rather than that they participate in a monogamous way of life because they approve of monogamy. Of course, the standards may be an idealization of the way of life from which they arise: the monogamy in which people participate maybe less complete, less rigid, than that of which it leads them to approve. This is not to say that moral judgements are purely conventional. Of course there have been and are moral heretics and moral reformers, people who have turned against the established rules and practices of their own communities for moral reasons, and often for moral reasons that we would endorse. But this can usually be understood as the extension, in ways which, though new and unconventional, seemed to them to be required for consistency, of rules to which they already adhered as arising out of an existing way of life. In short, the argument from relativity has some force simply because the actual variations in the moral codes are more readily explained by the hypothesis that they reflect ways of life than by the hypothesis that they express perceptions, most of them seriously inadequate and badly distorted, of objective values.

- *What is it about moral disagreements, as opposed to scientific ones, which Mackie thinks casts real doubt on objectivism?*

Mackie's 'argument from queerness' is as follows:

Even more important, however, and certainly more generally applicable, is the argument from queerness. This has two parts, one metaphysical, the other epistemological. If there were objective values, then they would be entities or qualities or relations of a very strange sort, utterly different from anything else in the universe. Correspondingly, if we were aware of them, it would have to be by some special faculty of moral perception or intuition, utterly different from our ordinary ways of knowing everything else.

....

Plato's Forms give a dramatic picture of what objective values would have to be. The Form of the Good is such that knowledge of it provides the knower with both a direction and an overriding motive; something's being good both tells the person who knows this to pursue it and makes him pursue it. An objective good would be sought by anyone who was acquainted with it, not because of any contingent fact that this person, or every person, is so constituted that he desires this end, but just because the end has to-be-pursuedness somehow built into it. Similarly, if there were objective principles of right and wrong, any wrong (possible) course of action would have not- to- be-doneness somehow built into it. Or we should have something like Clarke's necessary relations 'of fitness between situations and actions, so that a situation would have a demand for such-and-such an action somehow built into it.

- *Summarise what Mackie considers so 'queer' about objective values*

Mackie goes on to strengthen his argument by showing that we can easily explain why people would mistakenly believe in objective values:

Considerations of these kinds suggest that it is in the end less paradoxical to reject than to retain the common-sense belief in the objectivity of moral values, provided that we can explain how this belief, if it is false, has become established and is so resistant to criticisms. This proviso is not difficult to satisfy.

On a subjectivist view, the supposedly objective values will be based in fact upon attitudes which the person has who takes himself to be recognizing and responding to those values. If we admit what Hume calls the mind's 'propensity to spread itself on external objects', we can understand the supposed objectivity of moral qualities as arising from what we can call the projection or objectification of moral attitudes. This would be analogous to what is called the 'pathetic fallacy', the tendency to read our feelings into their objects. If a fungus, say, fills us with disgust, we may be inclined to ascribe to the fungus itself a non-natural quality of foulness. But in moral contexts there is more than this propensity at work. Moral attitudes themselves are at least [43] partly social in origin: socially established - and socially neccessary - patterns of behaviour put pressure on individuals, and each individual tends to internalize these pressures and to join in requiring these patterns of behaviour of himself and of others. The attitudes that are objectified into moral values have indeed an external source, though not the one assigned to them by the belief in their absolute authority. Moreover, there are motives that would support objectification. We need morality o regulate interpersonal relations, to control some of the ways in which people behave towards one another, often in opposiion to contrary inclinations. We therefore want our moral judgements to be authoritative for other agents as well as for ourselves: objective validity would give them the authority required.

- *Summarise the explanation*

C S Lewis

Mere Christianity

Book 1: 1 The Law of Human Nature

Every one has heard people quarrelling. Sometimes it sounds funny and sometimes it sounds merely unpleasant; but however it sounds, I believe we can learn something very important from listening to the kind of things they say. They say things like this: "How'd you like it if anyone did the same to you?"-"That's my seat, I was there first"-"Leave him alone, he isn't doing you any harm"- "Why should you shove in first?"-"Give me a bit of your orange, I gave you a bit of mine"-"Come on, you promised." People say things like that every day, educated people as well as uneducated, and children as well as grown-ups. Now what interests me about all these remarks is that the man who makes them is not merely saying that the other man's behaviour does not happen to please him. He is appealing to some kind of standard of behaviour which he expects the other man to know about. And the other man very seldom replies: "To hell with your standard." Nearly always he tries to make out that what he has been doing does not really go against the standard, or that if it does there is some special excuse. He pretends there is some special reason in this particular case why the person who took the seat first should not keep it, or that things were quite different when he was given the bit of orange, or that something has turned up which lets him off keeping his promise. It looks, in fact, very much as if both parties had in mind some kind of Law or Rule of fair play or decent behaviour or morality or whatever you like to call it, about which they really agreed.

And they have. If they had not, they might, of course, fight like animals, but they could not quarrel in the human sense of the word. Quarrelling means trying to show that the other man is in the wrong. And there would be nosense in trying to do that unless you and he had some sort of agreement as to what Right and Wrong are; just as there would be no sense in saying that a footballer had committed a foul unless there was some agreement about the rules of football.

Now this Law or Rule about Right and Wrong used to be called the Law of Nature. Nowadays, when we talk of the "laws of nature" we usually mean things like gravitation, or heredity, or the laws of chemistry. But when the older thinkers called the Law of Right and Wrong "the Law of Nature," they really meant the Law of Human Nature. The idea was that, just as all bodies are governed by the law of gravitation and organisms by biological laws, so the creature called man also had his law-with this great difference, that a body could not choose whether it obeyed the law of gravitation or not, but a man could choose either to obey the Law of Human Nature or to disobey it.

We may put this in another way. Each man is at every moment subjected to several different sets of law but there is only one of these which he is free to disobey. As a body, he is subjected to gravitation and cannot disobey it; if you leave him unsupported in mid-air, he has no more choice about falling than a stone has. As an organism, he is subjected to various biological laws which he cannot disobey any more than an animal can. That is, he cannot disobey those laws which he shares with other things; but the law which is peculiar to his human nature, the law he does not share with animals or vegetables or inorganic things, is the one he can disobey if he chooses.

This law was called the Law of Nature because people thought that every one knew it by nature and did not need to be taught it. They did not mean, of course, that you might not find an odd individual here and there who did not know it, just as you find a few people who are colour-blind or have no ear for a tune. But taking the race as a whole, they thought that the human idea of decent behaviour was obvious to every one. And I believe they were right. If they were not, then all the things we said about the war were nonsense. What was the sense in saying the enemy were in the wrong unless. Right is a real thing which the Nazis at bottom knew as well as we did and ought to have practised? If they had had no notion of what we mean by right, then, though we might still have had to fight them, we could no more have blamed them for that than for the colour of their hair.

I know that some people say the idea of a Law of Nature or decent behaviour known to all men is unsound, because different civilisations and different ages have had quite different moralities.

But this is not true. There have been differences between their moralities, but these have never amounted to anything like a total difference. If anyone will take the trouble to compare the moral teaching of, say, the ancient Egyptians, Babylonians, Hindus, Chinese, Greeks and Romans, what will really strike him will be how very like they are to each other and to our own. Some of the evidence for this I have put together in the appendix of another book called The Abolition of Man; but for our present purpose I need only ask the reader to think what a totally different morality would mean. Think of a country where people were admired for running away in battle, or where a man felt proud of double-crossing all the people who had been kindest to him. You might just as well try to imagine a country where two and two made five. Men have differed as regards what people you ought to be unselfish to-whether it was only your own family, or your fellow countrymen, or everyone. But they have always agreed that you ought not to put yourself first. Selfishness has never been admired. Men have differed as to whether you should have one wife or four. But they have always agreed that you must not simply have any woman you liked.

But the most remarkable thing is this. Whenever you find a man who says he does not believe in a real Right and Wrong, you will find the same man going back on this a moment later. He may break his promise to you, but if you try breaking one to him he will be complaining "It's not fair" before you can say Jack Robinson. A nation may say treaties do not matter, but then, next minute, they spoil their case by saying that the particular treaty they want to break was an unfair one. But if treaties do not matter, and if there is no such thing as Right and Wrong- in other words, if there is no Law of Nature-what is the difference between a fair treaty and an unfair one? Have they not let the cat out of the bag and shown that, whatever they say, they really know the Law of Nature just like anyone else?

It seems, then, we are forced to believe in a real Right and Wrong. People may be sometimes mistaken about them, just as people sometimes get their sums wrong; but they are not a matter of mere taste and opinion any more than the multiplication table.

James Rachels

Elements of Moral Philosophy

Chapter 2, The Challenge of Cultural Relativism

'Morality differs in every society, and is a convenient term for socially approved habits.'
Ruth Benedict, *Patterns of Culture* (1934)

2.1. How Different Cultures Have Different Moral Codes

Darius, a king of ancient Persia, was intrigued by the variety of cultures he encountered in his travels. He had found, for example, that the Callatians (a tribe of Indians) customarily ate the bodies of their dead fathers. The Greeks, of course, did not do that—the Greeks practiced cremation and regarded the funeral pyre as the natural and fitting way to dispose of the dead. Darius thought that a sophisticated understanding of the world must include an appreciation of such differences between cultures. One day, to teach this lesson, he summoned some Greeks who happened to be present at his court a n d asked them what they would take to eat the bodies of their dead fathers. They were shocked, as Darius knew they would be, and replied that no amount of money could persuade them to do such a thing.

Then Darius called in some Callatians, and while the Greeks listened asked them what they would take to b u r n their dead fathers' bodies. The Callatians were horrified and told Darius not even to mention such a dreadful thing. This story, recounted by Herodotus in his History, illustrates a recurring theme in the literature of social science: Different cultures have different moral codes. What is thought right within one group may be utterly abhorrent to the members of another group, and vice versa. Should we eat the bodies of the dead or burn them? If you were a Greek, one answer would seem obviously correct; but if you were a Callatian, the opposite would seem equally certain.

It is easy to give additional examples of the same kind. Consider the Eskimos (of which the largest group is the Inuit). They are a remote and inaccessible people. Numbering only about 25,000, they live in small, isolated settlements scattered mostly along the northern fringes of North America and Greenland. Until the beginning of the 20th century, the outside world knew little about them. Then explorers began to bring back strange tales.

Eskimo customs turned out to be very different from our own. The men often had more than one wife, and they would share their wives with guests, lending them for the night as a sign of hospitality. Moreover, within a community a dominant male might demand and get regular sexual access to other men's wives. The women however, were free to break these arrangements simply by leaving their husbands and taking up with new partners—free, that is, so long as their former husbands chose not to make trouble. All in all, the Eskimo practice was a volatile scheme that bore little resemblance to what we call marriage.

But it was not only their marriage and sexual practices that were different. The Eskimos also seemed to have less regard for human life. Infanticide, for example, was common. Knud Rasmussen, one of the most famous early explorers, reported that he met one woman who had borne 20 children but had killed 10 of them at birth. Female babies, he found, were especially liable to be destroyed, and this was permitted simply at the parents' discretion, with no social stigma attached to it. Old people also, when they became too feeble to contribute to the family, were left out in the snow to die. So there seemed to be, in this society, remarkably little respect for life.

To the general public, these were disturbing revelations. Our own way of living seems so natural and right that for many of us it is hard to conceive of others living so differently. And when we do hear of such things, we tend immediately to categorize the other peoples as "backward" or "primitive." But to anthropologists, there was nothing particularly surprising about the Eskimos. Since the time of Herodotus, enlightened observers have been accustomed to the idea that conceptions of right and wrong differ from culture to culture. If we assume that our ethical ideas will be shared by all peoples at all times, we are merely naive.

2.2. Cultural Relativism

To many thinkers, this observation — "Different cultures have different moral codes" — has seemed to be the key to understanding morality. The idea of universal truth in ethics, they say, is a myth. The customs of different societies are all that exist. These customs cannot be said to be "correct" or "incorrect," for that implies we have an independent standard of right and wrong by which they may be judged. But there is no such independent standard; every standard is culture-bound. The great pioneering sociologist William Graham Sumner, writing in 1906, put it like this:

> The "right" way is the way which the ancestors used and which has been handed down. The tradition is its own warrant. It is not held subject to verification by experience. The notion of right is in the folkways. It is not outside of them, of independent origin, and brought to test them. In the folkways, whatever is, is right. This is because they are traditional, and therefore contain in themselves the authority of the ancestral ghosts. When we come to the folkways we are at the end of our analysis.

This line of thought has probably persuaded more people to be skeptical about ethics than any other single thing. Cultural Relativism, as it has been called, challenges our ordinary belief in the objectivity and universality of moral truth. It says, in effect, that there is no such thing as universal truth in ethics; there are only the various cultural codes, and nothing more. Moreover, our own code has no special status; it is merely one among many. As we shall see, this basic idea is really a compound of several different thoughts. It is important to separate the various elements of the theory because, on analysis, some parts turn out to be correct, while others seem to be mistaken. As a beginning, we may distinguish the following claims, all of which have been made by cultural relativists:

1. Different societies have different moral codes.

2. The moral code of a society determines what is right within that society; that is, if the moral code of a society says that a certain action is right, then that action is right, at least within that society.

3. There is no objective standard that can be used to judge one society's code better than another's.

4. The moral code of our own society has no special status; it is merely one among many.

5. There is no "universal truth" in ethics; that is, there are no moral truths that hold for all peoples at all times.

6. It is mere arrogance for us to try to judge the conduct of other peoples. We should adopt an attitude of tolerance toward the practices of other cultures.

Although it may seem that these six propositions go naturally together, they are independent of one another, in the sense that some of them might be false even if others are true. In what follows, we will try to identify what is correct in Cultural Relativism, but we will also be concerned to expose what is mistaken about it.

2.3. The Cultural Differences Argument

Cultural Relativism is a theory about the nature of morality. At first blush it seems quite plausible. However, like all such theories, it may be evaluated by subjecting it to rational analysis; and when we analyze Cultural Relativism, we find that it is not so plausible as it first appears to be.

The first thing we need to notice is that at the heart of Cultural Relativism there is a certain form of argument. The strategy used by cultural relativists is to argue from facts about the differences between cultural outlooks to a conclusion about the status of morality. Thus we are invited to accept this reasoning:

(1) The Greeks believed it was wrong to eat the dead, whereas the Callatians believed it was right to eat the dead.

(2) Therefore, eating the dead is neither objectively right nor objectively wrong. It is merely a matter of opinion that varies from culture to culture.

Or, alternatively:

(1) The Eskimos see nothing wrong with infanticide, whereas Americans believe infanticide is immoral.

(2) Therefore, infanticide is neither objectively right nor objectively wrong. It is merely a matter of opinion, which varies from culture to culture.

Clearly, these arguments are variations of one fundamental idea. They are both special cases of a more general argument, which says:

(1) Different cultures have different moral codes.

(2) Therefore, there is no objective "truth" in morality. Right and wrong are only matters of opinion, and opinions vary from culture to culture.

We may call this the Cultural Differences Argument. To many people, it is persuasive. But from a logical point of view, is it sound?

It is not sound. The trouble is that the conclusion does not follow from the premise — that is, even if the premise is true, the conclusion still might be false. The premise concerns what people believe — in some societies, people believe one thing; in other societies, people believe differently. The conclusion, however, concerns what really is the case. The trouble is that this sort of conclusion does not follow logically from this sort of premise.

Consider again the example of the Greeks and Callatians. The Greeks believed it was wrong to eat the dead; the Callatians believed it was right. Does it follow, from the mere fact that they disagreed, that there is no objective truth in the matter? No, it does not follow; for it could be that the practice was objectively right (or wrong) and that one or the other of them was simply mistaken.

To make the point clearer, consider a different matter. In some societies, people believe the earth is flat. In other societies, such as our own, people believe the earth is (roughly)spherical. Does it follow, from the mere fact that people disagree, that there is no "objective truth" in geography? Of course not; we would never draw such a conclusion because we realize that, in their beliefs about the world, the members of some societies might simply be wrong. There is no reason to think that if the world is round everyone must know it. Similarly, there is no reason to think that if there is moral truth everyone must know it. The fundamental mistake in the Cultural Differences Argument is that it attempts to derive a substantive conclusion about a subject from the mere fact that people disagree about it.

This is a simple point of logic, and it is important not to misunderstand it. We are not saying (not yet, anyway) that the conclusion of the argument is false. That is still an open question. The logical point is just that the conclusion does not follow from the premise. This is important, because in order to determine whether the conclusion is true, we need arguments in its support. Cultural Relativism proposes this argument, but unfortunately the argument turns out to be fallacious. So it proves nothing.

2.4. The Consequences of Taking Cultural Relativism Seriously

Even if the Cultural Differences Argument is invalid, Cultural Relativism might still be true. What would it be like if it were true? In the passage quoted above, William Graham Sumner summarizes the essence of Cultural Relativism. He says that there is no measure of right and wrong other than the standards of one's society: "The notion of right is in the folkways. It is not outside of them, of independent origin, and brought to test them. In the folkways, whatever is, is right." Suppose we took this seriously. What would be some of the consequences?

1. We could no longer say that the customs of other societies are morally inferior to our own. This, of course, is one of the main points stressed by Cultural Relativism. We would have to stop condemning other societies merely because they are "different." So long as we concentrate on certain examples, such as the funerary practices of the Greeks and Callatians, this may seem to be a sophisticated, enlightened attitude.

   However, we would also be stopped from criticizing other, less benign practices. Suppose a society waged war on its neighbors for the purpose of taking slaves. Or suppose a society was violently anti-Semitic and its leaders set out to destroy the Jews. Cultural Relativism would preclude us from saying that either of these practices was wrong. (We would not even be able to say that a society tolerant of Jews is better than the anti-Semitic society, for that would imply some sort of transcultural standard of comparison.) The failure to condemn these practices does not seem enlightened; on the contrary, slavery and anti-Semitism seem wrong wherever they occur. Nevertheless, if we took Cultural Relativism seriously, we would have to regard these social practices as immune from criticism.

2. We could decide whether actions are right or wrong just by consulting the standards of our society. Cultural Relativism suggests a simple test for determining what is right and what is wrong: All one need do is ask whether the action is in accordance with the code of one's society. Suppose in 1975 a resident of South Africa was wondering whether his country's policy of apartheid—a rigidly racist system—was morally correct. All he has to do is ask whether this policy conformed to his society's moral code. If it did, there would have been nothing to worry about, at least from a moral point of view.

   This implication of Cultural Relativism is disturbing because few of us think that our society's code is perfect—we can think of all sorts of ways in which it might be improved. Yet Cultural Relativism not only forbids us from criticizing the codes of other societies; it also stops us from criticizing our own. After all, if right and wrong are relative to culture, this must be true for our own culture just as m u c h as for other cultures.

3. The idea of moral progress is called into doubt. Usually, we think that at least some social changes are for the better. (Although, of course, other changes may be for the worse.) Throughout most of Western history the place of women in society was narrowly circumscribed. They could not own properly; they could not vote or hold political office; and generally they were under the almost absolute control of their husbands. Recently much of this has changed, and most people think of it as progress.

   But if Cultural Relativism is correct, can we legitimately think of this as progress? Progress means replacing a way of doing things with a better way. But by what standard do we judge the new ways as better? If the old ways were in accordance with the social standards of their time, then Cultural Relativism would say it is a mistake to judge them by the standards of a different time. Eighteenth-century society was a different society from the one we have now. To say that we have made progress implies a judgment that present-day society is better, and that is just the sort of transcultural j u d g m e n t that, according to Cultural Relativism, is impossible.

Our idea of social reform will also have to be reconsidered. Reformers such as Martin Luther King, Jr., have sought to change their societies for the better. Within the constraints imposed by Cultural Relativism, there is one way this might be done. If a society is not living up to its own ideals, the reformer may be regarded as acting for the best; the ideals of the society are the standard by which we judge his or her proposals as worthwhile. But no one may challenge the ideals themselves, for those ideals are by definition correct. According to Cultural Relativism, then, the idea of social reform makes sense only in this limited way. These three consequences of Cultural Relativism have led many thinkers to reject it as implausible on its face. It does make sense, they say, to condemn some practices, such as slavery and anti-Semitism, wherever they occur. It makes sense to think that our own society has made some moral progress, while admitting that it is still imperfect and in need of reform. Because Cultural Relativism implies that these judgments make no sense, the argument goes, it cannot be right.

2.5. Why There Is Less Disagreement Than It Seems

The original impetus for Cultural Relativism comes from the observation that cultures differ dramatically in their views of right and wrong. But just how much do they differ? It is true that there are differences. However, it is easy to overestimate the extent of those differences. Often, when we examine what seems to be a dramatic difference, we find that the cultures do not differ nearly as much as it appears.

Consider a culture in which people believe it is wrong to eat cows. This may even be a poor culture, in which there is not enough food; still, the cows are not to be touched. Such a society would appear to have values very different from our own. But does it? We have not yet asked why these people will not eat cows. Suppose it is because they believe that after death the souls of humans inhabit the bodies of animals, especially cows, so that a cow may be someone's grandmother. Now shall we say that their values are different from ours? No; the difference lies elsewhere. The difference is in our belief systems, not in our values. We agree that we shouldn't eat Grandma; we simply disagree about whether the cow is (or could be) Grandma.

The point is that many factors work together to produce the customs of a society. The society's values are only one of them. Other matters, such as the religious and factual beliefs held by its members, and the physical circumstances in which they must live, are also important. We cannot conclude, then, merely because customs differ, that there is a disagreement about values. The difference in customs may be attributable to some other aspect of social life. Thus there may be less disagreement about values than there appears to be.

Consider again the Eskimos, who often kill perfectly normal infants, especially girls. We do not approve of such things; in our society, a parent who killed a baby would be locked up. Thus there appears to be a great difference in the values of our two cultures. But suppose we ask why the Eskimos do this. The explanation is not that they have less affection for their children or less respect for human life. An Eskimo family will always protect its babies if conditions permit. But they live in a harsh environment, where food is in short supply. A fundamental postulate of Eskimo thought is: "Life is hard, and the margin of safety small." A family may want to nourish its babies but be unable to do so.

As in many "primitive" societies, Eskimo mothers will nurse their infants over a much longer period of time than mothers in our culture. The child will take nourishment from its mother's breast for four years, perhaps even longer. So even in the best of times there are limits to the number of infants that one mother can sustain. Moreover, the Eskimos are a nomadic people—unable to farm, they must move about in search of food. Infants must be carried, and a mother can carry only one baby in her parka as she travels and goes about her outdoor work. Other family members help however they can.

Infant girls are more readily disposed of because, first, in this society the males are the primary food providers—they are the hunters, following the traditional division of labor—and it is obviously important to maintain a sufficient number of food providers. But there is an important second reason as well. Because the hunters suffer a high casually rate, the adult men who die prematurely far outnumber the women who die early. Thus if male and female infants survived in equal numbers, the female adult population would greatly outnumber the male adult population. Examining the available statistics, one writer concluded that "were it not for female infanticide . . . there would be approximately one-and-a-half times as many females in the average Eskimo local group as there are food-producing males."

So among the Eskimos, infanticide does not signal a fundamentally different attitude toward children. Instead, it is a recognition that drastic measures are sometimes needed to ensure the family's survival. Even then, however, killing the baby is not the first option considered. Adoption is common; childless couples are especially happy to take a more fertile couple's "surplus." Killing is only the last resort. I emphasize this in order to show that the raw data of the anthropologists can be misleading; it can make the differences in values between cultures appear greater than they are. The Eskimos' values are not all that different from our values. It is only that life forces upon them choices that we do not have to make.

2.6. How All Cultures Have Some Values in Common

It should not be surprising that, despite appearances, the Eskimos are protective of their children. How could it be otherwise? How could a group survive that did not value its young? It is easy to see that, in fact, all cultural groups must protect their infants. Babies are helpless and cannot survive if they are not given extensive care for a period of years. Therefore, if a group did not care for its young, the young would not survive, and the older members of the group would not be replaced. After a while the group would die out. This means that any cultural group that continues to exist must care for its young. Infants that are not cared for must be the exception rather than the rule.

Similar reasoning shows that other values must be more or less universal. Imagine what it would be like for a society to place no value at all on truth telling. When one person spoke to another, there would be no presumption that she was telling the truth, for she could just as easily be speaking falsely. Within that society, there would be no reason to pay attention to what anyone says. (I ask you what time it is, and you say "Four o'clock." But there is no presumption that you are speaking truly; you could just as easily have said the first thing that came into your head. So I have no reason to pay attention to your answer. In fact, there was no point in my asking you in the first place.) Communication would then be extremely difficult, if not impossible. And because complex societies cannot exist without communication among their members, society would become impossible. It follows that in any complex society there must be a presumption in favor of truthfulness. There may of course be exceptions to this rule: There may be situations in which it is thought to be permissible to lie. Nevertheless, these will be exceptions to a rule that is in force in the society.

Here is one further example of the same type. Could a society exist in which there was no prohibition on murder? What would this be like? Suppose people were free to kill other people at will, and no one thought there was anything wrong with it. In such a "society," no one could feel safe. Everyone would have to be constantly on guard. People who wanted to survive would have to avoid other people as much as possible. This would inevitably result in individuals trying to become as self-sufficient as possible — after all, associating with others would be dangerous. Society on any large scale would collapse. Of course, people might band together in smaller groups with others that they could trust not to harm them. But notice what this means:

They would be forming smaller societies that did acknowledge a rule against murder. The prohibition of murder, then, is a necessary feature of all societies. There is a general theoretical point here, namely, that there are some moral rules that all societies must have in common, because those rules are necessary for society to exist. The rules against lying and murder are two examples. And in fact, we do find these rules in force in all viable cultures. Cultures may differ in what they regard as legitimate exceptions to the rules, but this disagreement exists against a background of agreement on the larger issues. Therefore, it is a mistake to overestimate the amount of difference between cultures. Not every moral rule can vary from society to society.

2.7. Judging a Cultural Practice to Be Undesirable

In 1996, a 17-year-old girl named Fauziya Kassindja arrived at Newark International Airport and asked for asylum. She had fled her native country of Togo, a small west African nation, to escape what people there call "excision." Excision is a permanently disfiguring procedure that is sometimes called "female circumcision," although it bears little resemblance to the Jewish practice. More commonly, at least in Western newspapers, it is referred to as "female genital mutilation."

According to the World Health Organization, the practice is widespread in 26 African nations, and two million girls each year are "excised." In some instances, excision is part of an elaborate tribal ritual, performed in small traditional villages, and girls look forward to it because it signals their acceptance into the adult world. In other instances, the practice is carried out by families living in cities on young women who desperately resist.

Fauziya Kassindja was the youngest of five daughters in a devoutly Muslim family. Her father, who owned a successful trucking business, was opposed to excision, and he was able to defy the tradition because of his wealth. His first four daughters were married without being mutilated. But when Fauziya was 16, he suddenly died. Fauziya then came under the authority of his father, who arranged a marriage for her and prepared to have her excised. Fauziya was terrified, and her mother and oldest sister helped her to escape. Her mother, left without resources, eventually had to formally apologize and submit to the authority of the patriarch she had offended.

Meanwhile, in America, Fauziya was imprisoned for two years while the authorities decided what to do with her. She was finally granted asylum, but not before she became the center of a controversy about how we should regard the cultural practices of other peoples. A series of articles in the New York Times encouraged the idea that excision is a barbaric practice that should be condemned. Other observers were reluctant to be so judgmental—live and let live, they said; after all, our culture probably seems just as strange to them.

Suppose we are inclined to say that excision is bad. Would we merely be imposing the standards of our own culture? If Cultural Relativism is correct, that is all we can do, for there is no culture-neutral moral standard to which we may appeal. But is that true?

Is There a Culture-Neutral Standard of Right and Wrong? There is, of course, a lot that can be said against excision. Excision is painful and it results in the permanent loss of sexual pleasure. Its short-term effects include hemorrhage, tetanus, and septicemia. Sometimes the woman dies. Long-term effects include chronic infection, scars that hinder walking, and continuing pain.

Why, then, has it become a widespread social practice? It is not easy to say. Excision has no apparent social benefits. Unlike Eskimo infanticide, it is not necessary for the group's survival. Nor is it a matter of religion. Excision is practiced by groups with various religions, including Islam and Christianity, neither of which commend it.

Nevertheless, a number of reasons are given in its defense. Women who are incapable of sexual pleasure are said to be less likely to be promiscuous; thus there will be fewer unwanted pregnancies in unmarried women. Moreover, wives for whom sex is only a duty are less likely to be unfaithful to their husbands; and because they will not be thinking about sex, they will be more attentive to the needs of their husbands and children. Husbands, for their part, are said to enjoy sex more with wives who have been excised. (The women's own lack of enjoyment is said to be unimportant.) Men will not want unexcised women, as they are unclean and immature. And above all, it has been done since antiquity, and we may not change the ancient ways.

It would be easy, and perhaps a bit arrogant, to ridicule these arguments. But we may notice an important feature of this whole line of reasoning: It attempts to justify excision by showing that excision is beneficial—men, women, and their families are said to be better off when women are excised. Thus we might approach this reasoning, and excision itself, by asking whether this is true: Is excision, on the whole, helpful or harmful?

In fact, this is a standard that might reasonably be used in thinking about any social practice whatever: We may ask whether the practice promotes or hinders the welfare of the people whose lives are affected by it. And, as a corollary, we may ask if there is an alternative set of social arrangements that would do a better job of promoting their welfare. If so, we may conclude that the existing practice is deficient.

But this looks like just the sort of independent moral standard that Cultural Relativism says cannot exist. It is a single standard that may be brought to bear in judging the practices of any culture, at any time, including our own. Of course, people will not usually see this principle as being "brought in from the outside" to judge them, because, like the rules against lying and homicide, the welfare of its members is a value internal to all viable cultures.

Why, Despite All This, Thoughtful People May Nevertheless Be Reluctant to Criticize Other Cultures. Although they are personally horrified by excision, many thoughtful people are reluctant to say it is wrong, for at least three reasons.

First, there is an understandable nervousness about "interfering in the social customs of other peoples." Europeans and their cultural descendents in America have a shabby history of destroying native cultures in the name of Christianity and Enlightenment. Recoiling from this record, some people refuse to make any negative judgments about other cultures, especially cultures that resemble those that have been wronged in the past. We should notice, however, that there is a difference between (a) judging a cultural practice to be deficient, and (b) thinking that we should a n n o u n c e the fact, conduct a campaign, apply diplomatic pressure, or send in the army. The first is just a matter of trying to see the world clearly, from a moral point of view. The second is another matter altogether. Sometimes it may be right to "do something about it," but often it will not be.

People also feel, rightly enough, that they should be tolerant of other cultures. Tolerance is, no doubt, a virtue — a tolerant person is willing to live in peaceful cooperation with those who see things differently. But there is nothing in the nature of tolerance that requires you to say that all beliefs, all religions, and all social practices are equally admirable. On the contrary, if you did not think that some were better than others, there would be nothing for you to tolerate.

Finally, people may be reluctant to j u d g e because they do not want to express contempt for the society being criticized. But again, this is misguided: To condemn a particular practice is not to say that the culture is on the whole contemptible or that it is generally inferior to any other culture, including one's own. It could have many admirable features. In fact, we should expect this to be true of most human societies — they are mixes of good and bad practices. Excision happens to be one of the bad ones.

2.8. What Can Be Learned from Cultural Relativism

At the outset, I said that we were going to identify both what is right and what is wrong in Cultural Relativism. But I have dwelled on its mistakes: I have said that it rests on an invalid argument, that it has consequences that make it implausible on its face, and that the extent of moral disagreement is far less than it implies. This all adds up to a pretty thorough repudiation of the theory. Nevertheless, it is still a very appealing idea, and the reader may have the feeling that all this is a little unfair. The theory must have something going for it, or else why has it been so influential? In fact, I think there is something right about Cultural Relativism, and now I want to say what that is. There are two lessons we should learn from the theory, even if we ultimately reject it.

First, Cultural Relativism warns us, quite rightly, about the danger of assuming that all our preferences are based on some absolute rational standard. They are not. Many (but not all) of our practices are merely peculiar to our society, and it is easy to lose sight of that fact. In reminding us of it, the theory does a service.

Funerary practices are one example. The Callatians, according to Herodotus, were "men who eat their fathers" — a shocking idea, to us at least. But eating the flesh of the dead could be understood as a sign of respect. It could be taken as a symbolic act that says: we wish this person's spirit to dwell within us. Perhaps this was the understanding of the Callatians. On such a way of thinking, burying the dead could be seen as an act of rejection, and burning the corpse as positively scornful. If this is hard to imagine, then we may need to have our imaginations stretched. Of course we may feel a visceral repugnance at the idea of eating human flesh in any circumstances. But what of it? This repugnance may be, as the relativists say, only a matter of what is customary in our particular society.

There are many other matters that we tend to think of in terms of objective right and wrong that are really nothing more than social conventions. We could make a long list. Should women cover their breasts? A publicly exposed breast is scandalous in our society, whereas in other cultures it is unremarkable. Objectively speaking, it is neither right nor wrong — there is no objective reason why either custom is better. Cultural Relativism begins with the valuable insight that many of our practices are like this; they are only cultural products. Then it goes wrong by inferring that, because some practices are like this, all must be.

The second lesson has to do with keeping an open mind. In the course of growing up, each of us has acquired some strong feelings: We have learned to think of some types of conduct as acceptable, and others we have learned to reject. Occasionally, we may find those feelings challenged. For example, we may have been taught that homosexuality is immoral, and we may feel quite uncomfortable around gay people and see them as alien and "different." Now someone suggests that this may be a mere prejudice; that there is nothing evil about homosexuality; that gay people are just people, like anyone else, who happen, through no choice of their own, to be attracted to other of the same sex. But because we feel so strongly about the matter, we may find it hard to take this seriously. Even after we listen to the arguments, we may still have the unshakable feeling that homosexuals must, somehow, be an unsavory lot.

Cultural Relativism, by stressing that our moral views can reflect the prejudices of our society, provides an antidote for this kind of dogmatism. When he tells the story of the Greeks and Callatians, Herodotus adds:

> For if anyone, no matter who, were given the opportunity of choosing from amongst all the nations of the world the set of beliefs which he thought best, he would inevitably, after careful consideration of their relative merits, choose that of his own country. Everyone without exception believes his own native customs, and the religion he was brought up in, to be the best.

Realizing this can result in our having more open minds. We can come to understand that our feelings are not necessarily perceptions of the truth—they may be nothing more than the result of cultural conditioning. Thus when we hear it suggested that some element of our social code is not really the best, and we find ourselves instinctively resisting the suggestion, we might stop and remember this. Then we may be more open to discovering the truth, whatever that might be.

We can understand the appeal of Cultural Relativism, then, even though the theory has serious shortcomings. It is an attractive theory because it is based on a genuine insight, that many of the practices and attitudes we think so natural are really only cultural products. Moreover, keeping this thought firmly in view is important if we want to avoid arrogance and have open minds. These are important points, not to be taken lightly. But we can accept these points without going on to accept the whole theory.

Further Responses to Relativism

Pope Benedict XVI on the 'Dictatorship of Relativism'

Benedict XVI just before his election as Pope (April 2005), spoke of the "dictatorship of relativism".

How many winds of doctrine we have known in recent decades, how many ideological currents, how many ways of thinking. The small boat of thought of many Christians has often been tossed about by these waves - thrown from one extreme to the other: from Marxism to liberalism, even to libertinism; from collectivism to radical individualism; from atheism to a vague religious mysticism; from agnosticism to syncretism, and so forth. Every day new sects are created and what Saint Paul says about human trickery comes true, with cunning which tries to draw those into error (cf Ephesians 4, 14). Having a clear faith, based on the Creed of the Church, is often labeled today as a fundamentalism. Whereas, relativism, which is letting oneself be tossed and "swept along by every wind of teaching", looks like the only attitude acceptable to today's standards. We are moving towards a dictatorship of relativism which does not recognize anything as certain and which has as its highest goal one's own ego and one's own desires. However, we have a different goal: the Son of God, true man. He is the measure of true humanism. Being an "Adult" means having a faith which does not follow the waves of today's fashions or the latest novelties. A faith which is deeply rooted in friendship with Christ is adult and mature. It is this friendship which opens us up to all that is good and gives us the knowledge to judge true from false, and deceit from truth.

Sam Harris, The End of Faith (Page 179, The Demon of Relativism)

"The general retort to relativism is simple, because most relativists contradict their thesis in the very act of stating it. Take the case of relativism with respect to morality: moral relativists generally believe that all cultural practices should be respected on their own terms, that the practitioners of the various barbarisms that persist around the globe cannot be judged by the standards of the West, nor can the people of the past be judged by the standards of the present. And yet, implicit in this approach to morality lurks a claim that is not relative but absolute. Most moral relativists believe that tolerance of cultural diversity is better, in some important sense, than outright bigotry. This may be perfectly reasonable, of course, but it amounts to an overarching claim about how all human beings should live. Moral relativism, when used as a rationale for tolerance of diversity, is self-contradictory."

Richard Dawkins, The God Delusion (Pages 328-9, Childhood Abuse and Religion)

"It is the source of squirming internal conflict in the minds of nice liberal people who, on the one hand, cannot bear suffering and cruelty, but on the other hand have been trained by postmodernists and relativists to respect other cultures no less than their own. Female circumcision is undoubtedly hideously painful, it sabotages sexual pleasure in women (indeed, this is probably its underlying purpose), and one half of the decent liberal mind wants to abolish the practice. The other half, however, 'respects' ethnic cultures and feels that we should not interfere if 'they' want to mutilate 'their' girls."

Daniel C. Dennett, Breaking The Spell (Pages 375-6, Some More Questions About Science)

"The more one learns of the different passionately held convictions of peoples around the world, the more tempting it becomes to decide that there really couldn't be a standpoint from which truly universal moral judgments could be constructed and defended. So it is not surprising that cultural anthropologists tend to take one variety of moral relativism or another as one of their enabling assumptions. Moral relativism is also rampant in other groves of academia, but not all. It is decidedly a minority position among ethicists and other philosophers, for example, and it is by no means a necessary presupposition of scientific open-mindedness. We don't have to assume that there are no moral truths in order to study other cultures fairly and objectively; we just have to set aside, for the time being, the assumption that we already know what they are."

The Euthyphro Dilemma

The Euthyphro dilemma is a conundrum raised by the connection routinely made in Theology between God and the moral lives and standards of human beings. The name is taken from the Platonic dialogue in which it was raised in 380 BCE, and which is a fitting starting point for the study of the problem.

Plato's Euthyphro, translated by Benjamin Jowett

Euthyphro and Socrates are outside the court of King Archon. Socrates is being prosecuted by a young man named Meletus, who is accusing him of corrupting the youth of Athens. Euthyphro is prosecuting his father for the murder of a servant who had himself murdered another servant. Euthyphro seems confident in his controversial decision to pursue his own father and claims an intimate knowledge of matters of religion and piety. Socrates exclaims that he can do no better than to become Euthyphro's disciple and urges him to teach him about the questions in which he has such expertise. The passage below is a short extract from the ensuing discussion, highlighting the question which is our own concern in this section of the anthology. Unfortunately Euthyphro never manages to give Socrates a clear answer before muttering 'I am in a hurry, and must go now' and clearing off.

At the point where we join them they have already settled on a provisional definition of piety as follows: 'what all the gods love is pious and holy, and the opposite which they all hate, impious'

Socrates The point which I should first wish to understand is **whether the pious or holy is beloved by the gods because it is holy, or holy because it is beloved of the gods**.

Euthyphro I do not understand your meaning, Socrates.

Soc. I will endeavour to explain: we, speak of carrying and we speak of being carried, of leading and being led, seeing and being seen. You know that in all such cases there is a difference, and you know also in what the difference lies?

Euth. I think that I understand.

Soc. And is not that which is beloved distinct from that which loves?

Euth. Certainly.

Soc. Well; and now tell me, is that which is carried in this state of carrying because it is carried, or for some other reason?

Euth. No; that is the reason.

Soc. And the same is true of what is led and of what is seen?

Euth. True.

Soc. And a thing is not seen because it is visible, but conversely, visible because it is seen; nor is a thing led because it is in the state of being led, or carried because it is in the state of being carried, but the converse of this. And now I think, Euthyphro, that my meaning will be intelligible; and my meaning is, that any state of action or passion implies previous action or passion. It does not become because it is becoming, but it is in a state of becoming because it becomes; neither does it suffer because it is in a state of suffering, but it is in a state of suffering because it suffers. Do you not agree?

Euth. Yes.

Soc. Is not that which is loved in some state either of becoming or suffering?

Euth. Yes.

Soc. And the same holds as in the previous instances; the state of being loved follows the act of being loved, and not the act the state.

Euth. Certainly.

Soc. And what do you say of piety, Euthyphro: is not piety, according to your definition, loved by all the gods?

Euth. Yes.

Soc. Because it is pious or holy, or for some other reason?

Euth. No, that is the reason.

Soc. It is loved because it is holy, not holy because it is loved?

Euth. Yes.

Soc. And that which is dear to the gods is loved by them, and is in a state to be loved of them because it is loved of them?

Euth. Certainly.

Soc. Then that which is dear to the gods, Euthyphro, is not holy, nor is that which is holy loved of God, as you affirm; but they are two different things.

Euth. How do you mean, Socrates?

Soc. I mean to say that the holy has been acknowledge by us to be loved of God because it is holy, not to be holy because it is loved.

Euth. Yes.

Soc. But that which is dear to the gods is dear to them because it is loved by them, not loved by them because it is dear to them.

Euth. True.

Soc. But, friend Euthyphro, if that which is holy is the same with that which is dear to God, and is loved because it is holy, then that which is dear to God would have been loved as being dear to God; but if that which dear to God is dear to him because loved by him, then that which is holy would have been holy because loved by him. But now you see that the reverse is the case, and that they are quite different from one another. For one (theophiles) is of a kind to be loved cause it is loved, and the other (osion) is loved because it is of a kind to be loved. Thus you appear to me, Euthyphro, when I ask you what is the essence of holiness, to offer an attribute only, and not the essence-the attribute of being loved by all the gods. But you still refuse to explain to me the nature of holiness. And therefore, if you please, I will ask you not to hide your treasure, but to tell me once more what holiness or piety really is, whether dear to the gods or not (for that is a matter about which we will not quarrel) and what is impiety?

Euth. I really do not know, Socrates, how to express what I mean. For somehow or other our arguments, on whatever ground we rest them, seem to turn round and walk away from us

---

A contemporary version of the Euthyphro dilemma is this:

Is an action good because God commands it? Or does God command it because it is good?

Divine Command Theory states that the former is true. God's will defines moral goodness and rightness.

Both sides of the dilemma face serious challenges. The leading British philosopher Bertrand Russell (1872 - 02 Feb 1970) summarized the major difficulties as follows in his book *Why I Am Not a Christian*:

> If you are quite sure there is a difference between right and wrong, you are then in this situation: Is that difference due to God's fiat or is it not? If it is due to God's fiat, then for God Himself there is no difference between right and wrong, and it is no longer a significant statement to say that God is good. If you are going to say, as theologians do, that God is good, you must then say that right and wrong have some meaning which is independent of God's fiat, because God's fiats are good and not good independently of the mere fact that he made them. If you are going to say that, you will then have to say that it is not only through God that right and wrong came into being, but that they are in their essence logically anterior to God.

Russell's position is that the believer falls into incoherence or inconsistency whichever option she adopts. She would do better to leave God out of the discussion altogether. As you consider the different perspectives included here, you will be able to decide for yourself whether Russell is correct.

.

René Descartes (1596 – 1650)

Objections to the Meditations and Descartes's Replies

René Descartes Copyright ©2010–2015 All rights reserved. Jonathan Bennett

Sixth Objections; 8

OBJECTION: How can the truths of geometry or metaphysics, such as the ones you mention, be unchangeable and eternal and yet *not* be independent of God? What sort of causal dependence on God do they have? Could he have brought it about that there was never any such thing as *the nature of a triangle*? And how could he have made it untrue from eternity that twice four makes eight, or that a triangle has three angles?...

REPLY: Anyone who attends to the immeasurable greatness of God will find it utterly clear that there can't be *anything at all* that doesn't depend on him. This applies not just to all existing things, but also to all order, every law, and every reason for anything's being true or good. If this were not so, then, as I pointed out a little earlier, God would not have been completely indifferent with respect to the creation of what he did in fact create. If in advance of all God's decrees there had been a reason for something's being good, this would have determined God to choose the things that it was best to do; ·and this can't be right, because it is grossly impious to suggest that anything could determine God, i.e. act on him or sway him or incline him or anything like that·. The real story runs in the other direction: precisely *because* God resolved to prefer certain things, those things are, as Genesis says, 'very good'; they are good *because* God exercised his will to create them [the Latin could mean: '. . . exercised his will to make them good']. What kind of causality (you ask) is involved in the dependence of this goodness on God, or in the dependence on him of other truths, both mathematical and metaphysical? There doesn't have to be an answer to this; it wouldn't be surprising if we didn't have a label for this kind of causality; the various kinds of cause were listed ·and named· by thinkers who may not have attended to this type of causality. But in fact we *do* have a name for it—namely 'efficient causality', in the way in which a king may be called the efficient cause of a law, although the law is merely what they call a 'moral entity', not a thing that exists out there in the world. *How* could God could have brought it about from eternity that it was not true that twice four make eight? I admit that we have no understanding of how he could have done that. But there are two things that I *do* understand:

- There can't be any kind of entity that doesn't depend on God.
- Even with matters where we can't grasp the possibility of things' being other than the way they are, God could easily have brought it about that they were other than the way they are.

So it would be irrational for us to doubt things that we do understand correctly just because there is something that we don't understand and that there is no visible reason why we *should* understand. So let us not suppose that eternal truths depend on the human intellect, or on other existing things; they depend on God alone, who, as the supreme legislator, has ordained them from eternity.

G.W. Leibniz (1646 – 1716)

Discourse on Metaphysics

[Brackets] enclose editorial explanations. Small ·dots· enclose material that has been added, indenting of passages that are not quotations, are meant as aids to grasping the structure of a sentence or a thought. —-The division into sections is Leibniz's; the division of some sections into paragraphs is not. Leibniz wrote brief summaries of the 37 sections of this work, but did not include them in the work itself. Some editors preface each section with its summary, but that interrupts the flow. **1.** The most widely accepted and sharpest notion of God that we have can be expressed like this:

1. God is an absolutely perfect being;

but though this is widely accepted, its consequences haven't been well enough thought out. As a start on exploring them, let us note that there are various completely different ways of being perfect, and that God has them all, each in the highest degree. We also need to understand what a per- fection is. Here is one pretty good indicator: a property is not a perfection unless there is a highest degree of it; so number and shape are not perfections, because there cannot possibly be a largest number or a largest thing of a given shape— ·that is, a largest triangle, or square, or the like·. But there is nothing impossible about the greatest knowledge or about omnipotence [here = 'greatest possible power']. So power and knowledge are perfections, and God has them in unlimited form. It follows that the actions of God, who is supremely—indeed infinitely—wise, are completely perfect. This is not just metaphysical perfection, but also the moral kind. His moral perfection, so far as it concerns us, amounts to this: the more we come to know and understand God's works, the more inclined we shall be to find them excellent, and to give us everything we could have wished.

2. Some people— ·including Descartes·—hold that there are no rules of goodness and perfection in the nature of things, or in God's ideas of them, and that in calling the things God made 'good' all we mean is that God made them. I am far from agreeing with this. If it were right, then God would not have needed after the creation to 'see that they were good', as Holy Scripture says he did, because he already knew that the things in question were his work. In saying this— 'And God saw everything that he had made·, and, be- hold, it was very good' (*Genesis* 1:31)—Scripture treats God as like a man; but its purpose in doing this appears to be to get across the point that a thing's excellence can be seen by looking just at the thing itself, without reference to the entirely external fact about what caused it. Reinforcing that point is this one: the works must bear the imprint of the workman, because we can learn who he was just by inspecting them. I have to say that the contrary opinion strikes me as very dangerous, and as coming close to the view of the Spinozists that the beauty of the universe, and the goodness we attribute to God's works, are merely the illusions of people who conceive God as being like themselves. Furthermore, if you say ·as Descartes did · that things are good not because *they match up to objective standards of goodness, but only because *God chose them, you will unthinkingly destroy all God's love and all his glory. For why praise him for what he has done, if he would be equally praiseworthy for doing just the opposite? Where will his justice and wisdom be,

> if there is only a kind of despotic power, if *reason*'s
>
> place is taken by *will*, and if justice is tyrannically
>
> defined as what best pleases the most powerful?

[Leibniz here relies on his view that it is through reason that we learn what things are good.] And another point: it seems that any act of the will presupposes some reason for it—a reason that naturally precedes the act— ·so that God's choices must come from his reasons for them, which involve his knowledge of what would · be good; so they can't be the *sources* of the goodness of things. That is why I find it weird when Descartes says that the eternal truths of metaphysics and geometry, and therefore also the rules of goodness, justice, and perfection, are brought about by God's will. Against this, they seem to me to be results of his *understanding, and no more to depend on his *will than his intrinsic nature does.

3. Nor could I ever accept the view of some recent philosophers who have the nerve to maintain that God's creation is not utterly perfect, and that he could have acted much better. This opinion, it seems to me, has consequences that are completely contrary to the glory of God. Just as a lesser evil contains an element of good, so a lesser good contains an element of evil. To act with fewer perfections than one could have done is to act imperfectly; showing an architect that he could have done his work better is finding fault with it. Furthermore, this opinion goes against holy scripture's assurance of the goodness of God's works. ·That goodness can't consist simply in the fact that the works could have been worse; and here is why ·. Whatever God's work was like, it would always have been good in comparison with *some* possibilities, because there is no limit to how bad things could be. But being praiseworthy in *this* way is hardly being praiseworthy at all! I believe one could find countless passages in the holy scriptures and the writings of the holy fathers that support my opinion, and hardly any to support the modern view to which I have referred—a view that I think was never heard of in ancient times. It has arisen merely because we are not well enough acquainted with the general harmony of the universe and of the hidden reasons for God's conduct; and that makes us recklessly judge that many things could have been improved. Furthermore, these moderns argue—subtly but not soundly—from the false premise that however perfect a thing is, there is always something still more perfect. They also think that their view provides for God's freedom, ·through the idea that if God is free, it must be up to him whether he acts perfectly or not ·; but really it is the highest freedom to act perfectly, in accordance with sovereign reason. For the view that God sometimes does something without having any reason for his choice, besides seeming to be impossible, is hardly compatible with his glory.

Suppose that God, facing a choice between A and B, opts for A without having any reason for preferring it to B. I see nothing to praise in that, because all praise should be grounded in some reason, and in this case we have stipulated that there is none. By contrast, I hold that God does nothing for which he does not deserve to be glorified.

Thomas Aquinas

FIRST PART (FP)

The Goodness of God (Q6)

Article 1. Whether God is good?

Objection 1. It seems that to be good does not belong to God. For goodness consists in mode, species and order. But these do not seem to belong to God; since God is immense and is not ordered to anything else. Therefore to be good does not belong to God.

Objection 2. Further, the good is what all things desire. But all things do not desire God, because all things do not know Him; and nothing is desired unless it is known. Therefore to be good does not belong to God.

On the contrary, It is written (Lamentations 3:25): "The Lord is good to them that hope in Him, to the soul that seeketh Him."

I answer that, To be good belongs pre-eminently to God. For a thing is good according to its desirableness. Now everything seeks after its own perfection; and the perfection and form of an effect consist in a certain likeness to the agent, since every agent makes its like; and hence the agent itself is desirable and has the nature of good. For the very thing which is desirable in it is the participation of its likeness. Therefore, since God is the first effective cause of all things, it is manifest that the aspect of good and of desirableness belong to Him; and hence Dionysius (Div. Nom. iv) attributes good to God as to the first efficient cause, saying that, God is called good "as by Whom all things subsist."

Reply to Objection 1. To have mode, species and order belongs to the essence of caused good; but good is in God as in its cause, and hence it belongs to Him to impose mode, species and order on others; wherefore these three things are in God as in their cause.

Reply to Objection 2. All things, by desiring their own perfection, desire God Himself, inasmuch as the perfections of all things are so many similitudes of the divine being; as appears from what is said above (Question 4, Article 3). And so of those things which desire God, some know Him as He is Himself, and this is proper to the rational creature; others know some participation of His goodness, and this belongs also to sensible knowledge; others have a natural desire without knowledge, as being directed to their ends by a higher intelligence.

Article 4. Whether all things are good by the divine goodness?

Objection 1. It seems that all things are good by the divine goodness. For Augustine says (De Trin.

viii), "This and that are good; take away this and that, and see good itself if thou canst; and so thou shalt see God, good not by any other good, but the good of every good." But everything is good by its own good; therefore everything is good by that very good which is God.

Objection 2. Further, as Boethius says (De Hebdom.), all things are called good, accordingly as they are directed to God, and this is by reason of the divine goodness; therefore all things are good by the divine goodness.

On the contrary, All things are good, inasmuch as they have being. But they are not called beings through the divine being, but through their own being; therefore all things are not good by the divine goodness, but by their own goodness.

I answer that, As regards relative things, we must admit extrinsic denomination; as, a thing is denominated "placed" from "place," and "measured" from "measure." But as regards absolute things opinions differ. Plato held the existence of separate ideas (84, 4) of all things, and that individuals were denominated by them as participating in the separate ideas; for instance, that Socrates is called man according to the separate idea of man. Now just as he laid down separate ideas of man and horse which he called absolute man and absolute horse, so likewise he laid down separate ideas of "being" and of "one," and these he called absolute being and absolute oneness; and by participation of these, everything was called "being" or "one"; and what was thus absolute being and absolute one, he said was the supreme good. And because good is convertible with being, as one is also; he called God the absolute good, from whom all things are called good by way of participation.

Although this opinion appears to be unreasonable in affirming separate ideas of natural things as subsisting of themselves--as Aristotle argues in many ways--still, it is absolutely true that there is first something which is essentially being and essentially good, which we call God, as appears from what is shown above (Question 2, Article 3), and Aristotle agrees with this. Hence from the first being, essentially such, and good, everything can be called good and a being, inasmuch as it participates in it by way of a certain assimilation which is far removed and defective; as appears from the above (Question 4, Article 3).

Everything is therefore called good from the divine goodness, as from the first exemplary effective and final principle of all goodness. Nevertheless, everything is called good by reason of the similitude of the divine goodness belonging to it, which is formally its own goodness, whereby it is denominated good. And so of all things there is one goodness, and yet many goodnesses.

Brian Davies (b. 1951)

An Introduction to the Philosophy of Religion, Third Edition, 2003, OUP

Ch 12 Morality and Religion (extract)

What Is the Relation Between God and Moral Goodness?

But suppose that we do believe in God. And suppose that we also believe that there are moral truths which everyone should acknowledge. How should we connect the one belief to the other? Should we perhaps think of moral truths as deriving exclusively from God? Should we take them to be independent of God? Or should we adopt an altogether different viewpoint? These questions bring us to what is sometimes referred to as 'the Euthyphro dilemma'. In Plato's Euthyphro, Socrates asks: 'Is what is holy holy because the gods approve it, or do they approve it because it is holy?' Since Plato's time, philosophers have modified this question so as to ask: 'Is X morally good because God wills it, or does God will X because it is morally good?' And they have replied in different ways. Some have said that moral truths are nothing but expressions of God's will. According to this view, an action (or a refraining from action) is morally good (or is obligatory) simply because it is willed (or commanded) by God. On this account, whatever God wills us to do is the morally right thing to do just because God wills it. On this account, there is no moral standard apart from God's will. On this account, God's will establishes moral standards.

Other philosophers, however, have adopted exactly the opposite position. In their opinion, moral truth in no way derives from God's will. For them, it is independent of God, something to which even he must conform. For them, our knowing that God wills us to do X might constitute a reason for us to choose X. But only on the supposition that God has perfect knowledge of what is morally right and wrong independently of him.

How should we react to these two ways of thinking? Perhaps we can start by noting that there are questions which can be pressed against both of them. Take, to begin with, the notion that moral goodness and badness is constituted only by what God does or does not will. If that is so, then does it not follow that morality, at bottom, is arbitrary or even whimsical? Does it not also follow that morally wicked actions would be morally right if God so decreed? Yet, how can morality be grounded in nothing but a decision—even a divine decision? And how can even a divine decision make it to be true that, for example, genocide is morally good and feeding the starving is morally wrong?

On the other hand, however, can we seriously think of there being moral truths which are independent of God? If there are such truths, then, presumably, they are objects of God's knowledge distinct from God himself and in no way dependent on him. But can there be anything which does not owe its existence to God? And can we think of God as confronted by a series of commands and prohibitions which stand before him as things to which he morally ought to conform? We might think of God in this way. But, as I noted in Chapter 10, such a view does not square with how God is presented in the Bible. It is also at odds with ways in which some notable non-biblical writers have approached the topic of God and morality. Consider, for example, Soren Kierkegaard (1813 – 55).[1] In *Fear and Trembling* he considers the Old Testament story of of Abraham being told by God to sacrifice his son Isaac.[2] He says that Abraham was bound to do what God commanded, adding that

> here there can be no question of ethics in the sense of morality . . . Ordinarily speaking, a temptation is something which tries to stop a man from doing his duty, but in this case it is ethics itself which tries to prevent him from doing God's will. But what then is duty? Duty is quite simply the expression of the will of God.[3]

In this connection, Kierkegaard talks about 'a teleological suspension of the ethical', an idea which can also be found in the work of D. Z. Phillips, who writes:

> The religious concept of duty cannot be understood if it is treated as a moral concept. When the believer talks of doing his duty, what he refers to is doing the will of God. In making a derision, what is important for the believer is that it should be in accordance with the will of God. To a Christian, to do one's duty *is* to do the will of God. There is indeed no difficulty in envisaging the 'ethical' as the obstacle to 'duty' in this context.[4]

Yet, must we suppose *either* that X is morally good just because God wills it *or* that God wills X because it is morally good independently of him? Might we not rather seek to combine these views? Might we not suggest *both* that moral goodness is somehow constituted by God's will *and* that God wills moral goodness because of its very goodness? You may think that the answer to these questions has to be 'No'. But is that really true? At least one theistic philosopher thought that it is not. Here, once again, I refer to Aquinas, whose views on goodness and God are worth noting at this point.

Aquinas insists that God is certainly good. In fact, he says, God is supremely good' or 'the absolutely supreme good'[5]. But why does Aquinas think that this is so? You might instinctively suppose him to believe that God is good because God always conforms to sound moral standards. But that is not Aquinas's position. For one thing, he thinks (as most people do) that not all goodness is moral goodness. More importantly, however, his view is that the primary reason for calling God good lies in the fact that God is *desirable*. In approaching the topic of goodness and God, Aquinas takes his cue from Aristotle, according to whom the good is 'that at which everything aims'. [6]

For both Aquinas and Aristotle, goodness is not a distinct, empirical property possessed by all good things, as, for example, redness is a distinct, empirical property shared by all red things.[7] But they still think that we are saying something particular when calling things good. For them, goodness is always what is somehow wanted. And, says Aquinas, this is as true when it comes to God's goodness as it is when it comes to the goodness of anything else. For him, therefore, God is good because he is *attractive.*

But why does Aquinas take God to be attractive? Because he thinks of God as the unlimited source of the existence of everything other than himself. Considered as such, says Aquinas, God is (a) the transcendent cause of all that we can recognize as creaturely good, and (b) desirable (and good) on that count alone. Why? Because, as we saw in Chapter 7, Aquinas holds that what God produces must reflect what God is by nature. So he thinks of the goodness of creatures as somehow pre- existing in God before it exists in them. In Aquinas's way of thinking, the divine mind (not to be distinguished from God himself) is a kind of blueprint reflected by all creaturely goodness. For Aquinas, aiming at creaturely goodness consists (whether we realize it or not) in desiring what is *first* in God and *only secondarily* in creatures.

Aquinas, of course, does not mean that, for example, a good surgeon or a good bicycle *looks* like God. He does not think that anything looks like God. He does believe, however, that productive causes (which he calls 'efficient causes') express (show forth) their nature in their effects even if these belong to kinds which are different from those to which   their productive causes belong.[8] And for this reason Aquinas concludes that God is good. 'The perfection and form of an effect', he argues, 'is a certain likeness of the efficient cause, since every efficient cause produces an effect like itself ... [and]... since God is the first efficient cause of everything ... the aspect of good and desirable manifestly belong to him.' [9] According to this account, then, goodness in its many created forms is a kind of image of what God, in his own way, is in himself.

And, with this thought in mind, Aquinas has an answer to the Euthyphro dilemma, one that seeks to accommodate both of its alternatives.

Is X morally good because God wills it? Aquinas thinks it is since he takes people's moral goodness to depend on their nature as moral agents created by (and therefore willed by) God.

Does God will X because it is morally good? Aquinas responds that God, as good, always wills the good. But, he thinks, in willing us to be morally good, God is not respecting a standard distinct from himself. According to Aquinas, God creates a world in which we can make true moral judgements concerning our conduct. Yet Aquinas also holds that, in creating our world, and in willing us to do what is morally good, God is willing that we act in accordance with standards he himself has established by creating standards which reflect what he essentially is.

In his approach to morality, Aquinas is basically an Aristotelian. He thinks that people need virtues such as justice, prudence, temperate- ness, and courage. He also believes that we can come to see that this is so even without reference to belief in God. Aquinas's overall approach to morality is essentially a religious one. But he does not claim that we have to assume theological premises in order to argue cogently that certain ways of acting are morally bad and that others are morally good. What we need to do, he believes, is to look at the way the world works, to study human nature, and to draw reasonable conclusions when it comes to how people ought to behave given that they want to flourish as people.

But where does the world come from? And what is the source of people and their nature? For Aquinas, the answer to these questions is 'God'. So he takes our moral judgements to be ultimately grounded in what God is and in what he has willed to be. In this sense, he embraces the conclusion that X is morally good because God wills it. But he is not suggesting that what God wills is arbitrary or a matter of whim. He is not asserting that God could decide tomorrow that genocide is morally good or feeding the starving morally bad and that this is how things would be.[10].He is saying that reasons we can give for   arriving at true moral judgements concerning people depend on what God has created, though not with reference to standards binding on him. In this sense, Aquinas also accepts that God wills X because it is morally good.

But is Aquinas right in thinking as he does here? Not if God is a person who ought to art according to his moral duties and obligations. Aquinas can clearly make no sense of there being standards of goodness to which God must conform. For him, God is 'Goodness Itself. And his approach to the topic of God and morality is clearly flawed if he is wrong in thinking along these lines, as many philosophers take him to be. Then again, Aquinas's view on morality and God is wrong if moral standards for evaluating people cannot be derived from a knowledge of what people are by nature. As I have said, Aquinas commends Aristotelian ways of evaluating people. And the less sympathetic we are with those, the less we will sympathize with Aquinas. We will also find fault with Aquinas on God and morality if we reject his claim that created good- ness is a reflection of what God is by nature. But Aquinas's way of relating God and moral goodness is, at the least, something worth ser- iously considering. If nothing else, it offers an interesting approach to God and morality which, if correct, does not leave theists impaled on the horns of the Euthyphro dilemma.[11]

Are Religion and Morality at Odds with Each Other?

Many parents like their children to receive religious education in school since they think of this as likely to give them a basic grounding in ethics. But is not religion inimical to morality? Or, as I framed the question at the start of this chapter, are religion and morality at odds with each other?

(a) Some 'anti-religious' answers

Why should we suppose that they are? A popular answer holds **that** belief in God requires an attitude inappropriate to a truly moral person. Consider, for instance, the position of James Rachels. According to Rachels: (i) belief in God involves a total and unqualified commitment to obey God's commands, and (ii) such a commitment is not appropriate for a moral agent since 'to be a moral agent is to be an autonomous or self-directed agent... The virtuous man is therefore identified with the man of integrity, i.e. the man who acts according to precepts which he can, on reflection, conscientiously approve in his own heart'.[12] With this idea in mind, Rachels argues that it is even possible to disprove God's existence. He argues:

a If any being is God, he must be a fitting object of worship.

b No being could possibly be a fitting object of worship since worship requires the abandonment of one's role as an autonomous moral agent.

c Therefore, there cannot be any being who is God.

Rachels thinks that God's commands cannot constitute a reason for acting in any given way. For him, such a reason must be morally compel- ling in its own right. And this is also the position of Kant. As we have seen, he believes that there is an argument from morality to belief in God. But he also asserts that to say that we ought to do whatever God directs 'would form the basis for a moral system which would be in direct opposition to morality'. [13] Another line of thinking that has been defended by those who see religion and morality as being at odds notes that religious beliefs have led people to morally unacceptable ways of behaving or to morally suspect beliefs and policies. Hence, for example (and evidently on what he takes to be moral grounds), Bertrand Russell observes:

> Religion prevents our children from having a rational education; religion prevents us from removing the fundamental causes of war; religion prevents us from teaching the ethic of scientific co-operation in place of the old fierce doctrines of sin and punishment. It is possible that mankind is on the threshold of a golden age; but if so, it will be necessary first to slay the dragon that guards the door, and this dragon is religion.[14]

Russell has recently been echoed by Simon Blackburn. To begin with, Blackburn suggests that there are objections to be raised about ways in which God is depicted in texts like the Bible:

> Anyone reading the Bible might be troubled by some of its precepts. The Old Testament God is partial to some people above others, and above all jealous of his own pre-eminence, a strange moral obsession. He seems to have no problem with a slave-owning society, believes that birth control is a capital crime (Genesis 38: 9-10), is keen on child abuse (Proverbs 22:15, 23:13-14, 29: 15), and, for good measure, approves of fool abuse (Proverbs 26:3) . . . Things are usually supposed to get better in the New Testament... Yet the overall story of 'atonement' and 'redemption' is morally dubious, suggesting as it does that justice can be satisfied by the sacrifice of an innocent for the sins of the guilty.[15]

The New Testament portrait of Jesus of Nazareth has often been admired by moralists. But Blackburn's reaction to it is ethically hostile. The persona of Jesus in the Gospels, he says,

has his fair share of moral quirks. He can be sectarian: 'Go not into the way of the Gentiles, and into any city of the Samaritans enter ye not. But go rather to the lost sheep of the house of Israel' (Matt. 10: 5-6). In a similar vein, he refuses help to the non-Jewish woman from Canaan with the chilling racist remark, 'It is not meet to take the children's bread, and cast it to dogs' (Matt. 15: 26; Mark 7: 27). He wants us to be gentle, meek, and mild, but he himself is far from it. 'Ye serpents, ye generation of vipers, how can ye escape the damnation of hell?' (Matt. 23: 33). The episode of the Gadarene swine shows him to share the then-popular belief that mental illness is caused by possession by devils. It also shows that animal lives — also anybody else's property rights in pigs — have no value (Luke 8: 27-33). The events of the fig tree in Bethany (Mark 11:12-21) would make any environmentalist's hair stand on end.[16]

The demise of belief in God, Blackburn ends by suggesting, is 'far from being a threat to ethics'. It is 'a necessary clearing of the ground, on the way to revealing ethics for what it really is'.[17]

(b) Comments on these answers

Is Rachels right to suggest that morality provides us with a proof of God's non-existence? We might well conclude that he is were we to be power- fully struck by the conviction that we could never be morally justified in giving unqualified allegiance to anything but the truths of morality. But need even such a conviction lead to the conclusion proposed by Rachels?

Rachels supposes that, if there is a being worthy of worship, then there could not be autonomous moral agents. But there is an obvious reply to this supposition. For it is surely possible that there be a being worthy of worship who does nothing to interfere with people wishing to remain autonomous moral agents. And it is also possible that a being worthy of worship could positively require that people act as autonomous moral agents. This point is well brought out in a case against Rachels offered by Philip L. Quinn in his book *Divine Commands and Moral Requirements.* There he observes:

> An autonomous moral agent can admit the existence of God if he is prepared to deny that any putative divine command which is inconsistent with his hard-core reflective moral judgements really is a divine command. He can resolve the supposed role-conflict by allowing that genuine divine com- mands ought to be obeyed unconditionally but also maintaining that no directive which he does not accept on moral grounds is a genuine divine command. For the following propositions are logically compatible:

> God exists.   God sometimes commands agents to do certain things.   God never commands anything an autonomous and well-informed human moral agent would, on reflection, disapprove.[18]

Yet, might it not be argued that, if X is worthy of worship, then wor- shippers are bound to do whatever X wills? And does this not mean that worshippers cannot be autonomous moral agents? Rachels evidently supposes that the answer to these questions is 'Yes'. But is it? Cannot worshippers consistently say that they worship a being who always wills them to behave as autonomous moral agents? If a worshipper were to say this, then Rachels's case would clearly collapse. It would also col- lapse if someone who believes in and worships God were to say that God knows all moral truths and always directs people in accordance with them. Such a believer would be giving unqualified allegiance to God's commands. But it does not follow that the believer in question would thereby be abandoning autonomy as a moral agent.

Yet, what of the thesis that morality and religion should always be thought of as opposed to each other? If we think of certain religious beliefs, and if we think of certain moral ones, we might develop a case for their being at odds with each other (as Blackburn does). But can we defend the sweeping conclusion that morality (as such) is incompatible with religion (as such)?

One reason for saying that we cannot lies in the fact that the word 'morality' clearly has different associations for different people. What one person regards as morality another may dismiss as immorality, or as plain triviality. And it is often impossible to conclude that either party in such disputes is in some objective sense right. General statements about what morality is should be regarded with suspicion, for the boundaries dividing the moral and the non-moral are often very fuzzy.

A related reason for the same conclusion lies in the vagueness of the word 'religion'. If we insist that religion and morality are opposed to each other, we must surely be supposing that there is a fairly easily identifiable thing rightly referred to as 'religion'. But is there? Maybe not, as I indicated in Chapter 2. Many writers, in fact, would go so far as to say that 'religion' just cannot be defined. 'It is', says Ninian Smart, 'partly a matter of convention as to what is counted under the head of religion and what is not.' [19] Here Smart agrees with what William Alston writes on 'Religion' in *The Encyclopedia ofPhilosophy*. Alston notes vari- ous attempts to define 'religion' and suggests that none of them states necessary and sufficient conditions for something to be a religion. He concludes that the most that can be done is to note various characteristics of religion:

When enough of these characteristics are present to a sufficient degree, we have a religion. It seems that, given the actual use of the term 'religion', this is as precise as we can be. If we tried to say something like 'for a religion to exist, there must be the first two plus any three others', or 'for a religion to exist, any four of these characteristics must be present', we would be introducing a degree of precision not to be found in the concept of religion actually in use . . . The best way to explain the concept of religion is to elaborate in detail the relevant features of an ideally clear case of religion and then indicate the respects in which less clear cases can differ from this, without hoping to find any sharp line dividing religion from non-religion.[20]

The implication of such reflections, which seem reasonable ones, is that it is misleading to say that religion and morality are necessarily opposed to each other. And this means that we may challenge comments like those of Russell and Blackburn. A great deal that they con- sider bad may well have been perpetrated or encouraged by people in the name of religion. But many religious people would accept this conclusion while also objecting to the very things to which Russell and Blackburn object. They would, in fact, argue that many of the key values for which Russell and Blackburn stand are an essential part of religious aspiration. There are, for example, plenty of Christians who argue in favour of pluralistic and open education, for pacifism, for scientific cooperation, for non-sectarianism and anti-racism, for property rights, and for respect for the environment. And all this on theological grounds. Russell and Blackburn might reply that religion should still be seen as a source of evil which needs to be eradicated in order to make way for a kind of Utopia. But, as Mary Midgley observes, 'whatever may have been its plausibility in the eighteenth century, when it first took the centre of the stage', this view 'is just a distraction today'.[21]   Moral atrocity abounds even where the influence of religion is non-existent. And, as Midgley goes on to suggest, what might be required from thinkers is 'an atrociously difficult psychological inquiry' rather than 'a ritual warfare about the existence of God' and the like.[22]

But it ought to be added that there are evidently religious believers who see their religious beliefs as entailing moral judgements sharply at odds with those accepted by many other people. And sometimes it may be quite impossible to resolve the resulting disagreement. Take, for instance, the conflict between many secular moralists and theologians who disapprove of divorce in the light of what they take to be divine instruction. These people often share a great deal of common ground when it comes to criteria for arriving at moral judgements. Yet they can evidently reach deadlock in the long run because one group thinks that some sound moral teaching has been revealed by God while the other does not. And until they can come to agree on such matters as revelation, no solution to their final disagreement seems possible.

This kind of impasse may, of course, lead us to ask whether religion is inevitably inimical to morality. But this is not a question to answer in general terms, and maybe it is none too clear to begin with. As should be evident from the diversity of views presented in this chapter, anyone concerned with the relationship between morality and religion will need to proceed slowly and with reference to various understandings of both morality and religion.

[1] Kierkegaard is widely admired by many contemporary theologians. His writings include *Either-Or* (1843), *Philosophical Fragments* (1844), and *Concluding Unscientific Postscript* (1846). He is often said to be the founding father of the philosophical movement known as Existentialism. His writings had a particular influence on Martin Heidegger (1889-1976) and Jean-Paul Sartre (1905-80).

[2] Genesis 22.

[3] Soren Kierkegaard, *Fear and Trembling,* trans. Robert Payne (London, New York, and Toronto, 1939), pp. 84 f.

[4] D. Z. Phillips, 'God and Ought', in Ian Ramsey (ed.), *Christian Ethics and Contemporary Philosophy* (London, 1966), pp. 137 f.

[5] Thomas Aquinas, *Summa Theologiae,* la, 6, 2.1 quote from volume 2 of the Blackfriars edition of the *Summa Theologiae* (London and New York, 1964)

[6] Aristotle, *Nicomachean Ethics,* I, 1, 1094a. I quote from Roger Crisp (ed.), *Aristotle: Nicomachean Ethics* (Cambridge, 2000), p. 3.

[7] Cf. my account of Aquinas on the meaning of 'bad' (Chapter 10 above).

[8] Cf. Chapter 7 above.

[9] Aquinas, *Summa Theologiae,* la, 6,1.

[10] Aquinas thinks that God is immutable, so he would reject the notion of   God first willing this and then willing something different.

[11] Cf. Norman Kretzmann, 'Abraham, Isaac, and Euthyphro: God and the Basis of Morality', reprinted in Eleonore Stump and Michael J. Murray (eds.), *Philosophy of Religion: The Big Questions* (Oxford, 1999).

[12] James Rachels, 'God and Human Attitudes', *Religious Studies 7* (1971), p. 334.

[13] Immanuel Kant, *Groundwork of the Metaphysic of Morals,* ed. H. J. Paton (New York, 1964), p. 111.

[14] Bertrand Russell, *Why I am not a Christian* (London, 1927), p. 37.

[15] Simon Blackburn, *Being Good* (Oxford, 2001), pp. 10 ff.

[16] Ibid., pp. 12 f.

[17] Ibid., p. 19.

[18] Philip L. Quinn, *Divine Commands and Moral Requirements* (Oxford, 1978), pp. 6. F.

[19] Ninian Smart, *The Phenomenon of Religion* (London and Oxford, 1978), p. 10

[20] William Alston, 'Religion', in Paul Edwards (ed.), *The Encyclopedia of Philosophy, vol. 7* (New York and London, 1967)

[21] 47. Mary Midgely, Wickedness (London, 1984), p. 6.

[22] Ibid.

Spencer Case

1000 Word Philosophy

Because God Says So: On Divine Command Theory

What is the relationship between God's commands and morality? Given that God is morally perfect and so commands all and only good things, we may distinguish between two claims:

a. God commands what He does *because it is good*.

b. What is good is so *because of God's commands*.

If (a) is true, then facts about goodness exist independently of God's will. God's commands are a *response to* them. If (b) is true, God's commands *themselves create* all truths about goodness and badness. The philosophical fork in the road between (a) and (b) is known as the "Euthyphro Dilemma," since a version of it appears in Plato's dialogue the *Euthyphro*. To accept (b) is to accept Divine Command Theory about ethics (henceforth DCT), which shall be our focus here.

What Is Divine Command Theory?

Before we continue, let's first get clear about what DCT *isn't*. DCT isn't a theory about *which particular* actions are wrong and right, since it makes no claims about what God in fact commands. It also isn't a theory of how we come to *know* ethical truths. It is silent on how God makes His commandments known, or even *whether* He chooses to make them known.

Finally, DCT isn't inconsistent with atheism. The two are logically compatible, but together entail that there are no truths about morality, just as there would be no truths about what's legal in a state of anarchy.

We should also take care to distinguish DCT from Natural Law Theory (henceforth NLT). According to NLT, moral facts are grounded in the natural order of the universe and in the natures of human beings. Of course, theists who endorse NLT hold that God created that very natural order, thereby creating the moral order, but this position still differs from DCT. Both theories agree that God created a moral order to the universe, but one holds that God created the moral order through his creation of the natural order, while the other maintains he created the moral order by commanding and forbidding things.

Another way to look at the differences between NLT and DCT is this: If a defender of NLT decided that atheism was, after all, true, he need not abandon his moral theory in order to retain at least some of his moral beliefs. It is at least conceivable that an uncreated natural order grounds ethical truths. However, if a divine command theorist adopted atheism, then he would either have to change his moral theory or accept that there are no moral truths.

Two Worries for Divine Command Theory

While DCT is often appealed to in popular defenses of religion, it's controversial among religious thinkers. In Christianity, William of Ockham defended DCT, and so did many Protestants, but NLT is a much more common view among Christian philosophers. In Islam, the 'Asharite school of theology appeared to accept DCT, but the Mu'tazilite school rejected it. Even the views of most 'Asharites include important qualifications (al-Attar 99-140).

Why do so few really thoughtful believers accept DCT? Well, think about asking *why* God prohibits theft, lying, and adultery. We want to say: "Because these things are bad." But to give such a justification is to abandon DCT. Per DCT, *that God so wills* is supposed to be the explanatory foundation of morality. So, DCT makes God's commands totally arbitrary.

While one troubling consequence of DCT is arbitrariness, another is the possibility of God's commanding really horrible things. Think of the morally worst thing conceivable. Whatever you've just thought of, if DCT is true, then God *could* make that thing morally right by commanding it. Wes Morriston formalizes this thought into the following argument against DCT:

1. DCT entails that whatever God commands is morally obligatory.

2. God could command X.

3. So if DCT is true, X could be morally obligatory.

4. But X could not be morally obligatory.

Therefore, DCT is false. (Morriston 251)

DCT entails (1) and (3), so the defender of DCT must reject at least one of either (2) or (4). One could deny (2) by appealing to God's eternal and unchanging nature. Perhaps Robert M. Adams could be interpreted as rejecting (2). He endorses a modified version of DCT, according to which the commands must issue from a loving God (Adams 249-276; Morriston 254-259). So maybe God is constrained by his own loving nature. The problem surrounding the rejection of (2) is that it arguably undermines God's omnipotence.

Rejecting (4) is a kind of response philosophers call "biting the bullet," since most people who think about the possibility of X's being morally obligatory have a visceral intuition against it. Among Christian thinkers, William of Ockham comes close to biting that bullet, but even he seems to have wavered (King 239-240). Among Muslim philosophers, Al-'Ashari stands out as the best example of a thoroughgoing bullet-biter (al-Attar 111-122).

Are there any good arguments for DCT? Perhaps the best way to argue for DCT is to try to show that *if* you believe in God, *then* you should accept DCT as the correct moral theory. An appeal to God's power might be effective here:

1. God is the most powerful thing conceivable.

2. Something that can make things right or wrong by will is more powerful than something that can't.

3. So, if God can't make things right or wrong by will not the most powerful thing conceivable (since we can conceive of something that can).

4. But this is absurd.

Hence, God can make things right or wrong by will (definition of DCT).

This argument alone won't convince atheists of DCT, since it only works if you assume God exists. However, it could be employed in tandem with other arguments for God's existence (maybe one of Aquinas's five arguments, for instance).

Critics of DCT might reject (1) on the grounds that God, as they understand Him, isn't the most powerful being conceivable FULL STOP, but the most powerful being conceivable *who is consistent with all divine attributes*, including goodness. Most who have thought deeply on the matter would rather make concessions on omnipotence than accept a morally arbitrary God. Might, it is thought, doesn't make right. Not even God's might.

References

Adams, Robert Merrihew. *Finite and Infinite Goods: A Framework for Ethics*. Oxford University Press. (1999).

al-Attar, Mariam. *Islamic Ethics: Divine Command Theory in Arabo-Islamic Thought*. Routledge. New York. (2010).

King, Peter "Ockham's Ethical Theory." In *The Cambridge Companion to Ockham*. Edited by Paul Vincent Spade (1999).

Morriston, Wes. "What If God Commanded Something Terrible? A Worry for Divine-Command Meta-Ethics" *Religious Studies* 45, 249-267. Cambridge University Press (2009).

Plato. *Euthyphro*. Translated by G.M.A Grube. In *Complete Works*. Edited with introduction and notes by John M. Cooper. Hackett Publishing Company, Inc. (1997).

Spencer is currently pursuing a doctorate in philosophy at University of Colorado at Boulder. Previously, he served as a public affairs specialist for the U.S. Army in both the Iraq and Afghanistan wars. He also spent nine months in Egypt as a Fulbright Student Grant recipient to study Islamic philosophy. His main interests are ethics, meta-ethics, and comparative philosophy.

The Bible and the Goodness of God

Suggested tasks:

- *Read the various passages and use highlighting and annotation to note what they imply about God's goodness. (Is God presented as good? In what sense? Morally? What 'good' characteristics come across? Compassion? Love? What else?)*
- *Then write a 400 – 500 word answer to this question: Is the God of the Bible good?*

The Torah/Old Testament

(You may also wish to refer to Psalm 23 and the Genesis 1 Creation narrative which are relevant to God as good as well as to the idea of God as Creator).

The Flood and the Covenant

(covenant = a binding agreement)

Genesis 6-9

In Genesis 6-9 we find the story of Noah. God sees that human beings have become wicked and he floods the entire earth. However, he saves Noah and his family by instructing Noah to build an ark, since Noah is a righteous man. The ark also shelters pairs of animals of all species to repopulate the earth after the flood. When the waters recede and Noah and his companions leave the ark, God makes a promise to them:

9 8 Then God said to Noah and to his sons with him: 9 "I now establish my covenant with you and with your descendants after you 10 and with every living creature that was with you — the birds, the livestock and all the wild animals, all those that came out of the ark with you — every living creature on earth. 11 I establish my covenant with you: Never again will all life be destroyed by the waters of a flood; never again will there be a flood to destroy the earth."

12 And God said, "This is the sign of the covenant I am making between me and you and every living creature with you, a covenant for all generations to come: 13 I have set my rainbow in the clouds, and it will be the sign of the covenant between me and the earth. 14 Whenever I bring clouds over the earth and the rainbow appears in the clouds, 15 I will remember my covenant between me and you and all living creatures of every kind. Never again will the waters

become a flood to destroy all life. 16 Whenever the rainbow appears in the clouds, I will see it and remember the everlasting covenant between God and all living creatures of every kind on the earth."

17 So God said to Noah, "This is the sign of the covenant I have established between me and all life on the earth."

The Command to Sacrifice Isaac

Genesis 22:1-19

22 After these things God tested Abraham. He said to him, "Abraham!" And he said, "Here I am." 2 He said, "Take your son, your only son Isaac, whom you love, and go to the land of Moriah, and offer him there as a burnt offering on one of the mountains that I shall show you." 3 So Abraham rose early in the morning, saddled his donkey, and took two of his young men with him, and his son Isaac; he cut the wood for the burnt offering, and set out and went to the place in the distance that God had shown him. 4 On the third day Abraham looked up and saw the place far away. 5 Then Abraham said to his young men, "Stay here with the donkey; the boy and I will go over there; we will worship, and then we will come back to you." 6 Abraham took the wood of the burnt offering and laid it on his son Isaac, and he himself carried the fire and the knife. So the two of them walked on together. 7 Isaac said to his father Abraham, "Father!" And he said, "Here I am, my son." He said, "The fire and the wood are here, but where is the lamb for a burnt offering?" 8 Abraham said, "God himself will provide the lamb for a burnt offering, my son." So the two of them walked on together.

9 When they came to the place that God had shown him, Abraham built an altar there and laid the wood in order. He bound his son Isaac, and laid him on the altar, on top of the wood. 10 Then Abraham reached out his hand and took the knife to kill[a] his son. 11 But the angel of the Lord called to him from heaven, and said, "Abraham, Abraham!" And he said, "Here I am." 12 He said, "Do not lay your hand on the boy or do anything to him; for now I know that you fear God, since you have not withheld your son, your only son, from me." 13 And Abraham looked up and saw a ram, caught in a thicket by its horns. Abraham went and took the ram and offered it up as a burnt offering instead of his son. 14 So Abraham called that place "The Lord will provide";[b] as it is said to this day, "On the mount of the Lord it shall be provided."[c]

15 The angel of the Lord called to Abraham a second time from heaven, 16 and said, "By myself I have sworn, says the Lord: Because you have done this, and have not withheld your son, your only son, 17 I will indeed bless you, and I will make your offspring as numerous as the stars of heaven and as the sand that is on the seashore. And your offspring shall possess the gate of their enemies, 18 and by your offspring shall all the nations of the earth gain blessing for themselves, because you have obeyed my voice."

God leads the Israelites out of slavery

Exodus 14

Previous chapters have told the story of how the Israelites have been enslaved and have been working for the Pharoah of Egypt in cruel conditions for many years. God instructs Moses to lead them to freedom. He inflicts a series of plagues on the stubborn Egyptians until Pharoah eventually allows the Israelites to go after the worst plague - the death of all Egypt's eldest sons. However, having freed the slaves Pharoah decides to pursue them.

10 As Pharaoh drew near, the Israelites looked back, and there were the Egyptians advancing on them. In great fear the Israelites cried out to the Lord. 11 They said to Moses, "Was it because there were no graves in Egypt that you have taken us away to die in the wilderness? What have you done to us, bringing us out of Egypt? 12 Is this not the very thing we told you in Egypt, 'Let us alone and let us serve the Egyptians'? For it would have been better for us to serve the Egyptians than to die in the wilderness." 13 But Moses said to the people, "Do not be afraid, stand firm, and see the deliverance that the Lord will accomplish for you today; for the Egyptians whom you see today you shall never see again. 14 The Lord will fight for you, and you have only to keep still."

15 Then the Lord said to Moses, "Why do you cry out to me? Tell the Israelites to go forward. 16 But you lift up your staff, and stretch out your hand over the sea and divide it, that the Israelites may go into the sea on dry ground. 17 Then I will harden the hearts of the Egyptians so that they will go in after them; and so I will gain glory for myself over Pharaoh and all his army, his chariots, and his chariot drivers. 18 And the Egyptians shall know that I am the Lord, when I have gained glory for myself over Pharaoh, his chariots, and his chariot drivers."

19 The angel of God who was going before the Israelite army moved and went behind them; and the pillar of cloud moved from in front of them and took its place behind them. 20 It came between the army of Egypt and the army of Israel. And so the cloud was there with the darkness, and it lit up the night; one did not come near the other all night.

21 Then Moses stretched out his hand over the sea. The Lord drove the sea back by a strong east wind all night, and turned the sea into dry land; and the waters were divided. 22 The Israelites went into the sea on dry ground, the waters forming a wall for them on their right and on their left. 23 The Egyptians pursued, and went into the sea after them, all of Pharaoh's horses, chariots, and chariot drivers. 24 At the morning watch the Lord in the pillar of fire and cloud looked down upon the Egyptian army, and threw the Egyptian army into panic. 25 He clogged[a] their chariot wheels so that they turned with difficulty. The Egyptians said, "Let us flee from the Israelites, for the Lord is fighting for them against Egypt."

26 Then the Lord said to Moses, "Stretch out your hand over the sea, so that the water may come back upon the Egyptians, upon their chariots and chariot drivers." 27 So Moses stretched out his hand over the

sea, and at dawn the sea returned to its normal depth. As the Egyptians fled before it, the Lord tossed the Egyptians into the sea. ²⁸ The waters returned and covered the chariots and the chariot drivers, the entire army of Pharaoh that had followed them into the sea; not one of them remained. ²⁹ But the Israelites walked on dry ground through the sea, the waters forming a wall for them on their right and on their left.

³⁰ Thus the Lord saved Israel that day from the Egyptians; and Israel saw the Egyptians dead on the seashore. ³¹ Israel saw the great work that the Lord did against the Egyptians. So the people feared the Lord and believed in the Lord and in his servant Moses.

Psalm 103

¹ Praise the Lord, my soul;
   all my inmost being, praise his holy name.
² Praise the Lord, my soul,
   and forget not all his benefits —
³ who forgives all your sins
   and heals all your diseases,
⁴ who redeems your life from the pit
   and crowns you with love and compassion,
⁵ who satisfies your desires with good things
   so that your youth is renewed like the eagle's.

⁶ The Lord works

¹³ As a father has compassion on his children,
   so the Lord has compassion on those who
fear him;
¹⁴ for he knows how we are formed,
   he remembers that we are dust.
¹⁵ The life of mortals is like grass,
   they flourish like a flower of the field;
¹⁶ the wind blows over it and it is gone,
   and its place remembers it no more.
¹⁷ But from everlasting to everlasting
   the Lord's love is with those who fear him,
   and his righteousness with their children's
children —
¹⁸ with those who keep his covenant
   and remember to obey his precepts.

righteousness
   and justice for all the oppressed.

7 He made known his ways to Moses,

his deeds to the people of Israel:

8 The Lord is compassionate and gracious,

slow to anger, abounding in love.

9 He will not always accuse,

nor will he harbor his anger forever;

10 he does not treat us as our sins deserve

or repay us according to our iniquities.

11 For as high as the heavens are above the earth,

so great is his love for those who fear him;

12 as far as the east is from the west,

so far has he removed our transgressions from us.

Richard Dawkins (author of 'The God Delusion') describing God in the Old Testament:

"The God of the Old Testament is arguably the most unpleasant character in all fiction: jealous and proud of it; a petty, unjust, unforgiving control-freak; a vindictive, bloodthirsty ethnic cleanser; a misogynistic, homophobic, racist, infanticidal, genocidal, filicidal, pestilential, megalomaniacal, sadomasochistic, capriciously malevolent bully."

The New Testament – God as revealed in Jesus

God's love in Jesus

(In both the next two passages the speaker is Jesus)

John 3

16 For God so loved the world that he gave his one and only Son, that whoever believes in him shall not perish but have eternal life. 17 For God did not send his Son into the world to condemn the world, but to save the world through him.

John 10

11 "I am the good shepherd. The good shepherd lays down his life for the sheep. 12 The hired hand, who is not the shepherd and does not own the sheep, sees the wolf coming and leaves the sheep and runs away — and the wolf snatches them and scatters them. 13 The hired hand runs away because a hired hand does not care for the sheep. 14 I am the good shepherd. I know my own and my own know me, 15 just as the Father knows me and I know the Father. And I lay down my life for the sheep.

Jesus heals the sick

Mark 1

[29] As soon as they[n] left the synagogue, they entered the house of Simon and Andrew, with James and John. [30] Now Simon's mother-in-law was in bed with a fever, and they told him about her at once. [31] He came and took her by the hand and lifted her up. Then the fever left her, and she began to serve them.

[32] That evening, at sunset, they brought to him all who were sick or possessed with demons. [33] And the whole city was gathered around the door. [34] And he cured many who were sick with various diseases, and cast out many demons

§4 The Nature of Belief

The texts in this section aim to introduce students to debates surrounding faith and reason – whether they are at odds or complement each other; whether faith is propositional or non-propositional and varying degrees of rationalism contrasted with fideism.

Whereas the strong rationalist position is that, "in order for a religious belief-system to be properly and rationally accepted, it must be possible to prove that the belief-system is true" (Peterson et al), the fideist does not think that religious belief systems are (or should be) subject to rational evaluation or criticism. The quotation attributed to Tertulian, "*credo quia absurdum est*" [I believe because it is absurd] seems to champion the latter position; whereas Clifford's instance that, "it is wrong always, everywhere, and for anyone, to believe anything upon insufficient evidence" summarises the former.

Critical rationalism is, naturally, some point between the two positions, and Tennyson's observation that, "we have but faith, we cannot know" is a rational one.

As we have seen in Plato, some imagine the human epistemological journey as an ascent – out of the analogical 'Cave' of ignorance to enlightenment. For others, the journey is insurmountable without divine assistance. Thus the role of Revelation is of paramount significance to Theology. What constitutes (a) revelation is, naturally, matter of great debate between and within different faith traditions. Furthermore, whether (a) revelation is propositional (i.e. God reveals certain facts or truths) or non-propositional (something more ineffable) is also questioned.

Since different faith communities approach their sacred texts differently (some encouraging exegesis by the layperson; others preferring texts to be read in their original language, etc.) this section does not contain material from the Qur'an so that centres might choose for themselves what would be most appropriate for their students. The Judaeo-Christian concepts of God are focused on for our purposes but, as has been said before, the purpose of this Anthology is intended to be supplemented with other texts as appropriate.

Exodus 3

(NRSV. Author unknown. Traditional author: Moses)

[Moses at the Burning Bush]

1 Moses was keeping the flock of his father-in-law Jethro, the priest of Midian; he led his flock beyond the wilderness, and came to Horeb, the mountain of God. **2** There the angel of the LORD appeared to him in a flame of fire out of a bush; he looked, and the bush was blazing, yet it was not consumed. **3** Then Moses said, "I must turn aside and look at this great sight, and see why the bush is not burned up." **4** When the LORD saw that he had turned aside to see, God called to him out of the bush, "Moses, Moses!" And he said, "Here I am." **5** Then he said, "Come no closer! Remove the sandals from your feet, for the place on which you are standing is holy ground." **6** He said further, "I am the God of your father, the God of Abraham, the God of Isaac, and the God of Jacob." And Moses hid his face, for he was afraid to look at God.

7 Then the LORD said, "I have observed the misery of my people who are in Egypt; I have heard their cry on account of their taskmasters. Indeed, I know their sufferings, **8** and I have come down to deliver them from the Egyptians, and to bring them up out of that land to a good and broad land, a land flowing with milk and honey, to the country of the Canaanites, the Hittites, the Amorites, the Perizzites, the Hivites, and the Jebusites. **9** The cry of the Israelites has now come to me; I have also seen how the Egyptians oppress them. **10** So come, I will send you to Pharaoh to bring my people, the Israelites, out of Egypt." **11** But Moses said to God, "Who am I that I should go to Pharaoh, and bring the Israelites out of Egypt?" **12** He said, "I will be with you; and this shall be the sign for you that it is I who sent you: when you have brought the people out of Egypt, you shall worship God on this mountain."

13 But Moses said to God, "If I come to the Israelites and say to them, 'The God of your ancestors has sent me to you,' and they ask me, 'What is his name?' what shall I say to them?" **14** God said to Moses, "I AM WHO I AM."[1] He said further, "Thus you shall say to the Israelites, 'I AM has sent me to you.'"

---

[1] Exodus 3:14 Or *I am what I am* or *I will be what I will be*

15 God also said to Moses, "Thus you shall say to the Israelites, 'The LORD,[2] the God of your ancestors, the God of Abraham, the God of Isaac, and the God of Jacob, has sent me to you':

This is my name forever,
and this my title for all generations.

16 Go and assemble the elders of Israel, and say to them, 'The LORD, the God of your ancestors, the God of Abraham, of Isaac, and of Jacob, has appeared to me, saying: I have given heed to you and to what has been done to you in Egypt. **17** I declare that I will bring you up out of the misery of Egypt, to the land of the Canaanites, the Hittites, the Amorites, the Perizzites, the Hivites, and the Jebusites, a land flowing with milk and honey.' **18** They will listen to your voice; and you and the elders of Israel shall go to the king of Egypt and say to him, 'The LORD, the God of the Hebrews, has met with us; let us now go a three days' journey into the wilderness, so that we may sacrifice to the Lord our God.' **19** I know, however, that the king of Egypt will not let you go unless compelled by a mighty hand.[3] **20** So I will stretch out my hand and strike Egypt with all my wonders that I will perform in it; after that he will let you go. **21** I will bring this people into such favor with the Egyptians that, when you go, you will not go empty-handed; **22** each woman shall ask her neighbor and any woman living in the neighbor's house for jewelry of silver and of gold, and clothing, and you shall put them on your sons and on your daughters; and so you shall plunder the Egyptians."

---

[2] Exodus 3:15 The word "LORD" when spelled with capital letters stands for the divine name, *YHWH*, which is here connected with the verb *hayah,* "to be"
[3] Exodus 3:19 Gk Vg: Heb *no, not by a mighty hand*

Hebrews 11

(NRSV. Author unknown)

[The Meaning of Faith]

1 Now faith is the assurance of things hoped for, the conviction of things not seen. **2** Indeed, by faith[1] our ancestors received approval. **3** By faith we understand that the worlds were prepared by the word of God, so that what is seen was made from things that are not visible.[2]

The Examples of Abel, Enoch, and Noah

4 By faith Abel offered to God a more acceptable[3] sacrifice than Cain's. Through this he received approval as righteous, God himself giving approval to his gifts; he died, but through his faith[4] he still speaks. **5** By faith Enoch was taken so that he did not experience death; and "he was not found, because God had taken him." For it was attested before he was taken away that "he had pleased God." **6** And without faith it is impossible to please God, for whoever would approach him must believe that he exists and that he rewards those who seek him. **7** By faith Noah, warned by God about events as yet unseen, respected the warning and built an ark to save his household; by this he condemned the world and became an heir to the righteousness that is in accordance with faith.

The Faith of Abraham

8 By faith Abraham obeyed when he was called to set out for a place that he was to receive as an inheritance; and he set out, not knowing where he was going. **9** By faith he stayed for a time in the land he had been promised, as in a foreign land, living in tents, as did Isaac and Jacob, who were heirs with him of the same promise. **10** For he looked forward to the city that has foundations, whose architect and builder is God. **11** By faith he received power of procreation, even though he was too old — and Sarah herself was barren — because he considered him faithful who had promised.[5] **12** Therefore from one person, and this one as good as dead, descendants were born, "as many as the stars of heaven and as the innumerable grains of sand by the seashore."

---

[1] Hebrews 11:2 Gk *by this*
[2] Hebrews 11:3 Or *was not made out of visible things*
[3] Hebrews 11:4 Gk *greater*
[4] Hebrews 11:4 Gk *through it*
[5] Hebrews 11:11 Or By faith Sarah herself, though barren, received power to conceive, even when she was too old, because she considered him faithful who had promised.

13 All of these died in faith without having received the promises, but from a distance they saw and greeted them. They confessed that they were strangers and foreigners on the earth, **14** for people who speak in this way make it clear that they are seeking a homeland. **15** If they had been thinking of the land that they had left behind, they would have had opportunity to return. **16** But as it is, they desire a better country, that is, a heavenly one. Therefore God is not ashamed to be called their God; indeed, he has prepared a city for them.

17 By faith Abraham, when put to the test, offered up Isaac. He who had received the promises was ready to offer up his only son, **18** of whom he had been told, "It is through Isaac that descendants shall be named for you." **19** He considered the fact that God is able even to raise someone from the dead — and figuratively speaking, he did receive him back. **20** By faith Isaac invoked blessings for the future on Jacob and Esau. **21** By faith Jacob, when dying, blessed each of the sons of Joseph, "bowing in worship over the top of his staff." **22** By faith Joseph, at the end of his life, made mention of the exodus of the Israelites and gave instructions about his burial.[6]

The Faith of Moses

23 By faith Moses was hidden by his parents for three months after his birth, because they saw that the child was beautiful; and they were not afraid of the king's edict.[7] **24** By faith Moses, when he was grown up, refused to be called a son of Pharaoh's daughter, **25** choosing rather to share ill-treatment with the people of God than to enjoy the fleeting pleasures of sin. **26** He considered abuse suffered for the Christ[8] to be greater wealth than the treasures of Egypt, for he was looking ahead to the reward. **27** By faith he left Egypt, unafraid of the king's anger; for he persevered as though[9] he saw him who is invisible. **28** By faith he kept the Passover and the sprinkling of blood, so that the destroyer of the firstborn would not touch the firstborn of Israel.[10]

The Faith of Other Israelite Heroes

29 By faith the people passed through the Red Sea as if it were dry land, but when the Egyptians attempted to do so they were drowned. **30** By faith the walls of Jericho fell after they had been encircled

---

[6] Hebrews 11:22 Gk *his bones*
[7] Hebrews 11:23 Other ancient authorities add *By faith Moses, when he was grown up, killed the Egyptian, because he observed the humiliation of his people* (Gk *brothers*)
[8] Hebrews 11:26 Or *the Messiah*
[9] Hebrews 11:27 Or *because*
[10] Hebrews 11:28 Gk *would not touch them*

for seven days. **31** By faith Rahab the prostitute did not perish with those who were disobedient,[11] because she had received the spies in peace.

32 And what more should I say? For time would fail me to tell of Gideon, Barak, Samson, Jephthah, of David and Samuel and the prophets— **33** who through faith conquered kingdoms, administered justice, obtained promises, shut the mouths of lions, **34** quenched raging fire, escaped the edge of the sword, won strength out of weakness, became mighty in war, put foreign armies to flight. **35** Women received their dead by resurrection. Others were tortured, refusing to accept release, in order to obtain a better resurrection. **36** Others suffered mocking and flogging, and even chains and imprisonment. **37** They were stoned to death, they were sawn in two,[12] they were killed by the sword; they went about in skins of sheep and goats, destitute, persecuted, tormented— **38** of whom the world was not worthy. They wandered in deserts and mountains, and in caves and holes in the ground.

39 Yet all these, though they were commended for their faith, did not receive what was promised, **40** since God had provided something better so that they would not, apart from us, be made perfect.

---

[11] Hebrews 11:31 Or *unbelieving*
[12] Hebrews 11:37 Other ancient authorities add *they were tempted*

1 John

(NRSV. Author: St. John[?])

Chapter 1

1 We declare to you what was from the beginning, what we have heard, what we have seen with our eyes, what we have looked at and touched with our hands, concerning the word of life— **2** this life was revealed, and we have seen it and testify to it, and declare to you the eternal life that was with the Father and was revealed to us— **3** we declare to you what we have seen and heard so that you also may have fellowship with us; and truly our fellowship is with the Father and with his Son Jesus Christ. **4** We are writing these things so that our[1] joy may be complete.

5 This is the message we have heard from him and proclaim to you, that God is light and in him there is no darkness at all. **6** If we say that we have fellowship with him while we are walking in darkness, we lie and do not do what is true; **7** but if we walk in the light as he himself is in the light, we have fellowship with one another, and the blood of Jesus his Son cleanses us from all sin. **8** If we say that we have no sin, we deceive ourselves, and the truth is not in us. **9** If we confess our sins, he who is faithful and just will forgive us our sins and cleanse us from all unrighteousness. **10** If we say that we have not sinned, we make him a liar, and his word is not in us.[…]

Chapter 3

1 See what love the Father has given us, that we should be called children of God; and that is what we are. The reason the world does not know us is that it did not know him. **2** Beloved, we are God's children now; what we will be has not yet been revealed. What we do know is this: when he[2] is revealed, we will be like him, for we will see him as he is. **3** And all who have this hope in him purify themselves, just as he is pure.

4 Everyone who commits sin is guilty of lawlessness; sin is lawlessness. **5** You know that he was revealed to take away sins, and in him there is no sin. **6** No one who abides in him sins; no one who sins has either seen him or known him. **7** Little children, let no one deceive you. Everyone who does what is right is righteous, just as he is righteous. **8** Everyone who commits sin is a child of the devil; for the devil has been sinning from the beginning. The Son of God was revealed for this purpose, to destroy the works of the devil. **9** Those who have been born of God do not sin, because God's seed

---

[1] some manuscripts *your*

[2] or *it*

abides in them;[3] they cannot sin, because they have been born of God. **10** The children of God and the children of the devil are revealed in this way: all who do not do what is right are not from God, nor are those who do not love their brothers and sisters[4].

11 For this is the message you have heard from the beginning, that we should love one another. **12** We must not be like Cain who was from the evil one and murdered his brother. And why did he murder him? Because his own deeds were evil and his brother's righteous. **13** Do not be astonished, brothers and sisters, that the world hates you. **14** We know that we have passed from death to life because we love one another. Whoever does not love abides in death. **15** All who hate a brother or sister are murderers, and you know that murderers do not have eternal life abiding in them. **16** We know love by this, that he laid down his life for us — and we ought to lay down our lives for one another. **17** How does God's love abide in anyone who has the world's goods and sees a brother or sister in need and yet refuses help?

18 Little children, let us love, not in word or speech, but in truth and action. **19** And by this we will know that we are from the truth and will reassure our hearts before him **20** whenever our hearts condemn us; for God is greater than our hearts, and he knows everything. **21** Beloved, if our hearts do not condemn us, we have boldness before God; **22** and we receive from him whatever we ask, because we obey his commandments and do what pleases him.

23 And this is his commandment, that we should believe in the name of his Son Jesus Christ and love one another, just as he has commanded us. **24** All who obey his commandments abide in him, and he abides in them. And by this we know that he abides in us, by the Spirit that he has given us.

Chapter 4

1 Beloved, do not believe every spirit, but test the spirits to see whether they are from God; for many false prophets have gone out into the world. **2** By this you know the Spirit of God: every spirit that confesses that Jesus Christ has come in the flesh is from God, **3** and every spirit that does not confess Jesus is not from God. And this is the spirit of the antichrist, of which you have heard that it is coming; and now it is already in the world. **4** Little children, you are from God, and have conquered them; for the one who is in you is greater than the one who is in the world. **5** They are from the world; therefore what they say is from the world, and the world listens to them. **6** We are from God. Whoever knows

---

[3] or *because the children of God abide in him*
[4] Throughout the epistle the NRSV adds *and sisters* for inclusivity. The Greek only has 'brother' but is meant inclusively.

God listens to us, and whoever is not from God does not listen to us. From this we know the spirit of truth and the spirit of error.

7 Beloved, let us love one another, because love is from God; everyone who loves is born of God and knows God. **8** Whoever does not love does not know God, for **God is love**. **9** God's love was revealed among us in this way: God sent his only Son into the world so that we might live through him. **10** In this is love, not that we loved God but that he loved us and sent his Son to be the atoning sacrifice for our sins. **11** Beloved, since God loved us so much, we also ought to love one another. **12** No one has ever seen God; if we love one another, God lives in us, and his love is perfected in us.

13 By this we know that we abide in him and he in us, because he has given us of his Spirit. **14** And we have seen and do testify that the Father has sent his Son as the Savior of the world. **15** God abides in those who confess that Jesus is the Son of God, and they abide in God. **16** So we have known and believe the love that God has for us.

God is love, and those who abide in love abide in God, and God abides in them. **17** Love has been perfected among us in this: that we may have boldness on the day of judgment, because as he is, so are we in this world. **18** There is no fear in love, but perfect love casts out fear; for fear has to do with punishment, and whoever fears has not reached perfection in love. **19** We love[5] because he first loved us. **20** Those who say, "I love God," and hate their brothers or sisters, are liars; for those who do not love a brother or sister whom they have seen, cannot love God whom they have not seen. **21** The commandment we have from him is this: those who love God must love their brothers and sisters also.

Chapter 5

Everyone who believes that Jesus is the Christ[6] has been born of God, and everyone who loves the parent loves the child. **2** By this we know that we love the children of God, when we love God and obey his commandments. **3** For the love of God is this, that we obey his commandments. And his commandments are not burdensome, **4** for whatever is born of God conquers the world. And this is the victory that conquers the world, our faith. **5** Who is it that conquers the world but the one who believes that Jesus is the Son of God?

6 This is the one who came by water and blood, Jesus Christ, not with the water only but with the water and the blood. And the Spirit is the one that testifies, for the Spirit is the truth. **7** There are three

---

[5] Other ancient authorities add *him*; others add *God*
[6] or *Messiah*

that testify:[7] **8** the Spirit and the water and the blood, and these three agree. **9** If we receive human testimony, the testimony of God is greater; for this is the testimony of God that he has testified to his Son. **10** Those who believe in the Son of God have the testimony in their hearts. Those who do not believe in God have made him a liar by not believing in the testimony that God has given concerning his Son. **11** And this is the testimony: God gave us eternal life, and this life is in his Son. **12** Whoever has the Son has life; whoever does not have the Son of God does not have life.

[7] A few other authorities read (with variations) **7** There are three that testify in heaven, the Father, the Word, and the Holy Spirit, and these three are one. **8** And there are three that testify on earth:

St. Augustine of Hippo (354-430)

Confessions

Can any praise be worthy of the Lord's majesty?[1] How magnificent his strength! How inscrutable his wisdom![2] Man is one of your creatures, Lord, and his instinct is to praise you. He bears about him the mark of death, the sign of his own sin, to remind him that you *thwart the proud[3]*. But still, since he is a part of your creation, he wishes to praise you. The thought of you stirs him so deeply that he cannot be content unless he praises you, because you made us for yourself and our hearts find no peace until they rest in you.

Grant me, Lord, to know and understand whether a man is first to pray to you for help or to praise you, and whether he must know you before he can call you to his aid. If he does not know you, how can he pray to you? For he may call for some other help, mistaking it for yours.

Or are men to pray to you and learn to know you through their prayers? *Only, how are they to call upon the Lord until they have learned to believe in him? And how are they to believe in him without a preacher to listen to?[4]*

Those who look for the Lord will cry out in praise of him[5], because all who look for him shall find him, and when they find him they will praise him. I shall look for you, Lord, by praying to you and as I pray I shall believe in you, because we have had preachers to tell us about you. It is my faith that calls to you. Lord, the faith which you gave me and made to live in me through the merits of your Son, who became man, and through the ministry of your preacher.

---

[1] Psalm 145:3
[2] Psalm 147:5
[3] 1 Peter 5
[4] Romans 10:14
[5] Psalm 22:26

St. Thomas Aquinas (1225-1274)

Summma Theologica

FIRST PART (FP)

Treatise on Sacred Doctrine (Q1)

Whether, besides philosophy, any further doctrine is required?

Objection 1: It seems that, besides philosophical science, we have no need of any further knowledge. For man should not seek to know what is above reason: "Seek not the things that are too high for thee" (Ecclus. 3:22). But whatever is not above reason is fully treated of in philosophical science. Therefore any other knowledge besides philosophical science is superfluous.

Objection 2: Further, knowledge can be concerned only with being, for nothing can be known, save what is true; and all that is, is true. But everything that is, is treated of in philosophical science---even God Himself; so that there is a part of philosophy called theology, or the divine science, as Aristotle has proved (Metaph. vi). Therefore, besides philosophical science, there is no need of any further knowledge.

On the contrary, It is written (2 Tim. 3:16): "All Scripture, inspired of God is profitable to teach, to reprove, to correct, to instruct in justice." Now Scripture, inspired of God, is no part of philosophical science, which has been built up by human reason. Therefore it is useful that besides philosophical science, there should be other knowledge, i.e. inspired of God.

I answer that, It was necessary for man's salvation that there should be a knowledge revealed by God besides philosophical science built up by human reason. Firstly, indeed, because man is directed to God, as to an end that surpasses the grasp of his reason: "The eye hath not seen, O God, besides Thee, what things Thou hast prepared for them that wait for Thee" (Is. 66:4). But the end must first be known by men who are to direct their thoughts and actions to the end. Hence it was necessary for the salvation of man that certain truths which exceed human reason should be made known to him by divine revelation. Even as regards those truths about God which human reason could have discovered, it was necessary that man should be taught by a divine revelation; because he truth about God such as reason could discover, would only be known by a few, and that after a long time, and with the admixture of many errors. Whereas man's whole salvation, which is in God, depends upon the knowledge of this truth. Therefore, in order that the salvation of men might be brought about more fitly and more surely, it was necessary that they should be taught divine truths by divine revelation. It was therefore necessary that besides philosophical science built up by reason, there should be a sacred science learned through revelation.

Reply to Objection 1: Although those things which are beyond man's knowledge may not be sought for by man through his reason, nevertheless, once they are revealed by God, they must be accepted by faith. Hence the sacred text continues, "For many things are shown to thee above the understanding of man" (Ecclus. 3:25). And in this, the sacred science consists.

Reply to Objection 2: Sciences are differentiated according to the various means through which knowledge is obtained. For the astronomer and the physicist both may prove the same conclusion: that the earth, for instance, is round: the astronomer by means of mathematics (i.e. abstracting from matter), but the physicist by means of matter itself. Hence there is no reason why those things which may be learned from philosophical science, so far as they can be known by natural reason, may not also be taught us by another science so far as they fall within revelation. Hence theology included in sacred doctrine differs in kind from that theology which is part of philosophy.

Whether sacred doctrine is a science?

Objection 1: It seems that sacred doctrine is not a science. For every science proceeds from self-evident principles. But sacred doctrine proceeds from articles of faith which are not self-evident, since their truth is not admitted by all: "For all men have not faith" (2 Thess. 3:2). Therefore sacred doctrine is not a science.

Objection 2: Further, no science deals with individual facts. But this sacred science treats of individual facts, such as the deeds of Abraham, Isaac and Jacob and such like. Therefore sacred doctrine is not a science.

On the contrary, Augustine says (De Trin. xiv, 1) "to this science alone belongs that whereby saving faith is begotten, nourished, protected and strengthened." But this can be said of no science except sacred doctrine. Therefore sacred doctrine is a science.

I answer that, Sacred doctrine is a science. We must bear in mind that there are two kinds of sciences. There are some which proceed from a principle known by the natural light of intelligence, such as arithmetic and geometry and the like. There are some which proceed from principles known by the light of a higher science: thus the science of perspective proceeds from principles established by geometry, and music from principles established by arithmetic. So it is that sacred doctrine is a science because it proceeds from principles established by the light of a higher science, namely, the science of God and the blessed. Hence, just as the musician accepts on authority the principles taught him by the mathematician, so sacred science is established on principles revealed by God.

Reply to Objection 1: The principles of any science are either in themselves self-evident, or reducible to the conclusions of a higher science; and such, as we have said, are the principles of sacred doctrine.

Reply to Objection 2: Individual facts are treated of in sacred doctrine, not because it is concerned with them principally, but they are introduced rather both as examples to be followed in our lives (as in moral sciences) and in order to establish the authority of those men through whom the divine revelation, on which this sacred scripture or doctrine is based, has come down to us.

St. Thomas Aquinas (1225-1274)

Summa Theologica

SECOND PART OF THE SECOND PART (SS)

Treatise on the Theological Virtues (QQ[1]-46)

Of Faith (10 Articles)

Whether the object of faith is something complex, by way of a proposition?

Objection 1: It would seem that the object of faith is not something complex by way of a proposition. For the object of faith is the First Truth, as stated above (A[1]). Now the First Truth is something simple. Therefore the object of faith is not something complex.

Objection 2: Further, the exposition of faith is contained in the symbol. Now the symbol does not contain propositions, but things: for it is not stated therein that God is almighty, but: "I believe in God . . . almighty." Therefore the object of faith is not a proposition but a thing.

Objection 3: Further, faith is succeeded by vision, according to 1 Cor. 13:12: "We see now through a glass in a dark manner; but then face to face. Now I know in part; but then I shall know even as I am known." But the object of the heavenly vision is something simple, for it is the Divine Essence. Therefore the faith of the wayfarer is also.

On the contrary, Faith is a mean between science and opinion. Now the mean is in the same genus as the extremes. Since, then, science and opinion are about propositions, it seems that faith is likewise about propositions; so that its object is something complex.

I answer that, The thing known is in the knower according to the mode of the knower. Now the mode proper to the human intellect is to know the truth by synthesis and analysis, as stated in the FP, Q[85], A[5]. Hence things that are simple in themselves, are known by the intellect with a certain amount of complexity, just as on the other hand, the Divine intellect knows, without any complexity, things that are complex in themselves.

Accordingly the object of faith may be considered in two ways. First, as regards the thing itself which is believed, and thus the object of faith is something simple, namely the thing itself about which we have faith. Secondly, on the part of the believer, and in this respect the object of faith is something complex by way of a proposition.

Hence in the past both opinions have been held with a certain amount of truth.

Reply to Objection 1: This argument considers the object of faith on the part of the thing believed.

Reply to Objection 2: The symbol mentions the things about which faith is, in so far as the act of the believer is terminated in them, as is evident from the manner of speaking about them. Now the act of the believer does not terminate in a proposition, but in a thing. For as in science we do not form propositions, except in order to have knowledge about things through their means, so is it in faith.

Reply to Objection 3: The object of the heavenly vision will be the First Truth seen in itself, according to 1 Jn. 3:2: "We know that when He shall appear, we shall be like to Him: because we shall see Him as He is": hence that vision will not be by way of a proposition but by way of a simple understanding. On the other hand, by faith, we do not apprehend the First Truth as it is in itself. Hence the comparison fails.

Whether the object of faith can be something seen?

Objection 1: It would seem that the object of faith is something seen. For Our Lord said to Thomas (Jn. 20:29): "Because thou hast seen Me, Thomas, thou hast believed." Therefore vision and faith regard the same object.

Objection 2: Further, the Apostle, while speaking of the knowledge of faith, says (1 Cor. 13:12): "We see now through a glass in a dark manner." Therefore what is believed is seen.

Objection 3: Further, faith is a spiritual light. Now something is seen under every light. Therefore faith is of things seen.

Objection 4: Further, "Every sense is a kind of sight," as Augustine states (De Verb. Domini, Serm. xxxiii). But faith is of things heard, according to Rom. 10:17: "Faith . . . cometh by hearing." Therefore faith is of things seen.

On the contrary, The Apostle says (Heb. 11:1) that "faith is the evidence of things that appear not."

I answer that, Faith implies assent of the intellect to that which is believed. Now the intellect assents to a thing in two ways. First, through being moved to assent by its very object, which is known either by itself (as in the case of first principles, which are held by the habit of understanding), or through

174

something else already known (as in the case of conclusions which are held by the habit of science). Secondly the intellect assents to something, not through being sufficiently moved to this assent by its proper object, but through an act of choice, whereby it turns voluntarily to one side rather than to the other: and if this be accompanied by doubt or fear of the opposite side, there will be opinion, while, if there be certainty and no fear of the other side, there will be faith.

Now those things are said to be seen which, of themselves, move the intellect or the senses to knowledge of them. Wherefore it is evident that neither faith nor opinion can be of things seen either by the senses or by the intellect.

Reply to Objection 1: Thomas "saw one thing, and believed another" [*St. Gregory: Hom. xxvi in Evang.]: he saw the Man, and believing Him to be God, he made profession of his faith, saying: "My Lord and my God."

Reply to Objection 2: Those things which come under faith can be considered in two ways. First, in particular; and thus they cannot be seen and believed at the same time, as shown above. Secondly, in general, that is, under the common aspect of credibility; and in this way they are seen by the believer. For he would not believe unless, on the evidence of signs, or of something similar, he saw that they ought to be believed.

Reply to Objection 3: The light of faith makes us see what we believe. For just as, by the habits of the other virtues, man sees what is becoming to him in respect of that habit, so, by the habit of faith, the human mind is directed to assent to such things as are becoming to a right faith, and not to assent to others.

Reply to Objection 4: Hearing is of words signifying what is of faith, but not of the things themselves that are believed; hence it does not follow that these things are seen.

Whether those things that are of faith can be an object of science [*Science is certain knowledge of a demonstrated conclusion through its demonstration]?

Objection 1: It would seem that those things that are of faith can be an object of science. For where science is lacking there is ignorance, since ignorance is the opposite of science. Now we are not in ignorance of those things we have to believe, since ignorance of such things savors of unbelief, according to 1 Tim. 1:13: "I did it ignorantly in unbelief." Therefore things that are of faith can be an object of science.

Objection 2: Further, science is acquired by reasons. Now sacred writers employ reasons to inculcate things that are of faith. Therefore such things can be an object of science.

Objection 3: Further, things which are demonstrated are an object of science, since a "demonstration is a syllogism that produces science." Now certain matters of faith have been demonstrated by the philosophers, such as the Existence and Unity of God, and so forth. Therefore things that are of faith can be an object of science.

Objection 4: Further, opinion is further from science than faith is, since faith is said to stand between opinion and science. Now opinion and science can, in a way, be about the same object, as stated in Poster. i. Therefore faith and science can be about the same object also.

On the contrary, Gregory says (Hom. xxvi in Evang.) that "when a thing is manifest, it is the object, not of faith, but of perception." Therefore things that are of faith are not the object of perception, whereas what is an object of science is the object of perception. Therefore there can be no faith about things which are an object of science.

I answer that, All science is derived from self-evident and therefore "seen" principles; wherefore all objects of science must needs be, in a fashion, seen.

Now as stated above (A[4]), it is impossible that one and the same thing should be believed and seen by the same person. Hence it is equally impossible for one and the same thing to be an object of science and of belief for the same person. It may happen, however, that a thing which is an object of vision or science for one, is believed by another: since we hope to see some day what we now believe about the Trinity, according to 1 Cor. 13:12: "We see now through a glass in a dark manner; but then face to face": which vision the angels possess already; so that what we believe, they see. In like manner it may happen that what is an object of vision or scientific knowledge for one man, even in the state of a wayfarer, is, for another man, an object of faith, because he does not know it by demonstration.

Nevertheless that which is proposed to be believed equally by all, is equally unknown by all as an object of science: such are the things which are of faith simply. Consequently faith and science are not about the same things.

Reply to Objection 1: Unbelievers are in ignorance of things that are of faith, for neither do they see or know them in themselves, nor do they know them to be credible. The faithful, on the other hand, know them, not as by demonstration, but by the light of faith which makes them see that they ought to believe them, as stated above (A[4], ad 2,3).

Reply to Objection 2: The reasons employed by holy men to prove things that are of faith, are not demonstrations; they are either persuasive arguments showing that what is proposed to our faith is not impossible, or else they are proofs drawn from the principles of faith, i.e. from the authority of Holy Writ, as Dionysius declares (Div. Nom. ii). Whatever is based on these principles is as well proved in the eyes of the faithful, as a conclusion drawn from self-evident principles is in the eyes of all. Hence again, theology is a science, as we stated at the outset of this work (FP, Q[1], A[2]).

Reply to Objection 3: Things which can be proved by demonstration are reckoned among the articles of faith, not because they are believed simply by all, but because they are a necessary presupposition to matters of faith, so that those who do not known them by demonstration must know them first of all by faith.

Reply to Objection 4: As the Philosopher says (Poster. i), "science and opinion about the same object can certainly be in different men," as we have stated above about science and faith; yet it is possible for one and the same man to have science and faith about the same thing relatively, i.e. in relation to the object, but not in the same respect. For it is possible for the same person, about one and the same object, to know one thing and to think another: and, in like manner, one may know by demonstration the unity of the Godhead, and, by faith, the Trinity. On the other hand, in one and the same man, about the same object, and in the same respect, science is incompatible with either opinion or faith, yet for different reasons. Because science is incompatible with opinion about the same object simply, for the reason that science demands that its object should be deemed impossible to be otherwise, whereas it is essential to opinion, that its object should be deemed possible to be otherwise. Yet that which is the object of faith, on account of the certainty of faith, is also deemed impossible to be otherwise; and the reason why science and faith cannot be about the same object and in the same respect is because the object of science is something seen whereas the object of faith is the unseen, as stated above.

Summa Theologica

(First Part) Q12

How God is Known by us

Whether anyone in this life can see the essence of God?

Objection 1: It seems that one can in this life see the Divine essence. For Jacob said: "I have seen God face to face" (Gn. 32:30). But to see Him face to face is to see His essence, as appears from the words: "We see now in a glass and in a dark manner, but then face to face" (1 Cor. 13:12).

Objection 2: Further, the Lord said to Moses: "I speak to him mouth to mouth, and plainly, and not by riddles and figures doth he see the Lord" (Num. 12:8); but this is to see God in His essence. Therefore it is possible to see the essence of God in this life.

Objection 3: Further, that wherein we know all other things, and whereby we judge of other things, is known in itself to us. But even now we know all things in God; for Augustine says (Confess. viii): "If we both see that what you say is true, and we both see that what I say is true; where, I ask, do we see this? neither I in thee, nor thou in me; but both of us in the very incommutable truth itself above our minds." He also says (De Vera Relig. xxx) that, "We judge of all things according to the divine truth"; and (De Trin. xii) that, "it is the duty of reason to judge of these corporeal things according to the incorporeal and eternal ideas; which unless they were above the mind could not be incommutable." Therefore even in this life we see God Himself.

Objection 4: Further, according to Augustine (Gen. ad lit. xii, 24, 25), those things that are in the soul by their essence are seen by intellectual vision. But intellectual vision is of intelligible things, not by similitudes, but by their very essences, as he also says (Gen. ad lit. xiii, 24,25). Therefore since God is in our soul by His essence, it follows that He is seen by us in His essence.

On the contrary, It is written, "Man shall not see Me, and live" (Ex. 32:20), and a gloss upon this says, "In this mortal life God can be seen by certain images, but not by the likeness itself of His own nature."

I answer that, God cannot be seen in His essence by a mere human being, except he be separated from this mortal life. The reason is because, as was said above (A[4]), the mode of knowledge follows the mode of the nature of the knower. But our soul, as long as we live in this life, has its being in corporeal matter; hence naturally it knows only what has a form in matter, or what can be known by such a form. Now it is evident that the Divine essence cannot be known through the nature of material things. For it was shown above (AA[2],9) that the knowledge of God by means of any created similitude is not the vision of His essence. Hence it is impossible for the soul of man in this life to see the essence of God. This can be seen in the fact that the more our soul is abstracted from corporeal things, the more it is capable of receiving abstract intelligible things. Hence in dreams and alienations of the bodily senses divine revelations and foresight of future events are perceived the more clearly. It is not possible, therefore, that the soul in this mortal life should be raised up to the supreme of intelligible objects, i.e. to the divine essence.

Reply to Objection 1: According to Dionysius (Coel. Hier. iv) a man is said in the Scriptures to see God in the sense that certain figures are formed in the senses or imagination, according to some similitude representing in part the divinity. So when Jacob says, "I have seen God face to face," this does not mean the Divine essence, but some figure representing God. And this is to be referred to some high mode of prophecy, so that God seems to speak, though in an imaginary vision; as will later be explained (SS, Q[174]) in treating of the degrees of prophecy. We may also say that Jacob spoke thus to designate some exalted intellectual contemplation, above the ordinary state.

Reply to Objection 2: As God works miracles in corporeal things, so also He does supernatural wonders above the common order, raising the minds of some living in the flesh beyond the use of sense, even up to the vision of His own essence; as Augustine says (Gen. ad lit. xii, 26,27,28) of Moses, the teacher of the Jews; and of Paul, the teacher of the Gentiles. This will be treated more fully in the question of rapture (SS, Q[175]).

Reply to Objection 3: All things are said to be seen in God and all things are judged in Him, because by the participation of His light, we know and judge all things; for the light of natural reason itself is a participation of the divine light; as likewise we are said to see and judge of sensible things in the sun, i.e., by the sun's light. Hence Augustine says (Soliloq. i, 8), "The lessons of instruction can only be seen as it were by their own sun," namely God. As therefore in order to see a sensible object, it is not necessary to see the substance of the sun, so in like manner to see any intelligible object, it is not necessary to see the essence of God.

Reply to Objection 4: Intellectual vision is of the things which are in the soul by their essence, as intelligible things are in the intellect. And thus God is in the souls of the blessed; not thus is He in our soul, but by presence, essence and power.

Whether God can be known in this life by natural reason?

Objection 1: It seems that by natural reason we cannot know God in this life. For Boethius says (De Consol. v) that "reason does not grasp simple form." But God is a supremely simple form, as was shown above (Q[3], A[7]). Therefore natural reason cannot attain to know Him.

Objection 2: Further, the soul understands nothing by natural reason without the use of the imagination. But we cannot have an imagination of God, Who is incorporeal. Therefore we cannot know God by natural knowledge.

Objection 3: Further, the knowledge of natural reason belongs to both good and evil, inasmuch as they have a common nature. But the knowledge of God belongs only to the good; for Augustine says (De Trin. i): "The weak eye of the human mind is not fixed on that excellent light unless purified by the justice of faith." Therefore God cannot be known by natural reason.

On the contrary, It is written (Rom. 1:19), "That which is known of God," namely, what can be known of God by natural reason, "is manifest in them."

I answer that, Our natural knowledge begins from sense. Hence our natural knowledge can go as far as it can be led by sensible things. But our mind cannot be led by sense so far as to see the essence of God; because the sensible effects of God do not equal the power of God as their cause. Hence from the knowledge of sensible things the whole power of God cannot be known; nor therefore can His essence be seen. But because they are His effects and depend on their cause, we can be led from them so far as to know of God "whether He exists," and to know of Him what must necessarily belong to Him, as the first cause of all things, exceeding all things caused by Him.

Hence we know that His relationship with creatures so far as to be the cause of them all; also that creatures differ from Him, inasmuch as He is not in any way part of what is caused by Him; and that creatures are not removed from Him by reason of any defect on His part, but because He superexceeds them all.

Reply to Objection 1: Reason cannot reach up to simple form, so as to know "what it is"; but it can know "whether it is."

Reply to Objection 2: God is known by natural knowledge through the images of His effects.

Reply to Objection 3: As the knowledge of God's essence is by grace, it belongs only to the good; but the knowledge of Him by natural reason can belong to both good and bad; and hence Augustine says

(Retract. i), retracting what he had said before: "I do not approve what I said in prayer, 'God who willest that only the pure should know truth.' For it can be answered that many who are not pure can know many truths," i.e. by natural reason.

Whether by grace a higher knowledge of God can be obtained than by natural reason?

Objection 1: It seems that by grace a higher knowledge of God is not obtained than by natural reason. For Dionysius says (De Mystica Theol. i) that whoever is the more united to God in this life, is united to Him as to one entirely unknown. He says the same of Moses, who nevertheless obtained a certain excellence by the knowledge conferred by grace. But to be united to God while ignoring of Him "what He is," comes about also by natural reason. Therefore God is not more known to us by grace than by natural reason.

Objection 2: Further, we can acquire the knowledge of divine things by natural reason only through the imagination; and the same applies to the knowledge given by grace. For Dionysius says (Coel. Hier. i) that "it is impossible for the divine ray to shine upon us except as screened round about by the many colored sacred veils." Therefore we cannot know God more fully by grace than by natural reason.

Objection 3: Further, our intellect adheres to God by grace of faith. But faith does not seem to be knowledge; for Gregory says (Hom. xxvi in Ev.) that "things not seen are the objects of faith, and not of knowledge." Therefore there is not given to us a more excellent knowledge of God by grace.

On the contrary, The Apostle says that "God hath revealed to us His spirit," what "none of the princes of this world knew" (1 Cor. 2:10), namely, the philosophers, as the gloss expounds.

I answer that, We have a more perfect knowledge of God by grace than by natural reason. Which is proved thus. The knowledge which we have by natural reason contains two things: images derived from the sensible objects; and the natural intelligible light, enabling us to abstract from them intelligible conceptions.

Now in both of these, human knowledge is assisted by the revelation of grace. For the intellect's natural light is strengthened by the infusion of gratuitous light; and sometimes also the images in the human imagination are divinely formed, so as to express divine things better than those do which we receive from sensible objects, as appears in prophetic visions; while sometimes sensible things, or even voices, are divinely formed to express some divine meaning; as in the Baptism, the Holy Ghost was seen in the shape of a dove, and the voice of the Father was heard, "This is My beloved Son" (Mat. 3:17).

Reply to Objection 1: Although by the revelation of grace in this life we cannot know of God "what He is," and thus are united to Him as to one unknown; still we know Him more fully according as many and more excellent of His effects are demonstrated to us, and according as we attribute to Him some things known by divine revelation, to which natural reason cannot reach, as, for instance, that God is Three and One.

Reply to Objection 2: From the images either received from sense in the natural order, or divinely formed in the imagination, we have so much the more excellent intellectual knowledge, the stronger the intelligible light is in man; and thus through the revelation given by the images a fuller knowledge is received by the infusion of the divine light.

Reply to Objection 3: Faith is a kind of knowledge, inasmuch as the intellect is determined by faith to some knowable object. But this determination to one object does not proceed from the vision of the believer, but from the vision of Him who is believed. Thus as far as faith falls short of vision, it falls short of the knowledge which belongs to science, for science determines the intellect to one object by the vision and understanding of first principles.

Blaise Pascal (1623-1662)

Pensées

233. We know that there is an infinite, and are ignorant of its nature. As we know it to be false that numbers are finite, it is therefore true that there is an infinity in number. But we do not know what it is. It is false that it is even, it is false that it is odd; for the addition of a unit can make no change in its nature. Yet it is a number, and every number is odd or even (this is certainly true of every finite number). So we may well know that there is a God without knowing what He is. Is there not one substantial truth, seeing there are so many things which are not the truth itself?

We know then the existence and nature of the finite, because we also are finite and have extension. We know the existence of the infinite and are ignorant of its nature, because it has extension like us, but not limits like us. But we know neither the existence nor the nature of God, because He has neither extension nor limits.

But by faith we know His existence; in glory we shall know His nature. Now, I have already shown that we may well know the existence of a thing, without knowing its nature.

Let us now speak according to natural lights.

If there is a God, He is infinitely incomprehensible, since, having neither parts nor limits, He has no affinity to us. We are then incapable of knowing either what He is or if He is. This being so, who will dare to undertake the decision of the question? Not we, who have no affinity to Him.

Who then will blame Christians for not being able to give a reason for their belief, since they profess a religion for which they cannot give a reason? They declare, in expounding it to the world, that it is a foolishness, *stultitiam*;[1] and then you complain that they do not prove it! If they proved it, they would not keep their word; it is in lacking proofs that they are not lacking in sense. "Yes, but although this excuses those who offer it as such and takes away from them the blame of putting it forward without reason, it does not excuse those who receive it." Let us then examine this point, and say, "God is, or He

_____

[1] 1 Corinthians 1:21

is not." But to which side shall we incline? Reason can decide nothing here. There is an infinite chaos which separated us. A game is being played at the extremity of this infinite distance where heads or tails will turn up. What will you wager? According to reason, you can do neither the one thing nor the other; according to reason, you can defend neither of the propositions.

Do not, then, reprove for error those who have made a choice; for you know nothing about it. "No, but I blame them for having made, not this choice, but a choice; for again both he who chooses heads and he who chooses tails are equally at fault, they are both in the wrong. The true course is not to wager at all."

Yes; but you must wager. It is not optional. You are embarked. Which will you choose then? Let us see. Since you must choose, let us see which interests you least. You have two things to lose, the true and the good; and two things to stake, your reason and your will, your knowledge and your happiness; and your nature has two things to shun, error and misery. Your reason is no more shocked in choosing one rather than the other, since you must of necessity choose. This is one point settled. But your happiness? Let us weigh the gain and the loss in wagering that God is. Let us estimate these two chances. If you gain, you gain all; if you lose, you lose nothing. Wager, then, without hesitation that He is. "That is very fine. Yes, I must wager; but I may perhaps wager too much." Let us see. Since there is an equal risk of gain and of loss, if you had only to gain two lives, instead of one, you might still wager. But if there were three lives to gain, you would have to play (since you are under the necessity of playing), and you would be imprudent, when you are forced to play, not to chance your life to gain three at a game where there is an equal risk of loss and gain. But there is an eternity of life and happiness. And this being so, if there were an infinity of chances, of which one only would be for you, you would still be right in wagering one to win two, and you would act stupidly, being obliged to play, by refusing to stake one life against three at a game in which out of an infinity of chances there is one for you, if there were an infinity of an infinitely happy life to gain. But there is here an infinity of an infinitely happy life to gain, a chance of gain against a finite number of chances of loss, and what you stake is finite. It is all divided; where-ever the infinite is and there is not an infinity of chances of loss against that of gain, there is no time to hesitate, you must give all. And thus, when one is forced to play, he must renounce reason to preserve his life, rather than risk it for infinite gain, as likely to happen as the loss of nothingness.

For it is no use to say it is uncertain if we will gain, and it is certain that we risk, and that the infinite distance between the certainly of what is staked and the uncertainty of what will be gained, equals the finite good which is certainly staked against the uncertain infinite. It is not so, as every player stakes a certainty to gain an uncertainty, and yet he stakes a finite certainty to gain a finite uncertainty, without transgressing against reason. There is not an infinite distance between the certainty staked and the uncertainty of the gain; that is untrue. In truth, there is an infinity between the certainty of gain and the certainty of loss. But the uncertainty of the gain is proportioned to the certainty of the stake according to the proportion of the chances of gain and loss. Hence it comes that, if there are as many risks on one side as on the other, the course is to play even; and then the certainty of the stake is equal to the uncertainty of the gain, so far is it from fact that there is an infinite distance between them. And so our proposition is of infinite force, when there is the finite to stake in a game where there are equal risks of gain and of loss, and the infinite to gain. This is demonstrable; and if men are capable of any truths, this is one.

"I confess it, I admit it. But, still, is there no means of seeing the faces of the cards?" Yes, Scripture and the rest, etc. "Yes, but I have my hands tied and my mouth closed; I am forced to wager, and am not free. I am not released, and am so made that I cannot believe. What, then, would you have me do?"

True. But at least learn your inability to believe, since reason brings you to this, and yet you cannot believe. Endeavour, then, to convince yourself, not by increase of proofs of God, but by the abatement of your passions. You would like to attain faith and do not know the way; you would like to cure yourself of unbelief and ask the remedy for it. Learn of those who have been bound like you, and who now stake all their possessions. These are people who know the way which you would follow, and who are cured of an ill of which you would be cured. Follow the way by which they began; by acting as if they believed, taking the holy water, having masses said, etc. Even this will naturally make you believe, and deaden your acuteness. "But this is what I am afraid of." And why? What have you to lose?

But to show you that this leads you there, it is this which will lessen the passions, which are your stumbling-blocks.

The end of this discourse. — Now, what harm will befall you in taking this side? You will be faithful, humble, grateful, generous, a sincere friend, truthful. Certainly you will not have those poisonous pleasures, glory and luxury; but will you not have others? I will tell you that you will thereby gain in this life, and that, at each step you take on this road, you will see so great certainty of gain, so much nothingness in what you risk, that you will at last recognise that you have wagered for something certain and infinite, for which you have given nothing. "Ah! This discourse transports me, charms me," etc.

If this discourse pleases you and seems impressive, know that it is made by a man who has knelt, both before and after it, in prayer to that Being, infinite and without parts, before whom he lays all he has, for you also to lay before Him all you have for your own good and for His glory, that so strength may be given to lowliness.

234. **If we must not act save on a certainty, we ought not to act on religion, for it is not certain. But how many things we do on an uncertainty, sea voyages, battles! I say then we must do nothing at all, for nothing is certain,** and that there is more certainty in religion than there is as to whether we may see to-morrow; for it is not certain that we may see to-morrow, and it is certainly possible that we may not, see it. We cannot say as much about religion. It is not certain that it is; but who will venture to say that it is certainly possible that it is not? Now when we work for to-morrow, and so on an uncertainty, we act reasonably; for we ought to work for an uncertainty according to the doctrine of chance which was demonstrated above.

Saint Augustine has seen that we work for an uncertainty, on sea, in battle, etc. But he has not seen the doctrine of chance which proves that we should do so. Montaigne has seen that we are shocked at a fool, and that habit is all-powerful; but he has not seen the reason of this effect. All these persons have seen the effects, but they have not seen the causes. They are, in comparison with those who have discovered the causes, as those who have only eyes are in comparison with those who have intellect. For the effects are perceptible by sense, and the causes are visible only to the intellect. And although these effects are seen by the mind, this mind is, in comparison with the mind which sees the causes, as the bodily senses are in comparison with the intellect.

Section IV: On the Means of Belief

243. **It is an astounding fact that no canonical writer has ever made use of nature to prove God.** They all strive to make us believe in Him. David, Solomon, etc., have never said, "There is no void, therefore there is a God." They must have had more knowledge than the most learned people who came after them, and who have all made use of this argument. This is worthy of attention.

244. "Why! Do you not say yourself that the heavens and birds prove God?" No. "And does your religion not say so"? No. For although it is true in a sense for some souls to whom God gives this light, yet it is false with respect to the majority of men.

245. There are three sources of belief: reason, custom, inspiration. The Christian religion, which alone has reason, does not acknowledge as her true children those who believe without inspiration. It is not that she excludes reason and custom. On the contrary, the mind must be opened to proofs, must be

confirmed by custom and offer itself in humbleness to inspirations, which alone can produce a true and saving effect. *Ne evacuetur crux Christi*.[2]

248. A letter which indicates the use of proofs by the machine. — **Faith is different from proof**; the one is human, the other is a gift of God. *Justus ex fide vivit*.[3] It is this faith that God Himself puts into the heart, of which the proof is often the instrument, *fides ex auditu*[4]; but this faith is in the heart, and makes us not say *scio*, [I know] but *credo*. [I believe]

263. "A miracle," says one, "would strengthen my faith." He says so when he does not see one. Reasons, seen from afar, appear to limit our view; but when they are reached, we begin to see beyond. Nothing stops the nimbleness of our mind. There is no rule, say we, which has not some exceptions, no truth so general which has not some aspect in which it fails. It is sufficient that it be not absolutely universal to give us a pretext for applying the exceptions to the present subject and for saying, "This is not always true; there are therefore cases where it is not so." It only remains to show that this is one of them; and that is why we are very awkward or unlucky, if we do not find one some day.

265. Faith indeed tells what the senses do not tell, but not the contrary of what they see. It is above them and not contrary to them.

268. Submission. — We must know where to doubt, where to feel certain, where to submit. He who does not do so understands not the force of reason. There are some who offend against these three rules, either by affirming everything as demonstrative, from want of knowing what demonstration is; or by doubting everything, from want of knowing where to submit; or by submitting in everything, from want of knowing where they must judge.

269. Submission is the use of reason in which consists true Christianity.

270. Saint Augustine. — Reason would never submit, if it did not judge that there are some occasions on which it ought to submit. It is then right for it to submit, when it judges that it ought to submit.

---

[2] 1 Cor. 1:17. "Lest the cross of Christ should be made of none effect."
[3] Rom. 1:17. "The just shall live by faith."
[4] Rom. 10:17. "Faith cometh by hearing.

273. If we submit everything to reason, our religion will have no mysterious and supernatural element. If we offend the principles of reason, our religion will be absurd and ridiculous.

274. All our reasoning reduces itself to yielding to feeling.

But fancy is like, though contrary to, feeling, so that we cannot distinguish between these contraries. One person says that my feeling is fancy, another that his fancy is feeling. We should have a rule. Reason offers itself; but it is pliable in every sense; and thus there is no rule.

275. Men often take their imagination for their heart; and they believe they are converted as soon as they think of being converted.

276. M. de Roannez said: "Reasons come to me afterwards, but at first a thing pleases or shocks me without my knowing the reason, and yet it shocks me for that reason which I only discover afterwards." But I believe, not that it shocked him for the reasons which were found afterwards, but that these reasons were only found because it shocked him.

277. The heart has its reasons, which reason does not know. We feel it in a thousand things. I say that the heart naturally loves the Universal Being, and also itself naturally, according as it gives itself to them; and it hardens itself against one or the other at its will. You have rejected the one and kept the other. Is it by reason that you love yourself?

278. It is the heart which experiences God, and not the reason. This, then, is faith: God felt by the heart, not by the reason.

Faith is a gift of God; do not believe that we said it was a gift of reasoning. Other religions do not say this of their faith. They only give reasoning in order to arrive at it, and yet it does not bring them to it.

279. Faith is a gift of God; do not believe that we said it was a gift of reasoning. Other religions do not say this of their faith. They only gave reasoning in order to arrive at it, and yet it does not bring them to it.

280. The knowledge of God is very far from the love of Him.

Alfred Lord Tennyson (1808-1892)

Prologue from In Memoriam A.H.H.

Strong Son of God, immortal Love,
Whom we, that have not seen thy face,
By faith, and faith alone, embrace,
Believing where we cannot prove;

Thine are these orbs of light and shade;
Thou madest Life in man and brute;
Thou madest Death; and lo, thy foot
Is on the skull which thou hast made.

Thou wilt not leave us in the dust:
Thou madest man, he knows not why,
He thinks he was not made to die;
And thou hast made him: thou art just.

Thou seemest human and divine,
The highest, holiest manhood, thou.
Our wills are ours, we know not how;
Our wills are ours, to make them thine.

Our little systems have their day;
They have their day and cease to be:
They are but broken lights of thee,
And thou, O Lord, art more than they.

We have but faith: we cannot know;
For knowledge is of things we see
And yet we trust it comes from thee,
A beam in darkness: let it grow.

Let knowledge grow from more to more,

But more of reverence in us dwell;

That mind and soul, according well,

May make one music as before,

But vaster. We are fools and slight;

We mock thee when we do not fear:

But help thy foolish ones to bear;

Help thy vain worlds to bear thy light.

Forgive what seem'd my sin in me;

What seem'd my worth since I began;

For merit lives from man to man,

And not from man, O Lord, to thee.

Forgive my grief for one removed,

Thy creature, whom I found so fair.

I trust he lives in thee, and there

I find him worthier to be loved.

Forgive these wild and wandering cries,

Confusions of a wasted youth;

Forgive them where they fail in truth,

And in thy wisdom make me wise.

(Prologue composed 1849)

William Kingdom Clifford (1845-1879)

The Ethics of Belief

1 – The Duty of Inquiry

A Shipowner was about to send to sea an emigrant-ship. He knew that she was old, and not over-well built at the first; that she had seen many seas and climes, and often had needed repairs. Doubts had been suggested to him that possibly she was not seaworthy. These doubts preyed upon his mind, and made him unhappy; he thought that perhaps he ought to have her thoroughly overhauled and refitted, even though this should put him to great expense. Before the ship sailed, however, he succeeded in overcoming these melancholy reflections. He said to himself that she had gone safely through so many voyages and weathered so many storms, that it was idle to suppose she would not come safely home from this trip also. He would put his trust in Providence, which could hardly fail to protect all these unhappy families that were leaving their fatherland to seek for better times elsewhere. He would dismiss from his mind all ungenerous suspicions about the honesty of builders and contractors. In such ways he acquired a sincere and comfortable conviction that his vessel was thoroughly safe and seaworthy; he watched her departure with a light heart, and benevolent wishes for the success of the exiles in their strange new home that was to be ; and he got his insurance-money when she went down in mid-ocean and told no tales.

What shall we say of him? Surely this, that he was verily guilty of the death of those men. It is admitted that he did sincerely believe in the soundness of his ship; but the sincerity of his conviction can in nowise help him, because he had no right to believe on such evidence as was before him. He had acquired his belief not by honestly earning it in patient investigation, but by stifling his doubts. And although in the end he may have felt so sure about it that he could not think otherwise, yet inasmuch as he had knowingly and willingly worked himself into that frame of mind, he must be held responsible for it.

Let us alter the case a little, and suppose that the ship was not unsound after all; that she made her voyage safely, and many others after it. Will that diminish the guilt of her owner? Not one jot. When an action is once done, it is right or wrong for ever; no accidental failure of its good or evil fruits can possibly alter that . The man would not have been innocent, he would only have been not found out.

The question of right or wrong has to do with the origin of his belief, not the matter of it; not what it was, but how he got it; not whether it turned out to be true or false, but whether he had a a right to believe on such evidence as was before him.[…] It may be said, however, that …it is not the belief which is judged to be wrong, but the action following upon it. The shipowner might say, "I am perfectly certain that my ship is sound, but still I feel it my duty to have her examined, before trusting the lives of so many people to her." …

[I]t is not possible so to sever the belief from the action it suggests as to condemn the one without condemning the other. No man holding a strong belief on one side of a question, or even wishing to hold a belief on one side, can investigate it with such fairness and completeness as if he were really in doubt and unbiassed; so that the existence of a belief, not founded on fair inquiry, unfits a man for the performance of this necessary duty. Nor is that truly a belief at all which has not some influence upon the actions of him who holds it. He who truly believes that which prompts him to an action has looked upon the action to lust after it, he has committed it already in his heart… No real belief, however trifling and fragmentary it may seem, is ever truly insignificant; it prepares us to receive more of its like, confirms those which resembled it before, and weakens others; and so gradually it lays a stealthy train in our inmost thoughts, which may some day explode into overt action, and leave its stamp upon our character for ever.

And no one man's belief is in any case a private matter which concerns himself alone. Our lives are guided by that general conception of the course of things which has been created by society for social purposes. Our words, our phrases, our forms and processes and modes of thought, are common property, fashioned and perfected from age to age ; an heirloom, which every succeeding generation inherits as a precious deposit and a sacred trust, to be handed on to the next one, not unchanged, but enlarged and purified, with some clear marks of its proper handiwork. Into this, for good or ill, is woven every belief of every man who has speech of his fellows. An awful privilege, and an awful responsibility, that we should help to create the world in which posterity will live.

In the [case of the Shipowner] it has been judged wrong to believe on insufficient evidence, or to nourish belief by suppressing doubts and avoiding investigation. The reason of this judgment is not far to seek; it is that in both these cases the belief held by one man was of great importance to other men. But forasmuch as **no belief held by one man, however seemingly trivial the belief**, and however obscure the believer, **is** over actually insignificant or **without its effect on the fate of mankind**, we have no choice but to extend our judgment to all cases of belief whatever. Belief, that sacred faculty, which prompts the decisions of our will, and knits into harmonious working all the compacted energies of our being, is ours not for ourselves but for humanity[...]

It is not only the leader of men, statesman, philosopher, or poet, that owes this bounden duty to mankind. Every rustic who delivers in the village alehouse his slow, infrequent sentences, may help to kill or keep alive the fatal superstitions which clog his race. Every hard-worked wife of an artisan may transmit to her children beliefs which shall knit society together, or rend it in pieces. No simplicity of mind, no obscurity of station, can escape the universal duty of questioning all that we believe.[...]

The harm which is done by credulity in a man is not confined to the fostering of a credulous character in others, and consequent support of false beliefs. Habitual want of care about what I believe leads to habitual want of care in others about the truth of what is told to me. Men speak the truth to one another when each reveres the truth in his own mind and in the other's mind; but how shall my friend revere the truth in my mind when I myself am careless about it, when I believe things because I want to believe them, and because they are comforting and pleasant ? Will he not learn to cry, " Peace," to me, when there is no peace ? By such a course I shall surround myself with a thick atmosphere of falsehood and fraud, and in that I must live. It may matter little to me, in my cloud-castle of sweet illusions and darling lies; but it matters much to Man that I have made my neighbours ready to deceive. The credulous man is father to the liar and the cheat; he lives in the bosom of this his family, and it is no marvel if he should become even as they are... **To sum up: it is wrong always, everywhere, and for anyone, to believe anything upon insufficient evidence.** [...]

It may be permitted me to fortify this judgment with the sentence of Milton[1] —

> A man may be a heretic in the truth; and if he believe things only because his pastor says so, or the assembly so determine, without knowing other reason, though his belief be true, yet the very truth he holds becomes his heresy.

And with this famous aphorism of Coleridge:[2]

> He who begins by loving Christianity better than Truth, will proceed by loving his own sect or Church better than Christianity, and end in loving himself better than all.

Inquiry into the evidence of a doctrine is not to be made once for all, and then taken as finally settled. It is never lawful to stifle a doubt; for either it can be honestly answered by means of the inquiry already made, or else it proves that the inquiry was not complete.

" But," says one, " I am a busy man; I have no time for the long course of study which would be

---

[1] Areopagitica
[2] Aids to Reflection

necessary to make me in any degree a competent judge of certain questions, or even able to understand the nature of the arguments." Then he should have no time to believe.

2: The Weight of Authority

The goodness and greatness of a man do not justify us in accepting a belief upon the warrant of his authority, unless there are reasonable grounds for supposing that he knew the truth of what he was saying. And there can be no grounds for supposing that a man knows that which we, without ceasing to be men, could not be supposed to verify.

If a chemist tells me, who am no chemist, that a certain substance can be made by putting together other substances in certain proportions and subjecting them to a known process, I am quite justified in believing this upon his authority, unless I know anything against his character or his judgment. For his professional training is one which tends to encourage veracity and the honest pursuit of truth, and to produce a dislike of hasty conclusions and slovenly investigation. And I have reasonable ground for supposing that he knows the truth of what he is saying, for although I am no chemist, I can be made to understand so much of the methods and processes of the science as makes it conceivable to me that, without ceasing to be man, I might verify the statement. I may never actually verify it, or even see any experiment which goes towards verifying it; but still I have quite reason enough to justify me in believing that the verification is within the reach of human appliances and powers, and in particular that it has been actually performed by my informant. His result, the belief to which he has been led by his inquiries, is valid not only for himself but for others; it is watched and tested by those who are working in the same ground, and who know that no greater service can be rendered to science than the purification of accepted results from the errors which may have crept into them. It is in this way that the result becomes common property, a right object of belief, which is a social affair and matter of public business. Thus it is to be observed that his authority is valid because there are those who question it and verify it; that it is precisely this process of examining and purifying that keeps alive among investigators the love of that which shall stand all possible tests, the sense of public responsibility as of those whose work, if well done, shall remain as the enduring heritage of mankind.

But if my chemist tells me that an atom of oxygen has existed unaltered in weight and rate of vibration throughout all time, I have no right to believe this on his authority, for it is a thing which he cannot know without ceasing to be man. He may quite honestly believe that this statement is a fair inference from his experiments, but in that case his judgment is at fault. A very simple consideration of the character of **experiments** would show him that they **never can lead to results of such a kind; that being themselves only approximate and limited, they cannot give us knowledge which is exact and**

universal. No eminence of character and genius can give a man authority enough to justify us in believing him when he makes statements implying exact or universal knowledge. […]

[T]he aggregate testimony of our neighbours is subject to the same conditions as the testimony of any one of them. Namely, **we have no right to believe a thing true because everybody says so**, unless there are good grounds for believing that some one person at least has the means of knowing what is true, and is speaking the truth so far as he knows it. However many nations and generations of men are brought into the witness-box, they cannot testify to anything which they do not know. Every man who has accepted the statement from somebody else, without himself testing and verifying it, is out of court; his word is worth nothing at all. And when we get back at last to the true birth and beginning of the statement, two serious questions must be disposed of in regard to him who first made it: was he mistaken in thinking that he *knew* about this matter, or was he lying ? […]

A question rightly asked is already half answered, said Jacobi; we may add that the method of solution is the other half of the answer, and that the actual result counts for nothing by the side of these two. For an example let us go to the telegraph, where theory and practice, grown each to years of discretion, are marvellously wedded for the fruitful service of men. Ohm found that the strength of an electric current is directly proportional to the strength of the battery which produces it, and inversely as the length of the wire along which it has to travel. This is called Ohm's law; but the result, regarded as a statement to be believed, is not the valuable part of it. The first half is the question : what relation holds good between these quantities? So put, the question involves already the conception of strength of current, and of strength of battery, as quantities to be measured and compared; it hints clearly that these are the things to be attended to in the study of electric currents. The second half is the method of investigation ; how to measure these quantities, what apparatus are required for the experiment, and how are they to be used? **The student who begins to leam about electricity is not asked to believe in Ohm's law; he is made to understand the question, he is placed before the apparatus, and he is taught to verify it.** He learns to do things, not to think he knows things; to use instruments and to ask questions, not to accept a traditional statement. The question which required a genius to ask it rightly is answered by a tiro. If Ohm's law were suddenly lost and forgotten by all men, while the question and the method of solution remained, the result could be rediscovered in an hour. But the result by itself, if known to a people who could not comprehend the value of the question or the means of solving it, would be like a watch in the hands of a savage who could not wind it up, or an iron steamship worked by Spanish engineers.

In regard, then, to the sacred tradition of humanity, we learn that it consists, not in propositions or statements which are to be accepted and belieA-ed on the authority of the tradition, but in questions rightly asked, in conceptions which enable us to ask further questions, and in methods of answering questions. The value of all these things depends on their being tested day by day. The very sacredness of the precious deposit imposes upon us the duty and the responsibility of testing it, of purifying and enlarging it to the utmost of our power.

3 – The Limits of Inference

The question, in what cases we may believe that which goes beyond our experience, is a very large and delicate one, extending to the whole range of scientific method, and requiring a considerable increase in the application of it before it can be answered with anything approaching to completeness. But one rule, lying on the threshold of the subject, of extreme simplicity and A'ast practical importance, may here be touched upon and shortly laid down.

A little reflection will show us that every belief, even the simplest and most fundamental, goes beyond experience when regarded as a guide to our actions. A burnt child dreads the fire, because it believes that the fire will burn it to-day just as it did yesterday ; but this belief goes beyond experience, and assumes that the un- known fire of to-day is like the known fire of yesterday. Even the belief that the child was burnt yesterday goes beyond *present* experience, which contains only the memory of a burning, and not the burning itself; it assumes, therefore, that this memory is trustworthy, although we know that a memory may often be mis- taken. But if it is to be used as a guide of action, as a hint of what the future is to be, it must assume something about that future, namely, that it will be consistent with the supposition that the burning really took place yesterday; which is going beyond experience. Even the fundamental "I am," which cannot be doubted, is no guide to action until it takes to itself " I shall be," which goes beyond experience. The question is not, therefore, "May we believe what goes beyond experience?" for this is mvolved in the very nature of belief; but " How far and in what manner may we add to our experience in forming our beliefs ?"

And an answer, of utter simplicity and universality, is suggested by the example we have taken: a burnt child dreads the fire. We may go beyond experience by assuming that what we do not know is like what we do know ; or, in other words, we may add to our experience on the assumption of a uniformity in nature. What this uniformity precisely is, how we grow in the knowledge of it from generation to generation, these are questions which for the present we lay aside, being content to examine two instances which may serve to make plainer the nature of the rule. […]

For another example, let us consider the way in which we infer the truth of an historical event—say the siege of Syracuse in the Peloponnesian war. Our experience is that manuscripts exist which are said to be and which call themselves manuscripts of the history of Thucydides; that in other manuscripts, stated to be by later historians, he is described as living during the time of the War ; and that books, supposed to date from the revival of learning, tell us how these manuscripts had been preserved and were then acquired. We find also that men do not, as a rule, forge books and histories without a special motive ; we assume that in this respect men in the past were like men in the present; and we observe that in this case no special motive was present. That is, we add to our experience on the assumption of a uniformity in the characters of men. Because our knowledge of this uniformity is far less complete and exact than our knowledge of that which obtains in physics, inferences of the historical kind are more precarious and less exact than inferences in many other sciences. But if there is any special reason to suspect the character of the persons who wrote or transmitted certain books, the case becomes altered. If a group of documents give internal evidence that they were produced among people who forged books in the names of others, and who, in describing events, suppressed those things which did not suit them, while they amplified such as did suit them; who not only committed these crimes, but gloried in them as proofs of humility and zeal; then we must say that upon such documents no true historical inference can be founded, but only unsatisfactory conjecture.[…]

No evidence, therefore, can justify us in believing the truth of a statement which is contrary to, or outside of, the uniformity of nature.

To sum up:-

We may believe what goes beyond our experience, only when it is inferred from that experience by the assumption that what we do not know is like what we know.

We may believe the statement of another person, when there is reasonable ground for supposing that he knows the matter of which he speaks, and that he is speaking the truth so far as he knows it.

It is wrong in all cases to believe on insufficient evidence; and where it is presumption to doubt and to investigate, there it is worse than presumption to believe.

Karl Barth (1886-1968) and

Adolf von Harnack (1851-1930)

Revelation and Theology

The following is extracted from a series of correspondence between the two theologians. It was published in the German journal Christliche Welt *in 1923.*

The following text is from H Martin Rumscheidt's *doctoral thesis on the Barth-Harnack correspondence and explains some of the background. Karl Barth had been taught at the University of Berlin by Harnack in 1906 and was impressed with him but, two years later, Barth studied in Marburg under Wilhelm Herrmann.*

And here we must begin to trace the development that led Barth away from Harnack, for it was Herrmamn and not Harnack who became Barth's most revered and influential teacher. rom hill, whom Barth later called "the most pious of liberal theologians of his day", Barth learned the concept or doctrine of the **autopistia of faith. Its basic factors are the absolute transcendence of God and the impossibility of proving his existence scientifically. Faith is in no need of an ancillary science for its legitimization.** In Barth's theology this teaching became of fundamental importance for, as he is reported to have said, it is "the rat-poison against all sophistry (Spitzfindiglceiten) in theology." It is probably this teaching which Barth has in mind when he remarked that "Herrmann is the one from whom l have learned something most basic, something which, once l followed
it to its caused me to say everything else in a wholly different way, even to interpret that most basic matter quite differently from him."

It appears therefore that at Herrmann's feet Barth learned something which led him to a change in direction, something which caused him to stop and to reconsider his theological thinking. In other words, here is the beginning of Barth's differences with his previous teacher Harnack. Here begins the course which led Barth from being an enthusiastic pupil of Harnack's to that position which the latter called 'a despiser- of scientific theology"

Herrmann opposed what he called the intellectual interpretation of religion. What he has in mind is the cognition of God through the traditional proofs of his existence or through any other means of scientific cognition of objects. In an address to the Studentenkonferenz at Aarau in 1908 he said: **"A God who has been proven to exist is of the world and a God of the world is an idol."** Fifteen years later Barth wrote these words to Harnack: " One must not have any delusions that faith is an unprecedented event, that one must speak of the Holy Spirit here, if not all the objections Herrmann crammed us against 'mere credence of historical factors' apart from this basis of cognition are justified." The reference is to Herrmann's view that the God of faith is not a demonstrable reality or even a demonstrable possibility because God is God and not an object or subject like those of the world.

*

First Letter:

Harnack to Barth

FIFTEEN QUESTIONS TO THE DESPISERS OF SCIENTIFIC THEOLOGY

1) Is the religion of the Bible or its revelations so completely a unity that in relation to faith, worship and life one may simply speak of 'the Bible'? If this is not so may one leave the understanding of the content of the gospel solely to the individual's heuristic[1] knowledge, to his subjective 'experience', or does one not rather need historical knowledge here and critical reflection?

2) Is the religion of the Bible or its revelations so completely a unity and so clear that historical knowledge and critical reflection are not needed for a correct understanding their meaning? Or are they the converse , namely so incomprehensible and indescribable that one must simply wait until they radiate out in man's heart because no faculty of man's soul or mind can grasp them? Are not both these assumptions false? Do we not need for an understanding of the Bible next to an inner openness historical knowledge and critical reflection!

3) Is the experience of God different from the awakening of faith or identical with it? If it is different, what distinguishes it from uncontrollable fanaticism? If it is identical, how can it come about other than through the preaching of the gospel? And how can there be such preaching without historical knowledge and critical reflection?

4) If God and the world (life in God and life in the world) are complete opposites, how does education in Godliness, that is in goodness become possible? But how is education without historical knowledge and the highest valuation of morality?

---

[1] i.e. enabling someone to discover and learn for him/herself

8) If Goethe's Kant's conception of God or related points of view are merely opposites of the real statements of . Goâ, how can it be avoided that these statements are given over to barbarism?

9) But if the converse is true, namely that here as in all physical and spiritual development opposites are at one and the same time steps and steps are opposites, how can this basic knowledge be grasped and developed without historical knowledge and critical reflection?

10) If the knowledge that God is love is the highest and final knowledge of God and if love, joy and peace are his sphere, how may one forever remain between door and hinge, how may one give autonomous standing to what are transition points in Christian experience and thus perpetuate their dread?

14) If the person of Christ Jesus stands at the centre of the gospel, how else can the basis for a reliable and communal know- ledge of this person be gained but through critical-historical study so that an imagined Christ is not put in place of the real one? What else besides scientific theology is able to undertake this study?

Berlin-Grünewald   Adolf von Harnack

Second Letter:

Barth to Harnack

FIFTEEN ANSWERS TO PROFESSOR VON HARNACK

In reference to the title (of your questions): someone objecting to that form of Protestant theology which has become determinative since Pietism and the Enlightenment, especially during the last fifty years of German history, is not necessarily a "despiser of scientific theology." The point of the objection is that this particular theology might have moved f'urther f'rom its theme than is good. (The Reformation was the last instance where it was stated clearly).

1) **The one revelation of God might be considered as the theme of theology and this beyond the 'religion' and the 'revelations' of the Bible.** 'Historical knowledge' could tell us that the communication of the 'content of the gospel' can be accomplished, according to the assertion of the gospel itself', only through an aet of this 'content' itself. But 'critical reflection' could lead to the conclusion this assertion is founded in the essence of the matter (the relation of God and man) and is therefore to be seriously respected. The 'scientific character' of theology would then be its

adherence to the recollection that its object *was once subject* and must become that again and again, which has nothing to do whatever with 'one's heuristic knowledge' and 'experience' per se.

2) 'Inner openness, heuristic knowledge, experience, heart' and the like on the one hand and 'historical knowledge and critical reflection' on the other are possibilities which can be equally helpful, irrelevant or obstructive to the 'understanding' of the Bible. It is understood through neither this nor that 'function of the soul or mind' but through that spirit which is identical with the content of the Bible and that by faith!

3) The so-called 'experience of God' is therefore as different as heaven and earth from the faith awakened by God and is indeed indistinguishable from 'uncontrolled fanaticism'. But why *could* it not be a more distinct or more confused symptom of and a testimony to the awakening of faith? Faith does indeed come about through preaching, but preaching comes about through 'the Word of the Christ' (no matter in what state the preacher's historical knowledge and critical reflection are). The task of theology is at one with the task of preaching. It consists in the reception and transmission of the Word of the Christ. Why should 'historical knowledge and critical reflection' not be of preparatory service in this?

4) The faith awakened by God will never be able to avoid completely the necessity of a more or less radical protest against this world as surely as it is a hope for the promised but invisible gift. A theology, should it lose the understanding of the basic distance which faith posits between itself and this *world* would in the same measure have to lose from sight the knowledge of God the creator. For **the 'utter contrast' of God and the world, the cross, is the only way in which we as human beings can consider the original and final unity of creator and creature**. Sophistry is not the realisation that even our protest against the world cannot justify us before God. It is rather the common attempt to bypass the cross by means of a shallow doctrine of creation.

8) 'Real statements about God' are made in any way only where one is aware of being confronted by revelation and therefore of being placed under judgment instead of believing oneself to be on a pinnacle of culture or religion. Under this judgment stand with all other statements about this subject also those of Goethe and Kant. Schleiermacher's alarm about 'barbarism' is to be rejected as non-essential and irrelevant because the gospel has as much and as little to do with 'barbarism' as with culture.

9) It may be that in the sphere of human statements about God 'opposites are at one and the same time steps and steps are opposites, as in all physical and spiritual development', yet it is still true

that between God's truth (which may be expressed in human terms also) and truth there is only contrast, only an either - or. (It is more urgent, for theology in any case, to 'grasp' and to 'develop' this knowledge!) Humility, yearning and supplication will always be the first and also the last thing *for us.* The way from the old to the new world not a not a stairway, *not* a development in any sense whatsoever; it is a being born anew.

10) If the knowledge that 'God is love' is the highest and final knowledge about God, how can one consistently pretend to be in possession of it? Is not the 'transition point' just as long in duration as time? Is not our faith also unfaith? Or should we believe in our *faith*? Does not faith live by being faith in God's *promise*? Are we saved in a way other than in *hope*?

14) The reliability and communality of the knowledge of the person of Jesus Christ as the centre of the gospel can be none other than that of the God-awakened faith. Critical-historical study stands for the necessary end of those 'foundations' of this knowledge which are no foundations at all since they have not been laid by God himself. Whoever should not yet know (and still we all do not yet know it) that we *no* longer know Christ according to the flesh might let the critical study of the Bible tell him so. The more radically he is frightened the better for him and the matter involved might then turn out to be the service which 'historical knowledge' can render to the actual task of theology.

Göttingen   Karl Barth

Third Letter:

Harnack to Barth

OPEN LETTER TO PROFESSOR KARL BARTH

I thank you for replying to my 'fifteen questions.' They were addressed to you, *also*, yes, especially to you. Your answers have made a few things clearer to me but exactly because of that the opposition between us has become the more apparent to me. I shall try to show this in what follows. Other things have remained obscure for me or perhaps they have become so, especially your answer to my first question. Despite much hard effort it is wholly incomprehensible me. Since very much depends on this basic question, one of issues, namely your concept of revelation stays under the cover of a heavy fog.

Concerning the title of my questions and question 15: you see in contemporary scientific theology an unstable and. transitory product which has been in the making since Pietism and the Enlightenment and that has the value of an *opinio communis*[2] only. I see in it the only possible way of grasping the object epistemologically. This way is new and old at the same time, new because it has attained to greater clarity and maturity only since the

18th century and old because it began when man started thinking. You say that 'the task of theology is at one with the of preaching'; I reply that the task of theology is at one with the-task of science in general. The task of preaching is the pure presentation of the Christian's task as a witness to Christ. You transform the theological professorship into the pulpit-ministry (and desire to hand over to secular disciplines what is known as 'theology'). On the basis of the whole course of Church-history I predict that this undertaking will not lead to edification but to dissolution. Or is what you have to say meant to act only as a 'ferment'? No one could make this his and surely it is not part of your plan. Nevertheless, I acknowledge the ferment: the courage to be objective, the courage to be a witness. […]

Concerning question 6 (about the possibility of education in Godliness): you simply answer with John 6:44[3]. If that is all you have to say here, then you condemn all Christian pedagogy and sever, like Marcion[4], every link between faith and the human. In my view you have the example of Jesus against you.

Concerning questions 7 to 9: you assert that in each individual case it is an open question whether the cognition of God, evolved in the history of man, excepting revelation, protects against or sows atheism. This is only half an answer to my question as to whether God is not at all whatever is said about him on the basis of the development of culture, on the basis of the knowledge gathered by culture and on the basis of ethics. Or may I assume that you reject such an assertion with me? Hardly! For your sentence 'the gospel has as much and as little to do with barbarism as with culture' can be understood only as a radical denial of every valuable understanding of God within the history of man's thought and ethics. Your point of view becomes completely plain when you say that 'between God's truth and our truth there is

only contrast, only an either - or. The way from the old to the new world is not a stairway, not a development in any sense whatsoever, but rather a being born anew'. Does this not exclude the belief that one's own being a Christian happened precisely in that way, while at the same time one admits

---

[2] common opinion
[3] "No one can come to me unless the Father who sent me draws them, and I will raise them up at the last day."
[4] Marcion of Sinope (c.85-160AD) was decried as a heretic by the early Church Fathers for proposing two Gods. He tried to get rid of the Old Testament, declaring Christianity to be totally opposed to the Hebrew Scriptures and Judaism.

that God let this grow on this (kind of) stairway' on which eternal values had already been given? Remember Augustine's account of his becoming a Christian! […]

For question 14) l also miss a succinct answer. Does the awakening of faith, insofar as it includes the of the person of Jesus Christ as the centre of the gospel, take place without regard for his historical person? If this is to be answered negatively, can faith dispense with historical knowledge of this person? If this is to be answered affirmatively, can critical-historical study of this person with regard to faith be something irrelevant or is it rather not absolutely necessary? What you say *a propos* this in relation to biblical science may be formulated like this; the most radical biblical science is always right and thank heaven for this for now we may be rid of it. This point of view, known to the point of Dausea from recent second-rate Church- history, opens the gates to every suitable fantasy and to every theological dictatorship which dissolves the historical of our religion and seeks to torment the consciences of the ",others with one's own heuristic knowledge.

I do sincerely regret that the answers to my questions only point out the magnitude of the gap that divides us. But then neither my nor your theology matter. What does matter is that the gospel is correctly taught. Should however your way of doing this become predominant it will not be taught anymore; it. will rather be given over into the hands of the preachers of edification who freely create their own understanding of the Bible and who set up their dominion.

Yours respectfully,

von Harnack.

Fourth Letter:

Barth to Harnack

AN ANSWER TO PROFESSOR ADOLF VON HARNACK'S OPEN LETTER

Esteemed Dr. von Harnack,

It is not necessary to state particularly that your extensive discussion of my answers to your questions is an honour for which I am most grateful to you. Nevertheless I enter with hesitation upon the task of giving more information to you about my theological thoughts. The editor thought it a task which in view of your letter was the natural thing to do. But you yourself have intimated that my answers have shown you only the gap that divides us. Is it not pointless and annoying to pose further riddles to you now and more than likely to most readers of *Christliche Welt*? My position is unpleasant in yet another way: you have really raised questions for the first time which I, as one of those to whom they were addressed, had to answer and could answer as well or as badly as I was able. I have no intention of challenging your right in this, you who are one of my revered teachers of former times, but you confront me in your letter as someone who has accomplished his tasks, has obtained knowledge and who, because of the experience and the reflections of a rich life, has no time and ear not only for answers different from those he would give himself but also for questions other than his own. Is there anything else to be answered to your questions? Is the discussion not over? But since you wanted to tell me that it was not my answers you had in mind when you raised your original questions - something I never doubted - I think that I owe it to you and to our listeners to confess that I consider my answers quite disputable, but that for the time being and until I am shown a better way I reserve all else to myself. […]

You see in what you call 'scientific theology' 'the only possible way of grasping the object epistemologically' and you call it 'new because it has attained to greater clarity and maturity only since the 18th century, old since it began when man started to think! I hope that I am not reading anything into your position when on the basis of that explicit statement made in reference to the 18th century I assume that (together with that unfortunate generation of 'edificatory preachers') the reformers Luther and Calvin would fail to classify as 'scientific theologians', whereas Zwingli and Melanchthon might not. I would also assume that for you the idea of considering the apostle Paul (in addition to whatever else he was) as one of those theologians is totally foreign. However that may be I think I know 'thinking men' in old and new centuries who as theologians pursued wholly different ways from those which since the 18th century are regarded as the normal ones, men whose scientific quality (should 'scientific quality' mean objectivity) it would in my opinion be hazardous to question. The appeal to Paul's or Luther's theology is for you nothing but a presumptuous attempt at imitation. On this side of the 'gap' the process looks relatively simple.[…]

But the point really is not to keep the historical-critical method of biblical and historical research developed in the last centuries away from the work of theology, but rather to fit that method, and its refinement of the way questions are asked, into that work in a meaningful way. I think l said so in my answers 2,3 and 14 and may thus be allowed some astonishment that you still accuse me of regarding critical biblical science as something 'devious', of wishing 'to be rid' of it and must therefore be threatened with the punishment of occultism which is decreed by 'divine order' for **despisers of reason and science. The thing against which l defend myself is not historical criticism but rather the**

foregone conclusiveness with which - and this is characteristic also of your present statements - **the task of theology is** *emptied.*   That is to say, the way in which a so-called "simple gospel," discovered by historical criticism beyond the 'Scriptures' *and apart from* the 'Spirit', is given the place which the Reformers accorded to the 'Word' (the correlation of 'Scripture' and 'Spirit'). Such a 'gospel' is one which can be called 'God's Ward' only metaphorically because it is at best a human impression of it. The sentence so repugnant to you and others, namely that the task of theology is at one with the task of preaching is for me an inevitable statement of the programme (in the carrying out of which, of course, many things must still be considered). […]

But at this point appears your categorical statement that my **'concept of revelation'** is *'totally'* (the italics are yours!) 'incomprehensible' to you. In question 1) you asked how one might come to find out what the content of the gospel is without historical knowledge and critical reflection. I answered in the first instance that this understanding occurs exclusively through an action (through deed and word) of this 'content' itself (of God or Christ or the Spirit). Surely you will not demand individual citations for this thesis. In the second instance I said concerning critical reflection that **it cannot be good to reverse the order** and **to turn 'Thus says the lord' into 'Thus hears man'**. If there is a way to this 'content', then the content must be the way; the speaking voice must be the listening ear. All other ways do not lead to this goal, all other ears do not hear this voice. That God is himself the goal as well as the way is something - and I gladly concede this - which for me as for you is totally incomprehensible, not only 'fog', but darkness, as Luther said. If you were to tell me that one cannot believe in a way from God to us to which corresponds apparently no way from us to God (for **it is always most exclusively God's way to us**), I could only say to you that I think exactly the same deep down in my heart. But then does it not already **lie in the concept of revelation** (and really not only in *my* concept!), quite apart from what the Bible says about it on every page, that one cannot 'believe' it? Would it not be better to renounce this full-sounding word if revelation were only the designation of a very sublime or a very deep but yet a *possible human* discovery? Or if we were not willing to do this, should we theologians not get up the courage to let our theology begin with the perhaps thoroughly sceptical but nevertheless clear reminder of the indeed 'totally incomprehensible', inaudible and unbelievable, the *really* scandalous testimony that **God himself has said and done something, something** *new* **in fact outside of the correlation of all human words and things,** but which *as* this new thing he has put it *into* that correlation, a word and a thing next to others but *this* word and *this* thing? I am not talking now of the possibility of accepting this testimony. I only ask whether we should not for once reckon more soberly with the fact that what is called Christianity made its first and for us recognisable beginning with this testimony? I call this testimony in its totality 'the Scriptures', a testimony **which cannot be analysed**

enough by historical criticism. But it shall not cease being this testimony when thus analysed. The delineation of 'the Scriptures' against other scriptures appears to me a secondary question. Should an extra-canonical writing contain in a notable fashion this (but really this) testimony, there can be no *a priori* impossibility of letting this testimony speak through it also, no, quite on the contrary. From this observation, however, the canonization of 'Faust' for example is a long way which a sensible Church just will *not* travel.

The Scriptures then witness to revelation. One does not have to believe it; one cannot do it. But one should not deny that it witnesses to revelation, *genuine* revelation that is, and not a more or less **concealed religious possibility of man**, but rather the possibility of God, namely that he has acted in the form of a human possibility and this as *reality*. This testimony states that the Word became flesh, that God himself became a human-historical reality and this in the person of Jesus Christ. But f**or me it does not follow from that that this event can be the object of human-historical cognition**; this is excluded because and insofar as *this* reality is involved. The existence of a Jesus of Nazareth, for example, which can of course be discovered historically, is not *this* reality. A discernible 'simple gospel', discernible because it is humanly plausible, a 'simple gospel' which causes no scandal, a 'simple gospel' that is in your sense, a word or a deed of this Jesus which would really be nothing other than the realisation of

a human possibility - would not be *this* reality. l doubt that it is possible at any cogent point to separate one word or one deed of Jesus from. the background. of this reality when it is regarded only to separate it from the Scripture which testifies to revelation and therefore to the scandal and then proceed to interpret it as the' 'simple gospel' in your sense. l did indicate in answer 5 why l think this to be impossible for example in regard to the commandment of *love* for God and for the neighbour; you have admonished but not refuted me.[…]

The apostles and evangelists have made the object of the testimony known as revelation. As God's action it has been shrouded by them with an unsearchable hiddenness and protected against every desire to comprehend it directly, so much so in fact that not only all statements which obviously refer to this 'centre of the gospel', found. ,for example in that rather threatening bundle in the second article of the Creed and indeed also in the 'Sermon on the Mount', in the parabolic and polemical words of Jesus and in the account of his passion, leave the circumspect reader with the conclusion that there can be no question of speaking of a direct historical comprehensibility of this historical reality (of revelation) alleged here. What is comprehensible is always only the other, namely that which makes up the historical environment of the alleged revelation. Beyond this other the barrier goes up and the scandal, the fable or - the miracle threaten. The historical reality of Christ (as revelation, as 'centre of the gospel') is not the 'historical . Jesus' which an all too here. eager historical research wanted. to discern in disregard of those warnings which are made in the sources themselves, (coming upon a banality which has been and shall be proclaimed in. vain as a pearl of great priee). Nor is it as you said an imagined Christ but rather the risen one, or let us say with more restraint in view of our little faith: the Christ who is witnessed to us as the risen one. That is the 'historical Jesus Christ of the gospel and 'we now know him no longer' in other ways, that is apart from this testimony to him, apart from revelation which has to be believed. It is in this sense that I think I may legitimately appeal to II Cor. 5:16[5]. At the decisive point, when the answer to the question: what makes Jesus to be Christ? is given in terms of the reference to *the resurrection* there remains indeed from man's point of view what you called 'totally' incomprehensible. […]

I call the acceptance of this unbelievable testimony of the Scriptures faith. Again I am not saying that this is a discovery of theology. I do however ask what else faith could be – disregarding sentimentalities - but the obedience I give to a human word which, as if it were itself God's Word, witnesses to me the Word of God as a word addressed to me? One must not have any delusions here that this is an unprecedented event, that now one must speak of the Holy Spirit if not all the objections Herrmann crammed into our heads against a 'mere credence' of historical facts apart from. this basis of cognition are justified. Therefore I distinguish **faith as God's working on us (for only he can say to us audibly what *we* cannot hear,** 1 Corinthians 2:9[6]) from all known and unknown human organs and functions, even our so-called 'experiences of God'. Is that such a shocking novelty? […]

It has to be thus: whatever be said against the possibility of revelation can also be said with equal strength against the possibility of faith. What must remain as the second excluded possibility is this: God who according to the witness of the Scriptures has spoken 'the word of Christ' speaks that word also to me through the witness of the Scriptures empowered through the *testimonium spiritus sancti internum*[7] so that I *hear* that word and by hearing it *believe.* Is this the 'theory of the exclusive inner word' or one of the many 'other subjectivistic theories'? In your third question you yourself spoke of the awakening of faith. I agree but in the opinion that the point here as also in the 'understandable and comforting parable' of the prodigal son, Luke 15:32" is the awake- ning of someone dead, that is the miracle of God just as in revelation. Indeed **I have no confidence in any objectivity other than the one described in this way** or in terms of the correlated con- cepts of 'Scripture' and 'Spirit', least of all in

---

[5] "From now on, therefore, we regard no one from a human point of view; even though we once knew Christ from a human point of view, we know him no longer in that way."

[6] "But, as it is written, 'What no eye has seen, nor ear heard, nor the human heart conceived, what God has prepared for those who love him'"

[7] The internal witness of the Holy Spirit

the **pontifications of a science** which would have to demonstrate its absolute superiority over the subjectivistic activities of the 'preachers of edification' by means of actions. [...]

I think I also know that man's faith can at every moment completely he described as 'inner openness, heuristic knowledge, experience, critical reflection, historical knowledge, etc., just as the testimony of revelation also yes must be interpreted as a piece of dark history of man's spirit and culture (unless God himself-intervenes!). But I would not sever at all here or there (that would only be a completely senseless undertaking); I would rather say that **the human is the relative**, the testimony, the parable and thus not the absolute itself on some pinnacles or heights of evolution as one would certainly conclude from your statements. **It is rather the** (understood or not understood) **reference to the absolute**. In view of this the historically-psychologically discernible, that which we know in ourselves and others as 'faith' would be a witness to and a symptom of that action and miracle of God on us, of that faith in other words which, created through the 'Word' and 'steeped in the Word' is, as Luther said, our righteousness before God himself. The religions of the Bible, with which you began your first question, would in the same way be witness to and symptom of the historical reality of God's becoming man. But the basis of cognition of both justifying faith and revelation would be God's action on us through his Word. Does my point of view really not become clear to you? - However, and now I think that I am coming to the essence of all your objections: I am indeed content with the testimonial character of all which occurs here or there in time and as a result of man. I explicitly *deny* the possibility of positing anything relative as absolute anywhere and in any fashion, be it in history or ourselves or to say it in Kierkegaardian terms: to go from testimony to 'direct statement', which is and must remain in the most exclusive sense God's (if I do not wholly misunderstand the Bible and the Reformation). The fact that eternity becomes time, that the absolute becomes relative, that God becomes man (and with that - and only with that - every time the reverse also!), in other words the fact that the matter involved coincides with the sign pointing to it and with that the coincidence of the sign with the matter to which it points...is true only as the Ward and work of God', as the act of the Trinity itself. This act can only be witnessed to and believed because it is revealed. It is never a historical-psychological reality which becomes directly recognisable for example in our religious experience, in the denouments of our consciences, in the relations between man and man, even in the purest of them, in the thoughts of Goethe or Kant about God or in whatever towers of god-likeness you may mention. [...]

(Still in connection with the charge of Marcionism) you demand from me a full answer to the question 'whether God is simply unlike anything said about him on the basis of the development of culture, on the basis of the knowledge gathered by culture and on the basis of ethics.' Very well then, but may I ask you really to listen to my whole answer. NO God is 'absolutely not at all that', as surely as the creator not the creature or even the creation of the creature. But precisely in this NO, which can be uttered in its full severity only in the faith in

revelation, the creature recognises itself as the work and property of the creator. Precisely in this NO is God recognised as God, as the origin and goal of also the *thoughts* man is in the habit of forming about God in the darkness of his culture or his decadence. For this NO, posted with finality by revelation is not without 'the deep, secret YES under and over the NO' which we should 'grasp and hold with a steady faith in God's Word' and 'agree with God's judgement against us, " for thus we have won.' This is how it stands with that NO: 'nothing but YES in it, but always deep and secretly and it looks to be nothing but *NO*'. What lover of contradictoriness might have said that? Kierkegaard or Dostoyevsky? No, Martin Luther! [...]

Yet once again: I do not intend to entrench myself in those positions in which you, honoured Sir, and our voluntary-involuntary audience in these talks have seen me, simply because I know how frighteningly relative everything is that one can say about the great subject which occupies you and me. I know that it will be necessary to speak of it in a way quite different from that of my present insight. I would like to be able to listen attentively in the future to whatever you also will have to say. But I cannot concede at this time that you have driven me

off the field with your questions and answers, something that I will gladly suffer when it really takes place.

Respectfully yours

Karl Barth

A POSTSCRIPT TO MY OPEN LETTER TO PROFESSOR KARL BARTH

Prof. Barth has replied to my open letter very extensively.
I would like to thank hill for his full presentation. To my disappointment I cannot continue the discussion now and in this journal. The number and weight of the problems are simply too great to be dealt with here and with brevity. Yet two things which I would not like to leave unsaid. 1) Paul and Luther are for me indeed not primarily subjects but objects of scientific theology as is Prof, Barth and all those who express their Christianity as prophets or witnesses like preachers, whether they do it in biblical commentaries or in books of dogmatics etc. Scientific theology and witness are often enough mixed together in life, but neither can remain healthy when the demand to keep them separate

is in- validated. Both are objective, not only the witness, as one may conclude from Professor Barth's statements, but the kind of objec- tivity is a very different one in each case. A scientific-theo- logical presentation also set afire and edify, thanks to its object, but the scientific theologi8n whose aim it is to set afire and to edify brings a foreign flame to his altar; For as there is only scientific method there is also only scientific task: the pure cognition of its object. Whatever other fruit falls to science as a reward is an unexpected gift. 2) **the concept of revelation is no scientific concept**; science can neither draw together under generic concept nor explain in terms of 'revelation' the God-consciousness and the paradoxical preaching of founders of religion and prophets (and religious experiences in general). […]

In Barth's answers there becomes apparent in several places a certain which is intensified to the point where replies are said to sound like an 'admonition'. I cannot be judge in my own matters for which reason l say gladly that no other desire moved me in my letter than to reach clarity vis-à-vis a theologian friend.

Adolf von Harnack

Anthony Flew, (1923-2010)
RM Hare (1919-2002)
&
Basil Mitchell (1917-2011)

Theology and Falsification: A Symposium

ANTONY FLEW

Let us begin with a parable. I t is a parable developed from a tale told by John Wisdom in his haunting and revelatory article 'Gods'. Once upon a time two explorers came upon a clearing in the jungle. In the clearing were growing many flowers and many weeds. One explorer says, 'Some gardener must tend this plot.' The other disagrees, 'There is no gardener.' So they pitch their tents and set a watch. No gardener is ever seen. 'But perhaps he is an invisible gardener.' So they set up a barbed-wire fence. They electrify it. They patrol with bloodhounds. (For they remember how H. G. Wells's 'Invisible Man' could be both smelt and touched though he could not be seen.) But no shrieks ever suggest that some intruder has received a shock. No movements of the wire ever betray an invisible climber. The bloodhounds never give cry. Yet still the Believer is not convinced. 'But there is a gardener, invisible, intangible, insensible to electric shocks, a gardener who has no scent and makes no sound, a gardener who comes secretly to look after the garden which he loves.' At last the Sceptic despairs, 'But what remains of your original assertion? Just how does what you call an invisible, intangible, eternally elusive gardener differ from an imaginary gardener or even from no gardener at all?'

In this parable we can see how what starts as an assertion, that some- thing exists or that there is some analogy between certain complexes of phenomena, may be reduced step by step to an altogether different status, to an expression perhaps of a 'picture preference'. The Sceptic says there is no gardener. The Believer says there is a gardener (but invisible, etc.). One man talks about sexual behaviour. Another man prefers to talk of Aphrodite (but knows that there is not really a superhuman person additional to, and somehow responsible for, all sexual pheno- mena). The process of qualification may be checked at any point before the original assertion is completely withdrawn and something of that first assertion will remain (tautology). Mr. Wells's invisible man could not, admittedly, be seen, but in all other respects he was a man like the rest of us. But though the process of qualification may be, and of course usually is, checked in time, it is not always judiciously so halted. Some- one may dissipate his assertion completely without noticing that he has done so. A fine brash hypothesis may thus be killed by inches, the death by a thousand qualifications.

And in this, it seems to me, lies the peculiar danger, the endemic evil of theological utterance. Take such utterances as 'God has a plan', 'God created the world', 'God loves us as a father loves his children.' They look at first sight very much like assertions, vast cosmological assertions. Of course, this is no sure sign that they either are, or are intended to be, assertions. But let us confine ourselves to the cases where those who utter such sentences intend them to express assertions. (Merely remark- ing parenthetically that those who intend or interpret such utterances as crypto-commands, expressions of wishes, disguised ejaculations, con- cealed ethics, or as anything else but assertions, are unlikely to succeed in making them either properly orthodox or practically effective.)

Now to assert that such and such is the case is necessarily equivalent to denying that such and such is not the case. Suppose, then that we are in doubt as to what someone who gives vent to an utterance is asserting, or suppose that, more radically, we are sceptical as to whether he is really asserting anything at all, one way of trying to understand (or perhaps it will be to expose) his utterance is to attempt to find what he would regard as counting against, or as being incompatible with, its truth. For if the utterance is indeed an assertion, it will necessarily be equivalent to a denial of the negation of that assertion. And anything which would count against the assertion, or which would induce the speaker to withdraw it and to admit that it had been mistaken, must be part of (or the whole of) the meaning of the negation of that assertion. And to know the meaning of the negation of an assertion, is as near as makes no matter, to know the meaning of that assertion. And if there is nothing which a putative assertion denies then there is nothing which it asserts either: and so it is not really an assertion. When the Sceptic in the parable asked the Believer, 'Just how does what you call an invisible, intangible, eternally elusive gardener differ from an imaginary gardener at all?' he was suggesting that the Believer's earlier statement had been so eroded by qualification that it was no longer an assertion at all.

Now it often seems to people who are not religious as if there was no conceivable event or series of events the occurrence of which would be admitted by sophisticated religious people to be a sufficient reason for conceding 'There wasn't a God after all' or 'God does not really love us then.' Someone tells us that God loves us as a father loves his children. We are reassured. But then we see a child dying of inoperable cancer of the throat. His earthly father is driven frantic in his efforts to help, but his Heavenly Father reveals no obvious sign of concern. Some qualification is made - God's love is 'not a merely human love' or it is 'an inscrutable love', perhaps-and we realize that such sufferings are quite com- patible with the truth of the assertion that 'God loves us as a father (but, of course, ...).' We are reassured again. But then perhaps we ask: what is this assurance of God's (appropriately qualified) love worth, what is this apparent guarantee really a guarantee against? Just what would have to happen not merely (morally and wrongly) to tempt but also (logically and rightly) to entitle us to say

'God does not love us' or even 'God does not exist'? I therefore put to the succeeding symposiasts the simple central questions, 'What would have to occur or to have occurred to constitute for you a disproof of the love of, or of the existence of, God?'

RM HARE

I wish to make it clear that I shall not try to defend Christianity in particular, but religion in general-not because I do not believe in Christianity, but because you cannot understand what Christianity is, until you have understood what religion is.

I must begin by confessing that, on the ground marked out by Flew, he seems to me to be completely victorious. I therefore shift my ground by relating another parable. A certain lunatic is convinced that all dons want to murder him. His friends introduce him to all the mildest and most respectable dons that they can find, and after each of them has retired, they say, 'You see, he doesn't really want to murder you; he spoke to you in a most cordial manner; surely you are convinced now?' But the lunatic replies, 'Yes, but that was only his diabolical cunning; he's really plotting against me the whole time, like the rest of them; I know it I tell you.' However many kindly dons are produced, the reaction is still the same. Now we say that such a person is deluded. But what is he deluded about? About the truth or falsity of an assertion? Let us apply Flew's test to him. There is no behaviour of dons that can be enacted which he will accept as counting against his theory; and therefore his theory, on this test, asserts nothing. But it does not follow that there is no differ- ence between what he thinks about dons and what most of us think about them-otherwise we should not call him a lunatic and ourselves sane, and dons would have no reason to feel uneasy about his presence in Oxford.

Let us call that in which we differ from this lunatic, our respective *bliks*. He has an insane *blik* about dons; we have a sane one. It is important to realize that we have a sane one, not no *blik* at all; for there must be two sides to any argument-if he has a wrong *blik,* then those who are right about dons must have a right one. Flew has shown that a *blik* does not consist in an assertion or system of them; but nevertheless it is very important to have the right *blik*. Let us try to imagine what it would be like to have different *bliks* about other things than dons. When I am driving my car, it sometimes occurs to me to wonder whether my movements of the steering-wheel will always continue to be followed by corresponding alterations in the direction of the car. I have never had a steering failure, though I have had skids, which must be similar. Moreover, I know enough about how the steering of my car is made, to know the sort of thing that would have to go wrong for the steering to fail-steel joints would have to part, or steel rods break, or something-but how do I know that this won't happen? The truth is, I don't know; I just have a *blik* about steel and its properties, so that normally I trust the steering of my car; but I find it not at all difficult to imagine what it would be like to lose this *blik* and acquire the opposite one. People would say I was silly about steel; but there would be no mistaking the reality of the difference between our respective *bliks*- for example, I should never go in a motor-car. Yet I should hesitate to say that the difference between us was the difference between contradictory assertions. No amount of safe arrivals or bench- tests will remove my *blik* and restore the normal one; for my *blik* is compatible with any finite number of such tests.

It was Hume who taught us that our whole commerce with the world depends upon our *blik* about the world; and that differences between *bliks* about the world cannot be settled by observation of what happens in the world. That was why, having performed the interesting experiment of doubting the ordinary man's *blik* about the world, and showing that no proof could be given to make us adopt one *blik* rather than another, he turned to backgammon to take his mind off the problem. It seems, indeed, to be impossible even to formulate as an assertion the normal *blik* about the world which makes me put my confidence in the future reliability of steel joints, in the continued ability of the road to support my car, and not gape beneath it revealing nothing below; in the general non-homicidal tendencies of dons; in my own continued well-being (in some sense of that word that I may not now fully understand) if I con- tinue to do what is right according to my lights; in the general likelihood of people like Hitler coming to a bad end. But perhaps a formulation less inadequate than most is to be found in the Psalms: 'The earth is weak and all the inhabiters thereof: I bear up the pillars of it.'

The mistake of the position which Flew selects for attack is to regard this kind of talk as some sort of *explanation,* as scientists are accus- tomed to use the word. As such, it would obviously be ludicrous. We no longer believe in God as an *Atlas-nous n'avons pas besoin de cette hypothese.* But it is nevertheless true to say that, as Hume saw, without a *blik* there can be no explanation; for it is by our *bliks* that we decide what is and what is not an explanation. Suppose we believed that every- thing that happened, happened by pure chance. This would not of course be an assertion; for it is compatible with anything happening or not happening, and so, incidentally, is its contradictory. But if we had this belief, we should not be able to explain or predict or plan anything. Thus, although we should not be *asserting* anything different from those of a more normal belief, there would be a great difference between us; and this is the sort of difference that there is between those who really believe in God and those who really disbelieve in him.

The word 'really' is important, and may excite suspicion. I put it in, because when people have had a good Christian upbringing, as have most of those who now profess not to believe in any sort of religion, it is very hard to discover what they really believe. The reason why they find it so easy to think that they are not religious, is that they have never got into the frame of mind of one who suffers from the doubts to which religion is the answer. Not for them the terrors of the primitive jungle. Having abandoned some of the more picturesque fringes of religion, they think that they have abandoned the whole thing-whereas in fact they still have got, and could not live without, a religion of a com- fortably substantial, albeit highly sophisticated, kind, which differs from that of many 'religious people' in little more than this, that 'religious people' like to sing Psalms about theirs-a very natural and proper thing to do. But nevertheless there may be a big difference lying behind-the difference between two people who, though side by side, are walking in different directions. I do not know in what direction Flew is walking; perhaps he does not know either. But we have had some examples recently of various ways in which one can walk away from Christianity, and there are any number of possibilities. After all, man has not changed biologically since primitive times; it is his religion that has changed, and it can easily change again. And if you do not think that such changes make a difference, get acquainted with some Sikhs and some Mussul- mans of the same Punjabi stock; you will find them quite different sorts of people.

There is an important difference between Flew's parable and my own which we have not yet noticed. The explorers do not *mind* about their garden; they discuss it with interest, but not with concern. But my lunatic, poor fellow, minds about dons; and I mind about the steering of my car; it often has people in it that I care for. It is because I mind very much about what goes on in the garden in which I find myself, that I am unable to share the explorers' detachment.

BASIL MITCHELL

Flew's article is searching and perceptive, but there is, I think, some- thing odd about his conduct of the theologian's case. The theologian surely would not deny that the fact of pain counts against the assertion that God loves men. This very incompatibility generates the most in- tractable of theological problems-the problem of evil. So the theologian *does* recognize the fact of pain as counting against Christian doctrine. But it is true that he will not allow it-or anything-to count decisively

against it; for he is committed by his faith to trust in God. His attitude is not that of the detached observer, but of the believer.

Perhaps this can be brought out by yet another parable. In time of war in an occupied country, a member of the resistance meets one night a stranger who deeply impresses him. They spend that night together in conversation. The Stranger tells the partisan that he himself is on the side of the resistance- indeed that he is in command of it, and urges the partisan to have faith in him no matter what happens. The partisan is utterly convinced at that meeting of the Stranger's sincerity and con- stancy and undertakes to trust him.

They never meet in conditions of intimacy again. But sometimes the Stranger is seen helping members of the resistance, and the partisan is grateful and says to his friends, 'He is on our side.'

Sometimes he is seen in the uniform of the police handing over patriots to the occupying power. On these occasions his friends murmur against him; but the partisan still says, 'He is on our side.' He still believes that, in spite of appearances, the Stranger did not deceive him. Sometimes he asks the Stranger for help and receives it. He is then thankful. Some- times he asks and does not receive it. Then he says, The Stranger knows best.' Sometimes his friends, in exasperation, say, 'Well, what *would* he have to do for you to admit that you were wrong and that he is not on our side?' But the partisan refuses to answer. He will not consent to put the Stranger to the test. And sometimes his friends complain, 'Well, if *that's* what you mean by his being on our side, the sooner he goes over to the other side the better.'

The partisan of the parable does not allow anything to count decisively against the proposition 'The Stranger is on our side.' This is because he has committed himself to trust the Stranger. But he of course recognizes that the Stranger's ambiguous behaviour *does* count against what he believes about him. It is precisely this situation which constitutes the trial of his faith.

When the partisan asks for help and doesn't get it, what can he do? He can *(a)* conclude that the stranger is not on our side; or *(b)* maintain that he is on our side, but that he has reasons for withholding help.

The first he will refuse to do. How long can he uphold the second position without its becoming just silly?

I don't think one can say in advance. It will depend on the nature of the impression created by the Stranger in the first place. It will depend, too, on the manner in which he takes the Stranger's behaviour. If he blandly dismisses it as of no consequence, as having no bearing upon his belief, it will be assumed that he is thoughtless or insane. And it quite obviously won't do for him to say easily, 'Oh, when used of the Stranger the phrase "is on our side" *means* ambiguous behaviour of this sort.' In that case he would be like the religious man who says blandly of a terrible disaster, 'It is God's will.' No, he will only be regarded as sane and reasonable in his belief, if he experiences in himself the full force of the conflict.

It is here that my parable differs from Hare's. The partisan admits that many things may and do count against his belief: whereas Hare's lunatic who has a *blik* about dons doesn't admit that anything counts against his *blik*. Nothing *can* count against *bliks*. Also the partisan has a reason for having in the first instance committed himself, viz. the character of the Stranger; whereas the lunatic has no reason for his *blik* about dons-because, of course, you can't have reasons for *bliks*.

This means that I agree with Flew that theological utterances must be assertions. The partisan is making an assertion when he says, 'The Stranger is on our side.'

Do I want to say that the partisan's belief about the Stranger is, in any sense, an explanation? I think I do. It explains and makes sense of the Stranger's behaviour: it helps to explain also the resistance movement in the context of which he appears. In each case it differs from the interpretation which the others put up on the same facts.

'God loves men' resembles 'the Stranger is on our side' (and many other significant statements, e.g. historical ones) in not being conclusively falsifiable. They can both be treated in at least three different ways: (1) as provisional hypotheses to be discarded if experience tells against them; (2) as significant articles of faith; (3) as vacuous formulae (ex- pressing, perhaps, a desire for reassurance) to which experience makes no difference and which make no difference to life.

The Christian, once he has committed himself, is precluded by his faith from taking up the first attitude: 'Thou shalt not tempt the Lord thy God.' He is in constant danger, as Flew has observed, of slipping into the third. But he need not; and, if he does, it is a failure in faith as well as in logic.

FLEW

It has been a good discussion: and I am glad to have helped to provoke it. But now-at least in *University*[1]-it must come to an end: and the Editors of *University* have asked me to make some

---

[1] The journal in which this discussion first appeared, 1950-5

concluding remarks. Since it is impossible to deal with all the issues raised or to comment separately upon each contribution, I will concentrate on Mitchell and Hare, as representative of two very different kinds of response to the challenge made in 'Theology and Falsification'. The challenge, it will be remembered, ran like this. Some theological utterances seem to, and are intended to, provide explanations or express assertions. Now an assertion, to be an assertion at all, must claim that things stand thus and thus; *and not otherwise.* Similarly an explanation, to be an explanation at all, must explain why this particular thing occurs; *and not something else.* Those last clauses are crucial. And yet sophisti- cated religious people-or so it seemed to me-are apt to overlook this, and tend to refuse to allow, not merely that anything actually does occur, but that anything conceivably could occur, which would count against their theological assertions and explanations. But in so far as they do this their supposed explanations are actually bogus, and their seeming assertions are really vacuous.

Mitchell's response to this challenge is admirably direct, straight- forward, and understanding. He agrees 'that theological utterances must be assertions'. He agrees that if they are to be assertions, there must be something that would count against their truth. He agrees, too, that believers are in constant danger of transforming their would-be asser- tions into 'vacuous formulae'. But he takes me to task for an oddity in my 'conduct of the theologian's case. The theologian surely would not deny that the fact of pain counts against the assertion that God loves men. This very incompatibility generates the most intractable of theo- logical problems, the problem of evil.' I think he is right. I should have made a distinction between two very different ways of dealing with what looks like evidence against the love of God: the way I stressed was the expedient of qualifying the original assertion; the way the theologian usually takes, at first, is to admit that it looks bad but to insist that there

is-there must be-some explanation which will show that, in spite of appearances, there really is a God who loves us. His difficulty, it seems to me, is that he has given God attributes which rule out all possible saving explanations. In Mitchell's parable of the Stranger it is easy for the believer to find plausible excuses for ambiguous behaviour: for the Stranger is a man. But suppose the Stranger is God. We cannot say that he would like to help but cannot: God is omnipotent. We cannot say that he would help if he only knew: God is omniscient. We cannot say that he 'is not responsible for the wickedness of others: God creates those others. Indeed an omnipotent, omniscient God must be an acces- sory before (and during) the fact to every human misdeed! as well as being responsible for every non-moral defect in the universe. So, though I entirely concede that Mitchell was absolutely right to insist against me that the theologian's first move is to look for an *explanation,* I still think that in the end, if relentlessly pursued, he will have to resort to the avoiding action of *qualification.* And there lies the danger of that death by a thousand qualifications, which would, I agree, constitute 'a failure in faith as well as in logic'.

Hare's approach is fresh and bold. He confesses that 'on the ground marked out by Flew, he seems to me to be completely victorious'. He therefore introduces the concept of *blik.* But while I think that there is room for some such concept in philosophy, and that philosophers should be grateful to Hare for his invention, I nevertheless want to insist that any attempt to analyse Christian religious utterances as expressions or affirmations of a *blik* rather than as (at least would-be) assertions about the cosmos is fundamentally misguided. *First,* because thus interpreted, they would be entirely unorthodox. If Hare's religion really is a *blik,* involving no cosmological assertions about the nature and activities of a supposed personal creator, then surely he is not a Christian at all? *Second,* because thus interpreted, they could scarcely do the job they do. If they were not even intended as assertions then many religious activities would become fraudulent, or merely silly. If 'You ought *because* it is God's will' asserts no more than 'You ought', then the person who prefers the former phraseology is not really giving a reason, but a fraudulent substitution for one, a dialectical dud cheque. If 'My soul must be immortal *because* God loves his children, etc.' asserts no more than 'My soul must be immortal', then the man who reassures himself with theological arguments for immortality is being as silly as the man who tries to clear his overdraft by writing his bank a cheque on the same amount. (Of course neither of these utterances would be distinctively Christian: but this discussion never pretended to be so confined.) Religious utterances may indeed express false or even bogus assertions: but I simply do not believe that they are not both intended and inter- preted to be or at any rate to presuppose assertions, at least in the context of religious practice; whatever shifts may be demanded, in another context, by the exigencies of theological apologetic.

One final suggestion. The philosophers of religion might well draw upon George Orwell's last appalling nightmare 1984 for the concept of *doublethink.* '*Doublethink* means the power of holding two contradic- tory beliefs simultaneously, and accepting both of them. The party in- tellectual knows that he is playing tricks with reality, but by the exercise of *doublethink* he also satisfies himself that reality is not violated' (1984, p. 220). Perhaps religious intellectuals too are sometimes driven to doublethink in order to retain their faith in a loving God in face of the reality of a heartless and indifferent world. But of this more another time, perhaps.

Basil Mitchell (1917-2011)

The Justification of Religious Belief

In a ship at sea in stormy weather, the officer of the watch reports a lighthouse on a certain bearing. The navigating officer says he cannot have seen a lighthouse, because his reckoning puts him a hundred miles away from the nearest land. He must have seen a waterspout or a whale blowing or some other marine phenomenon which can be taken for a lighthouse. The officer of the watch is satisfied he must have made a mistake. Shortly afterwards, however, the lookout reports land on the starboard bow. The navigating officer, confident in his working, says it must be cloud — and it indeed very difficult to distinguish cloud from land in these conditions. But then a second cloud-looking-like-land or land-looking-like-cloud appears on another bearing. It really does begin to look as if the navigator might be out in his reckoning. He has, perhaps, underestimated the current, or his last star sight was not as good as he thought it was. The reported sightings are consistent with one another and indicate that he is approaching land.

If it is wartime and the coast is hostile, he had better assume that he is where the sightings place him. and get away from it quickly. It would be nice to be surer, but in the circumstances it would be prudent to act on the hypothesis which gives him the stronger reason for action. (Perhaps there is a moral to be drawn here for the ethics of belief. If so, now is not the time to draw it). The point at present is simply that the question whether there was a lighthouse there and the question whether the officer of the watch saw it or saw something else, or just imagined that he saw it. can only be answered in relation to some overall appraisal of the situation. The navigator's original appraisal, based on his dead reckoning, led him to say there was no lighthouse and the officer of the watch did not see it; and this was reasonable enough at that stage. But the other-reports, although their evidential value, taken singly, is as slight and as controversial as the first, do cumulatively amount to a convincing case for reading the whole situation differently. However, it does not in the least follow that, because the lighthouse hypothesis required the support of this sort of reasoning before it could properly be accepted, the lighthouse was for the lookout merely an inferred entity and not an experienced reality. Indeed that it was an experienced reality is precisely what the argument indicated.

Pope John Paul II (1920-2005)

Fides et Ratio

(Encyclical, 1998)

My Venerable Brother Bishops, Health and the Apostolic Blessing!

Faith and reason are like two wings on which the human spirit rises to the contemplation of truth; and God has placed in the human heart a desire to know the truth— in a word, to know himself—so that, by knowing and loving God, men and women may also come to the fullness of truth about themselves (cf. Ex 33:18; Ps 27:8- 9; 63:2-3; Jn 14:8; 1 Jn 3:2).

INTRODUCTION "KNOW YOURSELF"

1. In both East and West, we may trace a journey which has led humanity down the centuries to meet and engage truth more and more deeply. It is a journey which has unfolded—as it must—within the horizon of personal self-consciousness: the more human beings know reality and the world, the more they know themselves in their uniqueness, with the question of the meaning of things and of their very existence becoming ever more pressing. This is why all that is the object of our knowledge becomes a part of our life. The admonition Know yourself was carved on the temple portal at Delphi, as testimony to a basic truth to be adopted as a minimal norm by those who seek to set themselves apart from the rest of creation as "human beings", that is as those who "know themselves".

Moreover, a cursory glance at ancient history shows clearly how in different parts of the world, with their different cultures, there arise at the same time the fundamental questions which pervade human life: Who am I? Where have I come from and where am I going? Why is there evil? What is there after this life? These are the questions which we find in the sacred writings of Israel, as also in the Veda and the Avesta; we find them in the writings of Confucius and Lao-Tze, and in the preaching of Tirthankara and Buddha; they appear in the poetry of Homer and in the tragedies of Euripides and Sophocles, as they do in the philosophical writings of Plato and Aristotle. They are questions which have their common source in the quest for meaning which has always compelled the human heart. In fact, the answer given to these questions decides the direction which people seek to give to their lives.

2. The Church is no stranger to this journey of discovery, nor could she ever be. From the moment when, through the Paschal Mystery, she received the gift of the ultimate truth about human life, the Church has made her pilgrim way along the paths of the world to proclaim that Jesus Christ is "the way, and the truth, and the life" (Jn 14:6). It is her duty to serve humanity in different ways, but one way in particular imposes a responsibility of a quite special kind: the diakonia of the truth.(1) This mission on the one hand makes the believing community a partner in humanity's shared struggle to arrive at truth; (2) and on the other hand it obliges the believing community to proclaim the certitudes arrived at, albeit with a sense that every truth attained is but a step towards that fullness of truth which will appear with the final Revelation of God: "For now we see in a mirror dimly, but then face to face. Now I know in part; then I shall understand fully" (1 Cor 13:12).

3. Men and women have at their disposal an array of resources for generating greater knowledge of truth so that their lives may be ever more human. Among these is philosophy, which is directly concerned with asking the question of life's meaning and sketching an answer to it. Philosophy emerges, then, as one of noblest of human tasks. According to its Greek etymology, the term philosophy means "love of wisdom". Born and nurtured when the human being first asked questions about the reason for things and their purpose, philosophy shows in different modes and forms that the desire for truth is part of human nature itself. It is an innate property of human reason to ask why things are as they are, even though the answers which gradually emerge are set within a horizon which reveals how the different human cultures are complementary.

Philosophy's powerful influence on the formation and development of the cultures of the West should not obscure the influence it has also had upon the ways of understanding existence found in the East. Every people has its own native and seminal wisdom which, as a true cultural treasure, tends to find voice and develop in forms which are genuinely philosophical. One example of this is the basic form of philosophical knowledge which is evident to this day in the postulates which inspire national and international legal systems in regulating the life of society.

4. Nonetheless, it is true that a single term conceals a variety of meanings. Hence the need for a preliminary clarification. Driven by the desire to discover the ultimate truth of existence, human beings seek to acquire those universal elements of knowledge which enable them to understand themselves better and to advance in their own self-realization. These fundamental elements of knowledge spring from the wonder awakened in them by the contemplation of creation: human beings are astonished to discover themselves as part of the world, in a relationship with others like them, all sharing a common destiny. Here begins, then, the journey which will lead them to discover ever new frontiers of knowledge. Without wonder, men and women would lapse into deadening routine and little by little would become incapable of a life which is genuinely personal.

Through philosophy's work, the ability to speculate which is proper to the human intellect produces a rigorous mode of thought; and then in turn, through the logical coherence of the affirmations made and the organic unity of their content, it produces a systematic body of knowledge. In different cultural contexts and at different times, this process has yielded results which have produced genuine systems of thought. Yet often enough in history this has brought with it the temptation to identify one single stream with the whole of philosophy. In such cases, we are clearly dealing with a "philosophical pride" which seeks to present its own partial and imperfect view as the complete reading of all reality. In effect, every philosophical system, while it should always be respected in its wholeness, without any instrumentalization, must still recognize the primacy of philosophical enquiry, from which it stems and which it ought loyally to serve.

Although times change and knowledge increases, it is possible to discern a core of philosophical insight within the history of thought as a whole. Consider, for example, the principles of non-contradiction, finality and causality, as well as the concept of the person as a free and intelligent subject, with the capacity to know God, truth and goodness. Consider as well certain fundamental moral norms which are shared by all. These are among the indications that, beyond different schools of thought, there exists a body of knowledge which may be judged a kind of spiritual heritage of humanity. It is as if we had come upon an implicit philosophy, as a result of which all feel that they possess these principles, albeit in a general and unreflective way. Precisely because it is shared in some measure by all, this knowledge should serve as a kind of reference-point for the different philosophical schools. Once reason successfully intuits and formulates the first universal principles of being and correctly draws from them conclusions which are coherent both logically and ethically, then it may be called right reason or, as the ancients called it, orthós logos, recta ratio.

5. On her part, the Church cannot but set great value upon reason's drive to attain goals which render people's lives ever more worthy. She sees in philosophy the way to come to know fundamental truths about human life. At the same time, the Church considers philosophy an indispensable help for a deeper understanding of faith and for communicating the truth of the Gospel to those who do not yet know it.

Therefore, following upon similar initiatives by my Predecessors, I wish to reflect upon this special activity of human reason. I judge it necessary to do so because, at the present time in particular, the search for ultimate truth seems often to be neglected. Modern philosophy clearly has the great merit of focusing attention upon man. From this starting-point, human reason with its many questions has developed further its yearning to know more and to know it ever more deeply. Complex systems of thought have thus been built, yielding results in the different fields of knowledge and fostering the development of culture and history. Anthropology, logic, the natural sciences, history, linguistics and so forth—the whole universe of knowledge has been involved in one way or another. Yet the positive results achieved must not obscure the fact that reason, in its one-sided concern to investigate human subjectivity, seems to have forgotten that men and women are always called to direct their steps towards a truth which transcends them. Sundered from that truth, individuals are at the mercy of caprice, and their state as person ends up being judged by pragmatic criteria based essentially upon experimental data, in the mistaken belief that technology must dominate all. It has happened therefore that reason,

rather than voicing the human orientation towards truth, has wilted under the weight of so much knowledge and little by little has lost the capacity to lift its gaze to the heights, not daring to rise to the truth of being. Abandoning the investigation of being, modern philosophical research has concentrated instead upon human knowing. Rather than make use of the human capacity to know the truth, modern philosophy has preferred to accentuate the ways in which this capacity is limited and conditioned. This has given rise to different forms of agnosticism and relativism which have led philosophical research to lose its way in the shifting sands of widespread scepticism. Recent times have seen the rise to prominence of various doctrines which tend to devalue even the truths which had been judged certain. A legitimate plurality of positions has yielded to an undifferentiated pluralism, based upon the assumption that all positions are equally valid, which is one of today's most widespread symptoms of the lack of confidence in truth. Even certain conceptions of life coming from the East betray this lack of confidence, denying truth its exclusive character and assuming that truth reveals itself equally in different doctrines, even if they contradict one another. On this understanding, everything is reduced to opinion; and there is a sense of being adrift. While, on the one hand, philosophical thinking has succeeded in coming closer to the reality of human life and its forms of expression, it has also tended to pursue issues—existential, hermeneutical or linguistic—which ignore the radical question of the truth about personal existence, about being and about God. Hence we see among the men and women of our time, and not just in some philosophers, attitudes of widespread distrust of the human being's great capacity for knowledge. With a false modesty, people rest content with partial and provisional truths, no longer seeking to ask radical questions about the meaning and ultimate foundation of human, personal and social existence. In short, the hope that philosophy might be able to provide definitive answers to these questions has dwindled.

6. Sure of her competence as the bearer of the Revelation of Jesus Christ, the Church reaffirms the need to reflect upon truth. This is why I have decided to address you, my venerable Brother Bishops, with whom I share the mission of "proclaiming the truth openly" (2 Cor 4:2), as also theologians and philosophers whose duty it is to explore the different aspects of truth, and all
those who are searching; and I do so in order to offer some reflections on the path which leads to true wisdom, so that those who love truth may take the sure path leading to it and so find rest from their labours and joy for their spirit.

I feel impelled to undertake this task above all because of the Second Vatican Council's insistence that the Bishops are "witnesses of divine and catholic truth".(3) To bear witness to the truth is therefore a task entrusted to us Bishops; we cannot renounce this task without failing in the ministry which we have received. In reaffirming the truth of faith, we can both restore to our contemporaries a genuine trust in their capacity to know and challenge philosophy to recover and develop its own full dignity. There is a further reason why I write these reflections. In my Encyclical Letter Veritatis Splendor, I drew attention to "certain fundamental truths of Catholic doctrine which, in the present circumstances, risk being distorted or denied".(4) In the present Letter, I wish to pursue that reflection by concentrating on the theme of truth itself and on its foundation in relation to faith. For it is undeniable that this time of rapid and complex change can leave especially the younger generation, to whom the future belongs and on whom it depends, with a sense that they have no valid points of reference. The need for a foundation for personal and communal life becomes all the more pressing at a time when we are faced with the patent inadequacy of perspectives in which the ephemeral is affirmed as a value and the possibility of discovering the real meaning of life is cast into doubt. This is why many people stumble through life to the very edge of the abyss without knowing where they are going. At times, this happens because those whose vocation it is to give cultural expression to their thinking no longer look to truth, preferring quick success to the toil of patient enquiry into what makes life worth living. With its enduring appeal to the search for truth, philosophy has the great responsibility of forming thought and culture; and now it must strive resolutely to recover its original vocation. This is why I have felt both the need and the duty to address this theme so that, on the threshold of the third millennium of the Christian era, humanity may come to a clearer sense of the great resources with which it has been endowed and may commit itself with renewed courage to implement the plan of salvation of which its history is part.

Yann Martel (b. 1963)

Life of Pi

Pi Patel, the sole survivor of a shipwreck has told two insurance investigators – Mr Okamoto and Mr Chiba – how he survived in the company of a tiger, "Richard Parker." There are several fantastical elements to his story.

Chapter 99

Mr. Okamoto: "Mr. Patel, we don't believe your story."

"Sorry-these cookies are good but they tend to crumble. I'm amazed. Why not?" "It doesn't hold up."

"What do you mean?"

"Bananas don't float."

"I'm sorry?"

"You said the orangutan came floating on an island of bananas."

"That's right."

"Bananas don't float."

"Yes, they do."

"They're too heavy."

"No, they're not. Here, try for yourself. I have two bananas right here."

Mr. Chiba: <translation>"Where did those come from? What else does he have under his bedsheet?"

Mr. Okamoto: "Damn it.</translation> No, that's all right."

"There's a sink over there."

"That's fine."

"I insist. Fill that sink with water, drop these bananas in, and we'll see who's right."

"We'd like to move on."

"I absolutely insist."

[Silence]

Mr. Chiba: <translation>"What do we do?"

Mr. Okamoto: "I feel this is going to be another very long day."</translation>

[Sound of a chair being pushed back. Distant sound of water gushing out of a tap]

Pi Patel: "What's happening? I can't see from here."

Mr. Okamoto [distantly]: "I'm filling the sink."

"Have you put the bananas in yet?"

[Distantly] "No."

"And now?"

[Distantly] "They're in."

"And?"

[Silence]

Mr. Chiba: <translation>"Are they floating?"

[Distantly] "They're floating."</translation>

"So, are they floating?"

[Distantly] "They're floating."

"What did I tell you?"

Mr. Okamoto: "Yes, yes. But it would take a lot of bananas to hold up an orang-utan."

"It did. There was close to a ton. It still makes me sick when I think of all those bananas floating away and going to waste when they were mine for the picking."

"It's a pity. Now, about-"

"Could I have my bananas back, please?"

Mr. Chiba: <translation>"I'll get them."

[Sound of a chair being pushed back]

[Distantly] "Look at that. They really do float."</translation>

Mr. Okamoto: "What about this algae island you say you came upon?" Mr. Chiba: "Here are your bananas."

Pi Patel: "Thank you. Yes?"

"I'm sorry to say it so bluntly, we don't mean to hurt your feelings, but you don't really expect us to believe you, do you? Carnivorous trees? A fish-eating algae that produces fresh water? Tree-dwelling aquatic rodents? These things don't exist."

"Only because you've never seen them."

"That's right. We believe what we see."

"So did Columbus. What do you do when you're in the dark?"

"Your island is botanically impossible."

"Said the fly just before landing in the Venus flytrap."

"Why has no one else come upon it?"

"It's a big ocean crossed by busy ships. I went slowly, observing much." "No scientist would believe you."

"These would be the same who dismissed Copernicus and Darwin. Have scientists finished coming upon new plants? In the Amazon basin, for example?"

"Not plants that contradict the laws of nature."

"Which you know through and through?"

"Well enough to know the possible from the impossible."

Mr. Chiba: "I have an uncle who knows a lot about botany. He lives in the country near Hita-Gun. He's a bonsai master."

Pi Patel: "A what?"

"A bonsai master. You know, bonsai are little trees."

"You mean shrubs."

"No, I mean trees. Bonsai are little trees. They are less than two feet tall. You can carry them in your arms. They can be very old. My uncle has one that is over three hundred years old."

"Three-hundred-year-old trees that are two feet tall that you can carry in your arms?" "Yes. They're very delicate. They need a lot of attention."

"Whoever heard of such trees? They're botanically impossible."

"But I assure you they exist, Mr. Patel. My uncle-"

"I believe what I see."

Mr. Okamoto: "Just a moment, please. <translation>Atsuro, with all due respect for your uncle who lives in the country near Hita-Gun, we're not here to talk idly about botany."

"I'm just trying to help."

"Do your uncle's bonsai eat meat?"

"I don't think so."

"Have you ever been bitten by one of his bonsai?"

"No."

"In that case, your uncle's bonsai are not helping us.</translation> Where were we?"

Pi Patel: "With the tall, full-sized trees firmly rooted to the ground I was telling you about." "Let us put them aside for now."

"It might be hard. I never tried pulling them out and carrying them."

"You're a funny man, Mr. Patel. Ha! Ha! Ha!"

Pi Patel: "Ha! Ha! Ha!"

Mr. Chiba: "Ha! Ha! Ha! <translation>It wasn't that funny."

Mr. Okamoto: "Just keep laughing.</translation> Ha! Ha! Ha!"

Mr. Chiba: "Ha! Ha! Ha!"

Mr. Okamoto: "Now about the tiger, we're not sure about it either."

"What do you mean?"

"We have difficulty believing it."

"It's an incredible story."

"Precisely."

"I don't know how I survived."

"Clearly it was a strain."

"I'll have another cookie."

"There are none left."

"What's in that bag?"

"Nothing."

"Can I see?"

Mr. Chiba: <translation>"There goes our lunch."</translation>

Mr. Okamoto: "Getting back to the tiger..."

Pi Patel: "Terrible business. Delicious sandwiches."

Mr. Okamoto: "Yes, they look good."

Mr. Chiba: <translation>"I'm hungry."</translation>

"Not a trace of it has been found. That's a bit hard to believe, isn't it? There are no tigers in the Americas. If there were a wild tiger out there, don't you think the police would have heard about it by now?"

"I should tell you about the black panther that escaped from the Zurich Zoo in the middle of winter."

"Mr. Patel, a tiger is an incredibly dangerous wild animal. How could you survive in a lifeboat with one? It's-"

"What you don't realize is that we are a strange and forbidding species to wild animals. We fill them with fear. They avoid us as much as possible. It took centuries to still the fear in some pliable animals-domestication it's called-but most cannot get over their fear, and I doubt they ever will. When wild animals fight us, it is out of sheer desperation. They fight when they feel they have no other way out. It's a very last resort."

"In a lifeboat? Come on, Mr. Patel, it's just too hard to believe!"

"Hard to believe? What do you know about hard to believe? You want hard to believe? I'll give you hard to believe. It's a closely held secret among Indian zookeepers that in 1971 Bara the polar bear escaped from the Calcutta Zoo. She was never heard from again, not by police or hunters or poachers or anyone else. We suspect she's living freely on the banks of the Hugli River. Beware if you go to Calcutta, my good sirs: if you have sushi on the breath you may pay a high price! If you took the city of Tokyo and turned it upside down and shook it, you'd be amazed at all the animals that would fall out: badgers, wolves, boa constrictors, Komodo dragons, crocodiles, ostriches, baboons, capybaras, wild boars, leopards, manatees, ruminants in untold numbers. There is no doubt in my mind that feral giraffes and feral hippos have been living in Tokyo for generations without being seen by a soul. You should compare one day the things that stick to the soles of your shoes as you walk down the street with what you see lying at the bottom of the cages in the Tokyo Zoo-then look up! And you expect to find a tiger in a Mexican jungle! It's laughable, just plain laughable. Ha! Ha! Ha!"

"There may very well be feral giraffes and feral hippos living in Tokyo and a polar bear living freely in Calcutta. We just don't believe there was a tiger living in your lifeboat."

"The arrogance of big-city folk! You grant your metropolises all the animals of Eden, but you deny my hamlet the merest Bengal tiger!"

"Mr. Patel, please calm down."

"If you stumble at mere believability, what are you living for? Isn't love hard to believe?"

"Mr. Patel-"

"Don't you bully me with your politeness! Love is hard to believe, ask any lover. Life is hard to believe, ask any scientist. God is hard to believe, ask any believer. What is your problem with hard to believe?"

"We're just being reasonable."

"So am I! I applied my reason at every moment. Reason is excellent for getting food, clothing and shelter. Reason is the very best tool kit. Nothing beats reason for keeping tigers away. But be excessively reasonable and you risk throwing out the universe with the bathwater."

"Calm down, Mr. Patel, calm down."

Mr. Chiba: <translation>"The bathwater? Why is he talking about bathwater?"</translation> "How can I be calm? You should have seen Richard Parker!"

"Yes, yes."

"Huge. Teeth like this! Claws like scimitars!"

Mr. Chiba: <translation>"What are scimitars?"

Mr. Okamoto: "Chiba-san,, instead of asking stupid vocabulary questions, why don't you make yourself useful? This boy is a tough nut to crack. Do something!"</translation>

Mr. Chiba: "Look! A chocolate bar!"

Pi Patel: "Wonderful!"

[Long silence]

Mr. Okamoto: <translation>"Like he hasn't already stolen our whole lunch. Soon he'll be demanding tempura."</translation>

[Long silence]

Mr. Okamoto: "We are losing sight of the point of this investigation. We are here because of the sinking of a cargo ship. You are the sole survivor. And you were only a passenger. You bear no responsibility for what happened. We-"

"Chocolate is so good!"

"We are not seeking to lay criminal charges. You are an innocent victim of a tragedy at sea. We are only trying to determine why and how the Tsimtsum sank. We thought you might help us, Mr. Patel."

[Silence] "Mr. Patel?" [Silence]

Pi Patel: "Tigers exist, lifeboats exist, oceans exist. Because the three have never come together in your narrow, limited experience, you refuse to believe that they might. Yet the plain fact is that the *Tsimtsum* brought them together and then sank."

[Silence]

Mr. Okamoto: "What about this Frenchman?"

"What about him?"

"Two blind people in two separate lifeboats meeting up in the Pacific-the coincidence seems a little far-fetched, no?"

"It certainly does."

"We find it very unlikely."

"So is winning the lottery, yet someone always wins." "We find it extremely hard to believe."

"So did I."

<translation>"I knew we should have taken the day off. <translation> You talked about food?" "We did."

"He knew a lot about food."

"If you can call it food."

"The cook on the Tsimtsum was a Frenchman."

"There are Frenchmen all over the world."

"Maybe the Frenchman you met was the cook."

"Maybe. How should I know? I never saw him. I was blind. Then Richard Parker ate him alive." "How convenient."

"Not at all. It was horrific and it stank. By the way, how do you explain the meerkat bones in the lifeboat?" "Yes, the bones of a small animal were-"

"More than one!"

"-of some small animals were found in the lifeboat. They must have come from the ship."

"We had no meerkats at the zoo."

"We have no proof they were meerkat bones."

Mr. Chiba: "Maybe they were banana bones! Ha! Ha! Ha! Ha! Ha!" <translation>"Atsuro, shut up!"

"I'm very sorry, Okamoto-san. It's the fatigue."

"You're bringing our service into disrepute!"

"Very sorry, Okamoto-san." <translation>

Mr. Okamoto: "They could be bones from another small animal."

"They were meerkats."

"They could be mongooses."

"The mongooses at the zoo didn't sell. They stayed in India."

"They could be shipboard pests, like rats. Mongooses are common in India."

"Mongooses as shipboard pests?" "Why not?"

"Who swam in the stormy Pacific, several of them, to the lifeboat? That's a little hard to believe, wouldn't you say?"

"Less hard to believe than some of the things we've heard in the last two hours. Perhaps the mongooses were already aboard the lifeboat, like the rat you mentioned."

"Simply amazing the number of animals in that lifeboat." "Simply amazing."

"A real jungle."

"Yes."

"Those bones are meerkat bones. Have them checked by an expert."

"There weren't that many left. And there were no heads."

"I used them as bait."

"It's doubtful an expert could tell whether they were meerkat bones or mongoose bones." "Find yourself a forensic zoologist."

"All right, Mr. Patel! You win. We cannot explain the presence of meerkat bones, if that is what they are, in the lifeboat. But that is not our concern here. We are here because a Japanese cargo ship owned by Oika Shipping Company, flying the Panamanian flag, sank in the Pacific."

"Something I never forget, not for a minute. I lost my whole family." "We're sorry aboutt that."

"Not as much as I am."

[Long silence]

Mr. Chiba: <translation>"What do we do now?" Mr. Okamoto: "I don't know."<translation> [Long silence]

Pi Patel: "Would you like a cookie?"

Mr. Okamoto: "Yes, that would be nice. Thank you." Mr. Chiba: "Thank you."

[Long silence]

Mr. Okamoto: "It's a nice day."

Pi Patel: "Yes. Sunny."

[Long silence]

Pi Patel: "Is this your first visit to Mexico?"

Mr. Okamoto: "Yes, it is."

"Mine too."

[Long silence]

Pi Patel: "So, you didn't like my story?"

Mr. Okamoto: "No, we liked it very much. Didn't we, Atsuro? We will remember it for a long, long time."

Mr. Chiba: "We will."

[Silence]

Mr. Okamoto: "But for the purposes of our investigation, we would like to know what really happened."

"What really happened?"

"Yes."

"So you want another story?"

"Uhh...no. We would like to know what really happened."

"Doesn't the telling of something always become a story?"

"Uhh...perhaps in English. In Japanese a story would have an element of invention in it. We don't want any invention. We want the 'straight facts', as you say in English."

"Isn't telling about something-using words, English or Japanese-already something of an invention? Isn't just looking upon this world already something of an invention?"

"Uhh..."

"The world isn't just the way it is. It is how we understand it, no? And in understanding something, we bring something to it, no? Doesn't that make life a story?"

"Ha! Ha! Ha! You are very intelligent, Mr. Patel."

Mr. Chiba: <translation>"What is he talking about?"

"I have no idea."<translation>

Pi Patel: "You want words that reflect reality?" "Yes."

"Words that do not contradict reality?" "Exactly."

"But tigers don't contradict reality."

"Oh please, no more tigers."

"I know what you want. You want a story that won't surprise you. That will confirm what you already know. That won't make you see higher or further or differently. You want a flat story. An immobile story. You want dry, yeastless factuality."

"Uhh..."

"You want a story without animals."

"Yes!"

"Without tigers or orangutans."

"That's right."

"Without hyenas or zebras."

"Without them."

"Without meerkats or mongooses."

"We don't want them."

"Without giraffes or hippopotamuses."

"We will plug our ears with our fingers!"

"So I'm right. You want a story without animals."

"We want a story without animals that will explain the sinking of the Tsimtsum."

"Give me a minute, please."

"Of course. <translation>I think we're finally getting somewhere. Let's hope he speaks some sense."

<translation>

[Long silence]

"Here's another story."

"Good."

"The ship sank. It made a sound like a monstrous metallic burp. Things bubbled at the surface and then vanished. I found myself kicking water in the Pacific Ocean. I swam for the lifeboat. It was the hardest swim of my life. I didn't seem to be moving. I kept swallowing water. I was very cold. I was rapidly losing strength. I wouldn't have made it if the cook hadn't thrown me a lifebuoy and pulled me in. I climbed aboard and collapsed.

"Four of us survived. Mother held on to some bananas and made it to the lifeboat. The cook was already aboard, as was the sailor.

"He ate the flies. The cook, that is. We hadn't been in the lifeboat a full day; we had food and water to last us for weeks; we had fishing gear and solar stills; we had no reason to believe that we wouldn't be rescued soon. Yet there he was, swinging his arms and catching flies and eating them greedily. Right away he was in a holy terror of hunger. He was calling us idiots and fools for not joining him in the feast. We were offended and disgusted, but we didn't show it. We were very polite about it. He was a stranger and a foreigner. Mother smiled and shook her head and raised her hand in refusal. He was a disgusting man. His mouth had the discrimination of a garbage heap. He also ate the rat. He cut it up and dried it in the sun. I-I'll be honest-I had a small piece, very small, behind Mother's back. I was so hungry. He was such a brute, that cook, ill-tempered and hypocritical.

"The sailor was young. Actually, he was older than me, probably in his early twenties, but he broke his leg jumping from the ship and his suffering made him a child. He was beautiful. He had no facial hair at all and a clear, shining complexion. His features-the broad face, the flattened nose, the narrow, pleated eyes-looked so elegant. I thought he looked like a Chinese emperor. His suffering was terrible. He spoke no English, not a single word, not yes or no, hello or thank you. He spoke only Chinese. We couldn't understand a word he said. He must have felt very lonely. When he wept, Mother held his head in her lap and I held his hand. It was very, very sad. He suffered and we couldn't do anything about it.

"His right leg was badly broken at the thigh. The bone stuck out of his flesh. He screamed with pain. We set his leg as best we could and we made sure he was eating and drinking. But his leg became infected. Though we drained it of pus every day, it got worse. His foot became black and bloated.

"It was the cook's idea. He was a brute. He dominated us. He whispered that the blackness would spread and that he would survive only if his leg were amputated. Since the bone was broken at the thigh, it would involve no more than cutting through flesh and setting a tourniquet. I can still hear his evil whisper. He would do the job to save the sailor's life, he said, but we would have to hold him. Surprise would be the only anaesthetic. We fell upon him. Mother and I held his arms while the cook sat on his good leg. The sailor writhed and screamed. His chest rose and fell. The cook worked the knife quickly. The leg fell off. Immediately Mother and I let go and moved away. We thought that if the restraint was ended, so would his struggling. We thought he would lie calmly. He didn't. He sat up instantly. His screams were all the worse for being unintelligible. He screamed and we stared, transfixed. There was blood everywhere. Worse, there was the contrast between the frantic activity of the poor sailor and the gentle repose of his leg at the bottom of the boat. He kept looking at the limb, as if imploring it to return. At last he fell back. We hurried into action. The cook folded some skin over the bone. We wrapped the stump in a piece of cloth and we tied a rope above the wound to stop the bleeding. We laid him as comfortably as we could on a mattress of life jackets and kept him warm. I thought it was all for nothing. I couldn't believe a human being could survive so much pain, so much butchery. Throughout the evening and night he moaned, and his breathing was harsh and uneven. He had fits of agitated delirium. I expected him to die during the night.

"He clung to life. At dawn he was still alive. He went in and out of consciousness. Mother gave him water. I caught sight of the amputated leg. It cut my breath short. In the commotion it had been shoved aside and forgotten in the dark. It had seeped a liquid and looked thinner. I took a life jacket and used it as a glove. I picked the leg up.

"'What are you doing?' asked the cook.

"'I'm going to throw it overboard,' I replied.

"'Don't be an idiot. We'll use it as bait. That was the whole point.'

"He seemed to regret his last words even as they were coming out, for his voice faded quickly. He turned away.

"'The whole point?' Mother asked. 'What do you mean by that?' "He pretended to be busy.

"Mother's voice rose. 'Are you telling us that we cut this poor boy's leg off not to save his life but to get fishing bait?'

"Silence from the brute. "'Answer me!' shouted Mother.

"Like a cornered beast he lifted his eyes and glared at her. 'Our supplies are running out,' he snarled. 'We need more food or we'll die.'

"Mother returned his glare. 'Our supplies are not running out! We have plenty of food and water. We have package upon package of biscuits to tide us over till our rescue.' She took hold of the plastic container in which we put the open rations of biscuits. It was unexpectedly light in her hands. The few crumbs in it rattled. 'What!' She opened it. 'Where are the biscuits? The container was full last night!'

"The cook looked away. As did I.

"'You selfish monster!' screamed Mother. 'The only reason we're running out of food is because you're gorging yourself on it!'

"'He had some too,' he said, nodding my way.

"Mother's eyes turned to me. My heart sank.

"'Piscine, is that true?'

"'It was night, Mother. I was half asleep and I was so hungry. He gave me a biscuit. I ate it without thinking...' "'Only one, was it?' sneered the cook.

"It was Mother's turn to look away. The anger seemed to go out of her. Without saying another word she went back to nursing the sailor.

"I wished for her anger. I wished for her to punish me. Only not this silence. I made to arrange some life jackets for the sailor's comfort so that I could be next to her. I whispered, 'I'm sorry, Mother, I'm sorry.' My eyes were brimming with tears. When I brought them up, I saw that hers were too. But she didn't look at me. Her eyes were gazing upon some memory in mid-air.

"'We're all alone, Piscine, all alone,' she said, in a tone that broke every hope in my body. I never felt so lonely in all my life as I did at that moment. We had been in the lifeboat two weeks already and it was taking its toll on us. It was getting harder to believe that Father and Ravi had survived.

"When we turned around, the cook was holding the leg by the ankle over the water to drain it. Mother brought her hand over the sailor's eyes.

"He died quietly, the life drained out of him like the liquid from his leg. The cook promptly butchered him. The leg had made for poor bait. The dead flesh was too decayed to hold on to the fishing hook; it simply dissolved in the water. Nothing went to waste with this monster. He cut up everything, including the sailor's skin and every inch of his intestines. He even prepared his genitals. When he had finished with his torso, he moved on to his arms and shoulders and to his legs. Mother and I rocked with pain and horror. Mother shrieked at the cook, 'How can you do this, you monster? Where is your humanity? Have you no decency? What did the poor boy do to you? You monster! You monster!' The cook replied with unbelievable vulgarity.

"'At least cover his face, for God's sake!' cried my mother. It was unbearable to have that beautiful face, so noble and serene, connected to such a sight below. The cook threw himself upon the sailor's head and before our very eyes scalped him and pulled off his face. Mother and I vomited.

"When he had finished, he threw the butchered carcass overboard. Shortly after, strips of flesh and pieces of organs were lying to dry in the sun all over the boat. We recoiled in horror. We tried not to look at them. The smell would not go away.

"The next time the cook was close by, Mother slapped him in the face, a full hard slap that punctuated the air with a sharp crack. It was something shocking coming from my mother. And it was heroic. It was an act of outrage and pity and grief and bravery. It was done in memory of that poor sailor. It was to salvage his dignity.

"I was stunned. So was the cook. He stood without moving or saying a word as Mother looked him straight in the face. I noticed how he did not meet her eyes.

"We retreated to our private spaces. I stayed close to her. I was filled with a mix of rapt admiration and abject fear.

"Mother kept an eye on him. Two days later she saw him do it. He tried to be discreet, but she saw him bring his hand to his mouth. She shouted, 'I saw you! You just ate a piece! You said it was for bait! I knew it. You monster! You animal! How could you? He's human! He's your own kind!' If she had expected him to be mortified, to spit it out and break down and apologize, she was wrong. He kept chewing. In fact, he lifted his head up and quite openly put the rest of the strip in his mouth. 'Tastes like pork,' he muttered. Mother expressed her indignation and disgust by violently turning away. He ate another strip. 'I feel stronger already,' he muttered. He concentrated on his fishing.

"We each had our end of the lifeboat. It's amazing how willpower can build walls. Whole days went by as if he weren't there.

[…]

"He killed her. The cook killed my mother. We were starving. I was weak. I couldn't hold on to a turtle. Because of me we lost it. He hit me. Mother hit him. He hit her back.

[…]

"Then we fought and I killed him. He had no expression on his face, neither of despair nor of anger, neither of fear nor of pain. He gave up. He let himself be killed, though it was still a struggle. He knew he had gone too far, even by his bestial standards. He had gone too far and now he didn't want to go on living any more. But he never said 'I'm sorry.' Why do we cling to our evil ways? …

"He was such an evil man. Worse still, he met evil in me-selfishness, anger, ruthlessness. I must live with that. "Solitude began. I turned to God. I survived."

[Long silence]

"Is that better? Are there any parts you find hard to believe? Anything you'd like me to change?"

Mr. Chiba: <translation>"What a horrible story."

[Long silence]

Mr. Okamoto: "Both the zebra and the Taiwanese sailor broke a leg, did you notice that?"

"No, I didn't."

"And the hyena bit off the zebra's leg just as the cook cut off the sailor's."

"Ohhh, Okamoto-san, you see a lot."

[…]

"So what happened, Mr. Patel? We're puzzled.. Everything was normal and then...?" "Then normal sank."

"Why?"

"I don't know. You should be telling me. You're the experts. Apply your science." "We don't understand."

[Long silence]

Mr. Chiba: <translation>"Now what?"

Mr. Okamoto: "We give up. The explanation for the sinking of the Tsimtsum is at the bottom of the Pacific."

[Long silence]

Mr. Okamoto: "Yes, that's it. Let's go.<translation> Well, Mr. Patel, I think we have all we need. We thank you very much for your cooperation. You've been very, very helpful."

"You're welcome. But before you go, I'd like to ask you something." "Yes?"

"The Tsimtsum sank on July 2nd, 1977."

"Yes."

"And I arrived on the coast of Mexico, the sole human survivor of the Tsimtsum, on February 14th, 1978." "That's right."

"I told you two stories that account for the 227 days in between."

"Yes, you did."

"Neither explains the sinking of the Tsimtsum." "That's right."

"Neither makes a factual difference to you." "That's true."

"You can't prove which story is true and which is not. You must take my word for it." "I guess so."

"In both stories the ship sinks, my entire family dies, and I suffer."

"Yes, that's true."

"So tell me, since it makes no factual difference to you and you can't prove the question either way, which story do you prefer? Which is the better story, the story with animals or the story without animals?"

Mr. Okamoto: "That's an interesting question..."

Mr. Chiba: "The story with animals."

Mr. Okamoto: <translation>"Yes".<translation> The story with animals is the better story."

Pi Patel: "Thank you. And so it goes with God."

Charlotte and Peter Vardy

God Matters (2013)
Chapter 1: Faith and Reason

"I do not feel obliged to believe that the same God who has endowed us
with sense, reason, and intellect has intended us to forgo their use."
Galileo Galilei, Letter to the Grand Duchess Christina

Today, the common perception is that faith and reason are in opposition.
The polarisation of Religion and Science led to a shift in how people understand the nature of faith. Whereas in the past faith was understood as an intellectual response to any study of the universe and atheism seen as a mark of ignorance, following Darwin there seemed less and less need to posit a divine designer. Atheism is sometimes seen today as the mark of the informed mind and faith is portrayed in terms of weakness, stemming from a need for simple answers as well as a search for comfort and a basic fear of facing the Truth.
As scientists uncovered more about how the universe operates the creative role of God grew smaller; God was pushed into the gaps in human knowledge. Religious texts had to be re-interpreted to account for longer timescales, ice-ages, the existence of other hominid species and dinosaurs. This raised huge questions. If God's role and nature seemed to change according to the state of human knowledge, could that suggest that God is dependent on us, rather than we on God. If "revealed" wisdom falls short at precisely the same point as the state of human knowledge, could that imply that religious texts and traditions owe more to human authors than to divine inspiration?

The Tide Turns

In 1841 German writer Ludwig Feuerbach (1804-1872) wrote a book called *The Essence of Christianity*. Feuerbach was a "Young Hegelian", one of a group of radical thinkers inspired by the writings of Georg Hegel (1770-1831).
Hegel suggested that human history is dynamic, that ideas and society moves forward through a process of dialectic. The dominant philosophy is challenged by a new theory and, over time and out of the tension between the two, a new synthesis develops, which then becomes the dominant philosophy. Hegel's model was exciting partly because it suggested that things constantly change and progress and partly because it suggested that there could be more than one way of seeing the world, that "truth" to some extent depends on the world-view which dominates at the time. Young philosophers saw in Hegel's ideas hope that society could and would progress, that their radical ideas could challenge established orthodoxy and contribute to human advancement.

In the mid-19ᵗʰ Century Christianity dominated all life in Europe. In most cases, the Church held the keys to education and employment; it exerted a powerful influence on all governments, their laws and policies. Although many of the horror-stories of actual repression are untrue, in some cases the Church seemed to stand in the way of scientific progress; it was slow to accept new ideas and continued to invest in areas of study which seemed archaic and irrelevant. By Hegel's own theory, it was natural that some "Young Hegelians" would challenge the Church and propose radical, new ways of looking at and running the world. It was also natural that they should be inspired by scientific materialism, which offered a world-view diametrically opposed to that held by Christians.

Ludwig Feuerbach claimed to be *"a natural philosopher in the domain of the mind."*[1] He was a materialist and tried to apply scientific method to his study of society, history and philosophy. Starting with a definition of existence which limited what could be known to that which could be experienced, Feuerbach examined Christianity and concluded that *"Religion is the dream of the human mind"*[2] He explained how the religion had developed and changed over time and he noted that doctrines and structures seem to adapt in order to fulfil societal needs.

For example, in the power-vacuum after the decline of the Roman Empire the Church grew into a provider of governance. God was portrayed as emperor-judge and there was a great emphasis on teachings about heaven and hell. In a world with little infrastructure, no police service and few courts, Christianity transformed from a minority faith which encouraged believers to stand against social norms into a state religion which gradually assumed the functions of government.

As Feuerbach saw it, religion was a form of social control. In order to maximise its effectiveness, he argued that people were being encouraged to accept nonsensical things on the basis of authority, to suspend their critical faculties. He wrote [3] *"in these days illusion only is sacred, truth profane… Religion has disappeared and it has been substituted, even amongst Protestants, with the appearance of Religion – the Church – in order at least that "the Faith" might be imparted to the ignorant and indiscriminating multitude."*[4]

Feuerbach went on to argue that it is not just the Church which seems to respond to social needs and wants; the personal concepts of God held by different people often fulfil their needs and desires. Thus, a person without a strong Father figure sees God in this role, as authoritarian, whilst another person who lacked affection in their upbringing sees a God of love and forgiveness. For Feuerbach, faith in God is a form of subconscious wish-fulfilment.

It follows that analysing peoples' concepts of God can tell us much about their psychology and about the characteristics of their society, but it is difficult to escape the implication that the object of faith, God, has no independent existence. If God is simply a projection, a product of deep-seated imagination, then faith is not credible and not compatible with reason.

Sigmund Freud (1856-1939) was influenced by Feuerbach when he described faith in these terms. The child experiences the father as the source of fear and guilt, yet the child wants unconditional love from a father so creates an idealised image in God.

"The disturbed psyche projects images so that they appear to be outside of the mind. All human beings long for an unconditional, loving father figure who can accept them as they are and forgive all the dark sides of their character, so the religious idea of God is a projection of the human imagination and is the means whereby humans cope with the lack of love and the lack of meaning in the world."[5]

Religion is a neurosis albeit an attractive one; wishful thinking cannot create something that does not exist:

"It would be very nice if there were a God who created the world and was a benevolent providence, and if there were a moral order in the universe and an after-life; but it is a very striking fact that all this is exactly as we are bound to wish it to be."[6]

Feuerbach's work influenced others too. *The Essence of Christianity* was translated into English in 1853 by Marian Evans (1819-1880), who wrote novels under the name George Eliot.[7] Whilst Evans was working on the text the poet Matthew Arnold was writing the famous poem *Dover Beach* which reflects the devastating effect that ideas like those of Feuerbach had on British intellectuals in the 1850s. He wrote,

"The Sea of Faith

Was once, too, at the full, and round earth's shore

Lay like the folds of a bright girdle furled.

But now I only hear

Its melancholy, long, withdrawing roar,

Retreating, to the breath

Of the night-wind, down the vast edges drear

And naked shingles of the world."[8]

The development of Biblical Criticism led some Protestants, like Marian Evans, to lose their faith altogether – but it led others to cling to it in the face of rational objections. Reason and scholarship started to seem like the enemy of faith and religion. Many focussed on personal experiences of God, on feelings and emotions rather than on verifiable fact or argument.

In the second half of the 19th Century rational, bright and open neo-classical churches went out of fashion; neo-gothic swept in, embracing shadows and symbolism. The Gothic revival went further than bricks and mortar, making a case for *"a return to the faith and the social structures of the Middle Ages."* Faced with the fruits of scientific research, mass-industrialisation, urban migration, child-labour, poverty, ignorance, crime and social breakdown, people hankered after a golden age, before factories and the threat of famine. Christians saw in the Gospels a message of anti-materialism, simplicity and socialism which could help restore the world.

Whether in the works of novelists like Elizabeth Gaskell, designers like William Morris or the Pre-Raphaelite artists, suspicion of 'progress' and a longing for people to reengage with tradition, embrace myth and emotion and be suspicious of calculating reason is plain to see. The Church had never been so popular; it offered the possibility of blocking out the real world and nourishing the parts of humanity which modern life ignored – imagination, spirituality, beauty.

Nevertheless, the human horrors which led on from industrialisation, graphically described by Karl Marx and Friedrich Engels, led to worse horrors on the Western Front of WWI, in the gas-chambers of Auschwitz and in the streets of Hiroshima.

The Church failed to change and re-articulate its essential message in a way that could seem relevant. Christianity, at its best, appeals because it engages with the truth and with all it is and could be to be human. It does not defer to authority, get hung up in power-structures, belittle, ignore or exclude people. It is not obsessed with sex, however much it may seem to be today, and cares little for tradition and appearances. Jesus stood for what is good in humanity – for honesty, bravery, generosity, forgiveness, love – and against lies and injustice, cowardice and apathy, selfishness of all sorts. When people have turned to the Christian faith it is because they see it offering this sort of better life, not just an alternative political power-structure to submit to. This is why some forms of Islam are so popular and make it the fastest growing world religion. When religion offers a message of equality, justice and truth people flock to become part of it – but when it starts to prize unity and power over truth and fairness they disengage.

In the 20th Century it became more and more difficult to reconcile faith in an all-powerful and loving creator-God with the realities of life in an obviously imperfect world. Religion has offered little to make it any easier. Theology has become an obscure discipline; theologians write papers which will only ever be read by other theologians. The philosophy of religion has become a backwater, seldom considered even by academic philosophers. How can this be? Theology used to be the queen of the sciences, the capstone of education, providing the opportunity to ask the big questions about truth, origins and meaning. It has in all too many cases become relegated to being a sub-branch of the sociology department.

Because of this, in the face of glaring questions about how a good and powerful God could allow injustice, how the Scriptures can be reconciled with modern science and how people can just keep on believing, apparently in spite of the evidence rather than because of it, it might seem as if one might be justified in accepting Dawkins' characterisation of faith as *"anti-intellectual"*.

To do so would, however, ignore the fact that there have always been different types of faith. Broadly speaking, there are five different approaches to defining faith…

    d   Propositional Faith: faith is based on evidence and/or argument. It depends upon propositions and may be destroyed if its basis is destroyed.

    e   Non-propositional Faith: faith is not based on evidence or argument but may be enriched or explored through either.

    f   Fideism: faith is independent of reason, perhaps hostile to it and definitely superior to it in providing a complete account of the world.

g Voluntarism: belief is under our control, directly or indirectly. It is rational to will oneself to believe, at least to put oneself in a position whereby faith may develop, because doing so will yield positive results.

h Non-voluntarism: faith is not a matter of choice – God chooses some to believe and others not to, and we are not necessarily in a position to understand why.

Propositional Faith

Propositional Faith identifies faith with justified belief or knowledge. Faith that God exists may be compared with belief that evolution through natural selection occurs. Evidence (propositions) supports a conclusion, theory or explanation; if the evidence changes the conclusion will be *falsified* and the theory may have to change. Most, though not all, proponents of Propositional Faith use Natural Theology (arguments for God which start with observations of the natural world) to provide the propositions on which faith depends.

The traditional definition of faith is best articulated by St Thomas Aquinas (1215-1274), who wrote that *"from the perspective of the one believing … the object of faith is something composite in the form of a proposition"*[9]. Aquinas' five "ways" provide natural, rational grounds for belief in God. For Aquinas, the world is moved, caused, contingent and this suggests the God is unmoved, uncaused and fully actual and so *must* be understood in terms of omnipotence and omnibenevolence, at least as Aquinas interprets them.

It follows that although *natural theology* provides strong evidence to support belief, that evidence and the faith it supports is always subject to challenge. Arguably, Propositional Faith is not as strong as other forms of faith. Indeed, some would say that it is not really faith at all. Even Aquinas admitted that reason and natural theology cannot take us all the way to God. For Aquinas, it is as if Faith is a destination city served by two railway lines. The fast line, reason, stops just short of the city and leaves passengers to walk the final stage of the journey. The slow line, revelation, takes ages, is tortuous and prone to breaking down, but delivers passengers into the city-centre.

Today the mainstream Roman Catholic Church has a positive approach to Natural Theology and Propositional Faith. The Anti-Modernist oath promulgated by Pope Pius X required Catholics to affirm that *"God, the origin and end of all things, can be known with certainty by the natural light of reason from the created world (cf. Rom. 1:20), that is, from the visible works of creation, as a cause from its effects, and that, therefore, his existence can also be demonstrated..."*[10] Pope John Paul II's encyclical *Fides et Ratio* (1998) also affirms that reason is necessary for faith. He wrote... *"Faith and reason are like two wings on which the human spirit rises to the contemplation of truth; and God has placed in the human heart a desire to know the truth – in a word, to know himself – so that, by knowing and loving God, men and women may also come to the fullness of truth about themselves"*[11]

Non-Propositional Faith

CS Lewis wrote of faith, "*I am not asking anyone to accept Christianity if his best reasoning tells him that the weight of the evidence is against it. That is not the point at which Faith comes in. But supposing a man's reason once decides that the weight of the evidence is for it....There will come a moment when there is bad news, or he is in trouble, or is living among a lot of other people who do not believe it, and all at once his emotions will rise up and carry out a sort of blitz on his belief... I am not talking of moments at which any real new reasons against Christianity turn up. Those have to be faced and that is a different matter. I am talking about moments where a mere mood rises up against it. Now Faith, in the sense in which I am here using the word, is the art of holding on to things your reason has once accepted, in spite of your changing moods. For moods will change, whatever view your reason takes. I know that by experience...That is why Faith is such a necessary virtue: unless you teach your moods "where they get off," you can never be either a sound Christian or even a sound atheist, but just a creature dithering to and fro, with its beliefs really dependent on the weather and the state of its digestion. Consequently one must train the habit of Faith.*"[12]

For Lewis it is clear that faith is more than just an intellectual decision, it involves a commitment so that belief in God can survive the buffeting which life will bring. The Welsh Philosopher HH Price (1899-1984) distinguished between *believing in* something and *believing that* something. To *believe that* is propositional, the result of argument and so potentially falsified. It is an intellectual decision. To *believe in* however, is an attitude which requires that one's whole being changes. To believe that God exists is a matter of the intellect, to believe in God means to trust one's life to God. For Price, *believing in* is what Religious faith is really about – it cannot be reduced to believing that, whatever atheist philosophers seem to argue.

The Danish Philosopher Soren Kierkegaard (1813-1855) maintained a non-propositional definition of faith. Kierkegaard wrote "*I do not believe... that God exists, but I know it; whereas I believe that God has existed... even from the Greek point of view, the eternal truth by being for an existing person, becomes an object of faith and a paradox.*[13]" Faith is the individual's reaction to the paradox of Christianity expressed in the claim that Jesus is both fully human and also fully God. Since essential truth is far beyond our comprehension, it appears to us in the form of a paradox which can either be accepted or rejected. 'Paradox' is not the same as a logical contradiction – it is where two claims appear to be in tension and this tension cannot be resolved by the human mind. Since, for Kierkegaard, we cannot know the nature of God, the claim that Jesus is both God and man is a paradox and not a contradiction as, in a contradiction, both terms have to understood and known.

It is more likely that the human mind is limited than that the truth is limited by what the human mind can conceive. Kierkegaard would not have us believe the impossible or the contradictory, yet, because faith is necessarily puzzling and uncertain, "*when faith requires that he relinquish his understanding, then to have faith becomes just as difficult for the most intelligent person as it is for the person of the most limited intelligence, or it presumably becomes even more difficult for the former*"[14]

Kierkegaard is often identified with the idea that Faith requires irrational trust. Like in *"Indiana Jones and the Last Crusade"*[15], faith is not real unless it requires one to put one's weight on nothing, expecting it to hold. For Kierkegaard, *"there is no gradual accumulation of sensory data or rational proofs for God's existence or for the resurrection of Christ, etc. One performs a willed act of faith despite fear, doubt, and sin. The leap is not out of thoughtlessness, but out of volition."* The so-called "leap of faith" is not simply a suspension of one's critical faculties becoming certain of something beyond reason. For Kierkegaard, faith is the acceptance of the necessity of doubt and struggle with reality, a giving up of any hope of certainty but a commitment to stake one's life on one's belief. Existential engagement is crucial – as Kierkegaard said "As you have lived, so have you believed."

In his book *Dynamics of Faith*[16] Paul Tillich (1886-1965) explored the nature of faith. Faith involves a risk or wager, existential courage. It involves the certain acceptance of uncertainty, which can be overwhelming and lead us to live in what Kierkegaard called a state of *"fear and trembling"* or *"sickness unto death"*. Nevertheless, for Tillich God is nothing short of *"the ground of our being"*. It may be difficult to accept and live in relationship with God, but God concerns us ultimately and ignoring God is like ignoring reality itself.

For neither Kierkegaard nor Tillich is faith a comfortable state or an easy option!

1. Fideism

Alvin Plantinga defined fideism as *"exclusive or basic reliance upon faith alone, accompanied by a consequent disparagement of reason and utilized especially in the pursuit of philosophical or religious truth"*. He went on to define a fideist as someone who *"urges reliance on faith rather than reason, in matters philosophical and religious" and who "may go on to disparage and denigrate reason"*[17]. Reason and philosophy, therefore, are dismissed as groundings for faith – reason operates within faith and does not provide a basis for faith. Traditionally the fideist position was associated with the writings of Tertullian, a lawyer from Carthage who converted to Christianity sometime around the year 197AD. Tertullian asked the famous questions *"What does Athens have to do with Jerusalem? What have heretics to do with Christians?"*[18] For Tertullian, the Christian faith and pagan philosophy were polar opposites. The truth of Christianity had been revealed through the life of Christ and the scripture which recorded it. To use pagan philosophy to find God's message risked distorting it.

Famously, Tertullian wrote that *"The Son of God was crucified: I am not ashamed-because it is shameful. The Son of God died: It is immediately credible-because it is silly. He was buried, and rose again: It is certain-because it is impossible."*[19] The last phrase is sometimes translated as *"It is certain because it is impossible"* or even *"I believe because it is impossible!"*, yet it is important to appreciate that Tertullian's meaning is misrepresented by this.

Elsewhere in his writings Tertullian observed that *"reason is a property of God's, since there is nothing which God, the creator of all things, has not foreseen, arranged and determined by reason; moreover, there is nothing He does not wish to be investigated and understood by reason…"*[20] There are 340 passages in Tertullian where the word *ratio* appears, making it one of the most frequently used nouns in his work, so it is fair to say that he did not dismiss reason altogether. In fact, Tertullian utilized those elements of Greek philosophy and logic that he believed to be compatible with Christian belief; his faith was not based on rational argument, but he was not averse to using it in order to explore or defend that faith. When he does speak of the absurdity of Christian belief, Tertullian is referring to the unlikelihood that any human mind could conceive of God's plan. He meant much the same as Anselm when he said that *"God is that than which nothing greater can be conceived"* or Aquinas when he said that *"God is neither something nor nothing."*

Some Christians have interpreted Tertullian as meaning that faith is only really faith if its object is irrational, even absurd. The incarnation, miracles, the resurrection – they all run counter to reason and yet unless a Christian believes that they happened then many would question their faith. However, modern scholarship has largely abandoned the idea that Tertullian was the Father of fideism. Eric Osborne wrote, *"Not only did he never say 'credo quia absurdum', but he never meant anything like it and never abandoned the claims of Athens upon Jerusalem"*. He went on to explain that the context of the famous quotation is an argument with Marcion, who was held to be a heretic, and who believed in the resurrection but did not believe Christ had a real body, and that the flesh was shameful. Tertullian pointed out that Christ himself said that worldly wisdom was not to be trusted on such things, so if Marcion was following it, he must be in the wrong. Tertullian, Osborne concluded, was a *"most improbable fideist"*[21]

Another commonly used example of a fideist approach to faith is Martin Luther (1483-1546). Indeed, Luther wrote *"How, then should we be able to comprehend or understand the secret counsels of God's majesty, or search them out with our human sense, reason, or understanding? Should we then admire our own wisdom? I, for my part, admit myself a fool…"*[22] Indeed, he taught that *"All the articles of our Christian faith, which God has revealed to us in His Word, are in presence of reason sheerly impossible, absurd, and false…"*[23] continuing that *"Reason is the greatest enemy that faith has"*[24] Yet even Luther conceded that reason can be used to enhance faith, if not to create it. He also wrote, *"so it is with human reason, which strives not against faith, when enlightened, but rather furthers and advances it."*[25]

1. Voluntarism

In his *Pensees* Blaise Pascal (1623-1662) described a reason to believe which might convince an atheist. He wrote…

"If there is a God, He is infinitely incomprehensible… This being so… Who then will blame Christians for not being able to give a reason for their belief… Let us then examine this point, and say, "God is, or He is not." But to which side shall we incline? Reason can decide nothing here… What will you wager… according to reason, you can defend neither of the propositions… but you must wager. It is not optional. You are embarked. Which will you choose then… Let us weigh the gain and the loss in wagering that God is. Let us estimate these two chances. If you gain, you gain all; if you lose, you lose nothing. Wager, then, without hesitation that He is… there is here an infinity of an infinitely happy life to gain, a chance of gain against a finite number of chances of loss, and what

you stake is finite… there is no time to hesitate, you must give all… when one is forced to play, he must renounce reason to preserve his life, rather than risk it for infinite gain, as likely to happen as the loss of nothingness."[26] For Pascal, this did not constitute a good argument for the existence of God. God is *"infinitely incomprehensible"* and it is impossible to prove God's existence in the way that one might try to prove the existence of a new planet. Further, it does not explain why most people have faith; it is just a possible way of convincing somebody who was struggling to take the search for faith seriously. Pascal was not so crude as to suggest that we can force ourselves to believe, even when the reasons to do so are substantial. As Tillich observed, *"no command to believe and no will to believe can create faith."*[27] Pascal acknowledged the possibility that some people seem not to be made for faith, but suggested *"at least learn your inability to believe, since reason brings you to this, and yet you cannot believe. Endeavour then to convince yourself, not by increase of proofs of God, but by the abatement of your passions. You would like to attain faith, and do not know the way; you would like to cure yourself of unbelief, and ask the remedy for it. Learn of those who have been bound like you, and who now stake all their possessions. These are people who know the way which you would follow, and who are cured of an ill of which you would be cured. Follow the way by which they began; by acting as if they believed, taking the holy water, having masses said, etc. … What have you to lose?"*

Modern scholars distinguish between *direct voluntarism*, the idea that the choice over what to believe is under our immediate control, and *indirect voluntarism*, the idea that the choice is not under our immediate control but that we are able to influence what we come to believe by choosing to perform intermediary actions. Pascal was an indirect voluntarist. For Pascal, faith is not just the result of an intellectual decision but must be nurtured through developing a life of faith. People need to decide to put themselves in the best position for faith to develop, by being good, worshipping and integrating into the faith community. This is not just sensible in terms of a possible afterlife, but also in terms of this life. He asked, *"what harm will befall you in taking this side? You will be faithful, honest, humble, grateful, generous, a sincere friend, truthful. Certainly you will not have those poisonous pleasures, glory and luxury; but will you not have others? I will tell you that you will thereby gain in this life, and that, at each step you take on this road, you will see so great certainty of gain, so much nothingness in what you risk, that you will at last recognise that you have wagered for something certain and infinite, for which you have given nothing."* Pascal calls individuals to take the step of putting themselves in a position where they may acquire faith rather than to dismiss faith without enquiry or engagement. Pascal is really targeting indifference and seeking to persuade people to seek believe whilst recognising that they may not find it.

Two main objections are often raised to Pascal's argument. Firstly, to believe in God simply for some eventual reward is the wrong motive for belief. Such self-seeking individuals would not deserve eternal life, whatever they believed or did. Secondly, in order to be sure of a payoff, an individual would not know which God or gods to believe in to cover the conditions of the wager. Would the Wager also hold for another God? One would have to believe in all gods in order to be sure, but if there were only one God then this strategy would defeat itself. Nevertheless, it is worth considering that these criticisms could be based on an incomplete understanding of Pascal's position.

Pascal does not suggest that anybody could simply choose to believe for personal advantage; the best they could do is to be persuaded to live a good, religious life and to put themselves in the best position for faith to develop. Faith may or may not result.

Further, the idea that religions are mutually exclusive is not conclusive. It could be that different religious stories and modes of life are simply different interpretations of a single truth. It could be that being immersed in a Sikh life would be just as likely to result in faith as being immersed in a Catholic life. The differences could just be cultural and any claims to the contrary could be reflections of human beings' natural competitiveness rather than reality. Jesus seemed to indicate something on these lines in the parable of the sheep and the goats where what seems to matter most is how one lives rather than propositional belief.

1. Non-Voluntarism

A final understanding of faith is perhaps best represented by the stories of prophets in the Bible. God chose Moses as a leader for the Hebrews, Amos was "plucked" from his work as a farmer tending sycamore trees and sent to preach to the people of Judah and Jonah was chased across land and sea as he tried to escape God's mission for him. The Prophet Mohammed could be another example of somebody chosen by God for faith. For many people of faith it seems that their relationship with God is not the result of their own ordinary will or intellect, but is the will of God.

At its most basic level, a non-voluntarist approach to faith would suggest that some people are made for faith or commanded to believe. Whether we have faith or not is, to a large extent, out of our hands. The great Islamic philosopher Al Ghazali (1058-1111) described the process of acquiring faith in Chapter III of the *Munqidh*. Al Ghazali was a leading philosopher and teacher at the University of Baghdad. He started by looking for proof of God in normal forms of worship and through study, but realised that these would yield nothing. He wrote,

"I also perceived that I could not hope for eternal happiness unless I feared God and rejected all the passions, that is to say, I should begin by breaking my heart's attachment to the world. I needed to abandon the illusions of life on earth in order to direct my attention towards my eternal home with the most intense desire for God, the Almighty. This entailed avoiding all honours and wealth, and escaping from everything that usually occupies a person and ties him down... Turning to look inward, I perceived that I was bound by attachments on all sides. I meditated on all that I had done, teaching and instructing being my proudest achievements, and I perceived that all my studies were futile, since they were of no value for the Way to the hereafter... I thought of nothing else, all the time remaining undecided. One day, I would determine to leave Baghdad and lead a new life, but the next day I would change my mind... This tug of war between my emotions and the summons from the Hereafter lasted nearly six months, from the month of Rajab 488 A.H. (July 1095 A.D.), during which I lost my free will and was under compulsion... God tied my tongue and stopped me teaching... I grew weak. The physicians despaired of treating me. ... Feeling my impotence, my inability to come to a decision, I put myself in the hands of God, the

ultimate refuge of all those who are in need. I was heard by the one who hears those in need when they pray to Him. He made it easy for me to renounce honours, wealth, family and friends."[28]

For Al Ghazali, faith cannot arise from a normal life, from everyday experiences or unassisted reason. It arises from the realisation of the inadequacy of being human and from putting oneself in God's hands. God's grace makes it possible to know God in a new way, to have a certainty in His existence which is otherwise impossible. For Al Ghazali real faith is total certainty, which holds the *"soul so bound that nothing could detach it."*[29]

In the Christian tradition John Calvin (1509-1564) is most associated with a non-voluntarist approach to faith. For Calvin faith is *"a firm and certain knowledge of God's benevolence towards us, founded upon the truth of the freely given promise in Christ, both revealed to our minds and sealed upon our hearts through the Holy Spirit"*[30] For Calvin and modern followers of his tradition such as Alvin Plantinga, some people have a special cognitive faculty which makes them able to sense God and truly *know* His existence. For these people faith is not really a choice. God's reality impresses itself upon them and they cannot honestly deny it. For those without the special cognitive faculty however, God's existence appears no more than possible.

Modern *Reformed Epistemology*, following the ideas of William Alston (1921-2009), Nicholas Woltersdorff (b.1932) and Alvin Plantinga (b.1932), suggests that for some people, having a *"properly ordered noetic structure"*, belief in God is *"properly basic"*, reasonable though it is not held as an inference from other truths. For those with faith, reason must then be used to *"defeat the defeaters"*, to demonstrate the logical possibility of a faith position and that challenges, such as the existence of evil and suffering, do not destroy its credibility.

In *God and Other Minds* (1967), Plantinga argued that beliefs are *warranted* without regular evidence provided they are grounded and defended against known objections. Because it is conceivably possible that God has designed some minds to know God, faith is possibly warranted apart from argument. Plantinga challenges the dominance of evidentialism, suggesting that it has a limited view of warranted belief. He argues that Religious experiences, including everyday experiences such as awe and wonder, form an important part of the warrant of faith. Nevertheless it can be argued that this view applies a form of spiritual apartheid with some being chosen by God for faith and others for non-belief. Human freedom is radically compromised.

Summary

Although most people see faith as being opposed to reason today, in fact the place of reason in forming or supporting faith rather depends on one's denomination and/or definition of faith.

For Roman Catholics, many of whom have propositional faith, reason and argument will be of central importance.

For some Protestants, many of whose faith is non-propositional, reason will not lead to faith nor argument do much to support or erode it, though reason is the essential means of exploring and enriching faith.

For Evangelical Christians, many of whose faith is fideist, the relationship between faith and reason will be slight, though the attitude that faith and reason are naturally opposed is not held as widely as many people think.

For voluntarists reason and argument have an important part to play, not in terms of proving God's existence, but in demonstrating the benefits of believing in it and in seeking to persuade people away from indifference.

For Calvinists and members of the Reformed tradition who are non-voluntarists, reason and argument are irrelevant in forming faith, but may be used to explore its nature once it exists.

It must be recognised that these categories overlap. No Catholic thinks that faith should only be propositional and no fideist thinks that all Christian claims have to be absurd. Faith, in practice, is a complex phenomenon which both involves an interface between reason and faith, between voluntary assent and grace and between assent to propositions and existential engagement. Few people, therefore, belong solely in any one of the above categories.

§5: Conscience, Free Will and Determinism

Conscience

What is conscience? It is often described as a voice – the voice which tells you not to share someone's secret, or to save that last piece of cake for your sister rather than scoffing it yourself. But if it is useful to describe it as a 'voice', whose voice is it? The voice of your true self? The voice of God? Or the voice of your parents, or your society, which you have gradually absorbed into your own mind? Is the 'voice' metaphor misleading? Is it simply a matter of you, a complex human being, making up your mind about what to do?

The thinkers included in this anthology, from early in the history of Christianity up to the present day, have put forward diverse models of what conscience is. One way in which they could be categorized is represented by the diagram below, to which you may wish to add thinkers as your learn about them.

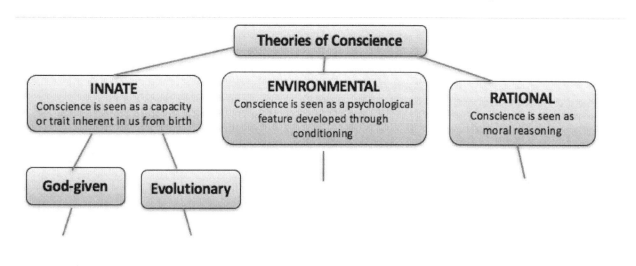

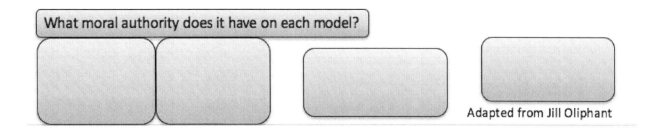

Adapted from Jill Oliphant

Any concept of conscience can be evaluated in terms of its *coherence* and its *plausibility in the light of personal/human experience*. For instance, when evaluating the Augustinian idea that conscience is an innate and God-given guide to right and wrong, we might ask whether anything follows from that idea which we cannot rationally accept. We might question how conscience could come from God when some people claim to be acting on conscience when they do dreadful things (terrorists of varying ideologies may provide some examples). We might also question whether conscience *feels* as if it comes from a divine source. Do we experience it as an external authority, or as an entirely human process of reflection on our moral lives?

Our understanding of what conscience is will inevitably affect how we think about its authority and the role it should play in moral life.

Over four thousand conscientious objectors were imprisoned during the First World War, some of whom faced very harsh treatment and physical abuse. Those whose claims to conscientious objection were accepted and who were allowed to do alternative work faced the contempt and ridicule of much of society. Some were religious people, such as Quakers, who hold the promptings of conscience in particular esteem. Some did not see the matter in religious terms but felt it humanly wrong to fight. One former butcher said simply 'I know what it is to kill a pig – I won't kill a man'. Were they right to honour the promptings of their consciences in the face of their country's needs or demands? Were those who broke the law on the basis of conscience right to do so? Your answer will depend on the status you accord to conscience, which in turn may depend on what you think it is.

Should one follow one's conscience over and above the teachings or rules of religious leaders or scriptures? If my conscience tells a person to assist in the suicide of a terminally ill and suffering loved one, while my church leaders as well as the laws of my country forbid it, am I doing the right thing? Again, we need to consider the nature and authority of conscience in giving an answer.

St Augustine (354 – 430)

On the Epistle of John

Return to your own conscience, question it. Do not consider what blossoms outwardly, but what root there is in the ground. Is lust rooted there? A show there may be of good deeds, truly good works there cannot be. Is charity rooted there? Have no fear: nothing evil can come of that... More accepted is the blow of charity than the alms of pride. Come then within, brethren; and in all things, whatsoever ye do, look unto God your witness.

- *While Augustine does not go into details, he seems to see conscience as an inner awareness of right and wrong which we can appeal to .*

-

1. *It enables us to judge not only what we do but also...*

As you will see in his Anti-Pelagian writings, Augustine considered that since the Fall of Adam, human beings are incapable of doing any good by themselves. Accordingly, for him conscience is dependent on the grace of God – his undeserved guidance and salvation. Conscience is innate; it is part of our God-given nature. But without God's direct gift of grace it is too corrupted by sin to enable us to act rightly. Augustine's wider theology also reveals the relation between conscience and the Church. The teaching of the Church which Christ has founded and sustains informs our conscience

The Catholic Church on conscience, in *Gaudium et Spes* - a major document of Church teachings produced by the Church's Second Vatican Council in 1965 (under Pope Paul VI):

Deep within his conscience man discovers a law which he has not laid upon himself but which he must obey. Its voice, ever calling him to love and to do what is good and to avoid evil, sounds in his heart at the right moment. . . . For man has in his heart a law inscribed by God. . . . His conscience is man's most secret core and his sanctuary. There he is alone with God whose voice echoes in his depths.

Augustine is one of the theologians which Gaudium et Spes quotes and draws upon.

2. *What is conscience according to this document?*

3. *At what times do we become aware of conscience?*

Cardinal John Henry Newman (1801 –1890)

(a summary of his view of conscience as an echo of the voice of God, the Divine Law within the individual)

Cardinal John Henry Newman (1801 –1890) was an influential theologian who began his career as an Anglican and later joined the Roman Catholic Church. He studied at Oxford and was a fellow of Oriel College (fifty years before Cecil Rhodes arrived to study there). He became vicar of the university church, St Mary's, in 1828 and was an important member of the Oxford Movement, an initiative within the Anglican church which resisted theological liberalism and valued ritual. In 1845 he became a Roman Catholic and went on to become a priest and ultimately a cardinal.

For Newman, conscience is **an echo of the voice of God.** It reveals the existence of God - 'an echo implies a voice, a voice a speaker, and that speaker I love and fear'.

He also understands it as the **Divine Law present in the individual**. In his Letter Addressed to the Duke of Norfolk he explains that God, who is morally good, implanted the Divine Law in all rational creatures. He goes on,

The Divine Law… is the rule of ethical truth, the standard of right and wrong, a sovereign, irreversible, absolute authority in the presence of men and Angels… This law, as apprehended in the minds of individual men, is called "conscience", and thou it may suffer refraction in passing into the intellectual medium of each [i.e. it may be distorted to some extent in our minds], it is not therefore so affected as to lose its character of being the Divine Law, but still has, as such, the prerogative of commanding obedience.

The **moral authority** to which Newman refers here, this 'prerogative of commanding obedience', **is supreme**. Newman's letter to the Duke of Norfolk, written after he joined the Catholic Church, addresses the seeming tension between the Pope's infallibility and the authority of conscience. He notes that the infallibility of the Pope only applies to general principles, whereas **conscience guides us in to particular situations**, so they will not directly clash. And it is the Pope's role to support the Divine Law present in conscience, guiding God's people in a world in which the voice of conscience may be drowned out by immoral influences.

Newman also makes it clear, though, that **the individual should obey her conscience even if it seems to conflict with the Pope's teachings**. She should respect those teachings and carefully consider whether she may be mistaken, but ultimately can never ignore conscience without losing her soul. Newman writes, 'if I am obliged to bring religion into after-dinner toasts, I shall drink — to the Pope, if you please, — still, to Conscience first, and to the Pope afterwards.'

Newman seems to see conscience as working in an **intuitive** manner. We sense/intuit rather than work out what the Divine Law demands in a particular situation. Conscience is seen as **innate.**

He also sees it as evidence for the existence of God:

If, as is the case, we feel responsibility, are ashamed, are frightened, at transgressing [going against] the voice of conscience, this implies there is One to whom we are responsible, before whom we are ashamed, whose claims upon us we fear. *The Grammar of Assent,* ch 5

Joseph Butler (1692 –1752)

Sermons

Sermon 1 (summarised points)

In this sermon Butler defines conscience as: 'the principle in man, by which he approves or disapproves his heart, temper, and actions'. *This principle* 'tends to restrain men from doing mischief to each other, and leads them to do good.' *It more reliably leads us to do good than feelings such as family affection.*

Butler claims that if we just consider how 'any common man' *reacts to examples of benevolent and unjust actions,* 'it cannot possibly be denied, that there is this principle of reflection or conscience in human nature.'

- *Do you agree that* 'it cannot possibly be denied'?

Sermon 2

Upon the Natural Supremacy of Conscience – 1 (extracts)

"For when the Gentiles, which have not the law, do by nature the things contained in the law, these having not the law, are a law unto themselves." Romans 2:14

A man can as little doubt whether his eyes were given him to see with, as he can doubt of the truth of the science of optics, deduced from occular experiments. And allowing the inward feeling, shame; a man can as little doubt whether it was given him to prevent his doing shameful actions, as he can doubt whether his eyes were given him to guide his steps. And as to these inward feelings themselves; that they are real; that man has in his nature passions and affections, can no more be questioned, than that he has external senses. Neither can the former be wholly mistaken, though to a certain degree liable to greater mistakes than the latter.

There can be no doubt but that several propensions or instincts, several principles in the heart of man, carry him to society, and to contribute to the happiness of it, in a sense and a manner in which no inward principle leads him to evil. These principles, propensions, or instincts, which lead him to do good, are approved of by a certain faculty within, quite distinct from these propensions themselves.

> Propension = propensity, tendency

But it may be said, "What is all this, though true, to the purpose of virtue and religion? these require, not only that we do good to others when we are led this way, by benevolence or reflection happening to be stronger than other principles, passions, or appetites; but likewise that the whole character be formed upon thought and reflection; that every action be directed by some determinate rule, some other rule than the strength and prevalency of any principle or passion. What sign is there in our nature that this was intended by its Author? It does not appear that there ever was a man who would not have approved an action of humanity rather than of cruelty; interest and passion being quite out of the case. But interest and passion do come in, and are often too strong for, and prevail over reflection and conscience.

Now, as brutes have various instincts, by which they are carried on to the end the Author of their nature intended them for; is not man in the same condition, with this difference only, that to his instincts (i. e. appetites and passions) is added the principle of reflection or conscience? And as brutes act agreeably to their nature, in following that principle or particular instinct which for the present is strongest in them; does not man likewise act agreeably to his nature, or obey the law of his creation, by following that principle, be it passion or conscience, which for the present happens to be strongest in him? Thus, different men are by their particular nature hurried on to pursue honor, or riches, or pleasure. There are also persons whose temper leads them in an uncommon degree to kindness, compassion, doing good to their fellow creatures; as there are others who are given to suspend their judgment, to weigh and consider things, and to act upon thought and reflection. Let everyone then quietly follow his nature; as passion, reflection, appetite, the several parts of it, happen to the strongest; but let not the man of virtue take upon him to blame the ambitious, the covetous, the dissolute; since these, equally with him, obey and follow their nature. Thus, as in some cases, we follow our nature in doing the works contained in the law, so in other cases we follow nature in doing contrary."

- *What objection to his idea of conscience as a clue to God's will does Butler recognise in the paragraphs above?*

Let us now take a view of the nature of man, as consisting partly of various appetites, passions, affections, and partly of the principle of reflection or conscience; leaving quite out all consideration of the different degrees of strength, in which either of them prevail; and it will further appear, that there is this natural superiority of one inward principle to another, or that it is even part of the idea of reflection or conscience.

Passion or appetite implies a direct simple tendency towards such and such objects, without distinction of the means by which they are to be obtained. Consequently, it will often happen there will be a desire of particular objects, in cases where they cannot be obtained without manifest injury to others. Reflection, or conscience comes in, and disapproves the pursuit of them in these circumstances; but the desire remains. Which is to be obeyed, appetite or reflection? Cannot this question be answered from the economy and constitution of human nature merely, without saying which is strongest? or need this at all come into consideration? Would not the question be intelligibly and fully answered by saying, that the principle of reflection or conscience being compared with the various appetites, passions, and affections in men the former is manifestly superior and chief, without regard to strength? And how often soever the latter happens to prevail, it is mere usurpation. The former remains in nature and in kind its superior; and every instance of such prevalence of the latter, is an instance of breaking in upon, and violation of the constitution of man.

All this is no more than the distinction which every body is acquainted with, between mere power and authority: only, instead of being intended to express the difference between what is possible, and what is lawful in civil government, here it has been shown applicable to the several principles in the mind of man. Thus, that principle by which we survey, and either approve or disapprove our own heart, temper, and actions, is not only to be considered as what is in its turn to have some influence; which may be said of every passion, of the lowest appetites: but likewise as being superior; as from its very nature manifestly claiming superiority over all others; insomuch that you cannot form a notion of this faculty, conscience, without taking in judgment, direction, superintendency. This is a constituent part of the idea, that is, of the faculty itself: and to preside and govern, from the very economy and constitution of man, belongs to it. Had it strength, as it has right; had it power, as it has manifest authority, it would absolutely govern the world.

This gives us a further view of the nature of man; shows us what course of life we were made for; not only that our real nature leads us to be influenced in some degree by reflection and conscience, but likewise in what degree we are to be influenced by it, if we will fall in with, and act agreeably to the constitution of our nature: that this faculty was placed within to be our proper governor; to direct and regulate all under principles, passions, and motives of action. This is its right and office: thus sacred is its authority. And how often soever men violate and rebelliously refuse to submit to it, for supposed interest which they cannot otherwise obtain, or for the sake of passion which they cannot otherwise gratify; this makes no alteration as to the natural right, and office of conscience.

- *What is the status of conscience within a human being?*

- *How has Butler answered the objection which he recognised above?*

Let us now turn the whole matter another way, and suppose there was no such thing at all as this supremacy of conscience; that there was no distinction to be made between one inward principle and another, but only that of strength; and see what would be the consequence….

If there be no difference between inward principles… we can make no distinction between a man killing his father and a man honouring his father, but in our coolest hours must approve or disapprove them equally: than which nothing can be reduced to a greater absurdity.

- *If the special status of conscience was not recognised, what does Butler say the result would be?*

NOTES:

[12] Ephes. ii. 3.

Sermon 3

Upon the Natural Supremacy of Conscience - 2

"The natural supremacy of reflection or conscience being thus established; we may from it form a distinct notion of what is meant by human nature, when virtue is said to consist in following it, and vice in deviating from it." Romans 2:14

As the idea of a civil constitution implies in it united strength, various subordinations, under one direction, that of the supreme authority; the different strength of each particular member of the society not coming into the idea; whereas, if you leave out the subordination, the union, and the one direction, you destroy and lose it: So reason, several appetites, passions, and affections, prevailing in different degrees of strength; is not that idea or notion of human nature; but that nature consists in these several principles considered as having a natural respect to each other, in the several passions being naturally subordinate to the one superior principle of reflection or conscience. Every bias, instinct, propension within, is a real part of our nature, but not the whole: add to these the superior faculty, whose office it is to adjust, manage, and preside over them, and take in this its natural superiority, and you complete the idea of human nature.

And as in civil government the constitution is broken in upon and violated, by power and strength prevailing over authority; so the constitution of man is broken in upon and violated by the lower faculties or principles within prevailing over that, which is in its nature supreme over them all. Thus, when it is said by ancient writers, that tortures and death are not so contrary to human nature as injustice; by this, to be sure, is not meant, that the aversion to the former in mankind is less strong and prevalent than their aversion to the latter: but that the former is only contrary to our nature, considered in a partial view, and which takes in only the lowest part of it, that which we have in common with the brutes; whereas the latter is contrary to our nature, considered in a higher sense, as a system and constitution, contrary to the whole economy of man. [13]

And from all these things put together, nothing can be more evident, than that, exclusive of revelation, man cannot be considered as a creature left by his Maker to act at random, and live at large up to the extent of his natural power, as passion, humor, wilfulness, happen to carry him; which is the condition brute creatures are in but that, from his make, constitution, or nature, he is the strictest and most proper sense, a law to himself. He hath the rule of right within: what is wanting is only that he honestly attend to it.

But, allowing that mankind hath the rule of right within himself, yet it maybe asked, "What obligations are we under to attend to and follow it?" I answer: it has been proved, that man by his nature is a law to himself, without the particular distinct consideration of the positive sanctions of that law; the rewards and punishments which we feel, and those which, from the light of reason, we have ground to believe are annexed to it. The question then carries its own answer along with it. Your obligation to obey this law, is its being the law of your nature. That your conscience approves of and attests to such a course of action, is itself alone an obligation. Conscience does not only offer itself to show us the way we should walk in, but it. likewise carries its own authority with it, that it is our natural guide, the guide assigned us by the Author of our nature: it therefore belongs to our condition of being: it is our duty to walk in that path, and follow this guide, without looking about to see whether we may not possibly forsake them with impunity.

- *Why ought we to obey conscience, according to Butler?*

- *Is his argument for obedience to conscience convincing?*

Joseph Butler

(A summary of his views on conscience as a reflective faculty with sacred authority)

Joseph Butler was Bishop of Durham in the 18th century and a notable philosopher and theologian. His best known religious work is *Analogy of Religion*, but his sermons also include significant theological ideas, including his explanation of conscience.

For him, conscience is an **innate, God-given reflective faculty. God has provided it for a reason – to allow us to judge our acts and impulses and discern what we ought to do** in particular instances. This intention should be clear to anyone who experiences feelings of shame due to conscience:

> We can as little doubt that a feeling of shame is intended to prevent certain kinds of actions as we can that our eyes were given to guide our steps.

Butler sees conscience as a reflective principle. It is not the same thing as natural impulses to kindness and compassion. We have to be a little wary of feelings; it is not always clear whether they are guiding us into the right path or leading us astray.

Butler sees conscience as:

> a superior principle of reflection.. in every man, which distinguishes between the internal principles of his heart, as well as his external actions; which **passes judgment upon himself** and them; pronounces determinately some actions to be in themselves just, right, good; others to be in themselves evil, wrong, unjust; which without being consulted, without being advised with, **magisterially exerts itself, and approves or condemns** him.

Conscience might sometimes be drowned out by our passions, but while it is not always the most powerful of our internal motivations, it is superior in being right. Its rightful place is at the top of the hierarchy of human motivations. **It has moral authority, and *ought* to rule our behaviour:**

> **Had it strength, as it has right; had it power, as it has manifest authority, it would absolutely govern the world.**

> This faculty was placed within to be our proper governor ; to direct and regulate all under principles, passions, and motives of action. This is its right and office: thus **sacred is its authority**.

The authority of conscience is not dependent on any system of reward and punishment.

Aquinas

Summa Theologica

FIRST PART (FP)

Treatise on Man (Q79)

Synderesis is a characteristic disposition rather than a power….as nature needs to implant in us the first principles concerning theoretical matters, so also does nature needs to implant in us the first principles concerning practical matters.

But the first principles about theoretical matters, principles implanted in us by nature, do not belong to any special power but to a special characteristic disposition, which we call "the understanding of principles"…and so the principles of practical matters, principles implanted in us by nature, likewise do not belong to a special power but to characteristic disposition from nature, and we call this disposition *synderesis*. And so we also say *synderesis* incites to good and complains of evil, since we progress from first principles to discovery and judge about the things we have discovered…so we judge by both reason and *synderesis*.

Conscience (*conscientia*) is an act, not a power. And this is evident both from the naming of the word and from the things that we in our ordinary way of speaking attribute to conscience. It signifies the relation of knowledge to something else, since we define *con-science* as knowledge with something else. But acts connect knowledge with things. And so it is clear from the meaning of the word that conscience is an act.

We say that conscience bears witness, morally obliges or stirs to action, and accuses or disquiets or reproves. And all of these things result from connecting some knowledge of ours to what we do.

This connection arises in three ways. It arises in one way as we recognize that we have or have not done something…and we accordingly say that conscience bears witness.

In a second way, we connect our knowledge to something as we by our conscience judge that we should or should not do something. And we accordingly say that conscience incites to action or morally obliges.

In a third way, we connect our knowledge to something as we by our conscience judge that we have or have not done something worthily. And we accordingly say that conscience excuses or accuses and disquiets.

But all three of these ways clearly result from the actual connection of knowledge to what we do. And so, properly speaking, conscience designates an act.

Aquinas On Law, Morality and Politics 2nd ed trans. Richard J. Regan (Hackett 2002)

- Explain in your own words the three ways in which conscience (*conscientia*) acts

- How does Aquinas use the Latin word *conscientia* to back up his statement that conscience is an act?

- What is the difference between *synderesis* and *conscientia*?

Freud

Conscience as Super-ego - Summary

The following information and the printed extracts are taken from Freud: the Key Ideas *by Ruth Snowden*

Sigmund Freud (1865-1939) was an Austrian doctor who lived and worked in Vienna for most of his life. His work largely concerns the unconscious mind. Before Freud, psychologists usually just described and observed behaviour. Freud wanted to go deeper, to analyse and explain it. He said that we have many inner motives for our behaviour, and that these are mostly sexual. Freud is famous because he founded a new system of psychology that he called psychoanalysis, which is still the basis of various therapies used today.

Freud distinguished different levels of the human mind:

- **The conscious mind is the part of the mind that is aware of its thoughts and actions.** This is where all conscious thought processes occur – it is the source of the conscious thinking, ideas and understanding.
- **The unconscious is seen as the part of the mind that is repressed**, the place where we put all the stuff that our conditioning does not allow us to look at. Information is the unconscious cannot easily be dug out.

As his career progressed he developed a more complex picture of the divisions of the mind, describing three parts as follows:

The id

What is it? What does it do? Where does it come from?

The ego

What is it? What does it do? Where does it come from?

The superego (aka CONSCIENCE)

What is it? What does it do? Where does it come from?

Freud's work was immensely influential. Among others, his insights on the unconscious, the significance of childhood experiences for the development of adult personality and the way we use defence mechanisms to protect our egos continue to be valued and developed today.

Criticisms of his work include the following:

- he places far too much emphasis on sex
- he claims to be scientific and yet his findings are often vague, inaccurate and based upon small samples of data.

Ruth Snowden

Freud: the Key Ideas (The McGraw Companies Inc, 2006)

Seeking an adult identity

In this chapter you will learn:
- *key features of Freud's new model of how the mind works*
- *theories about how the mind defends itself*
- *in more depth about how the adult character develops.*

Freud's new model of the mind

In the previous chapter we looked at Freud's ideas about how the adult personality develops and what can go wrong with this process. He also gradually developed theories about the ways in which the personality is actually formed and structured. For a long time he struggled with the problem of how neuroses arose. He knew that unacceptable or frightening ideas were repressed and banished to the unconscious, but where did this repression come from?

The original simple division of the mind into conscious and unconscious did not fully explain what was going on, so in 1923 Freud published his book *The Ego and the Id*, which proposed a new **dynamic model** of the mind.

Insight

A dynamic model is a simplified description of a system, emphasizing forces, motives and drives. It shows us how a thing works.

This was an attempt to describe the whole mind system, explaining how it works, and what are its main motives and drives. It involved three main parts: the id, ego and super-ego. These are not really physical parts of the brain but represent different aspects of the way we think, and so help to explain the apparent battle that goes on between different levels of consciousness. Freud didn't see them with exact boundaries like countries on a map, but rather as merging into one another, like the areas of colour mixed together by an artist. They did not *replace* the idea of conscious/unconscious – as we shall see later, they can sometimes operate on both levels.

Insight

Id: the unconscious part of the psyche that is concerned with inherited, instinctive impulses.
Ego: the part of the psyche which reacts to external reality and which a person thinks of as the 'self'.
Super-ego: the part of the psyche that acts like an 'inner parent', giving us a conscience and responding to social rules.

Freud explained that he was really suggesting new ways of looking at the psyche and the way in which it was arranged, rather than making startling new discoveries. Like so much of Freud's thinking, this was an ongoing process, so he constantly revised and modified what he thought to be true. This fact, coupled with the fact that the subject matter is somewhat abstract in any case, makes his ideas hard to grasp at times.

In exploring the way the mind is structured, Freud justified his use of clinical data from his work with patients by use of an analogy. If we throw a crystal on the floor, it tends to break along predetermined lines of weakness, inherent in its structure. Mental patients are split and broken in the same way, showing us the way the psyche is constructed. And the fact that they tend to turn away from external reality means that they know more about internal, psychical reality than most people, and so they can reveal things to us that would otherwise remain hidden.

Insight

'Id', 'ego' and 'super-ego' were not actually Freud's original words. He used words that can be translated as 'the It', 'the I' and 'the Over-I', which were perhaps rather more self-explanatory.

The id

From the Latin word for 'it', the id is the primitive, unconscious part of the mind that we are born with. The other parts of the mind are derived from this oldest, primeval part, which contains everything that is inherited. It is a dark, inaccessible area, seething with instinctive urges and its only reality is its own selfish needs. It is the source of the motive force behind the pleasure principle which involves avoiding states of tension or 'unpleasure', caused by the thwarting of a basic drive. In the young infant this is all about having its needs met immediately – as anyone who has looked after a baby for any length of time will know, the child will scream whenever it is hungry, or even the slightest bit uncomfortable in any way. So the id is concerned with simple biology and the basic needs of the organism.

As a child develops through the various oral, anal and phallic stages, it begins to realize that the world 'out there' is real too. This new awareness is closely linked to sexual development. Gradually, the child begins to realize that it cannot always instantly have what it wants, and begins to suppress the id urges in order to fit in with society. Adults who are very selfish or impulsive may be unable or unwilling to suppress the id.

The id is disorganized and illogical in nature, and much of its content is negative and selfish. It can make no value judgements – it is completely amoral. The desires of the id are commonly expressed in dreams and what little we know about it is partly gained from the study of dreams and partly from looking at neurotic symptoms. It uses a form of mental functioning that Freud called primary process, which involves the various mechanisms such as symbolization, condensation and so on discussed in Chapter 4. Because it is not logical, it ignores basic rational rules such as time and space, giving rise to the strange illogical fantasy world that most people are familiar with from their dreams.

Because the id has no concept of time it contains impulses and impressions that may have arisen from events that occurred decades before, but which still affect the person as if they were happening in the present. These can only be recognized as belonging to the past when they are made conscious by the work of analysis. Only then can they lose their importance and stop affecting the person's thinking and behaviour.

The ego

Named from the Latin word for 'I', the ego is the part of the mind that reacts to external reality and which a person thinks of as the 'self'. The ego is where consciousness comes from, although not all of its functions are carried out consciously.

- *The ego tells us what is real. It is a synthesizer – it helps us to combine ideas and make sense of things.*
- *It is practical and rational, involved in decision making.*
- *Anxiety arises from the ego. This is seen as a mechanism for warning us that there is a weakness somewhere in the ego's defences.*
- *The ego can observe itself – in fact, in a number of its functions it can split temporarily and then come together again afterwards.*
- *A whole system of unconscious* **defence mechanisms** *protects the ego. These are involuntary or unconscious ways of protecting the ego from undesirable feelings and emotions.*
- *The ego is seen as being rather weak in comparison with the id, but it is better organized and more logical, so that it usually maintains a tenuous upper hand.*

Insight

Defence mechanisms are unconscious ways of protecting the ego against undesirable effects. They help us to cope with the anxieties of life, and defend our self-image. Sometimes of course they are overdone, and then they can lead to problems. For example we have all met people who are 'over-defensive' and end up becoming aggressive.

Freud explains, somewhat confusingly, that the ego is part of the id that develops in order to cope with threats from the outside world. It is related to the system he refers to as the 'perceptual-conscious', which he sees as the most superficial portion of the mental apparatus. This could be described as a kind of protective skin which provides us with external perceptions at the same time as giving information about what is going on in the interior mind. This information is essential for the id because otherwise it would ignore the influence of the outer world and eventually be destroyed in one way or another in its blind pursuit of selfish satisfaction. For example, you need to learn that you can't just dash across the road to a cake shop without first checking to see if you will get run over by a bus. In other words, the main function of the ego is that of reality testing: it replaces the primitive pleasure principle of the id with a new reality principle, which ultimately promises more certainty and greater success in accomplishing goals.

Freud compares the ego and the id with a rider and his horse. The horse supplies the motor energy, but the rider decides where to go. The ego constantly has to devise little plans to satisfy the id in a controlled way. For example, a child is hungry but learns that it will have to wait until teatime until it gets a slice of cake. The problem-solving and reality-testing activities of the ego, which allow the id to take care of its needs as soon as an appropriate object can be found, are what Freud referred to as secondary process.

The super-ego

Some of Freud's patients suffered from delusions of being watched. Freud suggests that in a sense they were right, and that in each of us there is an agency that observes our behaviour and threatens to punish us – a sort of inner grown-up. In the delusional patients, this agency could simply have become sharply divided from the ego and mistaken for external reality.

A very young child is amoral and has little sense of inhibition. Any controls over its behaviour are provided by the parents and other carers who look after it. In normal development this state of affairs slowly changes. As the ego struggles to keep the id happy, it constantly meets up with both obstacles and helpers in the external world. It keeps a track record of these, and also of rewards and punishments that it has encountered, particularly from parents and other adults. This is how the super-ego develops: gradually a sort of inner parent evolves and the child develops feelings of guilt and of being watched and controlled. One aspect of this super-ego is what we would call the conscience – the part of ourselves that tells us what is right and what is wrong and judges our behaviour accordingly; but the super-ego also carries out self-observation, which is an essential preliminary to the judging process.
This is the work of the super-ego:

- *It gives us our sense of right and wrong, pride and guilt.*
- *It often gets us to act in ways that are acceptable to the society, rather than to the individual. For example, it might make a person feel guilty for having extra-marital sex. The super-ego incorporates the teachings of the past and of tradition, imparting a sense of morals.*
- *It monitors behaviour, decides what is acceptable and controls taboo areas, by means of repression. The fact that a person may not be aware of this repression shows that parts of the super-ego can operate unconsciously. In fact, Freud says that large parts of both the ego and the super-ego are normally unconscious.*
- *It allows the ego to measure itself and strive towards ever-greater perfection.*
- *It is rather bossy, always demanding perfection of the ego. In fact, it can be quite severe with the poor ego, humiliating it, ill-treating it and threatening it with dire punishments. Freud observed this sort of thing in his melancholic patients.*

The super-ego develops from and gradually takes the place of parental authority – observing, threatening and directing the ego in the same way as the parents did. Oddly, however, it seems to make a one-sided choice here, and seems not to regulate behaviour by means of loving care and encouragement. This is strange, given that the super-ego is all about what Freud calls the 'higher side' of human life and the striving towards perfection.

The super-ego develops as the Oedipus complex begins to be resolved, but if the resolution of the Oedipus complex is incomplete, the super-ego will remain stunted in its strength and growth and the child will remain over-identified with its parents. In the normal course of development, as the repression of Oedipal urges begins, the child feels a mixture of love, fear and hostility towards the parents.

The way the super-ego works is in a sense opposite to that of the id: the id just wants to satisfy the needs of the individual, regardless of what society wants. Like the ego, large parts of the super-ego can operate in unconscious ways. Freud acknowledges that the distinctions between id, ego and super-ego are not easy to grasp and that the three are not always sharply separated. If an adult has achieved a reasonably mature, mentally healthy personality, the id, ego and super-ego will be acting in a balanced way.

Freud explains that the child's super-ego is not really constructed on a model of the parents themselves, but rather of the parents' super-ego. In this sense it represents handed-down traditions and value judgements and so is a mirror for the workings of society itself. Freud defines a psychological group as a group of people who have introduced the same person into their super-ego and therefore, on the basis of this common element, identify with one another. Mankind never lives fully in the present, but is affected by inherited ideologies that are very slow to change. To understand the super-ego more fully would be to gain insight into many problems in the social behaviour of mankind, such as delinquency. Freud says that there is probably great variation among individuals in the development of the different parts of the psyche. The intention of psychoanalysis is really to strengthen the ego and make it more independent of the super-ego, so that it can widen its scope and take over fresh areas of the id. This is a huge task.

Piaget, Kohlberg, Gilligan, and Others on Moral Development

J. S. Fleming, PhD

(abbreviated article)

When confronted with a group of parents who asked me "How can we help make our children virtuous?" I had to answer as Socrates, "You must think I am very fortunate to know how virtue is acquired. The fact is that far from knowing whether it can be taught, I have no idea what virtue really is.". . . It appears, then, that we must either be totally silent about moral education or else speak to the nature of virtue

Piaget on Moral Development

Piaget's Methods for Studying Moral Development

Piaget believed that observing children playing games and querying them about the rules provided a realistic "lab on life" for understanding how morality principles develop. In his book The Moral Judgment of the Child (Piaget, 1932/1962), he studied children playing the game of marbles. The fact that only boys played this game seemed to impose a limitation on the generality of his findings, so he also studied a girl's game called ĭlet cachant, a kind of primitive hide-and-seek. But his most important observations were made on the boys – a fact that incurred later criticism, as will be seen shortly.

Piaget often used a practiced technique of feigned naivety: He pretended to be ignorant of the rules of the games and asked the children to explain them to him. In this way he was able to comprehend the way that the children themselves understood the rules, and to observe as well how children of different ages related to the rules and the game.

Piaget's Stages of Moral Development

Children's Moral Judgments. Piaget's studies of moral judgments are based both on children's judgments of moral scenarios and on their interactions in game playing. In terms of moral judgments, Piaget found that younger children (around ages four to seven) thought in terms of moral realism (compare to "realism" in Chapter 4) or moral heteronomy. These terms connote an absolutism, in which morality is seen in terms of rules that are fixed and unchangeable (heteronomy means "from without"). Guilt is determined by the extent of violation of rules rather than by intention.

The second stage in making moral judgments comes later, usually around age 10, when children come to realize that rules have arbitrariness and are formed by mutual consent for reasons of fairness and equity. This applies equally to society's laws, game rules, and familial standards of behavior. Older children realize that rules are not fixed and absolute, but that they can be changed as the need arises.

Piaget called this second stage moral autonomy.

Once again, egocentricism plays into moral heteronomy, as the child is unable to see rules from the broader perspective of another child or adult, or of society in general. Conversely, moral autonomy requires just such an ability.

Piaget also noted that the stages of moral understanding are not entirely discreet. Children become capable of certain autonomous judgments before others, depending on the situation, just as horizontal décalage characterized the understanding of his conservation tasks for cognitive development. In actuality, the stages of morality overlap one another to some degree.

Piaget's Method: Sample Dialog Between a Researcher and a Child

The following dialog is revealing (from Piaget, 1932/1962, pp. 124-125):

Q: Is one of the boys [who broke teacups] naughtier than the other?

A: The first is because he knocked over twelve cups.
Q: If you were the daddy, which one would you punish most? A: The one who broke twelve cups.
Q: Why did he break them?
A: The door shut too hard and knocked them. He didn't do it on purpose.
Q: And why did the other boy break a cup?
A: He wanted to get the jam. He moved too far. The cup got broken.
Q: Why did he want to get the jam?
A: Because he was all alone. Because his mother wasn't there. Q: Have you got a brother?
A: No, a little sister.
Q: Well, if it was you who had broken the twelve cups when

you went into the room and your little sister who had broken one cup when she was trying to get the jam, which of you would be punished more severely?
A: Me, because I broke more than one cup.

Gender and Moral Development

Piaget found that the games that girls played were nowhere near as complex as the boys and their marbles in terms of rules and options. Piaget did compare the stages of morality between the two sexes, noting both parallels and some differences. Both have stages of moral heteronomy and autonomy, for example. But the fact that the girls' games were simpler makes precise comparisons difficult. Piaget stated that: "The most superficial observation is sufficient to show that in the main the legal sense is far less developed in little girls than in boys. We did not succeed in finding a single collective game played by girls in which there were as many rules, and above all, as fine and consistent an organization and codification of these rules as in the game of marbles . . ." (p. 77). Piaget seemed to be saying that conclusions gender differences are necessarily tenuous because the observations were superficial and due to the lack of opportunity – the girls' games were simpler, and therefore comparisons were difficult. Yet he did see girls as being less concerned with (and less rigid about) rules in general, and more ready to relax them: They appeared to be less concerned with "legalities." But elsewhere Piaget appeared to equate concern with legalities as signs of advanced development: ". . . the juridico- moral discussions of the fourth stage [of moral development] may be compared to formal reasoning in general" (p. 47). Do girls then have a less sophisticated, and therefore deficient sense of moral understanding? Carol Gilligan (1982) believed that this was Piaget's message. She criticized Piaget and other (male) psychologists of harboring negative views of feminine morality, as will be seen following a consideration of Lawrence Kohlberg's extension of Piaget's work.

But in defense of Piaget, Eliot Turiel (2006, p. 807) noted that "In considering Piaget's ideas, Gilligan imposes certainty where ambiguity exists. Piaget did maintain that girls are less interested than boys in 'legal elaboration' and that 'the legal sense is far less developed in little girls than in boys' (Piaget, 1932[/1962], p. 69 & 75)" but that ". . . in Piaget's view, the developmentally advanced level of autonomous morality was organized by concerns with mutuality, reciprocity, and cooperation. Piaget saw a strict legal sense for fixed rules that left little room for innovation and tolerance as part of the less advanced form of heteronymous morality. Thus, it is not at all clear that Piaget regarded girls to be less advanced than girls because he thought that girls were oriented to tolerance, innovation with rules, and cooperation" (p. 807). Thus Piaget's observations do suggest that he observed some gender differences, but these differences are somewhat nuanced; and indeed, one could say that he actually saw **girls' moral understanding as in some ways actually more advanced than boys'.**

II. Kohlberg and Moral Development

Lawrence Kohlberg admired Piaget's approach to studying children's conceptions of morality. If Piaget saw children as little logicians, Kohlberg viewed them as moral philosophers. Unlike so many other psychologists who concerned themselves with morality, such as Freud, Skinner, and later Albert Bandura in his research on observation learning and role models, Kohlberg believed that it was not possible to study moral understanding without also coming to grips with philosophy, or more specifically, what could possibly be meant by "morality" (per the opening quote to this chapter; also see Kohlberg, 1968; Turiel, 2006).

In brief, Kohlberg assessed morality by asking children to consider certain moral dilemmas – situations in which right and wrong actions are not always clear. He was not concerned with whether the children decided that certain actions were right or wrong, but with their reasoning – at how they arrived at their conclusions. The story of "Heinz Steals the Drug" is one of his best known examples (Kohlberg, 1963, p. 19):

> In Europe, a woman was near death from a special kind of cancer. There was one drug that the doctors thought might save her. It was a form of radium that a druggist in the same town had recently discovered. The drug was expensive to make, but the druggist was charging ten times what the drug cost him to make. He paid $200 for the radium and charged $2,000 for a small dose of the drug. The sick woman's husband, Heinz, went to everyone he knew to borrow the money, but he could only get together about $1,000 which is half of what it cost. He told the

druggist that his wife was dying and asked him to sell it cheaper or let him pay for it later. But the druggist said: "No, I discovered the drug and I'm going to make money from it." So Heinz got desperate and broke into the man's store to steal the drug for his wife. Should the husband have done that?

Kohlberg's Levels and Stages of Morality

Based on his study of children's responses to such dilemmas, Kohlberg (1958, 1963) expanded Piaget's two stages into six, organized into three levels – each level consisting of two stages – as follows. Note that cross-references are made, where appropriate, to Piagetian and Freudian levels of development.

Level I: Preconventionl Morality. The preconventional child thinks of morality in terms of the consequences of disobedience to adult rules in order to avoid punishment. Behaviors are "good" or "bad" depending on their consequences, or in other words, behavior is guided by rewards and punishments. The child at this stage does not comprehend the rules of society.

• Stage 1. This first stage has been called "punishment and obedience," or "might makes right." Obey your parents, or these powerful authority figures will physically punish you. The child's understanding is that punishment must be avoided for her/his own comfort. The child is still unable to view the world from the perspective of others (Piaget's egocentricity), and behavior is largely guided by Freud's pleasure principle (is id dominated) – although the ego begins to emerge as the child understands that reality calls for discretion.

• Stage 2. By stage 2 the child recognizes that there is mutual benefit in cooperation. This stage has been called "instrumentalism" or "look out for number one" or "what's in it for me." The child is a bit less egocentric at this stage, recognizing that if one is good to others then they in terms will be good to you. There is now the notion that everyone looks out for their own needs, but that proper social exchanges are on a "tit-for-tat" basis. In Freudian terms, the reality principle has emerged to a greater extent at this stage.

Level II: Conventional Morality. At this level the child begins to grasp social rules and gains a more objective perspective on right and wrong. Freud would equate this level with superego development, or the formation of a conscience. In these stages Piaget's egocentrism has largely or entirely vanished.

• Stage 3. Stage 3 can be called "interpersonal relationships" or "good girl/boy." The major motivating factor in good behavior is social approval from those closest to the child.

• Stage 4. Maintaining social conventions or "law and order" are brief but apt descriptions of the fourth stage. This sense of order becomes generalized beyond close others to society at large. The concept of "doing one's duty" is crucial here.

Level III: Postconventional Morality. At this level the emphasis is no longer on conventional, societal standards of morality, but rather on personal or idealized principles.

- Stage 5. This can be called the "social contract" stage. The understanding is that laws, rules, and regulations are created for the mutual benefit of all citizens. Laws that are unjust ought to be changed. People at this stage understand and believe in democracy in action.

- Stage 6. This is the stage of "universal ethical principles." Right and wrong are not determined by rules and laws, but by individual reflection on what is proper behavior. One might think here of Kant's categorical imperative in which right and wrong apply equally to all, without regard to consequences (Chapter 3), except that modern ethicists understand the importance of the situation: What is wrong in most circumstances (e.g., lying) might be justifiable in others. But essentially, personal ethical values (e.g., a belief that all life is sacred) take precedence over any and all laws and conventions. In other words, laws are useful only as long as they serve the common good. Civil disobedience (such as the civil rights "sit- ins" in the 1960s) is justified by the circumstances (in this case segregation of the races). As a biblical example, think of Jesus, who said in response to the Pharisees that "The Sabbath was made for man, and not men for the Sabbath." Kohlberg believed that few people actually reach this stage, but those who do are of the stature of Mohandas Gandhi or Martin Luther King, Jr.

Table 7.1 shows some possible responses to the "Heinz" dilemma, both pro (Heinz should steal the drug) and con (Heinz should not steal the drug). At stage 6 no reasonable "con" response could be found for this particular dilemma. Note that these examples do not by any means exhaust the possibilities for children's or adults' rationalizations for Heinz's behavior.

The examples in Table 7.1 are reasonably straight forward; in fact, they are simpler than the more elaborate answers normally given by children. It takes some training as well as familiarity with guidelines (of Colby & Kohlberg, 1987) to become facile at classifying children according to their narrative reports.

Kohlberg's theory is really one of cognitive development (per Piaget) as applied to moral understanding because he believed that children developed their moral principles primarily though thinking about them. The progression through the stages cannot be accounted for by simple maturation or development of the nervous system. The child must grapple with these moral issues as they arise, and as with Piaget, disequilibrium occurs; for instance, when a child realizes that punishment for an unintentional infraction seems somehow unfair. Nor did Kohlberg believe that moral understanding was primarily due to learning of social mores because neither parents nor peers can teach new modes of thinking.

Kohlberg's (1958) doctoral dissertation, upon which he formulated his basic theory, studied 84 boys, most of whom he continued to study over the next couple of decades in his longitudinal research. As a result of his ongoing research he refined his methodology. He also dropped the sixth stage from his research program because so few people ever seem to reach this stage. Thus although this stage is not well-studied, it still retains some theoretical interest. But it is well to remember that the average person does not even attain the fifth stage; postconventional morality is rare, even among adults.

Although research generally supports Kohlberg's stage theory insofar as children's understanding of morality is concerned there are some notable exceptions.

Criticisms and Limitations of Kohlberg's Stage Theory

Cognition versus Affect. Kohlberg's studies stressed the cognitive factors in moral understanding. It should be easy to see in reviewing his stages that the higher levels require more advanced levels of cognitive development. But moral judgments can also be influenced by emotions. This is evident, for example, when a jury bases their verdict not strictly on the right or wrong in a defendant's actions, but also on their impression of his or her character.

Moral Understanding versus Moral Action. An assumption that one might all too easily make is that a person's moral understanding guides her moral behavior. While this is undoubtedly true to some extent, it cannot be said that moral behavior is anything close to perfectly predictable based on even the reliable classification of a person or child into one of Kohlberg's levels. To put it differently, understanding what is right does not necessarily translate into doing what is right. Social psychologists have come to understand the tremendous power of the situation in determining the course of behavior, as opposed to belief in abstract principles of morality. Someone may do a good deed like stopping to help a stranded motorist for any number of reasons; because it "seems right," because of guilt, because it will increase one's own self-image as a "good" person, because it might bring recognition from others, or simply because one has the time. One might fail to help because there are plenty of other people passing by, and surely one of them will stop (social psychologists refer to this diffusion of responsibility).

According to Harré (1983) people respond to different kinds of situations utilizing different levels of morality; and these are based more on societal expectations than on abstract moral reasoning. For example, Harré believed that people in the business world operate more at stage 2 (self-interest); that married couples are guided by stage 3 (mutual exchanges guided by the expectation of approval); and that the legal system is based on stage 4. (For other views on situational determinants of morality see Krebs and Denton, 2005).

Table 7.1

Brief Examples of Some Possible Responses to Kohlberg's "Heinz" Dilemma for Each Stage

I	1: Pro	Heinz should steal the drug: He could get in trouble with his wife and family otherwise.
I	1: Con	Heinz should not steal the drug: He could go to prison.
I	2: Pro	Heinz should steal the drug: He will be happy when his wife is cured she can again be there for him.
I	2: Con	Heinz should not steal the drug: The druggist deserves to be rewarded for his efforts in developing the drug.

II	3: Pro	Heinz should steal the drug: Heinz's wife and family will recognize that he did the right thing by them.
II	3: Con	Heinz should not steal the drug: People will think him a thief.
II	4: Pro	Heinz should steal the drug: He must do what's right for his wife, but he must also accept his punishment.
II	4: Con	Heinz should not steal the drug: Stealing is wrong, no matter the circumstance.
III	5: Pro	Heinz should steal the drug: His wife's need outweighs the druggist's. The law should be lenient with him, or even changed.
III	5: Con	Heinz should not steal the drug: Although druggist is unethical, he nonetheless is legally entitled to compensation.
III	6: Pro	Heinz should steal the drug: Saving his wife is morally a better choice than obeying the law because life itself is sacred.

Still, it can be argued that behaviors which are congruent with Kohlberg's stage descriptions depend on a cognitive understanding of that particular level of morality; which in turn assumes a certain degree of cognitive development. In other words, a person may have developed a high degree of moral reasoning in Kohlberg's hierarchy, yet under some conditions engage in behaviors that do not at all exemplify that presumed level of understanding. Furthermore, the motivations for a person's specific actions in a given situations are multifarious.

Cultural Variations. As with Piaget's stages of cognitive development, Kohlberg believed his stages to be universal. Despite differences in cultures with regard to manners and morals, Kohlberg still believed in the universality of his stages because they referred to general patterns of thinking rather than to specific cultural ideals. For example, if showing disrespect for one's father is taken more seriously in Shanghai than in Nova Scotia, this might differentially affect children's beliefs about the severity of punishment for such behavior within these two cultures, yet their reasoning processes would still be the same.

But still, the thinking underlying the stages may itself differ across cultures. Kohlberg's concepts of postconventional morality reflect Western philosophical ideals based on Enlightenment values of individualism freedom and rights. Kohlberg himself questioned the universality of the last two stages, finding these rarely reached by most of those he studied. His postconventional stage 6 in particular might represent a philosophical ideal that is accessible to select sages, such as Socrates, Buddha, Jesus, Gandhi, and so on; but certainly not to the average person. Also, just as Piaget's formal level of cognitive development may never emerge in certain cultures in which abstract reasoning (at least as we in our culture understand it), even stage 4 may not be attained in some village-centered agrarian or hunting/gathering cultures.

Also in contrast to individualistic cultures (such as the United States, Australia, and Western Europe), which place a high value on independence, collectivist cultures value harmony and interdependence within the group (family, community, or company), and these concerns usually outweigh those of the individual. To varying extents Asian, African, and Latin American cultures tend to be more collectivist than our own (see Markus & Kitayama, 1991; Triandis, 1995) 2. Differences in moral reasoning can thus be expected based on those different values.

A person from a collectivist society might place the responsibility for obtaining the drug less on Heinz himself and more on his family or on his community (Tietjen & Walker, 1985). Here, Kohlberg's scoring system, which positions a person at a higher level of morality (stage 4, for instance) based on her/his understanding of justice in a legalistic sense, would appear flawed when viewed in the context of a differing cultural perceptions.

Gender Differences. As was noted, Kohlberg's original work was done only on boys. Gilligan (1982) found this troubling; first, because results were necessarily limiting, based as they were on just one gender, and second, because Gilligan believed that girls and women use different standards from boys and men in making moral judgments. Her concerns are amplified in the next section.

IV. Other Views – Sigmund Freud, B. F. Skinner, and Albert Bandura

Freud, Skinner and Bandura are major theorists whose perspectives on development, including development of morality, are considered in great depth in later chapters. Here, for comparative purposes, some of their ideas concerning the specific area of morality are considered briefly.

Freud's Psychoanalytic Theory

Freud believed that the ego – the rational part of the human psyche – grew out of the primitive id, which was more instinctual. The id is the component of the personality that operates on the so-called pleasure principle. Present at birth, the id simply wants instant gratification. The ego develops later in response to the reality principle; in other words, the infant must learn to delay gratification.

Freud believed that around the ages of three to six the child develops sexual feelings toward the opposite sex parent. This introduces an element of competition and rivalry in family relations. The little girl, for example, feels competition with her mother for the affection of her father. The dynamics by which the child resolves these conflicts is referred to as the Oedipus complex in boys, and the Elektra complex in girls. In brief, due to anxiety, the child represses or eliminates from consciousness these feelings, which Freud considered to be sexual, and learns to identify with the opposite sex parent – girls with their mothers, boys with their fathers. In doing so, the child develops a conscience, or superego – that part of the personality that understands "should and shouldn't."

As will be seen later, there is more to all of this. But in short Freud believed that boys developed castration fears and girls envied boys their penises during this period of development, which were the causes of their anxieties. Because boys' castration fears were greater, their resolution task was harder, and thus they developed stronger superegos than did girls.

To quote Gilligan (1982, p. 7) on Freud:

> Having tied the formation of the superego or conscience to castration anxiety, Freud considered women to be deprived by nature of the impetus for a clear-cut Oedipal resolution. Consequently, women's superego – the heir to the Oedipus complex – was compromised: it was never "so inexorable, so impersonal, so independent of its emotional origins as we require it to be in men." From this observation of difference, that "for women the level of what is ethically normal is different from what it is in men," Freud concluded that women "show less sense of justice than men, that they are less ready to submit to the great exigencies of life, that they are more often influenced in their judgments by feelings of affection and hostility" (quotes are from Freud, 1925/1961, pp. 257-258, emphasis added).

Clearly Freud saw men as more rational and more ethical, at least in terms of their conceptions of justice. In contrast he saw women as more easily influenced by emotion. To him this implied that women were incomplete in their understanding of morality when compared to men.

The rest of this excellent chapter on psychological theories of moral development is available here: https://www2.warwick.ac.uk/fac/cross_fac/iatl/activities/modules/ugmodules/ethicalbeings/theoretical_approach_intro_reading.pdf

Piaget

Exercise: Examples of the Heteronomous and Autonomous Conscience

Passages a – d below are extracts of interviews of children with which Piaget illustrates his theory of the heteronomous and autonomous stages of morality (*Moral Judgment of the child*, 1932).

For each extract, decide whether the child is showing

- a heteronomous conscience (generally seen in children of 5-10 years old; moral requirements are imposed by others; it is punishment which makes an action bad) OR
- autonomous morality (generally seen in children of 10 years +; moral requirements are embraced by the individual based on understanding of social cooperation; an action is good or bad depending on intention)

A. Interviewer: Why must we not tell lies?
Child: Because God punishes them
Interviewer: And if God didn't punish them?
Child: Then we could tell them

B. Interviewer: Why is it naughty to tell a lie?
Child: Because you can't trust people any more

C. Interviewer: Why must we not lie?
Child: Because if everyone lied no one would know where they were

D. Interviewer: What happens when you tell lies?
Child: You get punished
Interviewer: And if you didn't get punished, would it be naughty to tell them?
Child: No.
Interviewer: I'm going to tell you two stories. There were two children and they broke a cup each. The first one says it wasn't him. His mother believes him and doesn't punish him. The second one also says that it wasn't him. But his mother doesn't believe him and punishes him. Are both lies that they told equally naughty?
Interviewer: No.
Interviewer: Which is the naughtiest?
Child: The one who was punished.

Kohlberg

Exercise: Six Stages of Moral Development

Based on slides from Edwin D. Bell, Ph.D., Winston-Salem State University:

- Stage 1: **Punishment and obedience** orientation. Punishment is what makes an action bad.
- Stage 2: Instrumental relativist orientation (**Self-interest**). What is right is what satisfies your own needs and occasionally the needs of others, e.g., the expectations of the family group or nation can be seen as valuable in own right.
- Stage 3: **"Good boy – good girl"** orientation – good behavior is what pleases or helps others and is **approved** by them
- Stage 4: **Law and order** orientation – right is doing one's duty, showing respect for authority, and maintaining social order for its own sake
- Stage 5: **Social contract** orientation – what is right is a function of individual rights and agreed upon standards.
- Stage 6: **Universal ethical principle** orientation – what is right is determined decision of conscience according to self-chosen ethical principles (these principles are abstract and ethical not specific moral prescriptions)

Which example illustrates which stage?

a. A little boy tidies the living room in return for a slice of cake.
b. A self-employed young man scrupulously fills in his first tax return because he is committed to contributing properly to public services and welfare.
c. A child lays the table for dinner without being asked because she knows her mum will be pleased.
d. A little girl is sent to her room when she pushes her little brother; she thinks it was wrong to push him.
e. A PTE student will never stretch the truth on her CV because she has embraced Kant's categorical imperative.
f. A child refuses to skip school with his friends because he respects the rules.

Erich Fromm (1900 – 1980)

Man for Himself

Erich Fromm was born in Frankfurt am Main, Germany, to Orthodox Jewish parents. He studied at the universities of Heidelberg and Munich, then at the Psychoanalytic Institute in Berlin. He emigrated in 1934, shortly after the Nazis gained power. His academic expertise was in psychoanalysis, and he is best known for application of the theory of psychoanalysis to social and cultural problems.

A. Authoritarian conscience

The contents of the authoritarian conscience are derived from the commands and taboos of the authority; its strength is rooted in the emotions of fear of, and admiration for, the authority. Good conscience is consciousness of pleasing the (external and internalized) authority; guilty conscience is the consciousness of displeasing it. The good (authoritarian) conscience produces a feeling of well being and security for it implies approval by, and greater closeness to, the authority; the guilty conscience produces fear and insecurity, because acting against the will of the authority implies the danger of being punished and – what is worse – of being deserted by the authority.

In order to understand the full impact of the last statement we must remember that character structure of the authoritarian person. He has found inner security by becoming, symbiotically, part of the authority felt to be greater and more powerful than himself. As long as he is part of that authority – at the expense of his own integrity – he feels that he is participating in the authority's strength. His feeling of certainty and identity depends on this symbiosis; to be rejected by the authority means to be thrown into a void, to face the horror of nothingness. Anything, to the authoritarian character, is better than this. To be sure, the love and approval of the authority give him the greatest satisfaction; but even punishment is better than rejection. The punishing authority is still with him, and if he has "sinned", the punishment is at least proof that the authority still cares.

As long as peoples relationships to the authority remains external, without ethical sanction, we can hardly speak of conscience; such conduct is merely expediential, regulated by fear of punishment and hope for reward, always dependent on the presence of these authorities, on their knowledge of what one is doing, and their alleged or real ability to punish and to reward. Often

> Expediential = concerning what is expedient – i.e. what is useful in achieving a goal

an experience which people take to be a feeling of guilt springing from their conscience is really nothing but their fear of such authorities. Properly speaking, these people do not feel guilty but afraid.

In the formation of the conscience, however, such authorities as the parents, the church, the state, public opinion are either consciously or unconsciously accepted as ethical and moral legislators whose laws and sanctions one adopts, thus internalizing them. The laws and sanctions of external authority become part of oneself, as it were, and instead of feeling responsible to something outside oneself, one feels responsible to something inside, to ones conscience. Conscience is a more effective regulator of conduct than fear of external authority; for while one can run from the latter, one can not escape from the internalized authority which has become part of oneself. While authoritarian conscience is different from fear if punishment and hope for reward, the relationship to the authority having become internalized, it is not very different in other essential respects. The most important point of similarity is the fact that the prescriptions of authoritarian conscience are not determined by one's own value judgment but exclusively by the fact that its commands and taboos are pronounced by authorities. If these norms happen to be good, conscience will guide man's actions in the direction of the good. However, they have not become the norms of conscience because they are good, but because they are the norms given by authority. If they are bad, they are just as much as part of conscience. A believer in Hitler, for instance, felt he was acting according to his conscience when he committed acts that where humanly revolting.

The prime offense in the authoritarian situation is rebellion against the authority's rule. Thus, disobedience becomes the "cardinal sin"; obedience, then cardinal virtue. Obedience implies the recognition of the authority's superior power and wisdom; his right to command, to reward, and to punish according to his own fiats. The authority demands submission not only because of the fear of its power, but out of the conviction of its moral superiority and right. The duty of recognizing the authority's superiority results in several prohibitions. The most comprehensive of these is the taboo against feeling oneself to be, or ever be able to become, like the authority, for this would contradict the latter's unqualified superiority and uniqueness. The real sin of Adam and Eve is the attempt to become like God; and it is a punishment for this challenge that they are expelled from the Garden of Eden.

The internalization of authority has two implications: one where man submits to the authority, the other where man takes over the role of the authority by treating himself with the same strictness and cruelty. Man thus becomes not only the obedient slave but also the strict taskmaster who treats himself as his own slave. This second implication is very important for the understanding of the psychological mechanisms of authoritarian conscience. The authoritarian character, being more or less crippled in his productiveness, develops a certain amount of sadism and destructiveness. These destructive energies are discharged by taking over the role of the authority and dominating oneself as the servant.

The dependence on irrational authority results in a weakening of will in the dependent person and, at the same time, whatever tends to paralyze the will makes for an increase in dependence. Thus, a vicious circle is formed. We ignore the fact that we too bow down to powers, not to that of a dictator and a political bureaucracy allied with him, but to the anonymous power of the market, of success and public opinion, of "common sense" – or rather, of common nonsense, and of the machine whose servants we have become. Our moral problem is man's indifference to himself. It lies in the fact that we have lost the sense of significance, that we have made ourselves into instruments for purposes outside ourselves, that we experience and treat ourselves as commodities and that our own powers have become alienated from ourselves. We have become things and our neighbors have become things. The result is that we are powerless and despise ourselves for our impotence. Since we do not trust our own power, we have no faith in man, no faith in ourselves or in what our own powers can create. We have no conscience in the humanistic sense, since we do not dare to trust our judgment.

Again the word "responsibility" has lost its original meaning and is usually used as a synonym for duty. The authoritarian conscience is essentially the readiness to follow the orders of the authorities to which one submits; it is glorified obedience. The humanistic conscience is the readiness to listen to the voice of one's own humanity and is independent of orders given by anyone else.

B. Humanistic conscience

Humanistic conscience is not the internalized voice of an authority whom we are eager to please and afraid of displeasing; it is our own voice, present in every human being and independent of external sanctions and rewards. What is the nature of this voice? Why do we hear it and why can we become deaf to it? Conscience judges our functioning as human beings; it is (as the root of the word con-scientia indicates) knowledge within oneself, knowledge of our respective success or failure in the art of living.

Actions, thoughts, and feelings which are conducive to the proper functioning and unfolding of our total personality produce a feeling of inner approval, of "rightness", characteristic of the humanistic "good conscience." On the other hand, acts, thoughts, and feelings injurious to our total personality produce a feeling of uneasiness and discomfort, characteristic of the " guilty conscience." Conscience is thus a reaction a re-action of ourselves to ourselves. It is the voice of our true selves, which summons us back to ourselves, to live productively, to develop fully and harmoniously – that is, to become fully what we potentially are. It is the guardian of our integrity.

It is the guardian of our integrity; it is the "ability to guarantee one's self with all due pride, and also at the same time to say yes to one's self (Nietsche, the Genealogy of Morals)." If love can be defined as the affirmation of the potentialities and the care for, and the respect of, the uniqueness of the loved person, humanistic conscience can be justly called the voice of our loving care for ourselves. Humanistic conscience represents not only the expression of our true selves; it contains also the essence of our moral experiences in life. In it we preserve the knowledge of our aim in life and of the principles through which attain it; those principles which we have discovered ourselves as well as those we have learned from others and which we have found to be true.

Humanistic conscience is the expression of man's self interest and integrity, while authoritarian conscience is concerned with man's obedience, self-sacrifice, duty, or his "social adjustment." The goal of humanistic conscience is productiveness and, therefore happiness, since happiness is the necessary concomitant of productive living. To cripple oneself by becoming a tool of others, no matter how dignified they are made to appear, to be "selfless, " unhappy, resigned, discouraged, is in opposition to the demands of one's conscience; any violation of the integrity and proper functioning of our personality, with regard to thinking as well as acting, and even with regard to such matters as taste for food or sexual behavior is acting against one's conscience.

But is our analysis of conscience not contradicted by the fact that in many people its voice is so feeble as not be heard and acted upon? Indeed, this fact is the reason for the moral precariousness of the human situation. If conscience always spoke loudly and distinctly enough, only a few would be mislead from their moral objective. One answer follows from the very nature of conscience itself: since its function is to be the guardian of man's true self-interest, it is alive to the extent to which the person has not lost himself entirely and become the prey of his own indifference and destructiveness. The relation to one's own productiveness is one of interaction. The more productively one lives, the stronger is one's conscience, and , in turn furthers one's productiveness. The less productive one lives, the weaker become one's conscience; the paradoxical – and tragic – situation of man is that his conscience is weakest when he needs it most.

Another answer to the question of the relative ineffectiveness of consciousness is our refusal to listen and – what is even more important – our ignorance of knowing how to listen. People are often under the illusion that their conscience will speak with a loud voice and its message will be clear and distinct; waiting for such a voice, they do not hear anything. But when the voice of conscience is feeble; it is indistinct; and one has to learn how to listen and understand it communication in order to act accordingly.

However, learning to understand the communications of one's conscience is exceedingly difficult, mainly for two reasons. In order to listen to the voice of our conscience we must be able to listen to ourselves, and this is exactly what most people in our culture have difficulties in doing. We listen to every voice and to everybody but not to ourselves. We are constantly exposed to the noise of opinions and ideas hammering at us from everywhere: motion pictures, newspapers, radio, idle chatter. If we had planned intentionally to prevent ourselves from ever listening to ourselves, we could have done no better

Listening to ourselves is so difficult because this art requires another ability, rare in modern man: that of being alone with oneself. In fact, we have developed a phobia of being alone; we prefer the most trivial and even obnoxious company, the meaningless activities, to being with ourselves; we seem to be frightened at the prospect of facing ourselves. Is it because we feel we would be such bad company? I think the fear of being alone with ourselves is rather a feeling of embarrassment, bordering sometimes on terror at seeing a person at once so well known and so strange; we are afraid and run away. We thus miss the chance of listening to ourselves, and we continue to ignore our conscience.

Listening to the feeble and indistinct voice of our conscience is difficult also because it does not speak to us directly and because we are often not aware that it is our conscience which disturbs us. We may feel only anxious (or even sick) for a number of reasons which have no apparent connection with our conscience. Perhaps the most frequent indirect reaction of our conscience to being neglected is a vague and unspecific feeling of guilt and uneasiness, of simply a feeling of tiredness or listlessness.

Sometimes such feelings are rationalized as guilt feelings for not having done this or that, when actually the omission one feels guilty about do not constitute genuine moral problems. But if the genuine though unconscious feeling of guilt has become so strong to be silenced by superficial rationalizations, it finds expression in deeper and more intense anxieties and even in physical and mental sickness.

Humanistic ethics takes the position that if man is alive he knows what is allowed; and to be alive means to be productive, to use one's powers not for any purpose transcending man, but for oneself, to make sense of one's existence, to be human. As long as anyone believes that his ideal and purpose is outside him, that it is above the clouds, in the past or in the future, he will go outside himself and seek fulfillment where it can not be found. He will look for solutions and answers at every point except the one where they can be found – in himself.

Richard Dawkins (b. 1941)

The God Delusion

Dawkins argues that our urges to be kind and altruistic are evolved. This behaviour, like all kinds of human behaviour, is ultimately explained by our genes, which programme us to ensure their own survival.

He explains how altruistic behaviour can be useful for our genes' survival:

There are circumstances – not particularly rare – in which genes ensure their own selfish survival by influencing organisms to behave altruistically. Those circumstances are now fairly well understood and they fall into two main categories. A gene that programs individual organisms to favour their genetic kin *[i.e. family]* is statistically likely to benefit copies of itself. Being good to one's own children is the obvious example, but it is not the only one. Bees, wasps, ants, termites and, to a lesser extent, certain vertebrates such as naked mole rats, meerkats and acorn woodpeckers, have evolved societies in which elder siblings care for younger siblings (with whom they are likely to share the genes for doing the caring). In general, as my late colleague W. D. Hamilton showed, animals tend to care for, defend, share resources with, warn of danger, or otherwise show altruism towards close kin because of the statistical likelihood that kin will share copies of the same genes.

The other main type of altruism for which we have a well worked-out Darwinian rationale is reciprocal altruism ('You scratch my back and I'll scratch yours').

What this does not explain so well is kindness to strangers – people who do not share our genes and are not likely to be able to help us out by returning the favour. However Dawkins considers that even this behaviour has a Darwinian explanation. Natural selection produces rules of thumb – inclinations to generally behave in a particular way which will tend to help our genes' survival. He goes on:

Rules of thumb, by their nature, sometimes misfire. In a bird's brain, the rule 'Look after small squawking things in your nest, and drop food into their red gapes' typically has the effect of preserving the genes that built the rule, because the squawking, gaping objects in an adult bird's nest are normally its own offspring. The rule misfires if another baby bird somehow gets into the nest, a circumstance that is positively engineered by cuckoos. Could it be that our Good Samaritan urges are misfirings, analogous to the misfiring of a reed warbler's parental instincts when it works itself to the bone for a young cuckoo?

Our altruistic urges developed in simpler societies, where more or less everyone we met would share our genes or be in a position to return favours. The altruistic rule of thumb 'misfires' in our more complex modern society so that we are sometimes kind to people who do not share our genes and will not be able to return the favour.

- *Give an example of an action which Dawkins would see as a 'misfiring' of the human altruistic rule of thumb*

Free Will and Determinism

In our day to day lives most people take it for granted that their actions are, for the most part, free. The unsuspecting non-philosopher sitting at her desk drinking a cup of tea would not be troubled by concerns over whether she was drinking it freely. However, the question of whether human actions are free, and in what sense, is a perplexing and ongoing topic of philosophical debate. Am I free in drinking this cup of tea simply because nobody is physically manipulating my arm and mouth to do so, or holding a gun to my head and saying 'drink up!'? Or are the pervasive influences of my genetic inheritance, upbringing and general social conditioning incompatible with any free action? Can I freely take my mug to the sink if God (who is omniscient and never makes mistakes) already knows that I am going to do so? Is it genuinely possible for me to either take my mug to the sink or to throw it out of the window, regardless of the influences of upbringing, genetics, God and so on?

Our conclusions about whether we have free will, and what it means, have a crucial bearing on our questions of human responsibility. Most people would say that someone should not be punished for something which they could not help doing. But when we think hard about freedom, we may find ourselves questioning whether any of us could ever have done otherwise.

The following terms are crucial to an accurate understanding of the debate.

Determinism:

The theory that all events, including human decisions and actions, are inevitable because they are necessitated by prior events and the laws of nature.

Hard determinism:

The theory that determinism is correct *and* that because of this no decision or action is free.

Soft determinism:

The theory that determinism is correct but that human beings can still act freely.

We act freely when we are able to do what we want (even if what we want is determined).

Libertarianism:

The theory that in at least some of our decisions, human beings are not determined; at least at times, when we make a decision we could genuinely have done otherwise in those same circumstances.

Compatibilism:

The theory that determinism and free will are compatible, i.e. that there is no contradiction between determinism being true and people being free. Soft determinists are compatibilists.

Theological determinism:

The theory that God determines every event that occurs in the world (including human actions).

Clarence Darrow's Determinist Defence

Extracts from speeches in Darrow's defence of Nathan Leopold and Richard Loeb

In 1924, in Chicago, the prominent defence attorney Clarence Darrow defended eighteen year old Richard Loeb and nineteen year old Nathan Leopold. They had murdered Robert Franks, who was just fourteen.

The killers had grown up with wealth and luxury, and both were extremely intellectually gifted. Loeb was obsessed with crime stories from a young age. They developed an intense relationship during the period when both were studying at Michigan University. Leopold was obsessed with Nietsche, and with Loeb. He saw Loeb as the sort of **ubermensch** *(superman) figure described by Nietsche, who is not bound by conventional morality but creates and imposes his own values. The teenagers started to cheat at cards and commit petty crimes together to prove their superiority. No longer satisfied with theft and arson, they planned to carry out the perfect crime, kidnapping and murdering a child and evading justice. They picked a victim at random, offering him a lift home from school. They bludgeoned him to death in their car, then poured acid on his body to make identification more difficult. His body was dumped in a drainage culvert. They were soon arrested because Leopold's glasses dropped out of his jacket while they moved the body.*

The passages which follow are taken from Darrow's defence of the boys at their trial.

No one knows what will be the fate of the child he gets or the child she bears; the fate of the child is the last thing they consider.

I am sorry for the fathers as well as the mothers, for the fathers who give their strength and their lives for educating and protecting and creating a fortune for the boys that they love; for the mothers who go down into the shadow of death for their children, who nourish them and care for them, and risk their lives, that they may live, who watch them with tenderness and fondness and longing, and who go down into dishonor and disgrace for the children that they love.

All of these are helpless. We are all helpless. But when you are pitying the father and the mother of poor Bobby Franks, what about the fathers and mothers of these two unfortunate boys, and what about the, unfortunate boys themselves, and what about all the fathers and all the mothers and all the boys and all the girls who tread a dangerous maze in darkness from birth to death?

Do you think you can cure the hatreds and the maladjustments of the world by hanging them? You simply show your ignorance and your hate when you say it. You may here and there cure hatred with love and understanding, but you can only add fuel to the flames by cruelty and hate.

…. I am always suspicious of righteous indignation. Nothing is more cruel than righteous indignation. To hear young men talk glibly of justice.

Who knows what it is? Does Mr. Savage know? Does Mr. Crowe know? Do I know? Does Your Honor know? Is there any human machinery for finding it out? Is there any man can weigh me and say what I deserve?

Can Your Honor? Let us be honest. Can Your Honor appraise yourself and say what you deserve? Can Your Honor appraise these two young men and say what they deserve? Justice must take account of infinite circumstances which a human being cannot understand….

These boys left this body down in the culvert and they came back telephoned home

How did it happen?

Let us take Dickie Loeb first.

I do not claim to know how it happened; I have sought to find out; I know that something, or some combination of things, is responsible for his mad act. I know that there are no accidents in nature. I know that effect follows cause. I know that if I were wise enough, and knew enough about this case, I could lay my finger on the cause. I will do the best I can, but it is largely speculation. The child, of course, is born without knowledge. Impressions are made upon its mind as it goes along. Dickie Loeb was a child of wealth and opportunity. Over and over in this court Your Honor has been asked, and other courts have been asked, to consider boys who have no chance; they have been asked to consider the poor, whose home had: been the street, with no education and no opportunity in life.

But Your Honor, it is just as often a great misfortune to be the child of the rich as it is to be the child of the poor. Wealth has its misfortunes. Too much, too great opportunity and advantage given to a child has its misfortunes. Can I find what was wrong? I think I can. Here was a boy at a tender age, placed in the hands of a governess, intellectual, vigorous, devoted, with a strong ambition for the welfare of this boy. He was, pushed in his studies, as plants are forced in hothouses. He had no pleasures, such as a boy should have, except as they were gained by lying and cheating. Now, I am not criticizing the nurse. I suggest that some day Your Honor look at her picture. It explains her fully. Forceful, brooking no Interference, she loved the boy, and her ambition was that he should reach the highest perfection. No time to pause, no time to stop from one book to another, no time to have those pleasures which a boy ought to have to create a normal life. And what happened?

Your Honor, what would happen? Nothing strange or unusual. This nurse was with him all the time, except when he stole out at night, from two to fourteen years of age. He, scheming and planning as healthy boys would do, to get out from under her restraint. She, putting before him the best books, which children generally do not want; and he, when she was not looking, reading detective stories, which he devoured, story after story, in his young life. Of all of this there can be no question. What is the result? Every story he read was a story of crime. We have a statute in this state, passed only last year, if I recall it, which forbids minors reading stories of crime. Why? There is only one reason. Because the legislature in its wisdom felt that it would produce criminal tendencies in the boys who read them. The legislature of this state has given its opinion, and forbidden boys to read these books. He read them day after day. He never stopped.

Now, these facts are beyond dispute. He early developed the tendency to mix with crime, to be a detective; as a little boy shadowing people on the street; as a little child going out with his fantasy of being the head of a band of criminals and directing them on the street. How did this grow and develop in him? Let us see. It seems to me as natural as the day following the night. Every detective story is a story of a sleuth getting the best of it; trailing some unfortunate individual through devious ways until his victim is finally landed in jail or stands on the gallows. They all show how smart the detective is, and where the criminal himself falls down....

They wanted to commit a perfect crime. There had been growing in this brain, dwarfed and twisted, not due to any wickedness of Dickie Loeb, for he is a child. It grew as he grew; it grew from those around him; it grew from the lack of the proper training until it possessed him.

We might as well be honest with ourselves, Your Honor. Before would tie a noose around the neck of a boy I would try to call back my mind the emotions of youth. I would try to remember what world looked like to me when I was a child. I would try to remember how strong were these instinctive, persistent emotions that moved life. I would try to remember how weak and inefficient was youth in presence of the surging, controlling feelings of the child.

But, Your Honor, that is not all there is to boyhood. Nature is strong and she is pitiless. She works in her own mysterious way, and we are her victims. We have not much to do with it ourselves. Nature takes this job in hand, and we play our parts. In the words of old Omar Khayyam, we are only

Impotent pieces in the game He plays

Upon this checkerboard if nights and days,

Hither and thither moves, and checks, and slays,

And one by one back in the closet lays.

What had this boy to do with it? He was not his own father; he was not his own mother; he was not his own grandparents. All of this was handed to him. He did not surround himself with governesses and wealth. He did not make himself and yet he is to be compelled to pay.

For God's sake, are we crazy? In the face of history, of every line of philosophy, against the teaching of every religionist and seer and prophet the world has ever given us, we are still doing what our barbaric, ancestors did when they came out of the caves and the woods.

Your Honor, I am almost ashamed to talk about it. I can hardly imagine that we are in the twentieth century. And yet there are men who seriously say that for what Nature has done, for what life has done, for what training has done, you should hang these boys.

I know that one of two things happened to Richard Loeb; that this terrible crime was inherent in his organism, and came from some ancestor, or that it came through his education and his training after he was born.

To believe that any boy is responsible for himself or his early training is an absurdity that no lawyer or judge should be guilty of today. Somewhere this came to the boy. If his failing came from his heredity, I do not know where or how. None of us are bred perfect and pure; and the color of our hair, the color of our eyes, our stature, the weight and fineness of our brain, and everything about us could, with full knowledge, be traced with absolute certainty to somewhere. If we had the pedigree it could be traced just the same in a boy as it could in a dog, a horse or a cow.

I do not know what remote ancestors may have sent down the seed that corrupted him, and I do not know through how many ancestors it may have passed until it reached Dickie Loeb.

All I know is that it is true, and there is not a biologist in the world who will not say that I am right.

If it did not come that way, then I know that if he was normal, if he had been understood, if he had been trained as he should have been it would not have happened. Not that anybody may not slip, but I know it and Your Honor knows it, and every schoolhouse and every church in the land is an evidence of it. Else why build them?

Every effort to protect society is an effort toward training the youth to keep the path. Every bit of training in the world proves it, and it likewise proves that it sometimes fails. I know that if this boy had been understood and properly trained – properly for him – and the training that he got might have been the very best for someone; but if it had been the proper training for him he would not be in this courtroom today with the noose above his head.

If there is responsibility anywhere, it is back of him; somewhere in the infinite number of his ancestors, or in his surroundings, or in both. And I submit, your Honor that under every principle of natural justice, under every principle of conscience, of right, and of law, he should not be made responsible for the acts of someone else."

Physics and Determinism

Newton's Laws of Motion

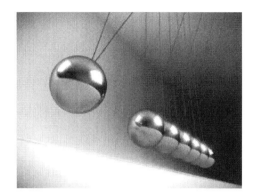

I.   Every object in a state of uniform motion (stationary, or moving at a constant speed in a constant direction) will stay in that state of motion unless an external force is applied to it

II.   The relationship between an object's mass m, its acceleration a, and the applied force F is $F = ma$. (So if we know what force is being applied to an object and what its mass is, why can work out how much it will accelerate)

III.   For every action there is an equal and opposite reaction.

1.   How could we describe the workings of the physical world as described by Newton?

2.   What has this to do with arguments about human free will?

Heisenberg's Uncertainty Principle

Werner Heisenberg (1901-1976), a Nobel prize winning pioneer of quantum mechanics, introduced the following principle:

We cannot know the position and the momentum of a subatomic particle at the same time. The more accurately we know the position of a particle in space, the more uncertainty there will be in our estimation of its momentum, and vice versa.

3.   Why might this principle be judged significant for discussions of free will?

4.   Does uncertainty at the subatomic level have an impact on the plausibility of free will?

John Locke (1632-1704)

Essay Concerning Human Understanding

Book II, Chapter XXI, Of Power

8. So far as a man has power to think or not to think, to move or not to move, according to the preference or direction of his own mind, so far is a man *free*. Wherever any performance or forbearance are not equally in a man's power; wherever doing or not doing will not equally *follow* upon the preference of his mind directing it, there he is not free... So that the idea of *liberty* is, the idea of a power in any agent to do or forbear any particular action, according to the determination or thought of the mind, whereby either of them is preferred to the other: where either of them is not in the power of the agent to be produced by him according to his volition, there he is not at liberty; that agent is under *necessity*. So that liberty cannot be where there is no thought, no volition, no will; but there may be thought, there may be will, there may be volition, where there is no liberty. A little consideration of an obvious instance or two may make this clear.

> Performance = doing
>
> Forbearance =

Q1 Under what conditions is a person free (at liberty)? In other words, what does it take for someone to be free?

9. A tennis-ball, whether in motion by the stroke of a racket, or lying still at rest, is not by any one taken to be a free agent. If we inquire into the reason, we shall find it is because we conceive not a tennis-ball to think, and consequently not to have any volition, or *preference* of motion to rest, or *vice versa*; and therefore has not liberty, is not a free agent; but all its both motion and rest come under our idea of necessary, and are so called. Likewise a man falling into the water, (a bridge breaking under him,) has not herein liberty, is not a free agent. For though he has volition, though he prefers his not falling to falling; yet the forbearance of that motion not being in his power, the stop or cessation of that motion follows not upon his volition; and therefore therein he is not free. So a man striking himself, or his friend, by a convulsive motion of his arm, which it is not in his power, by volition or the direction of his mind, to stop or forbear, nobody thinks he has in this liberty; every one pities him, as acting by necessity and constraint.

> herein = in this
>
> volition = will

Q2 Why is the tennis ball not free?

Q3 Why is the man in the example not free? (from 'Likewise a man falling...')

10 Again: suppose a man be carried, whilst fast asleep, into a room where is a person he longs to see and speak with; and be there locked fast in, beyond his power to get out: he awakes, and is glad to find

himself in so desirable company, which he stays willingly in, i.e. prefers his stay to going away. I ask, is not this stay voluntary? I think nobody will doubt it: and yet, being locked fast in, it is evident he is not at liberty not to stay, he has not freedom to be gone. So that liberty is not an idea belonging to volition, or preferring; but to the person having the power of doing, or forbearing to do, according as the mind shall choose or direct. Our idea of liberty reaches as far as that power, and no farther.

Q4 Why is the man in this example not free?

13. Wherever thought is wholly wanting, or the power to act or forbear according to the direction of thought, there necessity takes place.

Q5 Necessity occurs:

- **When there is no _____**
- **When you do not have the possibility of _____ or ____ _____according to _____ _____**

Q6 Give your own example of someone acting under necessity

14. If this be so, (as I imagine it is,) I leave it to be considered, whether it may not help to put an end to that long agitated, and, I think, unreasonable, because unintelligible question, viz. *Whether man's will be free or no?* For if I mistake not, it follows from what I have said, that the question itself is altogether improper; and it is as insignificant to ask whether man's *will* be free, as to ask whether his sleep be swift, or his virtue square: liberty being as little applicable to the will, as swiftness of motion is to sleep, or squareness to virtue. Every one would laugh at the absurdity of such a question as either of these: because it is obvious that the modifications of motion belong not to sleep, nor the difference of figure to virtue; and when any one well considers it, I think he will as plainly perceive that liberty, which is but a power, belongs only to agents, and cannot be an attribute or modification of the will, which is also but a power.

> Modifications = (here) attributes that change something

Q7 Why does it make no sense to talk of the freedom of the will, according to Locke?

EXTENSION

This, in an agent capable of volition, when the beginning or continuation of any action is contrary to that preference of his mind, is called compulsion; when the hindering or stopping any action is contrary to his volition, it is called restraint. Agents that have no thought, no volition at all, are in everything *necessary* agents.

E1 What is the difference between compulsion and restraint?

E2 Do you share Locke's view of necessity? Explain why/why not

Voluntary action and free action

5. This, at least, I think evident, — That we find in ourselves a power to begin or forbear, continue or end several actions of our minds, and motions of our bodies, barely by a thought or preference of the mind ordering, or as it were commanding, the doing or not doing such or such a particular action. This power which the mind has thus to order the consideration of any idea, or the forbearing to consider it; or to prefer the motion of any part of the body to its rest, and *vice versa*, in any particular instance, is that which we call the *Will*. The actual exercise of that power, by directing any particular action, or its forbearance, is that which we call *volition* or *willing*. The forbearance of that action, consequent to such order or command of the mind, is called *voluntary*. And whatsoever action is performed without such a thought of the mind, is called *involuntary*.

E3 What does Locke say makes an action voluntary?

E4 Do you agree with this definition?

E5 Give an example of involuntary action

7. Every one, I think, finds in himself a power to begin or forbear, continue or put an end to several actions in *himself*. From the consideration of the extent of this power of the mind over the actions of the man, which everyone finds in himself, arise the ideas of *liberty* and *necessity*.

E6 What are the ideas of liberty and necessity essentially about?

21. To return, then, to the inquiry about liberty, I think the question is not proper, *whether the will be free,*

but *whether a man be free*. Thus, I think, first, that so far as any one can, by the direction or choice of his mind, preferring the existence of any action to the non-existence of that action, and *vice versa*, make it to exist or not exist, so far *he* is free. For if I can, by a thought directing the motion of my finger, make it move when it was at rest, or *vice versa*, it is evident, that in respect of that I am free: and if I can, by a like thought of my mind, preferring one to the other, produce either words or silence, I am at liberty to speak or hold my peace: and as far as this power reaches, of acting or not acting, by the determination of his own thought preferring either, so far is a man free. For how can we think any one freer, than to have the power to do what he will? And so far as any one can, by preferring any action to its not being, or rest to any action, produce that action or rest, so far can he do what he will. For such a preferring of action to its absence, is the willing of it: and we can scarce tell how to imagine any being freer, than to be able to do what he wills. So that in respect of actions within the reach of such a power in him, a man seems as free as it is possible for freedom to make him.

Q8 What important rhetorical question does Locke ask here (a good quotation to include in an essay...)?

Q9 How would you answer that question?

22. But the inquisitive mind of man, willing to shift off from himself, as far as he can, all thoughts of guilt, is not content with this: freedom, unless it reaches further than this, will not serve the turn: and it passes for a good plea, that a man is not free at all, if he be not as *free to will* as he is to *act what he wills*. Concerning a man's liberty, there yet, therefore, is raised this further question, *Whether a man be free to will?* which I think is what is meant, when it is disputed whether the will be free. And as to that I imagine.

Q10 Locke thinks we have a morally dubious reason for asserting any other kind of freedom to the one he accepts. What is that reason?

EXTENSION

23. Secondly, That willing, or volition, being an action, and freedom consisting in a power of acting or not acting, a man in respect of willing or the act of volition, when any action in his power is once proposed to his thoughts, as presently to be done, cannot be free. The reason whereof is very manifest… For it is unavoidably necessary to prefer the doing or forbearance of an action in a man's power, which is once so proposed to his thoughts; a man must necessarily will the one or the other of them ….

E7 On what grounds does Locke here say that the will itself is not free? Are you convinced?

Besides to make a man free after this manner, by making the action of willing to depend on his will, there must be another antecedent will, to determine the acts of this will, and another to determine that, and so *in infinitum*: for wherever one stops, the actions of the last will cannot be free. Nor is any being, as far I can comprehend beings above me, capable of such a freedom of will, that it can forbear to will, i.e. to prefer the being or not being of anything in its power, which it has once considered as such.

E8 What does he say would be needed for the will to be free in this way? Why does he consider this idea absurd?

Q11 Can we have the kind of freedom Locke describes if determinism is correct?

Q12 Do you agree with Locke's view of what it takes to be free? Explain

David Hume

Enquiry Concerning Human Understanding

63 This has been the case in the long disputed question concerning liberty and necessity; and to so remarkable a degree that, if I be not much mistaken, we shall find, that all mankind, both learned and ignorant, have always been of the same opinion with regard to this subject, and that a few intelligible definitions would immediately have put an end to the whole controversy.

I hope, therefore, to make it appear that all men have ever agreed in the doctrine both of necessity and of liberty, according to any reasonable sense, which can be put on these terms; and that the whole controversy has hitherto turned merely upon words. We shall begin with examining the doctrine of necessity.

1. Why does Hume think disagreements arise about freedom (liberty) and necessity?

N.B. necessity for Hume is not the same as necessity according to Locke. For Locke it means being in a position of compulsion or constraint where you are effectively forced to do something or prevented from doing something (- the opposite of freedom). But for Hume necessity simply consists of this:

- _We observe that in the world some things regularly follow other things – e.g. a fire is started; it gets warmer_
- _We start to infer one from another – e.g. when we see a fire we expect heat._

Necessity consists just of the regularity with which 'effects' follow 'causes', and the connection our mind makes between the two. There is no mystical connection between cause and effect.

In the sections that follow the passage above he builds up his case to show that human actions are necessary.

There is, he claims, a 'remarkable degree of uniformity' (sameness) in human nature across times and places. In like circumstances, with like backgrounds, human beings tend to do the same things. He writes, 'Would you know the sentiments, inclinations, and course of life of the Greeks and Romans? Study well the temper and actions of the French and English.'

There is of course variation between people of difference ages, genders etc, but the variations are ultimately predictable; with enough knowledge we would be able to see exactly why two individuals act differently in different circumstances.

He comments on unexpected/irregular human actions as follows:

The most irregular and unexpected resolutions of men may frequently be accounted for by those who know every particular circumstance of their character and situation. A person of an obliging disposition gives a peevish answer: But he has the toothache, or has not dined. A stupid fellow discovers an uncommon alacrity in his carriage: But he has met with a sudden piece of good fortune...

> **2. Summarise his point in the passage above**

He continues:

The mutual dependence of men is so great in all societies that scarce any human action is entirely complete in itself, or is performed without some reference to the actions of others, which are requisite to make it answer fully the intention of the agent. The poorest artificer, who labours alone, expects at least the protection of the magistrate, to ensure him the enjoyment of the fruits of his labour.

In short, experimental inference and reasoning concerning the actions of others enters so much into human life that no man, while awake, is ever a moment without employing it. Have we not reason, therefore, to affirm that all mankind have always agreed in the doctrine of necessity according to the foregoing definition and explication of it?

> **3. To strengthen his case for the necessity of human action, Hume suggests that in fact that necessity is necessary for us to exist together. Why?**

73 But to proceed in this reconciling project with regard to the question of liberty and necessity; the most contentious question of metaphysics, the most contentious science; it will not require many words

---

EXTENSION: He goes on to consider why we mistakenly think human action is not necessary, in the face of this evidence... [Try this for a challenge!]

71 I have frequently considered, what could possibly be the reason why all mankind, though they have ever, without hesitation, acknowledged the doctrine of necessity in their whole practice and reasoning, have yet discovered such a reluctance to acknowledge it in words, and have rather shown a propensity, in all ages, to profess the contrary opinion. The matter, I think, may be accounted for after the following manner. If we examine the operations of body, and the production of effects from their causes, we shall find that all our faculties can never carry us farther in our knowledge of this relation than barely to observe that particular objects are constantly conjoined together, and that the mind is carried, by a customary transition, from the appearance of one to the belief of the other. But though this conclusion concerning human ignorance be the result of the strictest scrutiny of this subject, men still entertain a strong propensity to believe that they penetrate farther into the powers of nature, and perceive something like a necessary connexion between the cause and the effect. When again they turn their reflections towards the operations of their own minds, and feel no such connexion of the motive and the action; they are thence apt to suppose, that there is a difference between the effects which result from material force, and those which arise from thought and intelligence. But being once convinced that we know nothing farther of causation of any kind than merely the constant conjunction of objects, and the consequent inference of the mind from one to another, and finding that these two circumstances are universally allowed to have place in voluntary actions; we may be more easily led to own the same necessity common to all causes. And though this reasoning may contradict the systems of many philosophers, in ascribing necessity to the determinations of the will, we shall find, upon reflection, that they dissent from it in words only, not in their real sentiment. Necessity, according to the sense in which it is here taken, has never yet been rejected, nor can ever, I think, be rejected by any philosopher. It may only, perhaps, be pretended that the mind can perceive, in the operations of matter, some farther connexion between the cause and effect; and connexion that has not place in voluntary actions of intelligent beings. Now whether it be so or not, can only appear upon examination; and it is incumbent on these philosophers to make good their assertion, by defining or describing that necessity, and pointing it out to us in the operations of material causes.

E1 Why does Hume think we make the mistake of thinking that human action isn't necessary? (think about how he himself seems to understand necessity here...)

---

to prove, that all mankind have ever agreed in the doctrine of liberty as well as in that of necessity, and that the whole dispute, in this respect also, has been hitherto merely verbal. For what is meant by liberty, when applied to voluntary actions? We cannot surely mean that actions have so little connexion with motives, inclinations, and circumstances, that one does not follow with a certain degree of uniformity from the other, and that one affords no inference by which we can conclude the existence of the other. For these are plain and acknowledged matters of fact. By liberty, then, we can only mean a power of acting or not acting, according to the determinations of the will; that is, if we choose to remain at rest, we may; if we choose to move, we also may. Now this hypothetical liberty is universally allowed to belong to every one who is not a prisoner and in chains. Here, then, is no subject of dispute.

4. **Hume notes that there has always been widespread agreement that human beings are free. What does he think it means to be free?**

75 There is no method of reasoning more common, and yet none more blameable, than, in philosophical disputes, to endeavour the refutation of any hypothesis, by a pretence of its dangerous consequences to religion and morality. When any opinion leads to absurdities, it is certainly false; but it is not certain that an opinion is false, because it is of dangerous consequence. Such topics, therefore, ought entirely to be forborne; as serving nothing to the discovery of truth, but only to make the person of an antagonist odious. This I observe in general, without pretending to draw any advantage from it. I frankly submit to an examination of this kind, and shall venture to affirm that the doctrines, both of necessity and of liberty, as above explained, are not only consistent with morality, but are absolutely essential to its support.

5. **Hume warns against the blameworthy error of** _____

_____

76. The only proper object of hatred or vengeance is a person or creature, endowed with thought and consciousness; and when any criminal or injurious actions excite that passion, it is only by their relation to the person, or connexion with him. Actions are, by their very nature, temporary and perishing; and where they proceed not from some cause in the character and disposition of the person who performed them, they can neither redound to his honour, if good; nor infamy if evil.

Men are less blamed for such actions as they perform hastily and unpremeditately than for such as proceed from deliberation. For what reason? but because a hasty temper, though a constant cause or principle in the mind, operates only by intervals, and infects not the whole character. Again, repentance wipes off every crime, if attended with a reformation of life and manners. How is this to be accounted for? but by asserting that actions render a person criminal merely as they are proofs of criminal principles in the mind; and when, by an alteration of these principles, they cease to be just proofs, they likewise cease to be criminal. But, except upon the doctrine of necessity, they never were just proofs, and consequently never were criminal.

6. Hume considers that we blame people less for hasty or unpremeditated actions because they tell us less about _____.

We actually need necessity to blame people, because we blame them not so much for their actual actions but for their _____, and their actions will only tell us about this if there is a reliable connection between the two.

EXTENSION

78. I pretend not to have obviated or removed all objections to this theory, with regard to necessity and liberty. I can foresee other objections, derived from topics which have not here been treated of. It may be said, for instance, that, if voluntary actions be subjected to the same laws of necessity with the operations of matter, there is a continued chain of necessary causes, preordained and pre-determined, reaching from the original cause of all to every single volition of every human creature. No contingency anywhere in the universe; no indifference; no liberty. While we act, we are, at the same time, acted upon.

… He [God] foresaw, he ordained, he intended all those actions of men, which we so rashly pronounce criminal. And we must therefore conclude, either that they are not criminal, or that the Deity, not man, is accountable for them.

81…. It is not possible to explain distinctly, how the Deity can be the mediate cause of all the actions of men, without being the author of sin and moral turpitude. These are mysteries, which mere natural and unassisted reason is very unfit to handle; and whatever system she embraces, she must find herself involved in inextricable difficulties, and even contradictions, at every step which she takes with regard to such subjects. To reconcile the indifference and contingency of human actions with prescience; or to defend absolute decrees, and yet free the Deity from being the author of sin, has been found hitherto to exceed all the power of philosophy. Happy, if she be thence sensible of her temerity, when she pries into these sublime mysteries; and leaving a scene so full of obscurities and perplexities, return, with suitable modesty, to her true and proper province, the examination of common life; where she will find difficulties enough to employ her enquiries, without launching into so boundless an ocean of doubt, uncertainty, and contradiction!

E2 What problem does Hume note might be raised against the idea that human actions are necessary?

E3 What does he advise we do with this problem?

A.J. Ayer (1910 – 1989)

'Freedom and Necessity'

Chapter 12 of Philosophical Essays, 1954

WHEN I am said to have done something of my own free will it is implied that I could have acted otherwise; and it is only when it is believed that I could have acted otherwise that I am held to be morally responsible for what I have done. For a man is not thought to be morally responsible for an action that it was not in his power to avoid. But if human behaviour is entirely governed by causal laws, it is not clear how any action that is done could ever have been avoided. It may be said of the agent that he would have acted otherwise if the causes of his action had been different, but they being what they were, it seems to follow that he was bound to act as he did. Now it is commonly assumed both that men are capable of acting freely, in the sense that is required to make them morally responsible, and that human behaviour is entirely governed by causal laws: and it is the apparent conflict between these two assumptions that gives rise to the philosophical problem of the freedom of the will.

Confronted with this problem, many people will be inclined to agree with Dr. Johnson: 'Sir, we know our will is free, and *there's* an end on't'. But, while this does very well for those who accept Dr. Johnson's premiss, it would hardly convince anyone who denied the freedom of the will. Certainly, if we do know that our wills are free, it follows that they are so. But the logical reply to this might be that since our wills are not free, it follows that no one can know that they are: so that if anyone claims, like Dr. Johnson, to know that they are, he must be mistaken. What is evident, indeed, is that people often believe themselves to be acting freely; and it is to this 'feeling' of freedom that some philosophers appeal when they wish, in the supposed interests of morality, to prove that not all human action is causally determined. But if these philosophers are right in their assumption that a man cannot be acting freely if his action is causally determined, then the fact that someone feels free to do, or not to do, a certain action does not prove that he really is so. It may prove that the agent does not himself know what it is that makes him act in one way rather than another: but from the fact that a man is unaware of the causes of his action, it does not follow that no such causes exist.

So much may be allowed to the determinist; but his belief that all human actions are subservient to causal laws still remains to be justified. If, indeed, it is necessary that every event should have a cause, then the rule must apply to human behaviour as much as to anything else. But why should it be supposed that every event must have a cause? The contrary is not unthinkable. Nor is the law of universal causation a necessary presupposition of scientific thought. The scientist may try to discover causal laws, and in many cases he succeeds; but sometimes he has to be content with statistical laws, and sometimes he comes upon events which, in the present state of his knowledge, he is not able to subsume under any law at all. In the case of these events he assumes that if he knew more he would be able to discover some law, whether causal or statistical, which would enable him to account for them. And this assumption cannot be disproved. For however far he may have carried his investigation, it is always open to him to carry it further; and it is always conceivable that if he carried it further he would discover the connection which had hitherto escaped him. Nevertheless, it is also conceivable that the events with which he is concerned are not systematically connected with any others: so that the reason why he does not discover the sort of laws that he requires is simply that they do not obtain.

Now in the case of human conduct the search for explanations has not in fact been altogether fruitless. Certain scientific laws have been established; and with the help of these laws we do make a number of successful predictions about the ways in which different people will behave. But these predictions do not always cover every detail. We may be able to predict that in certain circumstances a particular man will be angry, without being able to prescribe the precise form that the expression of his anger will take. We may be reasonably sure that he will shout, but not sure how loud his shout will be, or exactly what words he will use. And it is only a small proportion of human actions that we are able to forecast even so precisely as this. But that, it may be said, is because we have not carried our investigations very far. The science of psychology is still in its infancy and, as it is developed, not only will more human actions be explained, but the explanations will go into greater detail. The ideal of complete explanation may never in fact be attained: but it is theoretically attainable. Well, this may be so: and certainly it is impossible to show *a priori* that it is not so: but equally it cannot be shown that it is. This will not, however, discourage the scientist who, in the field of human behaviour, as elsewhere, will continue to formulate theories and test them by the facts. And in this he is justified. For since he has no reason *a priori* to admit that there is a limit to what he can discover, the fact that he also cannot be sure that there is no limit does not make it unreasonable for him to devise theories, nor, having devised them, to try constantly to improve them.

But now suppose it to be claimed that, so far as men's actions are concerned, there is a limit: and that this limit is set by the fact of human freedom. An obvious objection is that in many cases in which a person feels himself to be free to do, or not to do, a certain action, we are even now able to explain, in causal terms, why it is that he acts as he does. But it might be argued that even if men are sometimes mistaken in believing that they act freely, it does not follow that they are always so mistaken. For it is not always the case that when a man believes that he has acted freely we are in fact able to account for his action in causal terms. A determinist would say that we should be able to account for it if we had more knowledge of the circumstances, and had been able to discover the appropriate natural laws. But until those discoveries have been made, this remains only a pious hope. And may it not be true that, in some cases at least, the reason why we can give no causal explanation is that no causal explanation is available; and that this is because the agent's choice was literally free, as he himself felt it to be?

The answer is that this may indeed be true, inasmuch as it is open to anyone to hold that no explanation is possible until some explanation is actually found. But even so it does not give the moralist what he wants. For he is anxious to show that men are capable of acting freely in order to infer that they can be morally responsible for what they do. But if it is a matter of pure chance that a man

306

should act in one way rather than another, he may be free but he can hardly be responsible. And indeed when a man's actions seem to us quite unpredictable, when, as we say, there is no knowing what he will do, we do not look upon him as a moral agent. We look upon him rather as a lunatic.

To this it may be objected that we are not dealing fairly with the moralist. For when he makes it a condition of my being morally responsible that I should act freely, he does not wish to imply that it is purely a matter of chance that I act as I do. What he wishes to imply is that my actions are the result of my own free choice: and it is because they are the result of my own free choice that I am held to be morally responsible for them.

But now we must ask how it is that I come to make my choice. Either it is an accident that I choose to act as I do or it is not. If it is an accident, then it is merely a matter of chance that I did not choose otherwise ; and if it is merely a matter of chance that I did not choose otherwise, it is surely irrational to hold me morally responsible for choosing as I did. But if it is not an accident that I choose to do one thing rather than another, then presumably there is some causal explanation of my choice : and in that case we are led back to determinism.

Again, the objection may be raised that we are not doing justice to the moralist's case. His view is not that it is a matter of chance that I choose to act as I do, but rather that my choice depends upon my character. Nevertheless he holds that I can still be free in the sense that he requires; for it is I who am responsible for my character. But in what way am I responsible for my character? Only, surely, in the sense that there is a causal connection between what I do now and what I have done in the past. It is only this that justifies the statement that I have made myself what I am: and even so this is an over-simplification, since it takes no account of the external influences to which I have been subjected. But, ignoring the external influences, let us assume that it is in fact the case that I have made myself what I am. Then it is still legitimate to ask how it is that I have come to make myself one sort of person rather than another. And if it be answered that it is a matter of my strength of will, we can put the same question in another form by asking how it is that my will has the strength that it has and not some other degree of strength. Once more, either it is an accident or it is not. If it is an accident, then by the same argument as before, I am not morally responsible, and if it is not an accident we are led back to determinism.

Furthermore, to say that my actions proceed from my character or, more colloquially, that I act in character, is to say that my behaviour is consistent and to that extent predictable: and since it is, above all, for the actions that I perform in character that I am held to be morally responsible, it looks as if the admission of moral responsibility, so far from being incompatible with determinism, tends rather to presuppose it. But how can this be so if it is a necessary condition of moral responsibility that the person who is held responsible should have acted freely? It seems that if we are to retain this idea of moral responsibility, we must either show that men can be held responsible for actions which they do not do freely, or else find some way of reconciling determinism with the freedom of the will.

It is no doubt with the object of effecting this reconciliation that some philosophers have defined freedom as the consciousness of necessity. And by so doing they are able to say not only that a man can be acting freely when his action is causally determined, but even that his action must be causally determined for it to be possible for him to be acting freely. Nevertheless this definition has the serious disadvantage that it gives to the word 'freedom' a meaning quite different from any that it ordinarily bears. It is indeed obvious that if we are allowed to give the word 'freedom' any meaning that we please, we can find a meaning that will reconcile it with determinism: but this is no more a solution of our present problem than the fact that the word 'horse' could be arbitrarily used to mean what is ordinarily meant by 'sparrow' is a proof that horses have wings. For suppose that I am compelled by another person to do something 'against my will'. In that case, as the word 'freedom' is ordinarily used, I should not be said to be acting freely: and the fact that I am fully aware of the constraint to which I am subjected makes no difference to the matter. I do not become free by becoming conscious that I am not. It may, indeed, be possible to show that my being aware that my action is causally determined is not incompatible with my acting freely: but it by no means follows that it is in this that my freedom consists. Moreover, I suspect that one of the reasons why people are inclined to define freedom as the consciousness of necessity is that they think that if one is conscious of necessity one may somehow be able to master it. But this is a fallacy. It is like someone's saying that he wishes he could see into the future, because if he did he would know what calamities lay in wait for him and so would be able to avoid them. But if he avoids the calamities then they don't lie in the future and it is not true that he foresees them. And similarly if I am able to master necessity, in the sense of escaping the operation of a necessary law, then the law in question is not necessary. And if the law is not necessary, then neither my freedom nor anything else can consist in my knowing that it is.

Let it be granted, then, that when we speak of reconciling freedom with determinism we are using the word 'freedom' in an ordinary sense. It still remains for us to make this usage clear: and perhaps the best way to make it clear is to show what it is that freedom, in this sense, is contrasted with. Now we began with the assumption that freedom is contrasted with causality: so that a man cannot be said to be acting freely if his action is causally determined. But this assumption has led us into difficulties and I now wish to suggest that it is mistaken. For it is not, I think, causality that freedom is to be contrasted with, but constraint. And while it is true that being constrained to do an action entails being caused to do it, I shall try to show that the converse does not hold. I shall try to show that from the fact that my action is causally determined it does not necessarily follow that I am constrained to do it: and this is equivalent to saying that it does not necessarily follow that I am not free.

If I am constrained, I do not act freely. But in what circumstances can I legitimately be said to be constrained? An obvious instance is the case in which I am compelled by another person to do what he wants. In a case of this sort the compulsion need not be such as to deprive one of the power of choice. It is not required that the other person should have hypnotized me, or that he should make it physically impossible for me to go against his will. It is enough that he should induce me to do what he wants by making it clear to me that, if I do not, he will bring about some situation that I regard as even more undesirable than the consequences of the action that he wishes me to do. Thus, if the man points a pistol at my head I may still choose to disobey him : but this does not prevent its being true that if I do fall in with his wishes he can legitimately be said to have compelled me. And if the circumstances are such that no reasonable person would be expected to choose the other alternative, then the action that I am made to do is not one for which I am held to be morally responsible.

A similar, but still somewhat different, case is that in which another person has obtained an habitual ascendancy over me. Where this is so, there may be no question of my being induced to act as the other person wishes by being confronted with a still more disagreeable alternative: for if I am sufficiently under his influence this special stimulus will not be necessary. Nevertheless I do not act freely, for the reason that I have been deprived of the power of choice. And this means that I have acquired so strong a habit of obedience that I no longer go through any process of deciding whether or not to do what the other person wants. About other matters I may still deliberate; but as regards the fulfilment of this other person's wishes, my own deliberations have ceased to be a causal factor in my behaviour. And it is in this sense that I may be said to be constrained. It is not, however, necessary that such constraint should take the form of subservience to another person. A kleptomaniac is not a free agent, in respect of his stealing, because he does not go through any process of deciding whether or not to steal. Or rather, if he does go through such a process, it is irrelevant to his behaviour. Whatever he resolved to do, he would steal all the same. And it is this that distinguishes him from the ordinary thief.

But now it may be asked whether there is any essential difference between these cases and those in which the agent is commonly thought to be free. No doubt the ordinary thief does go through a process of deciding whether or not to steal, and no doubt it does affect his behaviour. If he resolved to refrain from stealing, he could carry his resolution out. But if it be allowed that his making or not making this resolution is causally determined, then how can he be any more free than the kleptomaniac? It may be true that unlike the kleptomaniac he could refrain from stealing if he chose: but if there is a cause, or set of causes, which necessitate his choosing as he does, how can he be said to have the power of choice? Again, it may be true that no one now compels me to get up and walk across the room: but if my doing so can be causally explained in terms of my history or my environment, or whatever it may be, then how am I any more free than if some other person had compelled me? I do not have the feeling of constraint that I have when a pistol is manifestly pointed at my head; but the chains of causation by which I am bound are no less effective for being invisible.

The answer to this is that the cases I have mentioned as examples of constraint do differ from the others : and they differ just in the ways that I have tried to bring out. If I suffered from a compulsion neurosis, so that I got up and walked across the room, whether I wanted to or not, or if I did so because somebody else compelled me, then I should not be acting freely. But if I do it now, I shall be acting freely, just because these conditions do not obtain ; and the fact that my action may nevertheless have a cause is, from this point of view, irrelevant. For it is not when my action has any cause at all, but only when it has a special sort of cause, that it is reckoned not to be free.

But here it may be objected that, even if this distinction corresponds to ordinary usage, it is still very irrational. For why should we distinguish, with regard to a person's freedom, between the operations of one sort of cause and those of another? Do not all causes equally necessitate? And is it not therefore arbitrary to say that a person is free when he is necessitated in one fashion but not when he is necessitated in another?

That all causes equally necessitate is indeed a tautology, if the word 'necessitate' is taken merely as equivalent to `cause': but if, as the objection requires, it is taken as equivalent to 'constrain' or 'compel', then I do not think that this proposition is true. For all that is needed for one event to be the cause of another is that, in the given circumstances, the event which is said to be the effect would not have occurred if it had not been for the occurrence of the event which is said to be the cause, or vice versa, according as causes are interpreted as necessary, or sufficient, conditions: and this fact is usually deducible from some causal law which states that whenever an event of the one kind occurs then, given suitable conditions, an event of the other kind will occur in a certain temporal or spatio-temporal relationship to it. In short, there is an invariable concomitance between the two classes of events; but there is no compulsion, in any but a metaphorical sense. Suppose, for example, that a psycho-analyst is able to account for some aspect of my behaviour by referring it to some lesion that I suffered in my childhood. In that case, it may be said that my childhood experience, together with certain other events, necessitates my behaving as I do. But all that this involves is that it is found to be true in general that when people have had certain experiences as children, they subsequently behave in certain specifiable ways; and my case is just another instance of this general law. It is in this way indeed that my behaviour is explained. But from the fact that my behaviour is capable of being explained, in the sense that it can be subsumed under some natural law, it does not follow that I am acting under constraint.

If this is correct, to say that I could have acted otherwise is to say, first, that I should have acted otherwise if I had so chosen ; secondly, that my action was voluntary in the sense in which the actions, say, of the kleptomaniac are not; and thirdly, that nobody compelled me to choose as I did : and these three conditions may very well be fulfilled. When they are fulfilled, I may be said to have acted freely. But this is not to say that it was a matter of chance that I acted as I did, or, in other words, that my action could not be explained. And that my actions should be capable of being explained is all that is required by the postulate of determinism.

If more than this seems to be required it is, I think, because the use of the very word 'determinism' is in some degree misleading. For it tends to suggest that some person has arranged it, then the proposition is false. But if all that is meant is that it is possible, in principle, to deduce it from a set of particular facts about the past, together with the appropriate general laws, then, even if this is true, it does not in the least entail that I am the helpless prisoner of fate. It does not even entail that my actions make no difference to the future: for they are causes as well as effects; so that if they were different their consequences would be different also. What it does entail is that my behaviour can be predicted: but to say that my behaviour can be predicted is not to say that I am acting under constraint. It is indeed true that I cannot escape my destiny if this is taken to mean no more than that I shall do what I shall do. But this is a tautology, just as it is a tautology that what is going to happen is going to happen. And such tautologies as these prove nothing whatsoever about the freedom of the will.

Perspectives on Incompatibilism and Libertarianism

Peter Van Inwagen's case for incompatibilism – 'the consequence argument':

"If determinism is true, then our acts are the consequences of the laws of nature and events in the remote past. But it is not up to us what went on before we were born, and neither is it up to us what the laws of nature are. Therefore, the consequences of these things (including our present acts) are not up to us." (*Essay on Free Will*, 1983, p.16)

From Robert Kane, *Rethinking Free Will: New Perspectives on an Ancient Problem*

The Intelligibility Problem

But this approach to the incompatibility of free will and determinism raises a host of further extremely difficult questions about free will. How, for example, could acts lacking both sufficient causes and motives be free and responsible actions?... Can we make sense of such a notion of free will or is it an unintelligible, impossible or self-contradictory ideal, as Nietzsche and many other modern philosophers and scientists believe? And can it be reconciled with modern scientific conceptions of humans and the cosmos?

Doubts about the very possibility of an incompatibilist free will are related to an ancient dilemma: if free will is not compatible with determinism, it does not seem to be compatible with indeterminism either. Determinism implies that, given the past and laws, there is only one possible future. Indeterminism implies the opposite: Same past and laws, different possible futures. On the face of it, indeterminism may seem more congenial to the idea of an "open" future with branching pathways in decision making. But how is it possible one might ask that different actions or choices could arise voluntarily and intentionally for exactly the same past and (barring miraculous departures from the laws of nature) without occurring merely by luck or chance?

Indeterminism and Responsibility

(From 27.20 – 31.00 in clip) Our present question is the philosophical one that has boggled people's minds for centuries, from the time of the Epicureans onward: What could one do with indeterminism, assuming it was there in nature in the right places, to make sense of free will as something other than mere chance or randomness?

The first step in addressing this question is to note that indeterminism does not have to be involved in all acts done "of our own free wills" for which we are ultimately responsible, as argued earlier. Not all such acts have to be undetermined, but only those by which we made ourselves into the kinds of persons we are, namely "self-forming actions" or SFAs.

Now I believe these undetermined self-forming actions or SFAs occur at those difficult times of life when we are torn between competing visions of what we should do or become. Perhaps we are torn between doing the moral thing or acting from ambition, or between powerful present desires and long term goals, or we are faced with a difficult task for which we have aversions. In all such cases, we are faced with competing motivations and have to make an effort to overcome temptation to do something else we also strongly want. There is tension and uncertainty in our minds about what to do at such times, I suggest, that would be reflected in appropriate regions of our brains by movement away from thermodynamic equilibrium — in short, a kind of "stirring up of chaos" in the brain that makes it sensitive to micro-indeterminacies at the neuronal level. The uncertainty and inner tension we feel at such soul-searching moments of self-formation would thus be reflected in the indeterminacy of our neural processes themselves. What is experienced internally as uncertainty would correspond physically to the opening of a window of opportunity that would temporarily screen off complete determination by influences of the past.

When we do decide under such conditions of uncertainty, the outcome is not deter- mined because of the preceding indeterminacy — and yet it can be willed (and hence rational and voluntary) either way owing to the fact that in such self-formation, the agents' prior wills are divided by conflicting motives. Consider a businesswoman who faces such a conflict. She is on her way to an important meeting when she observes an assault taking place in an alley. An inner struggle ensues between her conscience, to stop and call for help, and her career ambitions which tell her she cannot miss this meeting. She has to make an effort of will to overcome the temptation to go on. If she overcomes this temptation, it will be the result of her effort, but if she fails, it will be because she did not allow her effort to succeed. And this is due to the fact that, while she willed to overcome temptation, she also willed to fail, for quite different and incommensurable reasons. When we, like the woman, decide in such circumstances, and the indeterminate efforts we are making become determinate choices, we make one set of competing reasons or motives prevail over the others then and there by deciding.

Full written paper available via student portal

His presentation of the paper available here: https://www.youtube.com/watch?v=rtceGVXgH8s

Nietzsche's critique of libertarian free will:

'The desire for "freedom of will" in the superlative, metaphysical sense, such as still holds sway, unfortunately, in the minds of the half-educated, the desire to bear the entire and ultimate responsibility for one's actions oneself, and to absolve God, the world, ancestors, chance, and society therefrom, involves nothing less than to be precisely this *causa sui*, and, with more than Munchausen daring, to pull oneself up into existence by the hair, out of the slough of nothingness.' *Beyond Good and Evil*, 21, tr. H. Zimmern.

Ted Honderich (b. 1933)

Determinism as True, Compatibilism and Incompatibilism as Both False, and the Real Problem

Should we accept determinism?

What is required for an event to have an explanation, in the fundamental sense, is for there to be something else of which it is the effect. That is, for there to be an answer to the fundamental question of <u>why</u> an event happened is for there to be something of which it was the effect. A standard effect is an event that had to happen, or could not have failed to happen or been otherwise than it was, given the preceding causal circumstance, this being a set of events. In more philosophical talk, the event was made necessary or necessitated by the circumstance.

In my life so far I have never known a single event to lack an explanation in the fundamental sense, and no doubt your life has been the same. No spoon has mysteriously levitated at breakfast. There has been no evidence at all, let alone proof, of there being no explanation to be found of a particular event. On the contrary, despite the fact that we do not seek out or arrive at the full explanations in question, my experience and yours pretty well consists of events that we take to have such explanations. If we put aside choices or decisions and the like -- the events in dispute in the present discussion of determinism and freedom -- my life and yours consists in nothing but events that we take to have fundamental explanations. Thus, to my mind, no general proposition of interest has greater inductive and empirical support than that all events whatever, including the choices or decisions and the like, have explanations.

Honderich's view is that...

What about apparent counterexamples in Quantum Theory?

The first thing to be noted of these supposed quantum events, events of true chance, by anyone inclined to determinism, is that there is no experimental evidence in a standard sense that there are any. There is no such evidence within physics. There is no such evidence, moreover, three quarters of a century after Heisenberg and Schrodinger developed quantum theory. In that very long time in science, including the recent decades of concern with Bell's Theorem, there has been <u>no direct and univocal experimental evidence</u> of the existence of quantum events.

…. It remains a clear possibility, indeed a probability, that physics has not started on the job, even 75 years late, of showing that there are events that lack explanations. This is so, simply, because it remains a probability that quantum events, so-called, are not events. They are not events in any of the senses gestured at in the first paragraph above. In brief, it is probable that they are not things that occur or happen, but are of the nature of numbers and propositions, out of space and time. They are theoretical entities in a special sense of that term, not events.

In summary, Honderich notes that

Extension: Honderich adds a number of further arguments against the significance of Quantum Theory for free will, including this:

There is a seventh respect in which the philosophers of origination are in more than trouble. Their doctrine suffers from another inconsistency that must stick in the craw of anyone not also on a mission to rescue our freedom. Say my lover writes to ask if I have been to bed with someone else, and I then form the intention to lie, and then I do lie. In order to save my freedom and responsibility as understood by them, my rescuers insert a quantum event between the question and my intention. In order to complete the rescue, however, or rather to defend it from itself, they need to <u>exclude</u> a quantum event between the intention and the lie. Otherwise I shall be doing some random lying -- neither freely nor responsibly.

How can they consistently do this? Does Quantum Theory as interpreted have some clause, hitherto unheard of, that its random events occur only in such places as to make us morally responsible in a certain sense? This objection of inconsistency, perhaps, is less effective with some uncommitted philosophers because they do not really take the philosophers of origination seriously. If it really <u>were</u> <u>ad hoc.</u> accepted as true that a random event could get in between the question and the intention, with great effect, then it would have to be accepted that one could get in between the intention and the lie, with as much effect.

In summary,...

Two sorts of hopes

Honderich rejects both incompatibilism and compatibilism. In stating that free will is compatible with determinism *or* that it is not they both assume that there one single idea of free will. Honderich considers this an error. He argues that we have two strong but different sets of idea and feelings concerning free will.

Neither is without its problems and importantly neither seems to account for all our ideas and feelings.

Honderich discusses the compatibilist side as follows:

[The compatibilist] conception, at its most simple, is of a choice or action that is not against the desire of the person in question. Freedom consists in choice or action flowing from the desire of the person in question -- or, a little less simply, from embraced rather than reluctant desire. Freedom is this absence of constraint or compulsion. Freedom is voluntariness -- quite other than origination. An unfree decision or action by contrast is one made as a result of the bars of the prison cell, or the threat to one's life, or the compulsion of kleptomania.

Against this idea as to our freedom, it may be objected that we could be free in this way and yet not be in control of our lives. This voluntariness is not control. Exactly this was a complaint of Incompatibilists. It gave rise to a struggle in response by our Compatibilists. It is plainly a mistake, we still hear from them, to suppose that if I was free in this sense today in my action of social deference, I was <u>subject to control</u>. What control would come to would be my being subject to the desires of another person, or something akin to another person, maybe within me. Given this proposition, evidently, it is not the case that determinism, which is indeed consistent with the Compatibilist idea to our freedom, deprives us of control of our lives. (Dennett, 1984)

So far so good, you may say, but clearly a question remains. Could what has been said by the Compatibilists be taken as coming near to establishing that there is but <u>one</u> way in which we can conceive of <u>not</u> being in control of our lives, the way where we are subject to someone or something else's desires? To put the question differently, and more pointedly, does this come near to establishing that there is but <u>one</u> way, the Compatibilist way, in which we can <u>be</u> in control of our lives, which is to say one way in which we conceive of being free? That all we think of or can care about is voluntariness?

There are rather plain difficulties in the way of this. There evidently is something very like another idea of self-control or freedom. Is it not against the odds, to say the least, that this dispute into which our Compatibilist is seriously entering is between his own conceptually respectable party and a party that has <u>no different idea at all</u>, nothing properly called an idea or anyway no idea worth attention, of what our freedom does or may consist in? There <u>is</u> what has been said of origination.

Let me mention yet more quickly the effort by some Compatibilists to make more explicit their idea of freedom. It is at bottom the effort to show why the kleptomaniac and other such unfortunates, on the Compatibilist account of freedom, are in fact unfree. Certainly it could be thought there was a problem for the account here, since the kleptomaniac in walking out of the department store yet again without paying for the blouses presumably <u>is</u> somehow doing what he wants to do, presumably is <u>not</u> acting against desire.

Our Compatibilist is indeed on the way to a solution if he supposes, a little bravely, that all kleptomaniacs not only desire to make off with the blouses, but also desire not to have that desire. By means of this idea of a hierarchy of desires, that is, the Compatibilist is indeed improving his conception of a free action -- it is, at least in the first part of the conception, an action such that we desire to desire to perform it. (Frankfurt 1971) Suppose more than that -- that the whole philosophical enterprise, this hierarchical theory of freedom, works like a dream, with no difficulties about a regress or about identifying a self with a particular level of desires or about anything else.

Will that have come near to establishing that there is no other conception of a free action? Will it come close to establishing that we have operating in our lives only the hierarchic conception? Will it come close to establishing the lesser thing that this conception is fundamental or dominant or most salient or in any other way ahead of another one? Come to think of it, <u>how</u> could it actually do that? Are we to suppose that from the premise that one conception of freedom has now been really perfected it follows that there is no other conception of freedom or none worth attention?

Libertarian accounts of free will have difficulty in providing an adequate account of how the undetermined agent causes her action/decision (the intelligibility problem). Further, Honderich notes the following:

There <u>is</u>, isn't there, a clear sense in which my action, necessary consequence though it was, may well have been <u>up to me</u> -- perfectly up to me. Suppose I was struck a month ago by Bradley's utterance that to wish to be better than the world is to be already on the threshold of immorality. Suppose I had then consciously determined after a month's serious reflection that henceforth I would consistently act on the side of my society. Suppose it had come about that a great desire drew me only to this -- and of course that I desired to have the desire, and so on. In fact my whole personality and character now supported my action of deference. I could not have been more for it. Does not this conjecture, or any more restrained one you like, come close to establishing that it must be a <u>very</u> brave Incompatibilist who maintains that there is no significant sense in which my action of compliance was up to me?

We all have hopes for our lives -- we all have a dominant hope in a particular stage of life, perhaps for more than one thing, perhaps a disjunctive hope. Like any hope, it is an attitude to a future possibility, at bottom a desire with respect to the possibility. Very likely indeed it is a desire with respect to our own future actions and their initiations in particular desires or whatever. To come to the crux quickly, such desires come in two sorts for all of us. One sort is for a future in which our actions will be voluntary, uncompelled and unconstrained. We won't be in jail or victims of our fearfulness. The other sort of desires is for a future in which our actions are also not fixed products of our natures and environments. We will not just be creatures of them. Each of us has the two sorts of desires, or at any rate each of us is more than capable of having them. One contains an ideas of our future actions as our own in being voluntary. The other sort makes them our own in also containing at least an image of our future actions as originated.

There is the same plain truth, as it seems to me, with respect to the trampled ground of moral responsibility, of which Incompatibilists in particular have had a too elevated notion. What determinism threatens here is also attitudinal. It is a matter of holding people responsible for particular actions and with crediting them with responsibility for particular actions. To do so is to approve or disapprove morally of them for the actions in question. We may do so on the contained assumption than an action was voluntary. Or we may do so, differently, on the contained assumption that the action was not only voluntary but originated. Different desires enter into the two sorts of attitudes -- retributive desires are attached to the idea that the person in question, just as things had been and were, could have done other than the thing he did.

What is more, we act and have institutions or parts of institutions that are owed to one assumption rather than the other. One good example of a general fact is preventive punishments, depending only on a conception of actions as voluntary, and retributive punishment, depending on a conception of actions as also originated. There is thus a behavioural proof of the existence and indeed the pervasiveness of two attitudes and two conceptions of freedom.

Intransience, dismay, affirmation

What all this leads to is the real problem of the consequences of determinism -- which is not the problem of proving something to be our one idea of freedom, or our only self-respecting one, or what you will along these lines. The real problem of the consequences of determinism is that of dealing with the situation in which we have both the idea of voluntariness and also the idea of voluntariness plus origination, and these two ideas run, shape or at least colour our lives, and the second conflicts with determinism. We may attempt to bluff, and to carry on intransigently in the pretence that what matters is only the first idea and what it enters into, one family of attitudes. This is a response of intransigence. On the other hand we may respond with dismay to the prospect of giving up the second idea and what it enters into, the other family of attitudes.

It is at this point among others that the question of the adequacy of the idea of origination comes up. Some philosophers say there is no adequate idea of it. What it comes to is only some piece of nonsense, literally speaking, like the old nonsense of speaking of a thing's causing itself. Hence, for one thing, it does not matter if determinism is true or false. If it is true, there is no more problem than if it is false, since there is no serious idea with which it conflicts. Also, Compatibilism has the field of discussion to itself, since Incompatibilism comes to nothing. The question of truth does not arise. (Cf. Strawson 1986)

This is a curious position that prompts speculation. Suppose I have no idea of why the petunias on the balcony need sun , but am persuaded they do, no doubt by good evidence. Despite the evidence, I have no acquaintance at all with photosynthesis, not even any boy's own science of the matter. It does not follow, presumably, that I lack the idea that the petunias need sun. I could have the idea, too, in a prescientific society where news of the science of the thing would for a long time make no sense. Could I not also have the idea, in a later society, if all of many attempts to explicate the need had broken down in obscurity and indeed contradiction?

At first sight, certainly, those who suppose that there is an adequate idea of origination are in just this sort of position. They speak no nonsense when they assert or offer for contemplation a certain thing. It is that there occur originations, these being events that are not effects, are in the control of the person in question, and render the person responsible in a certain way for ensuing actions -- his being held responsible can consist in an attitude having in it certain desires, notably retributive ones. The friends of origination speak no nonsense when they depend considerably for their characterization of the events of origination on these consequences. The friends still speak no nonsense when it transpires that they cannot in some way explain how it comes about that there is origination, or would come about if there were any. They still speak no nonsense in what went before if their attempts to explain are themselves pieces of nonsense.

No doubt more distinctions are needed here, but it remains my own view that determinism does threaten something important to us of which we have an adequate idea if not a tempting idea. The latter sort of thing, as you will expect, is an idea open to a kind of explanation, an idea of something along with an some explication of it. My untroubled view, too, until very recently, has been that the true problem of the consequences of determinism is the problem of giving up something of which we do have an adequate idea. It is not as if that problem does not arise for the clear-headed.

We can set out to try to deal with this problem of attitudes, at bottom desires. We can try to get away from the responses of intransigence and dismay, and oscillating between them, and make a response of affirmation. This, caricatured, is looking on the bright side. It is seeing the fullness and fineness of a life given much of its character by the attitudes consistent with determinism, and thus giving up the ones inconsistent with it. We can try this -- but we may not succeed. (Honderich 1993: 107-129; 1998: 488-612)

As it has seemed to me, what stands in our way, and in fact obstructs real belief in determinism despite all that can be said for it, is a great fact of our culture. We are so formed, first of all by mothers, those first agents of culture, as to be unable to escape the attitudes. We cannot dismiss one kind of our hopes, and we cannot escape other attitudes, such as those having to do with responsibility, notably when they are directed by ourselves onto ourselves.

Is this the only possible conclusion to the problem of determinism and freedom? For want of space, let me pass by some gallant work of originality and interest (Double 1991, 1996) and come on to something else, an idea of another alternative.

Honderich's change of heart

Having lately engaged explicitly in autobiography, rather than the kind of it in which philosophy is sometimes said to consist, I have been newly taken aback by the strength and durability of my attitudes to myself inconsistent with determinism. Is the stuff about culture really enough to explain them? I have been taken aback too by a seeming fact about a further kind of explanation -- picking out a cause within a causal circumstance and giving it special standing in connection with the effect. This has attitudes in it, all too evidently, but it also seems a business of truth. I do not mean that the attitudes direct and mislead explanation, but that they can seem somehow to enter into its constitution.

Thus a question has come up about attitudes inconsistent with determinism. Could they be owed not only to mothers and their successors in our culture but also have truth in them? Is <u>that</u> why they are so strong and durable? Will some dramatically different reconciliation of determinism and freedom one day be achieved? Certainly it will not be another appearance of that weary warhorse, Compatibilism. Will it have something to do with a connection between desire and truth? Again the point is not about desires affecting our pursuit of truth or obscuring it, but about their entering into the constitution of it. (Honderich 2000)

The extracts are from: Ted Honderich: Determinism as True, Compatibilism and Incompatibilism as Both False, and the Real Problem, published on the Determinism and Freedom Philosophy Website

Sandra LaFave, West Valley College

Free Will and Determinism

In these notes, I will describe three philosophically important positions on the question of free will. They are:

i   Hard Determinism (usually associated with social scientists such as B. F. Skinner, Freud, and Lorenz; usually rejected by philosophers)

j   Soft Determinism (Hobbes, Locke, Hume, and many others)

k   Indeterminism (Kant, Campbell, Taylor, existentialists)

I. HARD DETERMINISM

The basic argument of hard determinism is as follows: P1: No action is free if it must occur.

P2: For any event X there are antecedent causes that ensure the occurrence of X in accordance with impersonal, mechanical causal laws.

C: No action is free.   The hard determinist defends each premise as follows: P1 simply expresses what is meant by 'free'. Surely if an act must occur, it can't be free.

P2 is the Thesis of Determinism - the notion that every event is caused in accordance with causal laws, which account completely for its occurrence. Obviously (for the hard determinist), nothing is uncaused. We can't even imagine what it would mean for a thing to be 'uncaused'? The hard determinist claims that P2 is thus indubitable. (If you doubt P2 anyway, try to produce a counterexample - an instance of an uncaused event.)

Thus, since causes guarantee that their effects occur - that is, if the cause is present, the effect must occur - and since everything that happens is the effect of some cause or set of causes, everything must occur. So nothing is free.

Now, people often argue that P2 is true for the vast majority of events but is false for some human actions. Humans are different from mere things, people say. The hard determinist anticipates this objection, and gives the following argument to establish determinism for human actions:

P1: No action is free if it must occur.   P2: Human actions result from wants, wishes, desires, motivations, feelings, etc.

P3: Human wants, wishes, desires, motivations, feelings, etc. are caused in turn by specific antecedent conditions that ensure their occurrence.

C: Human actions are not free.

Thus, for the hard determinist, humans are no different from other things. Your present actions are part of a causal chain that extends back far before your birth, and each link of the chain determines the next link on the chain. Hence, although it may *appear* to you that you have control over your present actions and mental states, you really have no control. And if you have no control, you certainly can't be held morally responsible for what you do. Thus hard determinism, if true, is important as an challenge to the very enterprise of normative ethics, which usually assumes people can be held responsible for at least some of their actions.

Hard determinists can present their argument in a couple of other ways also. Both these arguments are of the *reductio ad absurdum* form, i.e., their strategy is to demonstrate that absurd consequences follow from the supposition that people are free.

Suppose your will were free. This would mean that your actions were not determined by causal laws. If no causal laws governed your actions, then it would be impossible to predict what you are going to do. But in fact people who know you *can* predict what you will do, with a fair amount of accuracy. And if they couldn't - if your actions were completely unpredictable - they'd probably say NOT that you were free, but that you were crazy. So your actions must be controlled by causal law.

Again, suppose your will were free. This means your actions are freely chosen, and you're morally responsible for them. How then do you make your choices? Either it's an accident that you choose as you do or it's not. If it's an accident, i.e., if you choose randomly or by chance, then it's just a matter of chance that you didn't choose otherwise. So how can you be held morally responsible for choosing as you did? On the other hand, if you didn't choose by accident, then that means there's a causal explanation for your choice, and this confirms hard determinism.   If hard determinism is correct, then,

There can be no freedom in the sense required for morality.

There is no point in punishing or blaming or putting down those who do 'wrong', since they cannot   help it. Indeed, there is no point in making value judgments of any kind about other people. People are not 'better' or 'worse'; they are only different. And if you differ from someone else, you differ, period. If you change, it's because you 'have it in you' already to change; if you don't change, you simply 'don't have it in you' and can't be blamed.

The notion of sin becomes incoherent. If sin is incoherent, then fundamental doctrines of Christianity (e.g., redemption from sin) are pointless.

Persons cannot be thought of as in any way 'special' or 'higher' than other animal species or physical objects. Thus, the interests of humans should not necessarily automatically be thought to override the interests of animals or plants.   However, the hard determinist does not think these consequences are necessarily bad. In fact, some hard determinists argue that the consequences might be very good. You can create a much better world, they argue, once you abandon the outdated notion of freedom. For example, B. F. Skinner argues that since people are the result of their conditioning, *and will get conditioned by their upbringing and environments anyway*, we ought to control people's upbringing and environments as much as possible to ensure that their conditioning is positive. The science of psychology, particularly Skinner's behaviorist principles of positive and negative reinforcement, can and should be applied to this task. Such a plan would be far better than the current situation, in which people's conditioning is more or less random; receiving positive conditioning is now just a matter of luck. But because people's actions and feelings are determined, you can create a perfect society simply by figuring out how to condition people so they don't do anything harmful, make a contribution to society, and have a happy consciousness.   Note that Skinner does not discount the importance of feeling free. Like all the interesting hard determinists, he acknowledges as an empirical fact of psychology that people prefer doing what they want to do, and prefer not to be coerced into doing what they don't want to do. Any happy society must take into account what people actually want. But since the hard determinist thinks that people's wants are determined by conditioning, s/he does not place any special emphasis on what people want right now, or what they have wanted at at various points in history. Social order depends on *manipulating* people's wants, so they voluntarily choose what they have actually been programmed to choose.   Freud and the ethologists (e.g., Konrad Lorenz) and sociobiologists (e.g., Richard Dawkins) are determinists of a different stripe, somewhat less optimistic and utopian than Skinner. Like Skinner, they discount the importance of people's actual desires. Actual conscious human wants are simply data, symptoms, residues of evolution or previous conditioning or manifestations of mental structures over which the individual has no

control. Human subjectivity has no special status or meaning. Unlike Skinner, Freud and the ethologists posit strong unconscious forces determining desire. These forces are built into human nature by evolution; thus, unfortunately, although these forces might be quite unsavory, they are not going to go away quickly. And they are quite unsavory. Freud, for example, holds that during the so-called 'Oedipal' period, everyone wants to have sex with the parent of the opposite sex and kill the parent of the same sex. Lorenz holds that aggression and territoriality and sexual competition are innate instinctive drives. Thus, we are destined to want (unconsciously) to dominate and subjugate others by violence, whether we consciously 'want' to or not.

All these theories agree that free will is an illusion. According to the hard determinists, since hard determinism is the only scientifically defensible way to understand humanity, the concept of free will only hides the real issues and interferes with true self-knowledge.

II. SOFT DETERMINISM

The soft determinist often begins by pointing out that the issue isn't nearly as complicated as the hard determinist thinks. After all, we don't have much trouble distinguishing free acts from unfree ones in ordinary life, do we? Sure, everything has a cause, but what does that have to do with it? That is, the soft determinist argues that an act can be *both caused and also free*. This is because, according to the soft determinist, the hard determinist mistakenly equates 'caused' with 'forced' or 'compelled'. Certainly every action is caused somehow; but not every action is compelled. In other words, an action can be both caused and uncompelled.

And, the soft determinist continues, this agrees with the way we use the words 'free' and 'unfree' in ordinary language. We say an act is free if it's voluntary (not forced or compelled); we say an act isn't free if it's involuntary (forced or compelled).

Note that the soft determinist position is probably the one most ordinary people would agree with. People assent if you ask them if everything is caused; and also assent if you ask them if some acts are free. The soft determinist position is also the one held most commonly by philosophers; both Descartes (in *Meditation* IV) and Hume (in the *Enquiry*) give versions of it.

Soft determinism is often called *compatibilism* because it holds that freedom and universal causation are compatible (can both exist).

The soft determinist agrees with the Thesis of Determinism (the claim that everything that happens must happen, because everything is caused in accordance with causal laws, which force effects which, in theory, can always be precisely predicted). That's why soft determinists are called soft *determinists*. They disagree with P1 of the HD argument, the claim that 'No act is free if it must occur'. The soft determinist says this premise is *equivocal* (i.e., is ambiguous because it can be read in more than one way). The following paragraphs explain why.

The HD reads 'No act is free if it must occur' as presupposing that all acts 'must occur' in the sense that they are all caused, and therefore not free. In other words, having a cause is sufficient to make an act unfree. The hard determinist assumes, that is, that causes are compelling; that is, that having a cause is exactly the same as being *forced*. Does this seem right to you?

It doesn't seem right to the soft determinist, who says the hard determinist abuses ordinary language. A free act on the hard determinist view would have to be an *uncaused* act, and naturally the HD position looks strong because it is hard to imagine what an uncaused event might look like. Thus it follows trivially for the HD that no acts are free, since no acts are uncaused. But it is absurd and weird to claim (as the HD does) that when we say an act is 'free', we really mean it has no cause at all! This is the kernel of the soft determinist position.

Think again about 'No act is free if it must occur', particularly the 'must occur' part. We always say an act 'must occur' if the act is *forced*; but we don't mean to imply that unforced (voluntary) acts have no causes at all! If the bank robber says, 'You must open the safe right now' while pointing a gun to your head, nobody would say that your subsequent opening the safe is a free act. You are *forced* to open the safe; and both the hard and

soft determinist would agree that your act is not free. But does that mean that if you weren't forced to open the safe, and you did anyway, that your voluntary act would have *no* cause? Not so either. The soft determinist agrees with the HD that all acts are caused; but points out that to say an act is caused is not the same as to say it's forced. And when we say an act is 'free', we mean simply that it's *not forced*.

Imagine having to open the safe at gunpoint, and compare that feeling to how you felt when you signed up for this class. Was anyone holding a gun to your head when you filled out your registration card? Most of you are probably taking this class to fulfill a requirement (e.g., Critical Thinking) that might also be fulfilled by another class (e.g., Philosophy 17). Was anyone saying 'Take Philosophy 3 or die!'? Probably not, right? You ended up writing 'Philosophy 3' on your reg card because in some sense you *wanted* to. Maybe you didn't want to *very much*, but I don't think you'd say you felt anything like what you'd have felt if you'd signed up at gunpoint.

If that example doesn't work for you (if signing up for this class felt exactly like signing up at gunpoint - poor you!), then substitute another example - a case where you clearly did not feel forced, e.g., choosing what to eat or what to wear, while scanning the menu or the closet.

The point is, sometimes we feel forced but sometimes we don't. And when we say an act is *free*, we just mean it was one of the ones where we didn't feel forced, i.e., it was voluntary. But that is not to say that our voluntary acts are uncaused; of course they are also caused. Both voluntary and involuntary acts are caused.

But we couldn't say any of this if HD is right. We couldn't make the distinction between forced and voluntary acts at all, since for the HD, all acts, voluntary and involuntary, are equally forced (since they all have causes).

Thus, the soft determinist charges that the hard determinist conflates two notions that should be kept distinct. There are two different senses of 'must occur'! Of course, everything 'must occur' in the sense that everything has a cause, and so nothing is free in this sense. We do not believe that anything is 'free' not to have a cause. But this does not mean that some actions aren't free in the other sense; that is, some actions can still be unforced, or voluntary.

For the SD, then, an unfree act is one that is forced or compelled or involuntary - the normal sense of 'not free'. But, the SD continues, let's not forget that many acts are voluntary; thus many acts are free, because 'free' *means* 'voluntary'. The soft determinist argues that only the SD definition of 'free' as 'voluntary' reflects ordinary language usage. When people say an act is 'free' they mean simply that it's voluntary; they certainly don't mean to say it's 'uncaused'!

The 20th-century philosopher A. J. Ayer sums up the soft determinist position when he says, 'If I suffered from a compulsion neurosis, so that I got up and walked across the room, whether I wanted to or not, or if I did so because sombody else compelled me, then I should not be acting freely. But if I do it now, I shall be acting freely, just because those conditions do not obtain; and the fact that my action may nevertheless have a cause is, from this point of view, irrelevant. For it is not when my action has any cause at all, but only when it has a special sort of cause, that it is reckoned not to be free.'

Besides, says the soft determinist, the hard determinist, in equating 'caused' with 'forced' is making a category mistake. The things that make an act unfree are things like having a gun pointed at you, or being attached to ropes, or being hypnotized, or sleepwalking, etc. All of these can be thought of as causes of behavior. That is, the notion of a cause of behavior is a much more general notion than any of these forces. Equating 'caused' with 'forced' is like equating 'fruit' with 'apple'; it's wrong in both cases because the second thing is a sub-class of the first. An act which is forced is a kind of caused act, just like an apple is a kind of fruit.

Hard Determinist / Indeterminist Reply to Soft Determinism

The hard determinist and indeterminist have similar critiques of soft determinism. The soft determinist wants to have both the thesis of determinism and freedom; but according to hard determinists and indeterminists, you can't have it both ways. If every act has a cause or a set of causes, and causes force their effects, then you can't admit the thesis of determinism and escape hard determinism; and only by denying the thesis of determinism altogether (the indeterminist approach) can you formulate a coherent notion of freedom.

The soft determinist places a lot of emphasis on whether or not an act is voluntary - an act is free if it's voluntary, unfree if it's not. But when we say an act is voluntary, we mean

2. We do it because we want to; and

3. Nobody is forcing us to do it.

The hard determinist and indeterminist both say neither of these criteria is adequate, since a person's wants are caused by the conditioning the person has received. The forces of conditioning might be so pervasive that although we might feel that our action is not forced, an impartial observer would say, 'Given that conditioning, s/he couldn't have done otherwise!' And if you *can't do otherwise* - if you have no genuine alternatives – you're not free.

In other words, the *feeling* of voluntariness seems to be what characterizes freedom for the soft determinist. But both the hard determinist and indeterminist say your feeling is irrelevant to the question of determinism. You might feel your acts are perfectly voluntary and yet they are determined by a series of causes anyway. Even your feeling that your act is voluntary is determined.

Sure, you often feel you are doing just as you wish; but are your wishes or desires themselves under your control? The hard determinist would say 'no'; your mental states are completely explained by reference to antecedent conditions and physical laws. It's fairly easy to think of cases that stump the soft determinist: cases where a person thinks and believes her acts are voluntary; all the world would agree the acts are voluntary; and yet we'd want to say they're nevertheless not free. E.g., people sometimes argue that women don't really want better-paying jobs, because they keep choosing low-status, low-paying jobs (nurse rather than doctor, secretary rather than boss, etc.). And it's true that women do in fact choose those jobs voluntarily. But what does that show? Feminists say it shows the strength of the conditioning that women receive. Their acts are voluntary and yet not really free.

Other Arguments Against Hard Determinism

Other influential arguments have been put forward in contemporary philosophy to refute hard determinism. They include the following.

2. The HD is using an outdated, 18th-century, mechanical misconception of causal laws. Modern scientific laws are construed more as probablistic and statistical than mechanical. Modern-day

laws always recognize the possibility of results happening contrary to prediction; but they state nonetheless that most probably the predicted results will occur.

3. The HD does not consider the possibility of chaotic, or truly unpredictable events. The new science of chaos theory is described for the general reader in James Gleick's recent book *Chaos*.

4. The HD's conclusion - 'No acts are free' - admits of no possible counterexamples. Thus, if it is intended as an empirical (factual) statement, it cannot be falsified; it is compatible with all states of affairs. But what, then, does it say? Does it have any content at all? Compare it with other unfalsifiable statements, such as 'Swimmers like to swim because their blood contains millions of tiny, invisible, non-sensible fish'. The claim is irrefutable, because the little fish are defined in such a way that you can't prove they don't exist, i.e., no counterexamples are possible. But then why believe that they do?

III. SUMMARY SO FAR

Thesis of determinism: Everything that happens must happen, because everything is caused in accordance with causal laws, which force effects which, in theory, can always be precisely predicted.

Hard determinism: Thesis of determinism is true and implies no freedom. If everything that happens *must* happen, everything is *forced* to happen. If an event is forced, it's not free.

Everything that happens is forced. So nothing is free.

Soft determinism: Thesis of determinism is true and is compatible with freedom, because freedom requires two elements: capability ('I can') and desire ('I want to'). A free act is a voluntary act that nothing prevents me from performing.

Everything that happens must happen. My wants happen. So I can't *want* otherwise. (This is the major flaw of SD, according to Indeterminists.) But I can often do what I want. Freedom is simply the *ability* to do what I *want* (capability + desire). Many acts are free, in this sense of freedom.

IV. INDETERMINISM

The indeterminist disagrees with both hard and soft determinism. Hard and soft determinists alike accept the thesis of determinism (the claim that all events are caused). The indeterminist attacks the thesis of determinism itself.

Here are some good reasons to reject the thesis of determinism:

2. In fact, the effects of some causal laws cannot be predicted precisely. This is why the Heisenberg uncertainty principle, and chaos theory are philosophically interesting.

3. The thesis of determinism is compatible with all states of affairs, can't be falsified.

4. The thesis of determinism does not elucidate - in fact, it flies in the face of - our ordinary experience.

5. The notion of mechanical causality applies to things but not to persons. When we account for the   behavior of persons, we must use *teleological explanations.*

Naturally, since the thesis of determinism constitutes an explicit premise of both the HD and SD arguments, these arguments immediately become unsound if the thesis of determinism can be shown to be false or dubious.

According to indeterminists, the hard determinist is right about one thing: if the thesis of determinism is true, then there is no freedom. Both the HD and the indeterminist agree that real freedom cannot exist if everything that happens must happen. For the indeterminist, the soft determinist compromise - the claim that freedom is compatible with the the thesis of determinism - just doesn't work. The indeterminist argues against SD as follows.

The Indeterminist Argument Against Soft Determinism

The libertarian definition of freedom Genuine freedom is contextual (always freedom with respect to something - call it X). Genuine   freedom with respect to X requires three conditions:

1. I can do X.

2. I want to do X.

3. I really can do something other than X.

The libertarian notes that the first and second conditions are often satisfied. I find I often can do what I want to do.

For the SD, this is enough for freedom. In fact, the SD must *deny* the third condition ("I really can do something other than X"), since it's incompatible with the thesis of determinism. As long as you maintain the thesis of determinism (the notion that everything that happens must happen), this third condition can *never* be satisfied, since if everything that happens must happen, my so-called 'free' choices must happen, too. My free choices are just like any other events in the world of universal causality: they can't be otherwise.

For the libertarian, however, condition (3) is just as necessary as (1) and (2). For the libertarian, there is no real freedom if my so-called 'free' choices can't be otherwise. This is the kernel of the indeterminist argument against SD.

So the libertarian notion of freedom depends on showing that the thesis of determinism is false or at least dubious.

There *are* both philosophical and scientific reasons to doubt the thesis of determinism. Philosophical Reasons

o The language of mechanical cause and effect simply does not apply in intentional contexts.

Teleological explanations are necessary.

o The thesis of determinism seems to contradict ordinary experience. o The thesis of determinism is compatible with all states of affairs.

Scientific Reasons

o Chaos theory   oR Heisenberg Uncertainty Principle (commits the fallacy of composition: although people are composed of atoms, what's true of atoms isn't necessarily true of people)

So if these reasons are sound, condition (3) can be met.

So genuine freedom can exist.   Reasons and Causes   Most philosophers nowadays acknowledge the necessity of teleological explanations of human behavior. One standard argument for teleological explanation comes from Kant.   Kant says persons are like things in the sense that physical laws apply to their bodies; the indeterminist might even admit that psychological 'laws' govern some of people's consciousness events. But persons are NOT like things because they can be conscious of the operation of these laws. (A thing is just subject to laws; it is not conscious of being subject to laws.) Even the hard determinist must admit this odd characteristic of persons. People can thus be aware of physical and psychological laws as observers, from the outside. These laws are viewed as things that can operate on me, but there is always a sense in which I view myself as apart from them - for example, right now, when I am reflecting about them.   When I think about how to behave, I consider *reasons*. I never think about causes, because insofar as I am an agent, they are never relevant. I have to make choices, and I choose on the basis of reasons. In other words, the model of physical causation does not fit at all when you try to apply it to human choices. Even if all human choices *were* determined, the HD model would still be completely inadequate to describe the perspective of the agent, which is what really matters for morality. The HD position is simply at odds with human experience because it continually asserts that as far as human experience is concerned, things are not what they seem. (What seems voluntary really isn't, for example.)   Now, the fact that a statement is at odds with our experiences does not show it is false. Many truths are counter-intuitive, e.g., that the earth revolves around the sun. But we accept those truths because they have independent confirmation, through experiments and mathematics. Hard determinism doesn't; in fact, it can't

---

have independent confirmation, since its assertions have no possible counter-examples. This makes it very suspicious. The indeterminist asks that you consider closely actual cases of human decision-making. Consider decisions in the realm of morality, for example. The indeterminist says you will find that there is undoubtedly a freedom to make or withhold moral effort, which exists no matter what a person's past conditioning has been.

Consider the following example: Take two people A and B. Suppose A has had a wonderful childhood - loving, supportive parents, no worries about money, good health, etc. Suppose B has had a terrible childhood - his parents didn't want him, beat him up, never enough money, etc. Suppose now that A and B are grown up. They have a mutual friend Z, who goes on vacation, and leaves a key to his apartment with A, and another key with B. Z has a watch that A and B both like very much; it occurs to both of them to steal it. Stealing it would be simple under the circumstances. Given their respective conditionings, what can we say about the relative strength of the temptation to steal the watch in A and in B? Probably, the temptation will be stronger for B. Another way of saying this is that the amount of moral effort required by B to resist the temptation will be greater than the amount required by A; for example, it might take 8 units of moral effort for B to resist the temptation, but only 2 unit of moral effort for A to resist the same temptation. Clearly, then, it will be easier for A to resist the temptation.

The indeterminist grants all this, but now comes to his major point: both A and B have to *decide* whether to expend the amount of moral effort required to resist the temptation. Both have to choose, and neither one's conditioning determines how they will choose. This choice is a free choice. Conditioning does not determine how they will choose - *it determines only the degree of difficulty* of different moral tasks for different people. Either A or B can choose either way.

So when we say some people are at a disadvantage because of their conditioning, we mean that choosing rightly will be harder for them, but not impossible. More moral effort will be required by a person with unfortunate conditioning; however, we always suppose that a person is responsible for the amount of moral effort he puts forth, no matter what his conditioning. Perhaps it is more likely that B will not put forth the effort; but A can slip too. Thus, by looking at actual cases of decision-making, the indeterminist says that freedom to make or withhold effort (moral effort, or other kinds of discipline, e.g., saving money, physical training) is clearly not illusory, and the existence of responsibility for choice can't be denied. Effort of the will is an illusion only if you deny your own experience.

The existentialist philosophy of Jean-Paul Sartre illustrates a kind of indeterminism. Sartre argues that because people have self-reflective ability, they can be genuinely creative with respect to their character. They can decide to break with their past. For Sartre, in fact, there is a radical gulf between a person and his past, such that a person must continually re-create and redefine himself. Sartre thinks that far from being determined, people are so free it terrifies them. They usually can't stand it, so they make up stories about how they are determined ...

St Augustine of Hippo

On the Free Choice of the Will

♦ A philosophical work written at a time when Augustine was engaged in a dispute with the Manicheans, who believed in an ultimate evil power as well as a good God

♦ Rejecting their ideas on the source of evil, he needed to explain where it came from, avoiding God seeming responsible

♦ *How might Augustine argue against any idea that God is responsible for evil?*

♦ Augustine **argues for a kind of free will which seems very similar to that proposed by modern Libertarian thinkers.**

♦ We are responsible, he considers, since 'the movement of the will by which it turns this way or that [is] under its own control.'

♦ This seems to claim that the will controls itself – it is not controlled by anything else.

Which passage(s) supports each of the statements below?

1. Augustine suggests that the *mind*, not just the person, must be free to do or not do.
2. Augustine argues that the will is not determined by nature.
3. Augustine considers that there is no doubt that human beings who do evil are blameworthy.
4. Augustine considers that the will is not caused by anything outside itself.
5. If the will were determined by nature we could not be held responsible for what we do.
6. Our wills alone are responsible if we become sinful.
7. Our wills alone are responsible for the kind of life we lead.

A. '… the movement by which the stone seeks the lowest place, is… a natural movement. If that's the sort of movement the soul has, then the soul's movement is also natural. And if it is moved naturally, it cannot justly be blamed; even if it is moved towards something evil, it is compelled by its own nature. But since we don't doubt that this movement is blameworthy, we must absolutely deny that it is natural, and so it is not similar to the natural movement of the stone.' OFCOTW 3.1

B. 'What could be the cause of the will before the will itself? Either it is the will itself, in which case the root of all evils is still the will, or else it is not the will, in which case there is no sin.' OFCOTW 3.17

C. The mind, the highest human faculty made to control our instincts and emotions, 'cannot be made a slave to inordinate desire by anything equal or superior to it, because such a thing would be just, or by anything inferior to it, because such a thing would be too weak. Just one possibility remains: only its own will and free choice can make the mind a companion of cupidity.' OFCOTW 1.11

D. 'Whatever these souls do, if they do it by nature and not will, that is, if they lack a movement of the mind free both for doing and not doing; if in fact they are not granted the power of refraining from operating, we cannot maintain that a sin is theirs.' From *On the two souls, against the Manicheans* by Augustine, written at around the same time as *On the Free Choice of the Will*.

E. 'It is by the will that we lead and deserve a praiseworthy and happy life, or a contemptible and unhappy one.' 1.13

Anti-Pelagian Writings

'I laboured indeed on behalf of the freedom of the human will, but God's grace overcame, and I could only reach that point where the apostle is perceived to have said with the most evident truth "for who makest thee to differ? And what hast thou that thou hadst not received?"'

• Later in his career, Augustine's understanding of human free will developed as he became increasingly preoccupied with defending the role of God's grace.

• He wrote 500 pages of letters to various recipients warning against the errors of the monk Pelagius. Pelagius and his follows denied original sin – the teaching that all human beings inherit sin and sinful tendencies from Adam, and hence are born guilty. They also suggested that God gives people grace - guidance and strength to be righteous - in response to their initial efforts to obey God.

• Augustine saw these ideas as denials of human beings' utter reliance on God's grace. He was convinced that human beings could do no good whatever without the undeserved gift of God's support and guidance. His own life experience probably supported this approach. In his *Confessions* he looks back on his childhood and sees himself as full of wickedness, dwelling on an incident in which he stole pears from an orchard with a group of youths. The writings of St Paul, who like Augustine underwent a powerful conversion experience, supported Augustine's preoccupation with dependence on undeserved grace.

In the *Anti-Pelagian Writings* Augustine continues to state that human beings have free will and responsibility. (At one point he bluntly states, 'It is your own fault that you are evil.' If we are condemned by God, he insists, this is fully deserved.) However, the meaning of freedom seems to have shifted. The passages below shed some light on the change.

[Commenting on Pelagius's teaching:] 'I am astonished that he can with any heart suppose that, even without the help of our Saviour's healing balm, it is in our own power to avoid sin, and the ability not to sin is of nature.' *Anti-Pelagian Writings*, 'On Nature and Grace', 56

'It came by the freedom of choice [Adam's] that man was with sin; but a penal corruption followed closely thereon, and out of liberty produced necessity'. *Anti-Pelagian Writings*, 'On Man's Perfection in Righteousness', 4(9)

- **Can a person stop sinning before God intervenes to assist them?**

The beginning of a good will is the gift of grace... Jesus said "No man can come to me, unless the Father who hath sent me draws him". He does not say, "unless He leads him" so that we can thus in any way understand that his will [the person being drawn] precedes. For who is "drawn," if he was already willing? And yet no man comes unless he is willing. Therefore he is drawn in wondrous ways to will, by Him who knows how to work within the very hearts of men. Not that men who are unwilling should believe, which cannot be, but that they should be made willing from being unwilling.

- **What does Augustine state is responsible for the will turning towards God and salvation?**

'...The Lord says: "Every man that hath heard and hath learned of the Father, cometh unto me." Of the man, therefore, who has not come, it cannot be correctly said: "He has heard and has learned that it is his duty to come to Him, but he is not willing to do what he has learned." It is indeed absolutely improper to apply such a statement to that method of teaching, whereby God teaches by grace. For is, as the Truth says, "Every man that hath learned cometh," it follows, of course, that whoever does not come has not learned.... When God teaches, it is not by the letter of the law, but by the grace of the Spirit. Moreover, He so teaches, that whatever a man learns, he not only sees with his perception, but also desires with his choice, and accomplishes in action.' (*Anti-Pelagian Writings*, 'On the Grace of Christ', 15)

- **According to Augustine's teaching here, if God intervenes in someone's life, what happens?**

- **What do these teachings mean for human freedom?**

- **How far does Augustine's position here differ from the position of *On the Free Choice of the Will?***

- **Which modern philosophical approach to free will is Augustine's later position closest to?**

Calvin, Freedom and Predestination

Extracts from John Calvin's (1509 – 1564) Institutes of the Christian Religion, chapter 21

THE covenant of life is not preached equally to all, and among those to whom it is preached, does not always meet with the same reception. This diversity displays the unsearchable depth of the divine judgment, and is without doubt subordinate to God's purpose of eternal election. But if it is plainly owing to the mere pleasure of God that salvation is spontaneously offered to some, while others have no access to it, great and difficult questions immediately arise, questions which are inexplicable, when just views are not entertained concerning election and predestination. To many this seems a perplexing subject, because they deem it most incongruous that of the great body of mankind some should be predestinated to salvation, and others to destruction. How ceaselessly they entangle themselves will appear as we proceed. We may add, that in the very obscurity which deters them, we may see not only the utility of this doctrine, but also its most pleasant fruits. We shall never feel persuaded as we ought that our salvation flows from the free mercy of God as its fountain, until we are made acquainted with his eternal election, the grace of God being illustrated by the contrast--viz. that he does not adopt all promiscuously to the hope of salvation, but gives to some what he denies to others. It is plain how greatly ignorance of this principle detracts from the glory of God, and impairs true humility. But though thus necessary to be known, Paul declares that it cannot be known unless God, throwing works entirely out of view, elect those whom he has predestined. His words are, "Even so then at this present time also, there is a remnant according to the election of grace. And if by grace, then it is no more of works: otherwise grace is no more grace. But if it be of works, then it is no more grace: otherwise work is no more work," (Rom. 11:6). If to make it appear that our salvation flows entirely from the good mercy of God, we must be carried back to the origin of election, then those who would extinguish it, wickedly do as much as in them lies to obscure what they ought most loudly to extol, and pluck up humility by the very roots. Paul clearly declares that it is only when the salvation of a remnant is ascribed to gratuitous election, we arrive at the knowledge that God saves whom he wills of his mere good pleasure, and does not pay a debt, a debt which never can be due. Those who preclude access, and would not have any one to obtain a taste of this doctrine, are equally unjust to God and men, there being no other means of humbling us as we ought, or making us feel how much we are bound to him. Nor, indeed, have we elsewhere any sure ground of confidence.

- **Calvin's doctrine is often referred to as *'double* predestination'. Why do you think this is?**

- **Why does Calvin think that belief in predestination is necessary for proper Christian faith?**

We, indeed, ascribe both prescience and predestination to God; but we say, that it is absurd to make the latter subordinate to the former (see chap. 22 sec. 1). When we attribute prescience to God, we mean that all things always were, and ever continue, under his eye; that to his knowledge there is no past or future, but all things are present, and indeed so present, that it is not merely the idea of them that is before him (as those objects are which we retain in our memory), but that he truly sees and contemplates them as actually under his immediate inspection. This prescience extends to the whole circuit of the world, and to all creatures. By predestination we mean the eternal decree of God, by which he determined with himself whatever he wished to happen with regard to every man. All are not created on equal terms, but some are preordained to eternal life, others to eternal damnation; and, accordingly, as each has been created for one or other of these ends, we say that he has been predestinated to life or to death.

- **What is the difference between God's prescience and God's predestination?**

- **What does Calvin think of the idea that predestination is an inevitable result of God's prescience?**

[*The following passage continues straight on from the one above*] This God has testified, not only in the case of single individuals; he has also given a specimen of it in the whole posterity of Abraham, to make it plain that the future condition of each nation lives entirely at his disposal: "When the Most High divided to the nations their inheritance, when he separated the sons of Adam, he set the bounds of the people according to the number of the children of Israel. For the Lord's portion is his people; Jacob is the lot of his inheritance," (Deut. 32:8, 9). The separation is before the eyes of all; in the person of Abraham, as in a withered stock, one people is specially chosen, while the others are rejected; but the cause does not appear, except that Moses, to deprive posterity of any handle for glorying, tells them that their superiority was owing entirely to the free love of God. The cause which he assigns for their deliverance is, "Because he loved thy fathers, therefore he chose their seed after them," (Deut. 4:37); or more explicitly in another chapter, "The Lord did not set his love upon you, nor choose you, because you were more in number than any people: for ye were the fewest of all people: but because the Lord loved you," (Deut. 7:7, 8). He repeatedly makes the same intimations, "Behold, the heaven, and the heaven of heavens is the Lord's thy God, the earth also, with all that therein is. Only the Lord had a delight in thy fathers to love them, and he chose their seed after them," (Deut. 10:14, 15). Again, in another passage, holiness is enjoined upon them, because they have been chosen to be a peculiar people; while in another, love is declared to be the cause of their protection (Deut. 23:5). This, too, believers with one voice proclaim, "He shall choose our inheritance for us, the excellency of Jacob, whom he loved," (Ps. 47:4). The endowments with which God had adorned them, they all ascribe to gratuitous love, not only because they knew that they had not obtained them by any merit, but that not even was the holy patriarch endued with a virtue that could procure such distinguished honor for himself and his posterity. And the more completely to crush all pride, he upbraids them with having merited nothing of the kind, seeing they were a rebellious and stiff-necked people (Deut. 9:6).

- **According to Calvin, why were the people of Israel chosen by God?**

Although it is now sufficiently plain that God by his secret counsel chooses whom he will while he rejects others, his gratuitous election has only been partially explained until we come to the case of single individuals, to whom God not only offers salvation, but so assigns it, that the certainty of the result remains not dubious or suspended…. Thus in the adoption of the family of Abraham, God gave them a liberal display of favor which he has denied to others; but in the members of Christ there is a far more excellent display of grace, because those ingrafted into him as their head never fail to obtain salvation.

- **What makes the election of Christians an even greater example of God's grace than his choosing of Abraham and his descendants?**

- **What are the implications of Calvin's doctrine for human freedom?**

- **What kind of freedom do we**

8177217R10198

Printed in Germany
by Amazon Distribution
GmbH, Leipzig